Insights into AI and Language Teaching and Learning

Edited by

Yijen Wang

Antonie Alm

Gilbert Dizon

Melbourne - London - Tokyo - New York

4th Floor, Silverstream House, 45 Fitzroy Street Fitzrovia, London W1T 6EB, United Kingdom
Level 9, 440 Collins Street, Melbourne, Victoria 3000, Australia
2nd Floor Daiya Building, 2-2-15 Hamamatsu-cho, Minato-ku, Tokyo 105-0013, Japan
447 Broadway, 2nd Floor #393, New York NY, 10013, United States

First published 2025 by Castledown Publishers, London

Information on this title:
www.castledown.com/reference/9781763711600

DOI: 10.29140/9781763711600

Insights into AI and Language Teaching and Learning
© (Editors) 2025

All rights reserved. This publication is copyright. Subject to statutory exception and to the provisions of relevant collective licencing agreements, no reproduction, transmission, or storage of any part of this publication by any means, electronic, mechanical, photocopying, recording or otherwise may take place without prior written permission from the author.

Typeset by Chennai Publishing Services Pvt. Ltd.
ISBN: 978-1-763711-60-0 (Paperback)
ISBN: 978-1-763711-61-7 (Digital)

Castledown Publishers takes no responsibility for the accuracy of URLs for external or third-party internet websites referred to in this publication. No responsibility is taken for the accuracy or appropriateness of information found in any of these websites.

Contents

Foreword   *v*

List of contributors   *xi*

Chapter 1   1
Introduction
Gilbert Dizon, Antonie Alm, and Yijen Wang

Part One   9
Overview of the issues

Chapter 2   11
ICALL and AI: Seven lessons from seventy years
Mathias Schulze

Chapter 3   32
Challenges of AI in language education
Yuwei Wan & Benjamin Luke Moorhouse

Chapter 4   53
Reconceptualising literacy as co-literacy in language education with AI
Antonie Alm

Chapter 5   77
AI and language assessment
Peter Crosthwaite & Qing Ma

Chapter 6   97
Ethical considerations of AI
Gilbert Dizon

Chapter 7   115
Research methods and AI
Yijen Wang

Part Two
Establishing the foundations of good practice — 133

Chapter 8
Motivational issues in AI integration — 135
Zhan Shi & Chun Lai

Chapter 9
AI and teaching communities — 153
Louise Ohashi

Chapter 10
Critical TPACK as a foundation for teaching with AI — 170
Jaeho Jeon & Seongyong Lee

Chapter 11
Teacher's practical pedagogical knowledge — 185
Zoe Handley

Chapter 12
Professional development and learner training for AI — 203
Glenn Stockwell

Part Three
AI in practice — 219

Chapter 13
Machine translation and writing — 221
Sangmin Michelle Lee & Nayeon Kang

Chapter 14
Generative AI and chatbots — 240
Curtis Green-Eneix & Lucas Kohnke

Chapter 15
AI-integrated language learning applications — 261
Eneyire Godwin Omuya, Xin Zhao & Minna Rollins

Chapter 16
Feedback and Automated Writing Evaluation (AWE) — 290
Inyoung Na, Mahdi Duris & Volker Hegelheimer

Index — *314*

Foreword
The added value of AI for language teaching and learning

Jozef Colpaert

Dear Reader,

What prompted you to purchase or borrow this book? Are you seeking to expand your horizons in the field of language teaching? Are you captivated by the advancements in AI technologies and eager to understand their implications? Are you searching for guidance on why, when, where, and how to utilize these technologies? Perhaps you feel pressured by your peers or fear that your students know more about AI than you do. Maybe you have specific needs as a language teacher and want to explore how AI can provide solutions.

Whatever your motivation, by opening this book, you are already swimming against the tide of misinformation and exaggerated expectations spread by self-proclaimed experts and hype-driven enthusiasts. A few months ago, I posted the following statement on several platforms: "The recent hype surrounding AI in education is based on poor technological knowledge, blatant wishful thinking, an outdated psychological-motivational paradigm, and a fundamental disregard for the achievements of the field." However, upon reviewing the work of my esteemed colleagues worldwide, I have adopted a more nuanced perspective. I agreed to write this foreword because this book is different. As a playful remark, I could say that writing a book on AI is courageous, as it risks becoming obsolete the moment it is published due to the rapid pace of technological advancements. Yet, this book is not about the hype or the technology itself, but about the core aspects that have intrigued us since the early days of Computer-Assisted Language Learning (CALL).

Since the 2020 pandemic, we have been inundated with announcements of breakthroughs in nuclear fusion, quantum processors, hypersonic jets, teleportation, and generative or agentic AI. Regarding AI, I remain skeptical due to my experience with previous waves of hype. Like many other developers, I am impressed not by the technology itself but by the speed at which these systems have emerged. The core technology has not changed much since the 1980s. The difference lies in the use of massive datasets and improved engines, processors, sensors, cameras, and servers—servers that consume vast amounts of energy, which surprisingly raises little ecological concern.

While AI systems are becoming more sophisticated, I do not yet perceive true intelligence, especially in the refined sense proposed by Piaget: "Intelligence is what you do when you do not know." If these systems possess any form of intelligence, it is hidden within neural networks—a black box that we cannot yet fully understand or analyze. The term 'Large Language Models' is misleading in this context because we do not truly know what the model is.

AI systems require training and fine-tuning, often performed by underpaid workers in modern digital sweatshops. Moreover, users must learn 'prompt engineering'—the skill of effectively instructing AI systems.

The pervasiveness of the term 'AI' should already raise concerns. Many products now claim to be "created with AI," even simple items like pencils. This ubiquity is not only pervasive but also persuasive. We see impressive systems (which Alan Cooper described as "Dancing Bearware") that captivate our imagination and spark both dreams and nightmares. The sudden AI wave has even overshadowed the Metaverse hype.

While I am impressed by some AI systems, I struggle to see how they meet my personal needs in daily life. Prime examples are the tedious process of ordering a meal, refurbishing a house, choosing a new car, searching for a partner or preparing an upcoming trip. This brings me back to my original question: AI offers impressive functionalities, but to what extent does it address the fundamental needs of students and teachers?

Academic journals are flooded with submissions, conferences with presentations, libraries with books, and social media with persuasive claims from overnight AI experts who lack deep technological understanding. History repeats itself—hype after hype. Instead of focusing on the maturity level of emerging technologies and predicting their trajectory in the Gartner Hype Cycle, the real issue is that each hype cycle since the 1980s has diverted attention from the actual needs of students and teachers. What are these needs exactly?

AI applications assist language learners and teachers in generating documents, subtitling, translating, and more. Researchers explore the challenges and opportunities related to reliability, accuracy, authenticity, creativity, and integrity. However, the deeper needs of autonomy, relatedness, and competence remain largely unaddressed.

Before answering this question, we must consider several issues. First, even marketers recognize it these days, people often do not know what they want or need when asked, as most factors influencing behavior are subconscious. Second, there is a difference between what learners and teachers want and what they need. That leads to our third consideration: we need to define needs more accurately.

The specification of needs emerges from a methodological process known as design. When crafting an optimal learning environment for a specific context, the process invariably identifies elements that are not yet present—these are termed requirements. Requirements encompass specific functionalities, such as corrective feedback, synchronous collaborative writing, or adaptive testing, which collectively form a multimodal learning environment. These functionalities can be mapped along various dimensions, including face-to-face versus remote, synchronous versus asynchronous, individual versus collaborative, and cohort-based versus independent learning. Importantly, requirements pertain not to individual learners but to the learning environment as an integrated ecosystem.

A crucial distinction lies between requirements and goals. Goals must be considered at the outset of the design process and can be categorized into pedagogical goals (explicit learning objectives) and personal goals (subconscious desires of learners and teachers). Effective design reconciles these potentially conflicting goals, such as fostering collaboration in a classroom where students are hesitant to work together.

In the context of artificial intelligence (AI), a pertinent question arises: How can AI contribute to the creation of an optimal multimodal language learning environment? I define the added value of educational technology as "the match between the requirements of the learning environment and the affordances of the technology."

This definition implies that the added value of AI—or any technology—depends on the specific context, including learning objectives, learner characteristics, teacher profiles, and infrastructure. Notably, the affordances of a technology are not fixed; they shift according to the context in which they are applied.

The concept of affordance is central to educational technology. Building on the work of Gibson and Norman, I adopt the term in the sense of "perceived contribution to goal realization." Two key elements stand out: 'perceived' and 'goal.'

The absolute, universal value of a given technology is less significant than its immediate, context-dependent value as perceived by learners and teachers when encountering new technology. This perspective aligns with the concepts of Perceived Ease-of-Use and Perceived Usefulness from the Technology Acceptance Model (TAM) and its successor, UTAUT (Unified Theory of Acceptance and Use of Technology).

The second critical element is goals. The perception of how a technology can contribute to achieving personal goals or reconciling conflicting personal and pedagogical goals significantly affects user acceptance, willingness to engage, and sense of identification with the technology. Given that goals vary and are context-dependent, so too are affordances.

A technology that learners and teachers perceive as fulfilling their goals—enhancing feelings of reward, support, autonomy, relatedness, or competence—will have a greater impact. The fundamental question is: To what extent can AI systems analyze the context and guide the design process toward selecting the most suitable technology?

No technology inherently possesses a measurable and generalizable effect on learning. This effect can only emerge from the learning environment as a whole—an ecology of learning. Moreover, the impact is proportional to the *designedness* of the learning environment, which refers to the degree to which the environment has been methodically designed, leading to the specification of requirements.

In this context, the added value of a technology is defined as the match between the specified requirements and the affordances of the technology. AI's potential lies in its ability to enhance this alignment through intelligent analysis of learning contexts and the facilitation of effective design processes.

Teachers should not be pressured to adopt specific technologies, including AI. They should not be portrayed as ignorant or resistant, as some proponents of models like TPACK suggest. During the pandemic, teachers demonstrated creativity, resilience, and natural intelligence in designing learning environments. They should view themselves as "master chefs" who create their own recipes rather than blindly following instructions.

Good design not only enhances learning environments but also empowers teachers to make context-specific choices and justify them. This continuous process of trial-and-error fosters new hypotheses and makes teaching more engaging for both teachers and students. This design approach relieves teachers of pressure, makes them more confident, makes teaching more fun and rewarding, and last but not least, allows them to turn their daily work into research...

This book aligns with this approach. It offers insights into the human mindset, focusing on learners' and teachers' perceptions, beliefs, needs, and goals. Building on the legacy of CALL, it identifies seven key needs: exposure to authentic language, contextual communication, appropriate error correction, varied interaction, learner behavior tracking, dynamic individualization, and gradual release of responsibility.

The book also addresses the didactic, ethical, and societal challenges of implementing AI in language education. It introduces "co-literacy," a framework that extends literacy to include critical engagement with AI-generated content, positioning AI as a collaborative agent in language learning.

Additionally, the book explores automated assessment tools, biases, and future AI research directions. It emphasizes the importance of self-efficacy, enjoyment, and supportive environments for boosting student motivation in integrating AI into language learning. Attention is given to academic skills, teacher communities, learner training, and professional development.

Finally, assessing effectiveness and perceptions will indeed be the crucial issue. For this reason, I am convinced that this book will provide valuable insights into the potential added value of AI in language learning and teaching.

List of contributors

Antonie Alm (PhD, UCLA) is an Associate Professor in the Languages and Cultures Programme at the University of Otago, New Zealand. Her work in computer-assisted language learning centres on learner autonomy and motivation, with a current focus on AI use in both informal and formal learning environments. She has published on educator and student perspectives on AI tools such as Google Translate and ChatGPT. Her recent work addresses AI literacy, the role of learner agency in AI-mediated environments, and ethical concerns arising from student engagement with generative AI tools. She is an associate editor for the *CALL Journal* and *JALT CALL Journal*.

Peter Crosthwaite is an Associate Professor in the School of Languages and Cultures at the University of Queensland. His areas of research and supervisory expertise include corpus linguistics and the use of corpora for language learning (known as 'data-driven learning'), as well as computer-assisted language learning, and English for General and Specific Academic Purposes. He has published over 60 articles to date in many leading Q1 journals in the field of applied linguistics. He is the Editor-in-Chief for the *Australian Review of Applied Linguistics* (from 2024), and currently serves on the editorial boards of the Q1 journals *IRAL*, *Journal of Second Language Writing*, *Journal of English for Academic Purposes*, *System*, and *Applied Corpus Linguistics*, a new journal covering the direct applications of corpora to teaching and learning.

Gilbert Dizon is an Associate Professor at Himeji Dokkyo University and holds a Doctor of Education from Indiana University. His research interests focus on technology-mediated informal language learning and the use of artificial intelligence in language education. His work has been published in journals such as *Computers and Education: Artificial Intelligence*, *Computer Assisted Language Learning*, *Language Learning & Technology*, and *Innovation in Language Learning and Teaching*.

Mahdi Duris is a Ph.D. candidate in Applied Linguistics & Technology at Iowa State University, focusing on the use of technology in second language pronunciation, second language writing, and AI applications in education. His research interests center on pronunciation, phonetics, and phonology, especially regarding the automation of intelligibility ratings, as well as Automated Writing Evaluation

(AWE) and the broader integration of AI in educational contexts. https://mahdiduris.com. Author ORCiD: https://orcid.org/0000-0002-1569-1655

Curtis Green-Eneix is a Research Assistant Professor in the Department of English Language Education at The Education University of Hong Kong. As an emerging critical educational linguist, he has published articles and book chapters in journals such as *System*, *TESOL Journal*, and *Urban Education*, as well as co-edited four special issues (*Australian Journal of Applied Linguistics*; *Chinese Journal of Applied Linguistics*; *Linguistics and Education*; *RELC Journal*) on various issues, such as langauge policy and planning in transnational contexts; raciolinguistic ideologies in teacher education, and critical implementation of AI to promote sustainable language teaching and learning. He is also the co-editor of *Applied Linguists Forum for TESOL International*.

Zoe Handley is Associate Professor of Language Education in the Department of Education at the University of York. Her research explores how the affordance of digital technologies might be harnessed to create the conditions and engage learners in the processes Second Language Acquisition (SLA) research suggests promote language learning. With a focus on speaking and writing, Dr Handley's research has explored the readiness of speech synthesis for language learning, and the impact of online writing platforms on collaboration and peer learning. She is also interested in teacher education, developed the EFL-TPACK survey and is currently exploring teachers' practical pedagogical knowledge for the deployment of technology to support language learning.

Volker Hegelheimer is Professor of Applied Linguistics in the Department of English at Iowa State University. He teaches courses on technology in language teaching and research, language assessment, and research methodology. His research interests include applications of technologies including Generative AI in language learning and language testing.

Jaeho Jeon is a Ph.D. Candidate in the Department of Curriculum and Instruction at Indiana University Bloomington. He will work as an Assistant Professor in the Department of Curriculum and Instruction at The University of Alabama from Fall 2025. His research focuses on AI in education, language learning, multilingualism, literacy, teacher education, and dynamic assessment, with a particular interest in integrating generative AI.

Nayeon Kang is a middle school teacher in the Gyeonggi-do Office of Education. She has been teaching English for about 20 years at secondary schools in South Korea. She holds a BA in English Education from Ewha Womans University and a MA in TESOL from the University of Edinburgh,

UK. Her research interests include the application of Artificial Intelligence (AI) in English education and the utilization of various Educational Technology tools for facilitating English language learning.

Lucas Kohnke's research focuses on technology-supported teaching and learning, and teacher professional development with emerging technologies. He has contributed over 60 articles to leading journals such as *Computers and Education: Artificial Intelligence*, *Educational Technology & Society*, *Education and Information Technologies*, *ReCALL*, *System*, and *RELC Journal*. His diverse teaching areas include integrating technology into language classrooms, AI in education, teacher training, and English language teaching methodologies. He is top 2% most cited scholar in education 2024.

Chun Lai is an Associate Professor at the Faculty of Education, the University of Hong Kong. Her research interests include self-directed language learning with technology beyond the classroom, technology-enhanced language learning, and teacher technology integration. She is the author of *Autonomous Language Learning with Technology beyond the Classroom* (Bloomsbury) and *Insights into Autonomy and Technology in Language Teaching* (Castledown Publishers).

Sangmin-Michelle Lee is a professor in the Department of Metaverse at Kyung Hee University, Korea. She received her Ph.D. from Pennsylvania State University, USA. Her research interests include technology-enhanced learning environments, machine translation, game-based learning, and computational creativity. She has published numerous articles in peer-reviewed journals, including *Computer Assisted Language Learning*, *ReCALL*, *Language Learning & Technology*, *BJET*, and *Education and Information Technologies*. She is currently conducting R&D projects in technology-enhanced learning, including AI digital textbooks, explainable AI for teachers, and an AI risk management framework and checklist. She is an associate editor of *Language Learning and Technology*, *Humanities and Social Sciences Communications*, and *JALT-CALL*.

Seongyong Lee is Assistant Professor of Applied Linguistics in School of Education and English at the University of Nottingham Ningbo China. His research interests include AI in L2 education, teacher education, and Global Englishes. His articles have appeared in international journals, such as *TESOL Quarterly*, *Computer Assisted Language Learning*, *Computers & Education*, *System*, *ELT Journal*, *Language Learning & Technology*, *International Journal of Bilingual Education and Bilingualism*, *Education & Information Technologies*, *Interactive Learning Environments*, *Educational Technology & Society*, *Applied Linguistics Review*, *Lingua*, *English Today*, and *Asian Englishes*. He is Editor-in-Chief of *Multimedia-Assisted Language Learning* sponsored by Korea Association of Multimedia-Assisted Language Learning.

Qing Ma (Angel) is an Associate Professor in the Department of Linguistics and Modern Language Studies and currently holds the position of Associate Dean (Research & Postgraduate Studies) in the Faculty of Humanities at The Education University of Hong Kong. Her research primarily focuses on second language vocabulary acquisition, computer-assisted language learning (CALL), mobile-assisted language learning (MALL), corpus linguistics, corpus-based literature studies, corpus-based language pedagogy (CBLP) and AI in language education.

Benjamin Luke Moorhouse is an Associate Professor in the Department of English, City University of Hong Kong, China. He has extensive experience as a primary school English language teacher. He has worked for the Education Bureau, Hong Kong Baptist University (HKBU), and The University of Hong Kong. He has received several teaching awards, including The President's Award for Outstanding Performance in Individual Teaching from HKBU in 2023. His research focuses on the lived experiences, competencies and professional learning of language teachers and teacher educators. Currently, he is exploring the impact of GenAI on language teaching and learning. He has published widely in international journals, including *Computers and Education: Artificial Intelligence*, *Journal of Education for Teaching*, *Asia-Pacific Journal of Teacher Education*, and *Studying Teacher Education*. According to Stanford University, Benjamin was in the top 2% of cited scholars worldwide in 2022, 2023, and 2024.

Inyoung Na is a Ph.D. student in Applied Linguistics and Technology at Iowa State University. Her research interests include second language pronunciation, speech intelligibility, and the integration of artificial intelligence technologies in language testing and assessment. She is currently working on her dissertation, which explores the use of generative AI technologies to develop and evaluate an AI-based test system for assessing interactional competence in second language oral communication. She is also investigating how learners interact with tools like ChatGPT to support language learning.

Louise Ohashi is Professor of Applied Linguistics in the Department of English Language and Cultures at Gakushuin University, Japan. She specializes in second language acquisition and L2 education. Her key research areas include learner autonomy, motivation, and the use of digital technology in language education. In recent years, she has been exploring the role of artificial intelligence in L2 teaching and learning. She actively brings educators together to explore these topics through her role as Chair of EUROCALL's AI SIG. She is also a keen language learner (日本語, italiano, français, español, Deutsch). Full bio at https://orcid.org/0000-0003-0218-7385

Eneyire Godwin Omuya (MSc.), a Data Science graduate of The University of Sheffield, England, UK, is a data scientist and researcher with expertise in computer engineering, machine learning, artificial intelligence and Generative AI. His work explores the intersection of AI and education, particularly the role of AI-powered tools in language learning and writing development. With experience in IT, data science, prompt engineering, and product management, he has contributed to projects that leverage AI for user engagement and skill enhancement. His research interests include human-inspired AI, Creative AI, and the ethical considerations of AI in educational settings. He has worked across diverse sectors, including IT infrastructure management, secondary school education, and product development. In addition to his research, he is passionate about AI-generated art and its applications in creative expression.

Minna Rollins (D.Sc.) is a Professor of Marketing at the University of West Georgia, USA. Her current research interests include international marketing and sales, gaming and esports, and Generative AI in learning and education. She has published her research in journals such as *Industrial Marketing Management* and the *Journal of Business Research*, as well as several international conference proceedings.

Mathias Schulze is the director of the Language Acquisition Resource Center and a professor of German Language and Literature in the Department of European Studies. He was born in Finsterwalde in Germany. He did his teacher training for German and Russian in Leipzig (Germany) and Kaluga (Russia) and got his PhD in Language Engineering (Applied Linguistics) from the University of Manchester Institute for Science and Technology (UMIST). For ten years, Mat worked at universities in Sunderland and Manchester (England) and for sixteen years at the University of Waterloo (Canada), where he was the director of the Waterloo Centre for German Studies. He was the co-editor of the *CALICO Journal* (on computer-assisted language learning (CALL)) for eight years. CALL is also his main area of research. His research interests are in language education and social bilingualism.

Zhan Shi is a PhD candidate in the Faculty of Education at The University of Hong Kong. His research interests focus on technology-assisted language learning, motivational issues and self-regulated learning. His previous research has been published in *Language Learning & Technology* and *TESOL Quarterly*.

Glenn Stockwell is Professor of Applied Linguistics at the Graduate School of International Culture and Communication Studies, Waseda University. He is author of *Mobile Assisted Language Learning: Concepts, Contexts and Challenges* (Cambridge University Press, 2022) and editor of *The Cambridge Handbook* of *Technology in Language Teaching and Learning* (Cambridge University Press, 2025) and *Computer Assisted Language Learning: Diversity in Research and Practice* (Cambridge University Press, 2012). He is Editor-in-Chief of *Computer Assisted Language Learning* and the *Australian Journal of Applied Linguistics*. His current research interests include the impact of technology on teaching and learning, professional development in using technology for language teaching, artificial intelligence in language education, teacher and learner training with technology, and the development of learner autonomy.

Yuwei Wan is a PhD candidate in the Department of Education and Psychology at Hong Kong Baptist University. Her current research interests include GenAI in language education, language teaching pedagogy, digital literacy, and professional development for language teachers. She has published articles in *RELC Journal*, *System*, *ELT Journal*, and *Computers and Education Open*.

Yijen Wang is an Assistant Professor at the School of International Liberal Studies, Waseda University. She specializes in computer-assisted language learning, with extensive research on the interplay between technology and psychology in language education. Dr. Wang is the Editor-in-Chief of *Technology in Language Teaching & Learning* and regularly reviews for multiple journals in the field. She has edited several major works, including *Insights into Teaching and Learning Writing*, *The Cambridge Handbook of Technology in Language Education*, and *The Cambridge Elements in Technology in Second Language Education*. Her current research interests include the impact of technology on teaching and learning, mobile-assisted language learning, generative AI in language education, and social justice in educational technology.

Xin Zhao (Skye) is a Lecturer in Generative AI for Education at the Manchester Institute of Education, University of Manchester, UK. She also serves as a Generative AI expert panellist for the United Nations and as a partner on the AI Competency Framework at UNESCO. Her primary research interests lie in Educational Technologies, particularly in Generative AI.

1
Introduction

Gilbert Dizon, Antonie Alm, and Yijen Wang

The public release of OpenAI's ChatGPT has not only brought artificial intelligence (AI) to the forefront of education but has also sparked widespread discussion beyond the field of language teaching. Educators and the general public have raised questions about large language models (LLMs) and generative AI, particularly their influence on formal language instruction (Hubbard, 2024; Ro, 2023). Although the full impact of AI on language education is still unfolding, it has the potential to transform the way languages are taught and learned (Du & Daniel, 2024; Tafazoli, 2024). Therefore, it is critical for stakeholders in language education – from teachers to researchers to administrators – to develop a thorough understanding of the affordances and limitations of AI in the context of language teaching and learning.

While AI has become a focal point in discussions on language education, its use in language teaching is not a new phenomenon. In 1988, Balin outlined the state of computer-assisted language learning (CALL) and discussed how AI was utilized at the time, including written feedback and drill-and-practice exercises. Later in the 1990s, grammar checkers (Levy & Garton, 1994), interactive speech technologies (Ehsani & Knodt, 1998), and intelligent tutoring programs (Yazdani, 1991) gained attention in CALL research. These early applications of AI laid the foundation for more advanced systems in the 2000s, such as automatic speech recognition (ASR) and automated writing evaluation (AWE) (Chen & Cheng, 2008; Derwing et al., 2000), two AI-based technologies that are still widely used today. With the advent of LLMs, AI's capabilities have grown significantly, allowing for more accurate language generation and automated feedback that closely mirrors human output and evaluation (Mizumoto et al., 2024; Shin & Lee, 2024). As these examples illustrate, AI does not refer to a single technology. Instead, it serves as an umbrella term for a range of computer systems designed to simulate human intelligence (Handley, 2024; Son et al., 2023). With that in mind, the aim of this book is to introduce language teachers to a wide range of AI tools so that they can confidently apply them to their own teaching contexts.

Understanding how AI tools function is only the beginning; this volume emphasizes the pivotal role of instructors in helping students make sense of AI's growing presence in language learning. As AI advances, students will continue to face uncertainty about its appropriate use, grappling with questions of academic integrity, reliability, and ethical considerations. For students to fully benefit from AI, they need support that helps them engage with its role in learning. This guidance should empower them to explore AI's potential to foster creativity, collaboration, and enhanced engagement with language learning. AI-assisted writing and speaking tasks, interactive feedback systems, and adaptive learning models offer opportunities for individualized and meaningful language practice. Teachers, therefore, serve as guides, helping students use AI to enrich their linguistic abilities, experiment with multimodal communication, and engage in more interactive learning experiences. This book aims to equip educators with the knowledge needed to integrate AI in ways that actively enhance students' language learning journeys.

Although AI offers language teachers and learners many affordances, including automated feedback and assessment, increased learner autonomy, and enhanced language skill development (Crompton et al., 2024), the use of AI poses several potential risks. One major concern is the accuracy and reliability of AI output, as errors or biases in the technology could lead to the spread of misinformation (UNESCO, 2023). Additionally, the use of AI may limit the development of essential cognitive skills such as creativity and critical thinking, resulting in an over-reliance on the technology (Mohebbi, 2025). Furthermore, privacy is a concern as many AI systems collect and store personal data, raising fears about data security and possible data misuse (Yan & Liu, 2024). These issues and others are discussed across many of the chapters in this edited volume to provide readers with a balanced look at the benefits and challenges of AI in language education and to offer practical strategies for mitigating AI-related risks.

This edited volume consists of three major sections: *Part I – Overview of the Issues*, summarizes key concepts and historical developments related to the emergence of AI in language teaching and learning; *Part II – Establishing the Foundations of Good Practice*, explores language teaching with AI and the pedagogical practices that foster effective and equitable use of AI in the classroom; *Part III – AI in Practice*, presents empirical research on AI and language learners, offering insights into students' perspectives and behaviors regarding AI-assisted language learning.

Part I: Overview of the issues

This book begins with Mathias Schulze's foundational overview in Chapter 2, tracing the evolution from early AI concepts to today's transformative GenAI within computer-assisted language learning (CALL). The author critically outlines the historical successes and limitations of Intelligent CALL (ICALL), setting the stage for understanding GenAI's potential and challenges in modern language education through seven key historical lessons. These lessons help frame the ongoing integration of GenAI into language education, suggesting that while GenAI offers new capabilities, there are significant pedagogical considerations that must be managed carefully.

In Chapter 3, Yuwei Wan and Benjamin Luke Moorhouse address the challenges brought by the integration of GenAI into language education, categorized into challenges directly associated with its use in educational settings and broader ethical and societal issues. It outlines how AI can be useful but potentially lead to challenges to both learners and educators. The chapter further suggests strategies for educators to overcome these challenges, including fostering communication with students about ethical GenAI use, developing professional competencies related to GenAI, engaging in continuous professional development, and maintaining a human-centered approach in educational practices.

In Chapter 4, Antonie Alm introduces the concept of 'co-literacy' to address the fundamental question, "What does literacy mean when machines can write?" Building on the multiliteracies framework and digital literacies, Alm reconceptualizes literacy as a collaborative process between humans and AI systems. The chapter compares human and machine literacies, highlighting their complementary strengths and limitations. Drawing on four conceptual approaches, Alm develops the concept of co-literacy to describe how humans and AI collaborate in co-constructing meaningful language experiences across modalities. She emphasizes that co-literacy should foster learner autonomy, critical engagement, and creative adaptation, preparing learners to traverse the 'AI wilderness' in ways that enrich their language learning.

Peter Crosthwaite and Qing Ma, in Chapter 5, discuss the integration of AI in second language (L2) assessment, focusing on its application in both productive and receptive language skills assessments. They detail AI's use in automated speech recognition (ASR) for spoken language assessments and automated essay scoring (AES) for written evaluations. The chapter highlights recent developments in GenAI and large language models (LLMs), which have expanded the possibilities for automated and scalable assessment methods across various contexts. On the other hand, the chapter also acknowledges persistent challenges such as issues of assessment integrity, equity, and reliability. To overcome these challenges, the chapter suggests enhancing AI literacy among educators to ensure ethical and effective integration of AI technologies in assessment practices.

Chapter 6, written by Gilbert Dizon, addresses the ethical considerations associated with the use of AI in language learning and teaching, a topic that has seen significant growth but insufficient scrutiny concerning its ethical implications. It particularly focuses on three prevalent AI technologies: automatic speech recognition, machine translation, and generative AI, and discusses the ethical concerns they raise, such as academic integrity, bias, and reliability. The chapter provides a comprehensive overview of the literature and suggests practical strategies to address these ethical issues, aiming to foster a more critical and equitable approach to AI in language education.

In Chapter 7, Yijen Wang provides a comprehensive exploration of current methodologies and trends in researching the integration and impact of AI tools in language learning. The chapter emphasizes the necessity of robust research frameworks to fully understand AI's capabilities and limitations in educational settings. It discusses various research approaches and topics, including the exploration of AI affordances, perceptions of AI among users, and the effectiveness of AI in enhancing language skills. Furthermore, the chapter critically evaluates the common biases and methodological challenges, proposing future directions for more comprehensive research.

Part II: Establishing the foundations of good practice

Chapter 8 by Zhan Shi and Chun Lai examines motivational issues in AI integration, presenting major motivational theories relevant to technological behaviors in educational contexts. The authors identify four key motivational mechanisms that support effective AI integration: building students' self-efficacy, enhancing perceived usefulness of AI, promoting enjoyment, and creating supportive environments. The chapter provides practical guidance for teachers on fostering students' intentions to integrate AI into their language learning, while addressing potential challenges such as overreliance and ethical concerns related to AI-generated content.

A teacher's ability to foster motivation is closely tied to the support they receive from professional communities, a topic explored in Chapter 9 by Louise Ohashi. Rather than approaching AI adoption in isolation, educators thrive through peer collaboration, particularly within teacher communities and professional networks. Drawing on the Communities of Practice (CoP) framework, the chapter illustrates how educators exchange ideas, refine best practices, and develop AI literacy together. Examples from both institutional and informal teacher networks show how collegial support strengthens educators' confidence and pedagogical decision-making. Through personal narratives and reflective prompts, Ohashi encourages readers to consider their own roles within teacher communities and offers a call to action for educators at all levels of the AI novice-expert spectrum.

While professional communities help educators build confidence in AI use, they also need clear theoretical frameworks to guide its integration. Chapter 10 by Jeon and Lee introduces an expanded version of the Technological, Pedagogical, and Content Knowledge (TPACK) framework, designed specifically for Generative AI (GenAI). Traditional models of technology integration, the authors argue, fail to account for the complexity of AI-generated content, which is inherently shaped by the values embedded in its training data. Recognizing GenAI as a value-laden technology that mediates meaning and influences the learning process, the chapter highlights the need for critical awareness of AI's biases, ethical considerations, and its potential to reinforce existing power structures. Their 'TPACK for GenAI' model incorporates a fourth dimension—critical engagement—which ensures that educators actively interrogate its role in learning. The chapter provides practical guidelines across four interpretive dimensions—concept, design, application, and critical thinking—to help teachers develop their own approaches to GenAI-assisted language classrooms.

Based on an interview study with English for Academic Purposes (EAP) tutors in the UK, Chapter 11 by Zoe Handley captures a range of perspectives on AI in higher education. Tutors voiced concerns about plagiarism, academic integrity, and shifting institutional policies, while also acknowledging AI's potential to support non-native English speakers. The findings reveal a lack of institutional clarity, forcing many educators to develop their own approaches to AI use in teaching and assessment. The chapter connects with earlier discussions on teacher training and community support, reinforcing the idea that AI integration must be an informed and collaborative process rather than an improvised response to technological change.

Teachers' ability to engage critically with AI depends on ongoing professional development, as Glenn Stockwell argues in Chapter 12. He examines how perceptions of stress, control, and social norms affect whether educators view AI as a threat or an opportunity, a challenge to be addressed, or a resource to enhance their teaching practices. Some educators adopt problem-focused strategies, integrating AI into their teaching, while others take an emotion-focused approach, limiting or rejecting its use. Stockwell emphasizes the importance of evaluating AI's fit within pedagogical goals and learner needs, ensuring that technology serves a meaningful role in language learning. Institutional inconsistencies—such as unclear AI policies and disparities in AI literacy—further complicate AI adoption. This chapter advocates for a reflective and collaborative approach to professional development, helping teachers develop both technical proficiency and pedagogical adaptability in assessing AI's role in education.

Part III: AI in practice

Chapter 13, the first chapter in Part III, focuses on machine translation (MT). Sangmin Michelle-Lee and Nayeon Kang look at Korean English as a foreign language (EFL) students' perception of MT and the variables that affect their use of the technology. While most studies on MT have explored the university context, the authors examined second language (L2) writing within a secondary school setting. The results from their study showed that the efficacy of MT was influenced by students' language proficiency and confidence in the L2, illustrating the significance of learner variables and the importance of sound instructional strategies that are adapted to learners' backgrounds and needs.

Chapter 14 also reports on students' views of AI, but within the context of generative AI in an English for Academic Purposes (EAP) course. Using a case study design, Curtis Green-Eneix and Lucas Kohnke examine the benefits and limitations of generative AI from the perspective of university students in Hong Kong. Overall, the students had favorable views of generative AI and used it to support their writing rather than to complete writing tasks. However, they also had concerns regarding the ethics of using generative AI, particularly in terms of privacy. As such, the authors strongly recommend that any implementation of generative AI in the classroom be complemented with critical AI literacy.

Chapter 15 examines an AI-integrated language learning application called Wordtune. In the chapter, Eneyire Godwin Omuya, Xin Zhao, and Minna Rollins take a mixed-methods approach to study how native English speakers and EFL students use Wordtune, investigate their views of the application, and identify key variables that are associated with its perceived effectiveness. Survey results indicated that close to two-thirds of the participants were EFL students, with many of them reporting frequent use of the application for all writing tasks. The use of Wordtune along with other AI-integrated language learning applications was also a commonly reported practice. A majority of the respondents reported improving their writing through feedback from Wordtune. Moreover, a strong association was identified between learner background and perceived benefits related to vocabulary, i.e., EFL students with high language proficiency valued the application's synonym suggestions more than native speakers. The findings from this study highlight the potential benefits of AI-integrated language learning applications in enhancing academic writing among native speakers and EFL students.

Using a CALL framework by Chapelle (2001), Inyoung Na, Mahdi Duris, and Volker Hegelheimer investigate students' interactional behaviors and perceptions of ChatGPT for L2 writing development in Chapter 16. Their study included English as a second language (ESL) students at an American university and incorporated multiple forms of data collection to achieve their goals. The authors found that the students most often asked ChatGPT for feedback and revisions on their writing output. However, the students reported that ChatGPT's feedback tended to be excessive, complicated, and overly positive. Another significant finding from the study was that many students copied and pasted suggested revisions by ChatGPT without any modifications. Given these findings, the authors suggest that language teachers collaborate with ChatGPT to provide writing feedback and guide students on ethical and effective ways to use AI to develop their writing skills.

The perspectives presented in this book examine how AI tools can support and enhance language education while acknowledging the irreplaceable human elements at the heart of teaching and learning. What emerges is a roadmap for critical engagement that respects both the potential of AI and the expertise of experienced educators. We invite readers to approach these pages with curiosity, drawing from them what best serves their teaching contexts while contributing to an ongoing conversation about the integration of AI in language education. In this remarkable moment of educational transformation, our hope is that this volume provides both practical guidance and conceptual clarity for language teachers forging new paths at the intersection of AI and pedagogy.

References

Balin, A. (1988). Artificial intelligence and computer-assisted language instruction: A perspective. *CALICO Journal, 5*(3), 25–45.

Chen, C. F. E., & Cheng, W. Y. E. C. (2008). Beyond the design of automated writing evaluation: Pedagogical practices and perceived learning effectiveness in EFL writing classes. *Language Learning & Technology, 12*(2), 94–112.

Crompton, H., Edmett, A., Ichaporia, N., & Burke, D. (2024). AI and English language teaching: Affordances and challenges. *British Journal of Educational Technology, 55*(6), 2503–2529. https://doi.org/10.1111/bjet.13460

Derwing, T., Munro, M., & Carbonaro, M. (2000). Does popular speech recognition software work with ESL speech? *TESOL Quarterly, 34*(3), 592–603. https://doi.org/10.2307/3587748

Du, J., & Daniel, B. K. (2024). Transforming language education: A systematic review of AI-powered chatbots for English as a foreign language speaking practice. *Computers and Education: Artificial Intelligence*, *6*, Article 100230. https://doi.org/10.1016/j.caeai.2024.100230

Ehsani, F., & Knodt, E. (1998). Speech technology in computer-aided language learning: Strengths and limitations of a new CALL paradigm. *Language Learning & Technology*, *2*(1), 54–73.

Handley, Z. L. (2024). Has artificial intelligence rendered language teaching obsolete? *The Modern Language Journal*, *108*(2), 548–555. https://doi.org/10.1111/modl.12929

Hubbard, P. (2024). Future directions in English language teacher education in a changing world. In J. S. Lee, D. Zou, & M. M. Gu (Eds.), *Technology and English language teaching in a changing world: A practical guide for teachers and teacher educators* (pp. 189–201). Springer.

Levy, M., & Garton, J. (1994). Adapting a grammar checker for learner writers. *ReCALL*, *6*(2), 3–8.

Mizumoto, A., Shintani, N., Sasaki, M., & Teng, M. F. (2024). Testing the viability of ChatGPT as a companion in L2 writing accuracy assessment. *Research Methods in Applied Linguistics*, *3*(2), Article 100116. https://doi.org/10.1016/j.rmal.2024.100116

Mohebbi, A. (2025). Enabling learner independence and self-regulation in language education using AI tools: a systematic review. *Cogent Education*, *12*(1), Article 2433814. https://doi.org/10.1080/2331186X.2024.2433814

Ro, S. (2023, June 23). Students switch to AI to learn languages. *BBC*. https://www.bbc.com/news/business-65849104

Shin, D., & Lee, J. H. (2024). Exploratory study on the potential of ChatGPT as a rater of second language writing. *Education and Information Technologies*, *29*, 24735–24757. https://doi.org/10.1007/s10639-024-12817-6

Son, J. B., Ružić, N. K., & Philpott, A. (2023). Artificial intelligence technologies and applications for language learning and teaching. *Journal of China Computer-Assisted Language Learning*. Advance online publication. https://doi.org/10.1515/jccall-2023-0015

Tafazoli, D. (2024). Exploring the potential of generative AI in democratizing English language education. *Computers and Education: Artificial Intelligence*, *7*, Article 100275. https://doi.org/10.1016/j.caeai.2024.100275

UNESCO. (2023). *Guidance for generative AI in education and research*. United Nations Educational, Scientific and Cultural Organization (UNESCO). https://doi.org/10.54675/EWZM9535

Yan, Y., & Liu, H. (2024). Ethical framework for AI education based on large language models. *Education and Information Technologies*. https://doi.org/10.1007/s10639-024-13241-6

Yazdani, M. (1991). The Linger project an artificial intelligence approach to second-language tutoring. *Computer Assisted Language Learning*, *4*(2), 107–116.

Part One

Overview of the issues

2
ICALL and AI: Seven lessons from seventy years[1]

Mathias Schulze
San Diego State University

> **Pre-reading questions:**
>
> 1) What do we know about artificial intelligence (AI) in language teaching and learning already?
> 2) What can we see if we look back more than two or so years?

In the last two years, discourses on generative AI (GenAI) in the academic literature on (language) education, writing, publishing, (machine) translation, computer science, and many other areas as well as in mainstream and specialized media have resulted in a multitude of articles, books, chapters, columns, essays, guidelines, opinion pieces, and tip sheets. Many of these will be discussed in the subsequent chapters of this book. Here, the time window will be much wider, to provide a more leveled, quasi-historical lens on the rapidly evolving AI approaches and tools in the context of language education (see also Stockwell [2024] for another brief retrospective). Three very early milestone years are important in this context: 1948, 1950, and 1955. In 1948, the first publication that connects AI and language learning came out. In it, Alan Turing, often called the father of AI, mentions a number of different ways in which computers would be able to demonstrate their intelligence in the future: "(i) Various games, for example, chess, noughts and crosses, bridge, poker; (ii) *The learning of languages*; (iii) *Translation of languages*; (iv) Cryptography; (v) Mathematics" (Turing [1948] quoted in Hutchins, 1986, pp. 26–27, my emphasis). Also in 1948, the then brand-new field of Applied Linguistics reached a noticeable

---

[1] My inspiration for this title came from the book Snyder, T. (2017). *On tyranny: Twenty lessons from the twentieth century*. Tim Duggan Books.

breakthrough with the publication of the first issue of *Language Learning. A Quarterly Journal of Applied Linguistics* (Reed, 1948). In 1950, what we call today the Turing Test was published as the "Imitation Game" (Turing, 1950). Seventy-four years passed before newspapers and magazines announced that ChatGPT-4 had passed the Turing Test. Researchers at UC San Diego had published a preprint (under review) about their replication of the Turing test (Jones & Bergen, 2024). "Human participants had a 5 minute conversation with either a human or an AI, and judged whether or not they thought their interlocutor was human. GPT-4 was judged to be a human 54% of the time" (p. 1). It was five years after the proposal of the Turing Test, which is meant to test the intelligence of a machine, that research and development in the field of artificial intelligence started. McCarthy et al. (1955) proposed "that a 2 month, 10 man study of artificial intelligence be carried out during the summer of 1956 at Dartmouth College in Hanover, New Hampshire," coining the name of the field – artificial intelligence.

The intersection of artificial intelligence and (computer-assisted) language learning has thus had a trajectory of about 70 years and had been termed Intelligent CALL (ICALL) up until the advent of GenAI, when AI became the buzzword and label. The documented development of ICALL software and systems occurred later; Bowerman notes that "Weischedel et al. (1978) produced the first ICALL system ..." (1993, p. 31). The system was a prototype German tutor implemented as an Augmented Transition Network with a semantic and syntactic component. Weischedel et al. (1978) reference earlier work in CALL, for example an article by Nelson et al. (1976). However, this and other earlier publications elsewhere seem to rely on string comparison, often character-by-character replacement, or regular expressions rather than natural language processing. It would only be the latter that is part of AI research and thus ICALL. ICALL played a significant role in Tutorial CALL (Heift & Schulze, 2015; Hubbard & Bradin-Siskin, 2004; Schulze, 2024) over many years, but it never became mainstream in CALL in terms of research and development. The label tutorial CALL captures the learning interaction of the student with the computer rather than interaction of the learner with other persons via the computer, as in computer-mediated communication. It is not only the utilization of AI that GenAI and ICALL have in common, GenAI has also brought a revival of the learner interacting with the machine and can thus be described as a form of tutorial CALL.

Heift and Schulze (2007) identified and discussed 119 ICALL projects over about thirty years, but with very rare exceptions these were research prototypes. Only a few ICALL projects had limited use in language classrooms (e.g., Heift, 2010; Nagata, 2002). In a review article, Schulze (2008a) used a list of nine key desiderata for ICALL by the applied linguist Rebecca Oxford (1993) to discuss developmental trajectories in ICALL:

1. Communicative competence must be the cornerstone of ICALL.
2. ICALL must provide appropriate language assistance tailored to meet student needs.
3. ICALL must offer rich, authentic language input.
4. The ICALL student model must be based in part on a variety of learning styles.
5. ICALL material is most easily learned through associations, which are facilitated by interesting and relevant themes and meaningful language tasks.
6. ICALL tasks must involve interactions of many kinds and these interactions need not be just student-tutor interactions.
7. ICALL must provide useful, appropriate error correction suited to the student's changing needs.
8. ICALL must involve all relevant language skills and must use each skill to support all other skills.
9. ICALL must teach students to become increasingly self-directed and self-confident language learners through explicit training in the use of learning strategies. (p. 174)

Here, these desiderata will be adapted and used as a *tertium comparationis* when drawing lessons from the 'history' of ICALL for the emerging use of GenAI in language education, using them also as a structuring criterion for this chapter as follows:

1. Exposure to rich, authentic language
2. Communication in context
3. Varied interaction in language learning tasks
4. Appropriate error correction and contingent feedback
5. Recording learner behavior and student modeling
6. Dynamic individualization
7. Gradual release of responsibility

A discussion of the work in ICALL as such over the decades is beyond the scope of this chapter; in addition to the review article mentioned above (Schulze, 2008a), overviews of ICALL research can be found in the monograph by Heift and Schulze (2007), which also provides an introduction to the main concepts and research questions in the field about 20 years ago, in a chapter (Nerbonne, 2003) in *The Oxford Handbook of Computational Linguistics*, and in articles (Gamper & Knapp, 2002; Matthews, 1993) in CALL journals. Many publications on ICALL appeared in edited volumes and in refereed conference proceedings and journals on computational linguistics, broadly conceived, and thus outside of the literature on CALL. This might be one of the reasons why GenAI was such a surprising novelty in language education in general and CALL in particular and why a focused retrospective can further our understanding of role and developmental trajectory of GenAI in language education today. We start with an excursion into a branch of AI that is relevant here – natural language processing (NLP).

Exposure to rich, authentic language

The texts – or the language – that a computer can understand or generate depend on its capacity for NLP. Computer scientists added the adjective 'natural' because the parsing of programming language(s) was possible, and necessary, before they turned to parsing texts produced by humans. In early NLP, computational linguists wrote grammatical rules and compatible dictionaries in programming languages such as Prolog and LISP. Rules and items were written by hand, relying on different (mathematical) grammar formalisms. This made the development process slow, error-prone, computationally expensive, and labor-intensive. This might be the main reason why the coverage and robustness of ICALL systems and applications remained limited over the years. Parsing a single sentence – the analysis of the grammatical constructions and the production of an equivalent information structure, something similar to a syntactic tree, which the computer could "understand" – took from a couple of seconds to a few minutes, depending on the computer hardware and the efficiency of the parsing algorithm. This approach to NLP is called symbolic, because it uses and processes symbols for syntactic phrases, such as NP for a noun phrase and VP for a verb phrase, and for lexical items, such as N for a noun and V for a verb, and their grammatical feature structures. Symbolic NLP in ICALL resulted in sentence-based language learning activities in a tutorial system. Since the dictionary was also hand-written and hence usually small, the language to which students using the ICALL system were exposed was limited to the vocabulary of a textbook at best.

In the 1990s, more electronic corpora (large, principled collections of texts) also in languages other than English became available. The approach to NLP that relies on the mathematical analysis of large corpora has been called statistical NLP. In this approach, language patterns are detected in corpus analyses. For these patterns or contiguous sequences of words – called n-grams with n being the number of words in each and every sequence – the probability of one word following the other(s) is calculated. In their simplest form, the probabilistic connection of linear word sequences is calculated. This results in a wider coverage of language, because of the underlying use of large corpora. However, the limitation was that, for example, long-distance dependencies as in the following sentence still posed a problem as they had in symbolic NLP.

The student who had finally given the right answer proceeded to ask the next question.

For any human reader, it is immediately clear that it is 'the student' who 'proceeded' and not 'the right answer'. For the computer, this connection between grammatical subject and finite verb poses a challenge because the words are not in the same n-gram(s) and the pattern cannot be detected easily.

This and other challenges were overcome by relying on artificial neural networks (ANNs), models that are inspired by the neural networks of human brains (for a comprehensive overview of how GPTs (generalized pre-trained transformers) work, see Wolfram, 2023, February 14). ANNs are multidimensional and do not only rely on linear sequences of words. Their individual nodes, the neurons, receive input and send output to other neurons. The processing of input to produce output is basically done through a mathematical equation. Thus, this output depends on the (probabilistically) weighted input. The network learns by adjusting the weights, which multiply different input values and biases, the latter are added independently of the input, to improve the accuracy of the result. If this machine learning relies on neurons organized in multiple layers – the input layer, the output layer, and in-between two or more hidden layers[2], then we talk about a deep network and deep learning (LeCun et al., 2015). Deep learning and ANNs are the underpinnings of the large language models (LLMs) (for an accessible overview of ANNs and LLMs, see Naveed et al., 2024), which in turn are the backbone of GenAI chatbots such as ChatGPT (OpenAI), Claude (Anthropic), Copilot (Microsoft), and Gemini (Google). Thus, LLMs essentially rely on enormous corpora of texts scraped from the internet and on machine-learned neural networks. In these ANNs, individual tokens – which can be individual letters, words, and parts of a word – are represented by long lists of numbers, which are called word vectors. The parameters in the network, which are tiny little rules and steps, help to determine which word follows the previous word.

---

[2] "GPT-3 has 96 layers. GPT-4's exact number of layers hasn't been publicly disclosed, but it is expected to be significantly larger than GPT-3." Microsoft Copilot. (2024, December 26). *How many nodes and layers does the ANN of the GPT large language model have?* Microsoft Copilot.

"GPT-3 has 175 billion parameters, which include the weights and biases of the neurons. GPT-4 is speculated to have trillions of parameters, though the exact number hasn't been confirmed" (Microsoft Copilot, 2024, December 26).

This new computational approach is far removed from the reliance on linguistic rules and items in early NLP and ICALL, because it is steeped in the complex calculations in the hidden layers of the LLM and arrays upon arrays of numbers. That's why GenAI's coverage, scope, and speed of NLP is vastly superior to previous systems in ICALL. Therefore, we can argue that students using GenAI are exposed to rich language at the paragraph and not only the sentence level. But is this generated language authentic? In an early paper on authenticity in the language classroom, Breen (1985) proposes that "that authentic texts for language learning are any sources of data which will serve as a means to help the learner to develop an authentic interpretation" (p. 68). The question then becomes: can a learner develop an authentic interpretation of a turn or text generated by a GenAI chatbot or a translation rendered by a GenAI machine translation tool? Since the generated texts are certainly well-formed and plausible, they appear to provide a good basis for the learner's interpretation and thus for language learning. Also, because they are based on actual language use as found in the texts on the internet, which were used to train the LLM, we have another indication that generated texts in chat with a GenAI or a translation from a GenAI potentially qualify as authentic. However, the real key to authenticity of language is found in communication.

Communication in context

Oxford (1993) desires that "communicative competence must be the cornerstone of ICALL" (p. 174), noting that many ICALL projects of her time did not meet that goal, although communication and by extension communicative language teaching have been central ideas in applied linguistics for decades. Canale and Swain (1980) transferred the concept of communicative competence by Dell Hymes – developed in opposition to the Chomskyan linguistic competence – from sociolinguistics to language learning. Hymes (1974) had introduced communicative competence with the mnemonic SPEAKING = **S**etting and Scene (time and place), **P**articipants (speaker and audience), **E**nds (purpose and outcome), **A**ct Sequence (progression of speech acts), **K**ey (tone, manner), **I**nstrumentalities (language modalities), **N**orms (social rules), and **G**enre (kind of speech act or text) (pp. 53–62). These different facets and components of communication go well beyond the idea of a generative grammar (Chomsky, 1957) and that of linguistic competence. In ICALL as in NLP generally, however, generative grammar and other formal grammars, which are sets of rules that rewrite strings using mathematical operations, are the backbone of a system. The partial disconnect between formal grammars, such as Head-driven Phrase Structure Grammar and Categorial Grammar, and communicative competence with its focus on meaning, situation, and context, as clearly illustrated also by Hymes' mnemonic, meant that ICALL systems did hardly play a role in communicative language teaching.

The GenAI chatbots, however, have been said to be a suitable conversation partner (Baidoo-anu & Owusu Ansah, 2023) and learning buddy (https://www.khanmigo.ai/). The GenAI output in a number of languages is certainly well-formed and plausible; GenAI's natural language understanding is fast and precise. But is a conversation with a chatbot the same as a human conversation? Is it a negotiation of meaning as understood in communicative language teaching? The NLP researcher Emily Bender and her colleagues compared GenAI chatbots to stochastic parrots, which skillfully aim but proceed by guesswork (see Merriam-Webster, n.d.), and argue that

> "coherence is in fact in the eye of the beholder. Our human understanding of coherence derives from our ability to recognize interlocutors' beliefs ... and intentions ... within context ... That is, human language use takes place between individuals who share common ground and are mutually aware of that sharing (and its extent), who have communicative intents which they use language to convey, and who model each others' mental states as they communicate." (Bender et al., 2021, p. 616)

In other words, the chatbot spits out forms that are plausible but that do not mean anything; the (student or teacher) reader imbues these hollow forms with meaning and thus anthropomorphizes the GenAI tool, by then reasoning about its 'intention' and basing their response on the result of the reasoning, as humans do in conversation. Computers, however, do not have or formulate intentions. Something was clicked, data was input, and a condition was met. This triggered a digital operation, and forms that are numbers to the computer and look like words to the human user of the device became visible or audible. We add meaning after the form of the text has been generated.

Varied interaction in language-learning tasks

The human-machine conversation often works because we are used to adhere – even if the machine cannot and is not – to Grice's four maxims of conversation (Grice, 1975): quantity (be informative), quality (be truthful), relation (be relevant), and manner (be clear). Interaction in dialog works because readers look at the mathematically compiled output of the GenAI and assume that it is informative, truthful, and relevant. Due to its generation of linguistically accurate and plausible text, the GenAI appears to be clear. Communicative interaction proceeds successfully as long as the human reader does not detect that the machine output is not truthful or factually accurate because of, for example, hallucinations (Nananukul & Kejriwal, 2024) or errors or is not relevant because of misinterpreting an ambiguity in different contexts (e.g., when asked about bats, giving information about the mammal rather than the intended sports instrument).

Besides these hurdles, GenAIs have become interesting verbal interactants in language education. On the other hand, ICALL systems, mainly due to their limited language coverage (see above), have provided limited interaction. Systems with or without AI worked with branching trees and canned text, for example in Quandary, a software of the Hot Potatoes suite (Arneil & Holmes, n.d.), which does not have NLP built in. Other systems were more like Chatbots whose conversation was limited to one topic or topic area (e.g., Underwood, 1982). Such CALL chatbots were inspired by Weizenbaum's Eliza (for his reflection see Weizenbaum (1976)) and SHRDLU (Winograd, 1971) and often relied on regular expressions (Computer Science Field Guide, n.d.) and keyword searches. More sophisticated NLP was employed in the interactive games *Spion* (Sanders & Sanders, 1995) and *Kommissar* (DeSmedt, 1995). These early examples of the direct interaction of a learner with a machine with some AI capabilities, especially a level of NLP, show that GenAI has opened a door to the possibility of many more complex and comprehensive verbal interactions and role plays in a variety of languages.

Of course, language learning tasks (see Willis [1996] for an early introduction to the now commonly applied Task-based Language Teaching) are not only rooted in conversations and role plays. GenAI can also generate model answers for different task components or be employed for brainstorming first ideas in the pre-task steps, for example. This was impossible with the ICALL systems based on symbolic NLP and (limited) expert systems. A discussion of the affordances and challenges of this powerful generation of (partial) task outcomes and components both by the student or the teacher is beyond the confines of this chapter, but it is an area within the application of GenAI in language education that is in urgent need of discussion. This agentive collaboration in dialog, possible scaffolding, and student guidance can either support or hinder and even prevent learning.

Appropriate error correction and contingent feedback

Rather than focusing on engaging the learner in communicative interaction, learning with ICALL systems was often based on the assumption that corrective feedback on learner language is of great importance. ICALL research particularly in the 1990s and early 2000s focused on corrective feedback and relied on the three steps of traditional error analysis: effective recognition, description, and explanation (Heift & Schulze, 2007, chapter 3: Error analysis and description). Error analysis (Corder, 1974) was the main approach in second-language acquisition research in the 1960s and 1970s. It's contributions to language education, applied linguistics, and ICALL are manifold and impacted language teaching to this day. Although error correction is still a part common teaching practices today, applied linguistics research has shifted the focus away from deficits in the learner's language to operationalizing and encouraging their abilities (compare the National Council of State Supervisors for Languages (NCSSFL) and the American Council on the Teaching of Foreign Languages (ACTFL) Can-Do Statements, which were introduced in 2013). This has changed the perspective on corrective feedback in language education. More nuances were introduced and also ICALL began to look at providing help and guidance to learners through text augmentation by, for example, enriching a reading text with linked online glossaries and information on morphological paradigms (e.g., Amaral & Meurers, 2011; Wood, 2011). Text augmentation appears to be as yet underexplored in GenAI and language education research since late 2022.

How does ICALL with its symbolic NLP compare with language feedback and guidance to GenAI with its LLMs and ANNs? The texts GenAI produces are mostly well-formed, especially if the text's language is English or one of the other languages in which many texts on the internet are written (Schulze, in press). So, how suitable would a GenAI be for appropriate error correction and contingent feedback? In an ICALL system, a fragment of the grammar of the learnt language would be described with rules and items, using a formal grammar, in the expert model and parser. This computational grammar could 'understand' the linguistically well-formed words, phrases, and sentences, which were covered by the rules of the expert model. To be able to parse student errors, the expert model needed to be adapted. Errors were captured in an error grammar – the buggy rules that were parallel to the rules that covered error-free linguistic units – or in relaxed constraints (Dini & Malnati, 1993). An example of a buggy rule and its error-free counterpart in German is (in pseudo-code for legibility):

> default rule(subject-verb agreement) := if subject(NUMBER) = verb(NUMBER) and
>   subject(PERSON) = verb(PERSON)
>   then parse successfully and move on
>   else buggy rule(subject-verb agreement)
>
> buggy rule(subject-verb agreement) := if subject(NUMBER_S) <> verb(NUMBER_V)
>   then give feedback("The subject is in",
>   [subject(NUMBER_S)],
>   ". You need to choose a verb ending that indicates
>   [subject(NUMBER_S)],
>   ", too. The verb in your sentence is in",
>   [verb(NUMBER_V)])
>   else next
>   then if subject(PERSON_S) <> verb(PERSON_V)
>   then give feedback("The subject is in", [subject(PERSON_S)],
>   ". You need to choose a verb ending that indicates
>   [subject(PERSON_S)],
>   ", too. The verb in your sentence is in",
>   [verb(PERSON_V)])
>   else next
>   then parse successfully and move on

Buggy rules required a high level of error anticipation, because to cover an error, a particular buggy rule needed to be written. Since buggy rules are deterministic, if they were sufficient to parse the student input, they were robust in the feedback they provided. Relaxed constraints reached a slightly wider coverage and required less error anticipation, because the constraint that, for example, the subject and finite verb of German sentence needed to agree in number and person has been relaxed. This means that whether or not subject and verb agree the sentence is parsed successfully with one less constraint rule:

> relaxed rule(subject-verb agreement) = subject(NUMBER_S) and verb(NUMBER_V)
>   and subject(PERSON_S) and verb(PERSON_V)
>   if NUMBER_S = NUMBER_V
>   then next
>   else give feedback("The subject is in", [subject(NUMBER_S)],

". You need to choose a verb ending that indicates [subject(NUMBER_S)],
", too. The verb in your sentence is in",
[verb(NUMBER_V)])
then if PERSON_S = PERSON_V
then next
else give feedback("The subject is in", [subject(PERSON_S)],
". You need to choose a verb ending that indicates [subject(PERSON_S)],
", too. The verb in your sentence is in",
[verb(PERSON_V)])
then parse successfully and move on

This pseudo-code illustration shows how labor-intensive the coding of symbolic NLP for ICALL with its focus on error correction and feedback was. The lack of coverage of the computational lexica and grammars and the additional parsing challenges introduced with including parser coverage of errors learners make meant that even the few ICALL systems that were used by students had limited coverage (e.g., Heift, 2010; Nagata, 2002).

Coverage is not a problem for GenAI, as we saw above. However, LLMs and multidimensional ANNs were not intended to provide corrective feedback to language learners. Their error correction of GenAI can be illustrated best with the automatic correction of spelling errors. The prompt "Tell me please what the capitel of germany is." with its two spelling errors yields the following result: "The capital of Germany is **Berlin** ..." (Microsoft Copilot, 2025, January 17, my emphasis) For languages with LLMs, the automatic error correction in the natural language understanding is accurate and comprehensive, as can be seen from the answer in the example. However, the feedback on such errors, only given when specifically requested, is all too often flawed in parts or incomplete. Stated in brief, GenAIs are good at error correction and are limited in providing appropriate corrective feedback. Many teachers, and language learners, have at least anecdotal evidence that metalinguistic explanations are not suitable for language learners and that errors are often underreported or over-flagged. This is understandable if one considers that GenAIs are working with probabilistic patterns in the LLM for their error correction, diagnosis, and (metalinguistic) feedback. This works often for the correction, but is shaky at best for diagnosis and feedback. The computational linguist and ICALL researcher Detmar Meuers (2024) argued in this context that assuming a GenAI is a suitable language teacher is worse than asking a speaker of that language to start teaching systematic language classes. His argument was also based on the fact the a GenAI has no 'knowledge' of the prior learning history, language abilities and beliefs, and the general profile of the learner.

Recording learner behavior and student modeling

The intelligent tutoring systems in ICALL had this knowledge stored in a student model (Schulze, 2012). Student modeling (e.g., Bull, 1993; Bull, 1994, 2000; Mabbott & Bull, 2004; McCalla, 1992; Michaud & McCoy, 2000; Schulze, 2008b; Self, 1974; Tsiriga & Virvou, 2003) is a challenging endeavor; student data needs to be recorded and structured into a student profile, then inferences can be drawn to construct a student model over time. The model has structured information about prior learning, learner beliefs, strategies, and preferences, and language beliefs. Basically, it models the information teachers have about their students both through student records and the teacher's experience. Such information helps to tailor instructional sequences, guidance and help, and corrective feedback individually so that it becomes relevant and most effective. GenAIs have LLMs which contain enormous information about language and languages (Wolfram, 2023, February 14); their knowledge of the learner is often non-existent or serendipitous at best. Currently and in the context of language education and especially in the context of previous research in ICALL and student modeling in general, the lack of a student model means that GenAIs cannot be treated nor employed as an intelligent tutoring system (ITS), because ITS consist of a knowledge base, a student model, and a pedagogical module (Wikipedia contributors, 2024, December 20) to imitate the behavior of a human tutor and provide individualized tutoring.

Dynamic individualization

Even though a GenAI is not an ITS, as some ICALL systems were, can it consider and appropriately respond to individual learner differences (Dörnyei, 2006)? On the one hand, the limits of appropriate corrective feedback GenAIs can give curtail the possibilities for individualized help learners receive. On the other, the probabilistic, nonlinear approach and other (hidden) traits of LLMs mean that the experience of text generation is unique to each user (Wolfram, 2023, February 14). In other words, the same prompt put in twice will normally generate (at least slightly) different texts. This is a feature of GPTs because they contain slight distortions to make their generated text more human-like. Texts can also be generated using different voices, styles, and registers as well as for different language proficiency and readability levels. Thus, providing an individualized textual experience is a strength of GenAIs that are based on LLMs.

As discussed above, LLMs are machine-learnt ANNs, which were trained on a very large number of texts from the internet. They did not gain 'their experience' with a large group of students who they got to know over the years. This is what teachers do, and this is what student models contribute in an AI system. GPTs are not meant or designed to function as an intelligent tutoring system, because they have little to no information about the individual student, planned instructional sequences, and the curricular context of an activity or lesson. Information about an individual student is stored in a student profile. Virtual learning environments and quiz tools, for example, store scores, time on task, resources accessed, etc. in the system. This structured information can be used in a student model of an intelligent language tutoring system to 'reason' about the student's learning and language beliefs, which then informs the next steps of the system: what feedback is given when, what help is offered, which resources are shown or hidden, which activity is pushed next, … And GenAI's strength is in the generation of plausible texts and not in the administering of meaningful and effective learning sequences. GenAIs can collect further textual data to further refine their LLM, but they do not (yet) collect learner information like bespoke learning environments and apps do. Thus, the individualization of learning processes – also when employing GenAI tools – is still the remit and responsibility of the teacher and must not be delegated to the machine. GenAI can adapt the generated text to the user's prompt, but it is not designed to deliver or implement adaptive instruction (Schulze et al., 2025 in press). Adaptation of the machine to the learner was in ICALL because of the student model and pre-programmed feedback algorithms, for example. Also, tutorial CALL software in the early phase of CALL had instructional sequences of its activities hard-wired and had limited capability of adapting to the learning path of individual students and their learning preferences through inbuilt branching between activities, for example based on prior answers in the previous activities or overall score thresholds.

Gradual release of responsibility

Instructional sequences and other learning processes are structured according to pedagogical guidelines and principles and specific teaching methods. For reasons of brevity, we chose one commonly employed method – the gradual release of responsibility (Fisher & Frey, 2021). In an instructional sequence, the responsibility for the process and its outcomes is shifted from the teacher to the learner. Starting with Focused Instruction (I do it) and moving to Guided Instruction (We do it), more and more responsibility is transferred to the student in the latter two phases Collaborative Learning (You do it together) and Independent Learning (You do it alone). It is mainly the locus of control that shifts gradually from the teacher to the learner.

If the sequences of learning activities and the algorithm for guidance and feedback are hardwired in the system and hardly adapt to an individual learner and their behavior – as was the case in most ICALL and in tutorial CALL in general – then the control of processes is largely with the machine. To put it polemically, the learner's choices are limited to using the ICALL or tutorial app or not. At first sight, this is different with GenAI. Learners can request specific texts and then request something different. Everything can be translated from one language into another, all questions will get an answer – it might not be correct – and all prompts get a reply. The student decides what and how much will be generated at what time. The generation is fast and often faster than most humans can type. This means that the locus of control is largely with the learner in this respect.

The GenAI controls the generation process. The many hidden layers of the ANN mean that how the GPT transforms the input, for example the prompt, to the output the learner can read, for example an answer to a question. The problem here is for learner to be able to learn, they need to be able trust the truth value and relevance of text they received. Since the GPT with its LLM remains impenetrable even for the computer scientists who ran the deep (machine) learning to train the model and thus the artificial neural network due its enormous complexity, it is almost impossible to check the generated text output within the system. Currently, because all GenAI users are new users, teachers and students can rely on previously learned information – information that was not generated by a GenAI – to compare the output they received to what they know already. However, one can conduct a thought experiment already: if we learn more and more from generated texts, then we have less and less prior 'independent' information that we can use to check the GenAI output for errors …

The more immediate conundrum is the trust all learners need to put into information they are being taught and do not know (and thus cannot check easily). Because of their institutionalized power and prior training and accreditation, teachers normally get the trust of their students; students trust the information they are taught. Especially during the phase of Focused Instruction, if this instruction is given via GenAI generated text, learners do not know how much trust they can place in the information they obtain from the text. Here again, it is the responsibility of the teacher to control the process and, if need be, check the taught information. This means that the gradual release of responsibility from the teacher to the student must be almost parallel to the 'release of responsibility' from the teacher to the machine. Whereas an ICALL ITS was a rigid and often limited 'tutor', GenAI must not replace the human teacher and can only be useful as the learning partner in the third phase of Collaborative Learning (You [learner and GenAI] do it together) and as a helper in the Guided Instruction phase (You [teacher, GenAI, and learner] do it) with the teacher in the lead. It appears that the current GenAI does not have a role in the individual teacher phase (Focused instruction [I do it]) nor in the individual student phase (independent Learning [You do it]). Teachers should not abdicate their role in the initial teaching of new material; and students cannot have their independent learning done for them by a machine.

Seven lessons

In conclusion, we will recapitulate and condense the seven lessons that we can learn from 'good old-fashioned AI' and ICALL with its declarative knowledge, engineered algorithms, and symbolic NLP and see how they can be applied to GenAI with its machine-learnt complex artificial neural networks.

1. **Exposure to rich, authentic language**
   GenAI is capable of providing ample exposure to rich language just in time, on the right topic, and at the right level. Generated texts consist of mostly accurate language forms and are plausible, so that they lend themselves to an interpretation in context by the students. This gives such a text an authentic feel. Here GenAI compares very well to the limited linguistic scope of ICALL systems.
2. **Communication in context**
   GenAI, also because of the comprehensive coverage of the LLMs, can sustain conversations with learners on different topics. Its natural language understanding is such that it can take into consideration prior textual context, making any conversation more natural. This was impossible with ICALL systems and chatbots of the past. However, teachers and students need to be aware that they are communicating with a machine, a stochastic parrot (Bender et al., 2021). This requires informed reflection on a new form of communication and learning, to avoid the anthropomorphizing of machine and its output.
3. **Appropriate error correction and contingent feedback**
   This is the area where we can learn most from ICALL and tutorial CALL. Especially with giving metalinguistic feedback, GenAI has too many shortcomings. Researchers need to explore how the automatic error correction, which happens frequently, impacts aspects of language learning such as noticing.

4. **Varied interaction in language learning tasks**
   This is the area where we have many new opportunities to explore, although we can take inspiration particularly from projects in ICALL and game-based language learning. GenAI is most suitable as a partner in conversation and learning.
5. **Recording learner behavior and student modeling**
   Student modeling has a long tradition – not just in ICALL – in AI and education. GenAI tools by themselves are that – tools and not tutors. They can be embedded in other learning systems, but they cannot be used as virtual tutors, because their information about learners and the learning context are serendipitous at best.
6. **Dynamic individualization**
   GenAI provides teachers and students with an individual experience with generated texts of high quality. The adaptive instruction (Schulze et al., 2025 in press), however, which has been an ambition of ICALL research, has not yet been achieved. Broader research and development in AI, beyond GenAI, is still necessary to achieve dynamic individualization in what can truly be termed ICALL.
7. **Gradual release of responsibility**
   Since the instructional sequences, pedagogical approaches, and teaching methods are not present in GenAI, teachers need to design the use of GenAI as one of the tools in the learning process carefully. Teachers must not render the control of curricular and pedagogical decisions about activity design, learning goals, lesson contents, and learning materials to the machine.

GenAI, due to its powerful LLMs, has lifted AI in language education to a new quality. Such a disruptive technology shows great promise, provides many additional opportunities, and poses some challenges for teachers, students, and researchers alike.

Post-reading questions:

1) Considering the emphasis on communicative competence in language learning, how would you want AI systems to be designed to better support meaningful and contextually appropriate interactions?
2) What communication is better human to human and what type of interaction can be a good practice opportunity with a GenAI?
3) Looking at Lesson 7, how can teachers gradually release responsibility for the learning design to the machine? Where can GenAI help; where does the teacher need to retain control?

Further reading

1. If you are interested in what happened with AI and language learning, the article in CALICO Journal provides a brief overview: Schulze, M. (2008). AI in CALL - Artificially inflated or almost imminent? *CALICO Journal, 25*(3), 510–527.
2. The blogpost Wolfram, S. (2023, February 14). *What is ChatGPT doing ... and why does it work? Stephen Wolfram Writings.* https://writings.stephenwolfram.com/2023/02/what-is-chatgpt-doing-and-why-does-it-work. offers an accessible introduction to large language models with many examples. A basic understanding of LLMs is very helpful when working with powerful GenAIs. Stephen Wolfram is a well-known British-American computer scientist.
3. LLMs are created through deep learning, a form of machine learning. Again, it is important to understand the basics, to have better insight into the capabilities and limitations of current GenAIs. The article LeCun, Y., Bengio, Y., & Hinton, G. (2015). Deep learning. *Nature, 521*, 436–444 is a good introduction. The three authors have been called the "Godfathers of Deep Learning."

References

Amaral, L., & Meurers, W. D. (2011). On using Intelligent computer-assisted language learning in real-life foreign language teaching and learning. *ReCALL, 23*(1), 4–24.

Arneil, S., & Holmes, M. (n.d.). *Quandary.* Retrieved January 17 from https://hcmc.uvic.ca/project/quandary/

Baidoo-anu, D., & Owusu Ansah, L. (2023). Education in the era of generative artificial intelligence (AI): Understanding the potential benefits of ChatGPT in promoting teaching and learning. *Journal of AI, 7*(1), 52–62.

Bender, E. M., Gebru, T., McMillan-Major, A., & Shmitchell, S. (2021). On the dangers of stochastic parrots. In *Proceedings of the 2021 ACM Conference on Fairness, Accountability, and Transparency* (pp. 610–623). https://doi.org/10.1145/3442188.3445922

Bowerman, C. (1993). *Intelligent computer-aided language learning. LICE: A system to support undergraduates writing in German* [PhD Thesis, UMIST]. Manchester.

Breen, M. P. (1985). Authenticity in the language classroom. *Applied Linguistics, 6*(1), 60–70. https://doi.org/10.1093/applin/6.1.60

Bull, S. (1993). Towards user/system collaboration in developing a student model for intelligent computer-assisted language learning. *Computer Assisted Language Learning, 8*, 3–8.

Bull, S. (1994). Student modeling for second language acquisition. *Computers and Education, 23*(1–2), 13–20.

Bull, S. (2000). 'Do it yourself' student models for collaborative student modelling and peer interaction. In B. P. Goettl, H. M. Halff, C. Redfield Luckhardt, & V. J. Shute (Eds.), *Intelligent Tutoring Systems. 4th International Conference, ITS '98, San Antonio, Texas, USA, August 16–19, 1998 Proceedings* (pp. 176–185). Springer Verlag.

Canale, M., & Swain, M. (1980). Theoretical bases of communicative approaches to second language teaching and testing. *Applied Linguistics, 1*(1), 1–47.

Chomsky, N. (1957). *Syntactic structures*. Mouton.

Computer Science Field Guide. (n.d.). *Regular expressions - Formal Languages*. Retrieved January 27 from https://www.csfieldguide.org.nz/en/chapters/formal-languages/regular-expressions/

Corder, P. (1974). Error analysis. In J. P. B. Allen & P. Corder (Eds.), *The Edinburgh course in applied linguistics. Volume 3 - Techniques in applied linguistics* (pp. 122–131). Oxford University Press.

DeSmedt, W. H. (1995). Herr Kommissar: An ICALL Conversation simulator for intermediate German. In V. M. Holland, J. D. Kaplan, & M. R. Sams (Eds.), *Intelligent language tutors: Theory shaping technology* (pp. 153–174). Lawrence Erlbaum Associates.

Dini, L., & Malnati, G. (1993). Weak constraints and preference rules. In P. Bennett & P. Paggio (Eds.), *Preference in Eurotra* (pp. 75–90). Commission of the European Communities.

Dörnyei, Z. (2006). Individual differences in second language acquisition. *AILA Review, 19*, 42–68.

Fisher, D., & Frey, N. (2021). *Better learning through structured teaching: A framework for the gradual release of responsibility* (3rd ed.). ASCD.

Gamper, J., & Knapp, J. (2002). A review of intelligent CALL systems. *Computer Assisted Language Learning, 15*(4), 329–342.

Grice, H. P. (1975). Logic and conversation. In D. Cole & J. Morgan (Eds.), *Syntax and semantics: Speech acts* (pp. 41–58). Academic Press.

Heift, T. (2010). Developing an intelligent tutor. *CALICO Journal, 27*(3), 443–459.

Heift, T., & Schulze, M. (2007). *Errors and intelligence in CALL. Parsers and pedagogues*. Routledge.

Heift, T., & Schulze, M. (2015). Tutorial CALL. *Language Teaching, 48*(4), 471–490.

Hubbard, P., & Bradin-Siskin, C. (2004). Another look at tutorial CALL. *ReCALL, 16*(2), 448–461.

Hutchins, J. (1986). *Machine translation - Past, present and future*. Ellis Horwood.

Hymes, D. H. (1974). *Foundations in sociolinguistics: An ethnographic approach*. University of Pennsylvania Press.

Jones, C. R., & Bergen, B. K. (2024). *People cannot distinguish GPT-4 from a human in a Turing test.* http://dx.doi.org/10.48550/arXiv.2310.20216

LeCun, Y., Bengio, Y., & Hinton, G. (2015). Deep learning. *Nature, 521*, 436–444.

Mabbott, A., & Bull, S. (2004). Alternative views on knowledge: Presentation of open learner models. In J. C. Lester, R. M. Vicari, & F. Paraguacu (Eds.), *Intelligent Tutoring Systems: 7th International Conference* (pp. 689–698). Springer-Verlag.

Matthews, C. (1993). Grammar frameworks in intelligent CALL. *CALICO Journal, 11*(1), 5–27.

McCalla, G. I. (1992). The centrality of student modelling to intelligent tutoring systems. In E. Costa (Ed.), *New directions for intelligent tutoring systems* (pp. 107–131). Springer Verlag.

McCarthy, J., Minsky, M. L., Rochester, N., & Shannon, C. E. (1955). *A proposal for the Dartmouth Summer Research Project on Artificial Intelligence.* Retrieved Sep 30 from http://www-formal.stanford.edu/jmc/history/dartmouth/dartmouth.html

Merriam-Webster. (n.d.). *Stochastic.* In *Merriam-Webster's unabridged dictionary.* Retrieved December 30 from https://unabridged.merriam-webster.com/unabridged/stochastic

Meurers, D. (2024). #3x07 - Intelligente Tutorielle Systeme (mit Prof. Dr. Detmar Meurers) In *Auftrag:Aufbruch. Der Podcast des Forum Bildung Digitalisierung.* https://auftrag-aufbruch.podigee.io/30-intelligente-tutorielle-systeme-mit-detmar-meurers

Michaud, L. N., & McCoy, K. F. (2000). Supporting intelligent tutoring in CALL by modeling the user's grammar. In *Proceedings of the Thirteenth Annual International Florida Artificial Intelligence Research Symposium, May 22–24, 2000, Orlando, Florida* (pp. 50–54). AAAI Press.

Microsoft Copilot. (2024, December 26). *How many nodes and layers does the ANN of the GPT large language model have?* Microsoft Copilot.

Microsoft Copilot. (2025, January 17). *Tell me please what the capitel of germany is.* Microsoft Copilot.

Nagata, N. (2002). BANZAI: An application of natural language processing to web-based language learning. *CALICO, 19*(3), 583–599.

Nananukul, N., & Kejriwal, M. (2024). HALO: An ontology for representing and categorizing hallucinations in large language models. Proc. SPIE 13058, *Disruptive Technologies in Information Sciences VIII*, 130580B (6 June 2024).

Naveed, H., Khan, A. U., Qiub, S., Saqib, M., Anwar, S., Usman, M., Akhtar, N., Barnes, N., & Mian, A. (2024). *A comprehensive overview of large language models.* https://dx.doi.org/10.48550/arxiv.2307.06435 http://arxiv.org/pdf/2307.06435

Nelson, G. E., Ward, J. R., Desch, S. H., & Kaplow, R. (1976). Two new strategies for computer-assisted language instruction (CALI). *Foreign Language Annals, 9*(1), 28–37.

Nerbonne, J. A. (2003). Computer-assisted language learning and natural language processing. In R. Mitkov (Ed.), *The Oxford handbook of computational linguistics* (pp. 670–698). Oxford University Press.

Oxford, R. L. (1993). Intelligent computers for learning languages: The view for Language Acquisition and Instructional Methodology. *Computer Assisted Language Learning, 6*(2), 173–188.

Reed, D. W. (1948). Editorial. *Language Learning, 1*(1), 1–2.

Sanders, R. H., & Sanders, A. F. (1995). History of an AI spy game: Spion. In V. M. Holland, J. D. Kaplan, & M. R. Sams (Eds.), *Intelligent language tutors: Theory shaping technology* (pp. 141–151). Lawrence Erlbaum Associates.

Schulze, M. (2008a). AI in CALL – artificially inflated or almost imminent? *CALICO Journal, 25*(3), 510–527.

Schulze, M. (2008b). Modeling SLA processes using NLP. In C. Chapelle, Y.-R. Chung, & J. Xu (Eds.), *Towards adaptive CALL: Natural language processing for diagnostic assessment.* (pp. 149–166). Iowa State University. https://apling.engl.iastate.edu/wp-content/uploads/sites/221/2015/05/5thTSLL2007_proceedings.pdf

Schulze, M. (2012). Learner modeling. In C. A. Chapelle (Ed.), *The encyclopaedia of applied linguistics. 10 volumes* (pp. online n.p.). Wiley-Blackwell.

Schulze, M. (2024). Tutorial CALL – Language practice with the computer. In R. Hampel & U. Stickler (Eds.), *Bloomsbury handbook of language learning and technologies* (pp. 35–47). Bloomsbury Publishing.

Schulze, M. (in press). The impact of artificial intelligence (AI) on CALL pedagogies. In L. Klimanova & L. Lomicka Anderson (Eds.), *The Palgrave encyclopedia on computer-assisted language learning*.

Schulze, M., Caws, C., Hamel, M.-J., & Heift, T. (2025 in press). Adaptive instruction. In G. Stockwell (Ed.), *Cambridge handbook of technology in language teaching and learning* (pp. t.b.d.). Cambridge University Press.

Self, J. A. (1974). Student models in computer-aided instruction. *International Journal of Man-Machine Studies, 6*, 261–276.

Snyder, T. (2017). *On tyranny: Twenty lessons from the twentieth century*. Tim Duggan Books.

Stockwell, G. (2024). ChatGPT in language teaching and learning: Exploring the road we're travelling. *Technology in Language Teaching & Learning, 6*(1), 1–9.

Tsiriga, V., & Virvou, M. (2003). Modelling the student to individualise tutoring in a web-based ICALL. *International Journal of Continuing Engineering Education and Life-Long Learning, 13*(3–4), 350–365.

Turing, A. (1950). Computing machinery and intelligence. *Mind*, *LIX*(236), 433–460.
Underwood, J. H. (1982). Simulated conversation as CAI strategy. *Foreign Language Annals*, *15*, 209–212.
Weischedel, R. M., Voge, W. M., & James, M. (1978). An artificial intelligence approach to language instruction. *Artificial Intelligence*, *10*, 225–240.
Weizenbaum, J. (1976). *Computer power and human reason: From judgment to calculation*. W. H. Freeman.
Wikipedia contributors. (2024, December 20). Intelligent tutoring system. In *Wikipedia, The Free Encyclopedia*.
Willis, J. R. (1996). *A framework for task-based learning*. Longman.
Winograd, T. (1971). *Procedures as a representation for data in a computer program for understanding natural language*. https://hci.stanford.edu/winograd/shrdlu/AITR-235.pdf
Wolfram, S. (2023, February 14). *What is ChatGPT doing ... and why does it work? Stephen Wolfram Writings*. https://writings.stephenwolfram.com/2023/02/what-is-chatgpt-doing-and-why-does-it-work
Wood, P. (2011). Computer assisted reading in German as a foreign language. Developing and testing an NLP-based application. *CALICO Journal*, *28*(3), 662–676.

3
Challenges of AI in language education

Yuwei Wan

Benjamin Luke Moorhouse

> **Pre-reading questions:**
>
> 1) What challenges might language learners face when using GenAI in their language learning?
> 2) What challenges might language teachers face when using GenAI in their language teaching practices?
> 3) What ethical and social issues do you think the development of GenAI has created?

Introduction

Whenever there are new technological developments, the initial debates and discussions are inevitably about the challenges they bring and the effects they will have on the status quo. Language teaching, as with other professions, has developed specific practices and ways of thinking and doing that overtime have become established – universally recognised best practice (Jones & Hafner, 2021). Technology can disrupt these established practices and require a shift in thinking and doing in order for the profession to stay relevant, but also capitalize on the technology in developing new and (hopefully) more effective teaching practices. For example, the development of machine translation tools. Tools such as Google Translate have increased the opportunity for students to engage in self-directed learning and learner autonomy (Lee, 2021). Yet, these same technologies can bring challenges for language students and teachers. Teachers and students may not know how to use these technologies to support their learning and teaching, and at the same time, they could have a negative effect on learning, if used in certain ways.

Take the example of machine translation again. Although these tools are very easy to use, implementing them effectively in the classroom to support learning can be challenging and will require specific pedagogical knowledge and skills (Moorhouse & Yan, 2023). Teachers need to develop suitable learning activities and provide guidance on when and how students could use them to support their language learning. At the same time, teachers may feel concerned that machine translation may undermine learning if students become over reliant on them (e.g., writing everything in their L1 and simply using tools to translate them into their target language), or use them deceptively. Therefore, as well as understanding the pedagogical benefits of technological developments for language teaching and learning, teachers also need a comprehensive understanding of the challenges they bring, and find ways to mitigate these challenges.

Understandably, the development of artificial intelligence (AI), and most recently, generative artificial intelligence (GenAI) has led to intense speculation regarding their effects on the status quo within language education and the effect they will have on the thinking and doing of language teaching and learning (Jeon & Lee, 2023; Crompton & Burke, 2024). They can perform a variety of tasks commonly associated with human intelligence without additional training by the user. These tasks include, text generation, text summarization, translation, analysis, as well as image, code, audio, and video generation (Ali et al., 2023). Language teachers can use them as a knowledge resource and developer, to support their instructional preparation and planning, support personalized learning, and assist their assessment and feedback practices (See Moorhouse, 2024 for examples of uses of AI in language teaching and learning). However, the generative capabilities of these tools provide unique challenges to language education.

In this chapter, we provide an overview of the challenges of AI in language education. We have organized the identified challenges into those associated with using GenAI in language education and the challenges GenAI has created in the field of language education. We believe that students and teachers can both experience challenges when using GenAI, while there are also wider ethical and social challenges the development of these tools have created. Figure 1 summaries the challenges discussed in this chapter. Throughout the chapter we provide practical examples to illustrate the challenges. After the challenges are introduced, we provide some ways language teachers may address them in order to effectively and responsibly use GenAI to assist their language teaching and help students achieve their language learning aims.

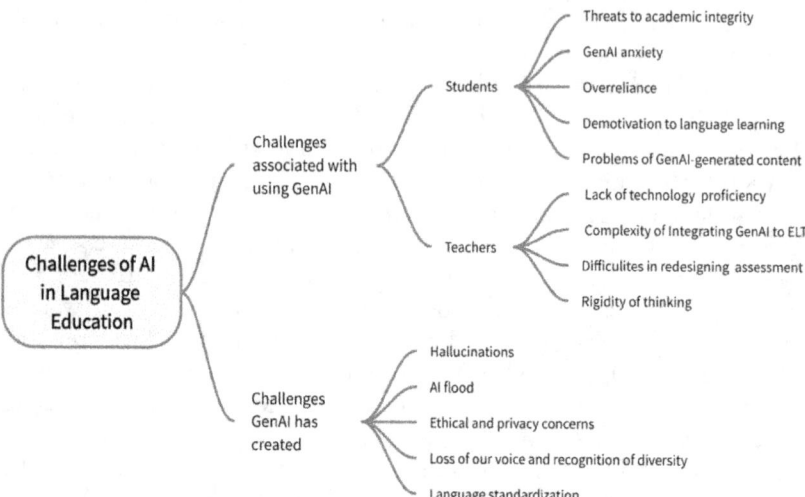

Figure 3.1 *Challenges of AI in language education.*

Challenges associated with using GenAI

A growing number of studies have demonstrated the potential applications of GenAI tools in language education (e.g., Kohnke et al., 2023; Wan & Moorhouse, 2024; Wang et al., 2024; Thorburn, 2023). However, integrating these GenAI tools into practices brings several practical challenges for both teachers and students. In the following section, we will discuss the potential challenges associated with using GenAI in language teaching and learning from students' and teachers' perspectives.

Students

This section outlines five challenges associated with students' use of GenAI: threats to academic integrity, GenAI anxiety, over-reliance, demotivation to language learning, and problems with GenAI-generated content.

Threats to academic integrity

GenAI tools have been widely used by students to assist with writing or completing tasks, sometimes deliberately and sometimes inadvertently without awareness. This practice can blur the lines of academic integrity, increasing the risk of plagiarism and cheating

(Kohnke et al., 2023; Xiao & Zhi, 2023; Yeo, 2023). Grade Point Averages (GPA) often serve as a key metric for assessing students' academic performance (Ayoub & Aladwan, 2021). College students, in particular, face significant pressure to achieve high GPAs to enhance their chances of being accepted into good postgraduate programs and securing competitive job opportunities after graduation. Thus, students may prioritize task completion over the learning process. Tools like ChatGPT, powered by large language models (LLMs), can perform well in helping students manage their workloads, particularly in language writing tasks. Students with low motivation to learn might resort to using GenAI as a "ghostwriter," seeking shortcuts to complete their assignments (Xiao & Zhi, 2023). A student participant in Xiao and Zhi's (2023) study honestly stated that since ChatGPT already helps with brainstorming, it seems reasonable to let it write the entire essay. Without proper guidance on the responsible use of GenAI, these mindsets could become widespread among students, leading to increased inequality and decreased learning quality.

GenAI anxiety

The pressure to succeed academically not only drives students towards potentially unethical use of GenAI but also contributes to students' anxiety over GenAI use. AI anxiety is rooted in computer anxiety, such as technophobia or computer phobia (Li & Huang, 2020; Wang & Wang, 2022), which is defined as the propensity of a person to feel uneasy, apprehensive, or fearful about current or future use of computers (Parasuraman & Igbaria, 1990). With the emergence of GenAI, AI anxiety has further evolved to represent the fear arising from changes in personal or social life brought about by AI and its potential threats (Kaya et al., 2024; Wang et al., 2024). For students, the development of GenAI has significantly changed many aspects of their lives. Their anxiety associated with using GenAI largely comes from the lack of clear policies and guidelines from teachers and institutions. They are uncertain about whether or not they should use and how to use GenAI for language learning but often find themselves unable to resist its "allure" (Zou & Huang, 2023). They might use GenAI with trepidation, unsure if doing so is against academic integrity. In the latest study of Chan (preprint), students expressed their anxiety and fear of being judged by peers, teachers, and society for using GenAI to facilitate academic work. They are concerned about being tagged as "lazy", "dishonest", and lacking "intellectual effort", viewing it as a "social stigma."

Over-reliance

Additionally, some scholars have expressed concern over students' over-reliance on GenAI tools (e.g., Al-khresheh, 2024; Kasneci et al., 2023; Bai et al., 2023; Ulla et al., 2023). The immediate responses these tools generate can lead students to overestimate their capabilities, especially without positive guidance from teachers. They might depend on the tools to accomplish many language-related activities, including information search, summarization, brainstorming, text generation, and revision. From a cognitive standpoint, Bai et al. (2023) argued that learners' over-reliance on AI may impair "memory retention," reinforce "societal biases," and reduce "human interaction." Using GenAI can make reaching conclusions and finding solutions easier, which might reduce students' enthusiasm and motivation for independent thinking and research (Kasneci et al., 2023). Similarly, considering the document upload and summary feature of many tools (e.g., ChatPDF), Dwivedi et al. (2023) cautioned against students' "superficial learning" by using tools to facilitate the reading and comprehending process. The lack of thoughtful engagement can impact the development of their language skills and limit their high-order thinking skills, such as creativity, problem-solving, and critical thinking.

Demotivation to language learning

Some studies have indicated a positive correlation between AI-assisted language instruction and L2 motivation (e.g., Wei, 2023; Dai & Liu, 2024). However, the AI tools referred to in these studies have not covered the wide range of different GenAI tools, but some applications like Duolingo (e.g., Wei, 2023). Additionally, most of the studies emphasize the use of AI within structured language instruction, not students' personal use in language learning. From a broader perspective, the wide use of GenAI in various aspects of daily life in the future may have a negative impact on some ESL students' motivation for language learning (Stockwell & Wang, 2024). Students might start to feel that mastering English is less critical because GenAI tools now offer powerful language and real-time translation capabilities. Their perceived ease of use and usefulness of the tools might overshadow the intrinsic value of mastering a second/foreign language, leading to their demotivation of learning and affecting students' engagement with their language studies.

Problems of GenAI-generated content

Admittedly, some motivated students are using GenAI to personalize their learning experience. GenAI can act as a personal language tutor to give students guidance and prompt feedback (Kohnke et al., 2023; Wan & Moorhouse, 2024). However, there are concerns regarding the content generated by GenAI. Although GenAI tools, such as ChatGPT, can perform well with grammar and vocabulary in English teaching, they were found to fall short of fully comprehending and conveying the "cultural nuances" inherent in language instruction (Al-khresheh, 2024). For example, when students upload their writing and ask for corrective feedback, these tools may be competent in correcting grammar mistakes and providing a polished revised version with complex sentence patterns and advanced vocabulary, but they often lack the ability to provide detailed and personalized explanations necessary for understanding critical aspects of language rules, such as intercultural communication, and applying them across different contexts. In other words, the unpredictability and superficiality of GenAI-generated content may not adequately prepare students for real-world interactions, which are dynamic and context-based (Crompton et al., 2024).

Teachers

Similarly, teachers also face significant hurdles in effectively incorporating GenAI into their teaching practices. This section explores four primary challenges faced by teachers: lack of technology proficiency and accessibility, complexity of integrating GenAI into ELT, difficulties in redesigning assessments, and rigidity of thinking.

Lack of technology proficiency and accessibility

For teachers, their lack of GenAI competencies is one of the major challenges. Besides mainstream large language models (LLMs) like OpenAI's GPT and Anthropic's Claude, new tools with embedded GenAI functions are released daily, overwhelming teachers with an array of choices (Moorhouse, 2024). Without sufficient training, teachers may not know how to properly use these tools and maximize their potential. For example, some studies have emphasized the importance of mastering prompt engineering skills or prompt literacy (e.g., Cain, 2024; Maloy & Gattupalli, 2024), which is the ability to effectively ask questions to get the desired output from LLMs. However, many teachers are struggling with this, not knowing the key elements of a good prompt and how to interact with LLMs iteratively to accomplish the task. Another significant issue is teachers' inaccessibility to certain GenAI tools. While some tools may offer free trials for several days or weeks, they eventually require a subscription, with costs ranging from a few dollars to several hundred dollars. Some websites might allow users to generate a limited number of lesson plans. Once users get a taste of the usefulness, they have to subscribe for further access. Each tool has unique features and specific applications that can facilitate language instruction, but without institutional support, it is not practical for teachers to purchase subscriptions to all useful tools. This financial barrier prevents teachers from fully leveraging GenAI tools in their teaching practices.

Complexity of integrating GenAI to ELT

Moreover, the complexity of integrating GenAI into the classroom extends beyond the basic use of asking questions. Teachers need to understand how to align GenAI tools with their pedagogical goals and customize them to fit their specific language teaching context. GenAI can help brainstorm and generate various activities and materials based on teachers' needs, making the classroom rich and engaging. However, it places higher demands on teachers. Teachers need to have profound pedagogical insight to ensure that GenAI tools complement curricular objectives rather than disrupt them (Kostka & Toncelli, 2023). Suppose teachers merely stack GenAI-generated materials and activities without thoughtful adjustment. In that case, English classes might seem dynamic and interactive, but whether students achieve the intended learning outcomes is open to doubt. This highlights the critical need for teachers to use GenAI judiciously to cater to the specific teaching content and students' diverse needs.

Difficulties in redesigning assessment

Considering the threats to the validity of assessment practices brought about by students' wide use of GenAI in accomplishing tasks, teachers are expected to redesign assessments to focus not only on the results (Moorhouse et al., 2023; Kostka & Toncelli, 2023). In Liu's 2024 study of 17 teachers from 10 universities, more than half perceived threats or challenges related to assessment posed by GenAI. As LLMs can assist with most language learning tasks and generate human-like content, it is difficult for people to distinguish between human and AI-generated writing. By asking reviewers to do a judgment task, Casal and Kessler (2023) found that even linguists were unsuccessful in distinguishing human and AI-generated research abstracts. Although there are some AI detection tools available in the market, the reliability of most of these tools is open to doubt (Moorhouse et al., 2023). This creates an urgent need for teachers to rethink their original assessment tasks and come up with innovative ideas that are process-oriented and can cultivate students' high-order thinking skills in language learning. However, without institutional support and resources, it is challenging for teachers to undertake such comprehensive changes on their own. An easy solution is to convert all take-home assignments into in-class assessment (Moorhouse et al., 2023), but such a shift could place great pressure on classroom time and resources, and may be perceived as a step backward in educational progress.

Rigidity of thinking

Notably, the increasing integration of GenAI tools in education can also lead to teachers' rigidity of thinking, which may hinder their ability to generate novel instructional ideas and negatively affect the quality of classroom instruction (Farrokhnia et al., 2023). GenAI tools can assist with lesson planning, material development, and assessment, potentially improving efficiency and reducing teachers' workload (Kohnke et al., 2023; Thorburn, 2023). Because of these capabilities, language teachers often turn to GenAI for advice and information whenever they encounter problems. As GenAI tools rarely reject teachers' requests and consistently provide answers that are plausible, some teachers may mistakenly believe that GenAI is omnipotent, mastering both content and pedagogical knowledge. Some studies found that when teachers utilize AI tools that are tailored to meet certain goals in education, they become a supplement to the tools rather than making tools as facilitators (Holstein & Aleven, 2022). For instance, if a language teacher enters their requirement to a lesson plan generator (e.g., magicschool.ai) and asks it to follow a specific teaching approach, such as Task-Based Language Teaching (TBLT), it can produce a plan with detailed teaching steps and supporting texts and activities. Figure 2 is the screenshot of a lesson plan generator. Teachers can create a tailored lesson plan with several clicks. Then, teachers might ask, "If these tools are so powerful and even more knowledgeable than me, why bother thinking?" Over time, this reliance on tools may turn teachers into passive AI recipients, making teachers less likely to explore diverse teaching methods and making classrooms monotonous for students. Because of this, some studies on in-service language teachers' perspectives of GenAI have pointed out their feelings of insecurity and fear of being replaced by AI in the future (e.g., Moorhouse, 2024).

Challenges GenAI has created to the society

In the previous section, we have discussed the practical, day-to-day challenges that teachers and students face when they interact with

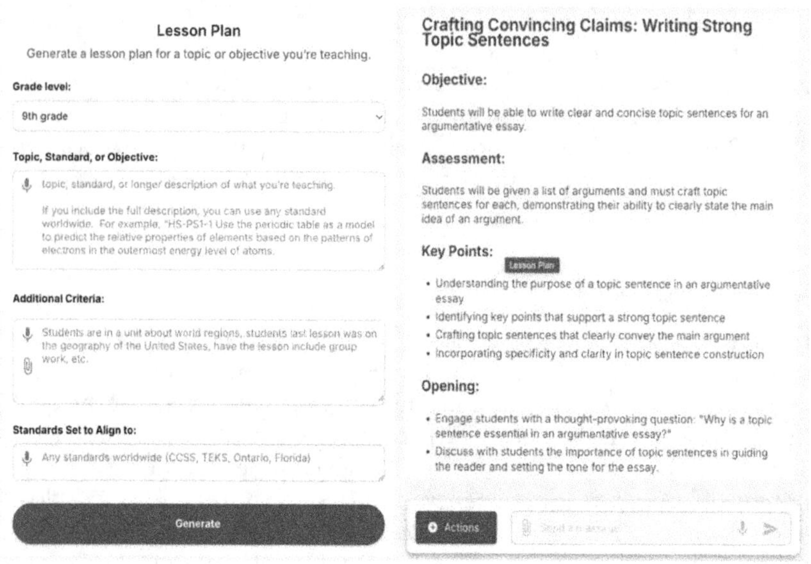

Figure 3.2 *Interface of a lesson plan generator.*

GenAI tools and implement them in the context of language education. In this section, we will introduce broader and systemic challenges that have inherently been created by GenAI, including technical, ethical, and social dimensions.

Hallucinations

The term *hallucination* has been constantly mentioned and recognized as one of the major drawbacks of generative AI. It refers to instances where LLMs generate false, misleading, or unsubstantiated information (Walters & Wilder, 2023). While LLMs are trained on vast datasets, they generate responses based on patterns and probabilities rather than pre-defined answers and verifying facts (Perković et al., 2024). Most LLMs, such as ChatGPT and Claude, do not provide the sources of their generated responses. The algorithm makes them capable of responding to any type of questions, but if the information is unknown or not as prevalent in their database, LLM generates hallucinations. They can fabricate names, numbers, locations, cases, fake quotations, and even non-existent academic references (Babl & Babl, 2023; Rawte et al., 2023; Walters & Wilder, 2023). In the study by Walters and Wilder (2023), an examination of 636 citations within 84 literature reviews generated by ChatGPT-3.5 and GPT-4 revealed that 55% of GPT-3.5 citations and 18% of GPT-4 citations were fabricated. Additionally, 43% of the real GPT-3.5 citations and 24% of the real GPT-4 citations contained significant errors. This indicates the importance of critically evaluating GenAI-generated content. Otherwise, fabricated citations may be mistakenly published by journals, and others who reference these journals may further cite these erroneous sources, leading to widespread misinformation and potentially undermining the credibility of subsequent research. Another form of hallucination can be "sentence contradiction" (Perković et al., 2024), where the content generated by LLMs in one iteration may contradict the previous output, and prompting the same question multiple times may yield entirely different answers. Many teachers and students may not be aware of the issue of hallucination and use GenAI as a search engine like Google, unconditionally trusting GenAI-generated content.

AI flood

Another significant problem is the AI flood. In other words, GenAI-generated content, such as text and images, floods and becomes ubiquitous in human's daily lives. A prominent example is Amazon, where thousands of AI-written e-books have inundated the marketplace (Terech, 2023). The pictures and texts generated by GenAI are so human-like and impressive that they are almost indistinguishable from human-created works. With GenAI assistance, anyone can generate endless books and sell them on the Amazon eBook store. Recent reports indicate that AI-generated books even appear in Kindle's lock screen advertisements (Reisinger, 2024). People can utilize text generators like ChatGPT alongside image generators like Midjourney and Stable Diffusion to produce fully illustrated children's books created entirely from simple prompts. Some GenAI-embedded websites even claim that you can create your own ebook with just several clicks. As a result, it is suspected that the majority of Amazon bestsellers in the Teen & Young Adult Contemporary Romance eBooks category are generated by AI (Terech, 2023). This overwhelming volume of GenAI-produced content not only saturates traditional dissemination channels, such as books and articles but also raises concerns about the quality and authenticity of the material being consumed. In response to the AI flood, Amazon updated its Kindle content guidelines by introducing a new policy that requires authors to disclose AI involvement as AI-generated or AI-assisted (Bishop, 2023). However, concerns remain about the transparency and quality of the content.

Ethical and privacy concerns

The wide use of GenAI also sparked concerns about the potential ethical and privacy problems. GenAI-generated content sometimes perpetuates biases related to race, gender, minority groups (Kasneci et al., 2023; Stahl & Eke, 2024; Wang et al., 2024), disabilities, and political ideologies. These biases from original databases can be unintentionally embedded in the training data and subsequently reflected in the outputs, reinforcing stereotypes, discrimination, and misinformation (Wang et al., 2024). The emergence of GenAI also exacerbates issues of equality of access and widens the digital divide (Lim et al., 2023). Developed countries and affluent institutions or individuals may have better access to high-quality GenAI tools by subscription, giving them a significant advantage. Copyright issues present another layer of complexity. The materials used to train AI models often include copyrighted content, raising questions about intellectual property rights (Lucchi, 2023). There is ambiguity regarding who holds the authorship for the material generated by GenAI: the user, the developer of the GenAI, or another entity (Draxler et al., 2024). Notably, privacy risks are also a major concern. The underlying algorithms of GenAI are complex and not fully transparent (Stahl & Eke, 2024). The data users input into GenAI tools might be used to further train these models or even disclose to third parties, potentially leading to data breaches and misuse of personal information (Lund et al., 2023). Figure 3 shows OpenAI's privacy policy, which states their intention to protect users' personal information, but also explicitly clarifies that the policy will not apply to content processed on behalf of customers using their API, potentially leaving our data unprotected. Sensitive and private data may be exposed or exploited without the users' consent, leading to serious consequences.

> We at OpenAI OpCo, LLC (together with our affiliates, "OpenAI", "we", "our" or "us") respect your privacy and are strongly committed to keeping secure any information we obtain from you or about you. This Privacy Policy describes our practices with respect to Personal Information we collect from or about you when you use our website, applications, and services (collectively, "Services"). This Privacy Policy does not apply to content that we process on behalf of customers of our business offerings, such as our API. Our use of that data is governed by our customer agreements covering access to and use of those offerings.
>
> For information about how we collect and use training information to develop our language models that power ChatGPT and other Services, and your choices with respect to that information, please see this help center article.

Figure 3.3 *OpenAI's privacy policy (OpenAI, 2023).*

service. However, many of us use GenAI-embedded tools that rely on OpenAI's API, potentially leaving our data unprotected. Sensitive and private data may be exposed or exploited without the users' consent, leading to serious consequences.

Loss of our voice and recognition of diversity

It should be noted that the capabilities of LLMs may lead to the loss of autonomy and our own voice, particularly in terms of creativity and authenticity (Dwivedi et al., 2023). LLMs can generate vast amounts of information and list numerous choices upon request. While this offers an array of possibilities, it can actually trap us within an "Echo Chamber" (Stahl & Eke, 2024). Stahl and Eke (2024) emphasized that LLMs could potentially reinforce existing beliefs and opinions by providing information that aligns with a user's preconceptions, leading to the narrowing of perspectives. LLMs can constantly generate convincing responses with supporting details. Their persuasive capabilities can influence individuals' decision-making, potentially undermining their autonomy and ability to make informed choices and find their own unique voices. This can result in a diminished appreciation for the richness of human diversity in thoughts and experiences.

Language standardization

GenAI has also increased language standardization because it relies on large datasets that mostly feature "standard" language varieties, such as Standard American English or Standard British English (Smith et al., 2024). These datasets are more readily available and widely used, leading LLMs to prioritize these language use. Additionally, it is found that some words and expressions are being overused by GenAI. By tracking papers published after the release of ChatGPT, some words that were not widely used before–like "delve," "intricate," "meticulous," and "commendable" – are increasingly being used (Strokel-Walker, 2024). This indicates that GenAI may have infiltrated scientific publishing and reinforced language standardization. However, this language standardization has several negative effects. It reinforces hierarchies between language varieties, privileging "standard" forms while marginalizing others (Milroy, 2001). By providing a narrow view of language, English language learners might mistakenly believe that these are the only "correct" ways to speak. They might miss out on the richness and diversity of different dialects and cultural expressions. This can limit their understanding of how English is used in various contexts and may lead to difficulties in communicating with speakers of non-standard varieties.

What is more concerning is that GenAI is data-driven, but many of the world's languages lack standardized written forms and have very few electronic texts. According to Trosterud (2023), between 98% and 99% of the world's languages are infrequently taught in school but spoken widely. Most of them are marginalized languages from former colonies or indigenous people. For instance, in parts of Africa, the local languages people use in daily life are typically not their national official languages. The wide and long-time use of GenAI could contribute to the decline of these marginalized languages.

Ways to address AI challenges in language education

By now, you probably have a good understanding of the possible challenges associated with using GenAI as well as the challenges GenAI has created. The knowledge you have gained already and the critical awareness you have developed of the potential risks and concerns inherent to GenAI can make you better prepared to use GenAI in language education. However, we do also want to give you some ideas that could help you address the AI challenges in language education. We have divided this section up into four sub-sections: (1) Communicating with students; (2) Developing professional GenAI competence; (3) Engaging in continuous professional development; and (4) Adopting a human-centered mindset.

Communicating with students

Given the number of challenges associated with students' use of GenAI, it is important for language teachers to have sustained open and honest communication with students about these tools. Students can be unaware of how these tools can be used to assist their learning, and could be considered that any use of these tools could lead them to get in trouble. Language teachers can provide policies and guidelines on how they can be used with justification provided for any restrictions on specific functions or tasks (Moorhouse et al., 2023). Providing clarity can help reduce anxiety and raise students' awareness of the appropriate use of the tools. Teachers can also highlight the benefit of learning language to our self-improvement and lived experiences, along with the common functional reasons for learning - to increase students' motivation to learn language in a world of competent AI tools.

Developing professional GenAI competence

The release of GenAI tools has led to the need for language teachers to develop specific professional GenAI competence (P-GenAI-C) – the skills and knowledge needed to use GenAI tools effectively within their professional practices. The more competent a teacher feels, the more able and confident they will feel to overcome challenges in using GenAI tools. Building on previous models, Moorhouse et al. (2024) conceptualize P-GenAI-C as including five aspects:

1. GenAI technological proficiency (TP)
2. Pedagogical compatibility of GenAI in English language teaching (PC)
3. Teachers' professional work (PW)
4. Risk, well-being and the ethical use of GenAI (EU)
5. Preparation of students for a GenAI world (PS) (see Table 1 for the descriptors of each aspect.)

Table 1 *Descriptors of P-GenAI-C aspects (Moorhouse et al., 2024)*

P-GenAI-C Descriptor aspects	Descriptor
TP	TP is concerned with teachers' awareness of a variety of GenAI tools, including their functions, uses, and affordances.
PC	PC refers to teachers' use of GenAI tools to supplement and enhance their students' English language learning, including using GenAI tools to help them achieve their learning objectives.
PW	PW is concerned with the use of GenAI tools in teachers' professional work outside of the classroom, including grading and giving feedback, communicating with stakeholders and school administration.
EU	EU refers to teachers' awareness of the risks associated with using AI, the effects GenAI tools may have on teacher and learner well-being, and the ethical issues pertaining to the use of GenAI tools.
PS	PS relates to a teacher's abilities to prepare their students with the knowledge and skills needed to critically and productively engage in GenAI tools in their learning, recreation time, and future work.

By focusing on developing each aspect of GenAI, language teachers will be better positioned to overcome the challenges identified in this chapter.

Engaging in continuous professional development

The rapid development of these tools means language teachers need to continuously engage in related professional development. Luckily, there are a myriad of resources teachers can access to learn more about

GenAI. video hosting platforms such as YouTube have a wide range of content related to GenAI and education, technology companies, such as open.ai, Google and Microsoft have developed interactive online training packages providing information on the technological features of GenAI tools, and there are now an increasing number of journal and magazine articles and special issues regarding the use of GenAI in language education. Teachers can consider creating communities of practice and engaging in practitioner research to address possible challenges they experience with the use of GenAI. These bottom-up approaches can lead to contextual relevant solutions and sustained impact on practice (Kostaka & Toncelli, 2023).

Adopting a human-centered mindset

The capabilities of GenAI tools can often 'wow' the user and make them feel they cannot compete with their competence. Language learning is complex and challenging in itself and requires sustained effort. To overcome the challenges of GenAI, it is important to adopt a human-centered mindset. With this mindset, the goal of learning becomes about self-improvement rather than accomplishing a task. To facilitate this, teachers should emphasize the value of learning, pushing oneself to outperform their abilities, and learn from mistakes. The process of completing a task becomes more important than the final product. In this way, language learners will engage in their learning activities for what it brings to them, rather than for external recognition (which could lead them to use GenAI to cover-up any perceived weaknesses). At the same time, the learners can be shown how to use AI to assist them with the human being the main decision maker within a collaborative AI/Human process. For example, a language learner could work with an LLM in exploring ways to improve their written work.

Conclusion

This chapter has outlined the challenges of AI in language education. Clearly, these tools have been highly disruptive to the current status quo within language education and have required us to analyze and critique our practices to come up with something fit for purpose in the GenAI age. We introduced challenges for students and teachers, as well as additional ethical and social challenges GenAI tools have created. By becoming aware of the challenges, it is hoped that language teachers can be better prepared and confident to use GenAI tools to assist their professional practices. Yet, these technologies are developing at a rapid pace and each new release will bring about new capabilities and challenges. Language teachers need to engage in continuous professional development to stay up-to-date with these advancements.

> 1) Look at your answers to the pre-reading questions, are the challenges similar or different from those mentioned in this chapter?
> 2) What did you learn from this chapter that could help you effectively integrate the use of GenAI into your language teaching practices?
> 3) How might you continue your professional learning about AI and language education?

Further reading

1. Moorhouse, B. L. (2024). Generative artificial intelligence and ELT, *ELT Journal*, 2024, ccae032, https://doi.org/10.1093/elt/ccae032
2. Wang, N., Wang, X., & Su, Y.-S. (2024). Critical analysis of the technological affordances, challenges and future directions of Generative AI in education: A systematic review. *Asia Pacific Journal of Education*, 44(1), 139–155. https://doi.org/10.1080/02188791.2024.2305156
3. Chan, C. K. Y & Colloton, T. (2024). *Generative AI in higher education: The ChatGPT effect.* Taylor & Francis.

References

Ali, J. K. M., Shamsan, M. A. A., Hezam, T. A., & Mohammed, A. A. (2023). Impact of ChatGPT on learning motivation: Teachers and students' voices. *Journal of English Studies in Arabia Felix*, 2(1), 41–49. https://doi.org/10.56540/jesaf.v2i1.51

Al-khresheh, M. H. (2024). Bridging technology and pedagogy from a global lens: Teachers' perspectives on integrating ChatGPT in English language teaching. *Computers and Education. Artificial Intelligence*, 6, 100218-. https://doi.org/10.1016/j.caeai.2024.100218

Ayoub/Al-Salim, M. I., & Aladwan, K. (2021). The relationship between academic integrity of online university students and its effects on academic performance and learning quality. *Journal of Ethics in Entrepreneurship and Technology*, 1(1), 43–60. https://doi.org/10.1108/JEET-02-2021-0009

Babl, F. E., & Babl, M. P. (2023). Generative artificial intelligence: Can ChatGPT write a quality abstract? *Emergency Medicine Australasia*, 35(5), 809–811. https://doi.org/10.1111/1742-6723.14233

Bai, L., Liu, X., & Su, J. (2023). ChatGPT: The cognitive effects on learning and memory. *Brain-X*, *1*(3). https://doi.org/10.1002/brx2.30

Bishop, T. (2023, September 11). Amazon distinguishes between AI 'generated' and 'assisted' content in new policy for Kindle authors. *Geekwire*. https://www.geekwire.com/2023/amazon-distinguishes-between-ai-generated-and-assisted-content-in-new-policy-for-kindle-authors/

Cain, W. (2024). Prompting Change: Exploring Prompt Engineering in Large Language Model AI and Its Potential to Transform Education. *TechTrends*, *68*(1), 47–57. https://doi.org/10.1007/s11528-023-00896-0

Casal, J. E., & Kessler, M. (2023). Can linguists distinguish between ChatGPT/AI and human writing? A study of research ethics and academic publishing. *Research Methods in Applied Linguistics*, *2*(3), 100068. 168-182. https://doi.org/10.1016/j.rmal.2023.100068

Chan, C. K. Y. (preprint) Exploring the Factors of "AI Guilt" Among Students -- Are You Guilty of Using AI in Your Homework?

Chu, W. [@wes_chu]. (2023, June 27). *Amazon self publishing is going through a thing right now*....Twitter. https://twitter.com/wes_chu/status/1673699269252112384/photo/1?ref_src=twsrc%5Etfw%7Ctwcamp%5Etweetembed%7Ctwterm%5E1673699269252112384%7Ctwgr%5E8e74e2157507bf99782ae54555bb810719ce-7bec%7Ctwcon%5Es1_&ref_url=https%3A%2F%2Fwww.vice.com%2Fen%2Farticle%2Fv7b774%2Fai-generated-books-of-nonsense-are-all-over-amazons-bestseller-lists

Crompton, H., & Burke, D. (2024). The educational affordances and challenges of ChatGPT: State of the Field. *TechTrends*, *68*(2), 380–392. https://doi.org/10.1007/s11528-024-00939-0

Crompton, H., Jones, M. V., & Burke, D. (2022). Affordances and challenges of artificial intelligence in K-12 education: a systematic review. *Journal of Research on Technology in Education*, *56*(3), 248–268. https://doi.org/10.1080/15391523.2022.2121344

Dai, K., & Liu, Q. (2024). Leveraging artificial intelligence (AI) in English as a foreign language (EFL) classes: Challenges and opportunities in the spotlight. *Computers in Human Behavior*, 108354. https://doi.org/10.1016/j.chb.2024.108354

Draxler, F., Werner, A., Lehmann, F., Hoppe, M., Schmidt, A., Buschek, D., & Welsch, R. (2024). The AI ghostwriter effect: When users do not perceive ownership of AI-generated text but self-declare as authors. *ACM Transactions on Computer-Human Interaction*, *31*(2), 1–40. https://doi.org/10.1145/3637875

Dwivedi, Y. K., Kshetri, N., Hughes, L., Slade, E. L., Jeyaraj, A., Kar, A. K., Baabdullah, A. M., Koohang, A., Raghavan, V., Ahuja, M.,

Albanna, H., Albashrawi, M. A., Al-Busaidi, A. S., Balakrishnan, J., Barlette, Y., Basu, S., Bose, I., Brooks, L., Buhalis, D., ... Wright, R. (2023). Opinion paper: "So what if ChatGPT wrote it?" Multidisciplinary perspectives on opportunities, challenges and implications of generative conversational AI for research, practice and policy. *International Journal of Information Management, 71*, 102642. https://doi.org/10.1016/j.ijinfomgt.2023.102642

Farrokhnia, M., Banihashem, S. K., Noroozi, O., & Wals, A. (2023). A SWOT analysis of ChatGPT: Implications for educational practice and research. *Innovations in Education and Teaching International, 61*(3), 460–474. https://doi.org/10.1080/14703297.2023.2195846

Holstein, K., & Aleven, V. (2022). Designing for human–AI complementarity in K-12 education. *AI Magazine, 43*(2), 239–248. https://doi.org/10.1002/aaai.12058

Jeon, J., & Lee, S. (2023). Large language models in education: A focus on the complementary relationship between human teachers and ChatGPT. *Education and Information Technologies, 28*(12), 15873–15892. https://doi.org/10.1007/s10639-023-11834-1

Jones, R. H., & Hafner, C. A. (2021). *Understanding digital literacies: A practical introduction* (Second edition.). Routledge.

Kasneci, E., Sessler, K., Küchemann, S., Bannert, M., Dementieva, D., Fischer, F., Gasser, U., Groh, G., Günnemann, S., Hüllermeier, E., Krusche, S., Kutyniok, G., Michaeli, T., Nerdel, C., Pfeffer, J., Poquet, O., Sailer, M., Schmidt, A., Seidel, T., ... Kasneci, G. (2023). ChatGPT for good? On opportunities and challenges of large language models for education. *Learning and Individual Differences, 103*, 102274. https://doi.org/10.1016/j.lindif.2023.102274

Kaya, F., Aydin, F., Schepman, A., Rodway, P., Yetişensoy, O., & Demir Kaya, M. (2022). The roles of personality traits, AI anxiety, and demographic factors in attitudes toward artificial intelligence. *International Journal of Human–Computer Interaction, 40*(2), 497–514. https://doi.org/10.1080/10447318.2022.2151730

Kohnke, L., Moorhouse, B. L., & Zou, D. (2023). ChatGPT for language teaching and learning. *RELC Journal, 54*(2), 537–550. https://doi.org/10.1177/00336882231162868

Kostka, I., & Toncelli, R. (2023). Exploring applications of ChatGPT to English language teaching: Opportunities, challenges, and recommendations. *TESL-EJ (Berkeley, Calif.), 27*(3), 1–19. https://doi.org/10.55593/ej.27107int

Lee, Y.-J. (2021). Still taboo? Using machine translation for low-level EFL writers. *ELT Journal, 75*(4), 432–441. https://doi.org/10.1093/elt/ccab018

Li, J., & Huang, J. S. (2020). Dimensions of artificial intelligence anxiety based on the integrated fear acquisition theory. *Technology in Society*, *63*, 101410. https://doi.org/10.1016/j.techsoc.2020.101410

Lim, W. M., Gunasekara, A., Pallant, J. L., Pallant, J. I., & Pechenkina, E. (2023). Generative AI and the future of education: Ragnarök or reformation? A paradoxical perspective from management educators. *The International Journal of Management Education*, *21*(2), 100790. https://doi.org/10.1016/j.ijme.2023.100790

Liu, X. (2024). Navigating uncharted waters: Teachers' perceptions of and reactions to AI-induced challenges to assessment. *The Asia-Pacific Education Researcher*. https://doi.org/10.1007/s40299-024-00890-x

Lucchi, N. (2023). ChatGPT: A case study on copyright challenges for generative artificial intelligence systems. *European Journal of Risk Regulation*, 1–23. https://doi.org/10.1017/err.2023.59

Lund, B. D., Wang, T., Mannuru, N. R., Nie, B., Shimray, S., & Wang, Z. (2023). ChatGPT and a new academic reality: Artificial Intelligence-written research papers and the ethics of the large language models in scholarly publishing. *Journal of the Association for Information Science and Technology*, *74*(5), 570–581. https://doi.org/10.1002/asi.24750

Maloy, R. W., & Gattupalli, S. (2024). Prompt literacy. *EdTechnica*, 209–215. https://doi.org/10.59668/371.14442

Milroy, J. (2001). Language ideologies and the consequences of standardization. *Journal of sociolinguistics*, *5*(4), 530–555. https://doi.org/10.1111/1467-9481.00163

Moorhouse, B. L., & Yan, L. (2023). Use of digital tools by English language schoolteachers. *Education Sciences*, *13*(3), 226. *https://doi.org/10.3390/educsci13030226*

Moorhouse, B. L. (2024). Generative artificial intelligence and ELT, *ELT Journal*, 78(4), 378–392.p https://doi.org/10.1093/elt/ccae032

Moorhouse, B. L., Yeo, M., & Wan, Y. (2023). Generative AI tools and assessment: Guidelines of the world's top-ranking universities, *Computers & Education Open*. *5*, 100151. https://doi.org/10.1016/j.caeo.2023.100151

OpenAI (2023). Privacy Policy. https://openai.com/policies/privacy-policy/

Parasuraman, S., & Igbaria, M. (1990). An examination of gender differences in the determinants of computer anxiety and attitudes toward microcomputers among managers. *International Journal of Man-Machine Studies*, *32*(3), 327–340. https://doi.org/10.1016/S0020-7373(08)80006-5

Perković, G., Drobnjak, A., & Botički, I. (2024, May). Hallucinations in LLMs: Understanding and addressing challenges. In *2024 47th MIPRO ICT and Electronics Convention (MIPRO)* (pp. 2084–2088). IEEE.

Rawte, V., Chakraborty, S., Pathak, A., Sarkar, A., Tonmoy, S. M., Chadha, A., ... & Das, A. (2023). The troubling emergence of hallucination in large language models–an extensive definition, quantification, and prescriptive remediations. *arXiv preprint arXiv:2310.04988*.

Reisinger, D. (2024, April 1). AI-generated books are flooding Kindle lock screens, and Amazon doesn't care. *ZDNET*. https://www.zdnet.com/article/ai-generated-books-are-flooding-kindle-lock-screens-and-amazon-doesnt-care/

Smith, G., Fleisig, E., Bossi, M., Rustagi, I., & Yin, X. (2024). Standard language ideology in AI-generated language. *arXiv preprint arXiv:2406.08726*.

Stahl, B. C., & Eke, D. (2024). The ethics of ChatGPT–Exploring the ethical issues of an emerging technology. *International Journal of Information Management, 74*, 102700. https://doi.org/10.1016/j.ijinfomgt.2023.102700

Stockwell, G., & Wang, Y. (2024). Expanding the learning ecology and autonomy of language learners with mobile technologies. *Educational Technology & Society, 27*(2), 60–69. https://doi.org/10.30191/ETS.202404_27(2).SP05

Strokel-Walker, C. (2024, May 1). AI chatbots have thoroughly infiltrated scientific publishing. *SciAm*. https://www.scientificamerican.com/article/chatbots-have-thoroughly-infiltrated-scientific-publishing/

Terech, K. (2024, June 4). Amazon has a big problem as AI-generated books flood Kindle Unlimited. *Techradar*. https://www.techradar.com/computing/artificial-intelligence/amazon-has-a-big-problem-as-ai-generated-books-flood-kindle-unlimited

Thorburn R. (2023). Creating teaching materials with ChatGPT and DALL-E2. Retrieved from https://hongkongtesol.com/blog/creating-teaching-materials-chatgpt-and-dall-e2

Trosterud, T. (2023, August 17). *CALL for all languages? Why languages differ and what consequences that has for CALL* [Keynote presentation]. EUROCALL 2023.

Ulla, M. B., Perales, W. F., & Busbus, S. O. (2023). 'To generate or stop generating response': Exploring EFL teachers' perspectives on ChatGPT in English language teaching in Thailand. *Learning: Research and Practice, 9*(2), 168-182.

Walters, W. H., & Wilder, E. I. (2023). Fabrication and errors in the bibliographic citations generated by ChatGPT. *Scientific Reports, 13*(1), 14045–14045. https://doi.org/10.1038/s41598-023-41032-5

Wan, Y., & Moorhouse, B. L. (2024). Using Call Annie as a generative artificial intelligence speaking partner for language learners. *RELC Journal*. https://doi.org/10.1177/00336882231224813

Wang, N., Wang, X., & Su, Y.-S. (2024). Critical analysis of the technological affordances, challenges and future directions of Generative AI in education: a systematic review. *Asia Pacific Journal of Education*, *44*(1), 139–155. https://doi.org/10.1080/02188791.2024.2305156

Wang, Y. Y., & Wang, Y. S. (2019). Development and validation of an artificial intelligence anxiety scale: An initial application in predicting motivated learning behavior. *Interactive Learning Environments*, *30*(4), 619–634. https://doi.org/10.1080/10494820.2019.1674887

Wei, L. (2023). Artificial intelligence in language instruction: impact on English learning achievement, L2 motivation, and self-regulated learning. *Frontiers in Psychology*, *14*, 1261955–1261955. https://doi.org/10.3389/fpsyg.2023.1261955

Xiao, Y., & Zhi, Y. (2023). An exploratory study of EFL learners' use of ChatGPT for language learning tasks: Experience and perceptions. *Languages (Basel)*, *8*(3), 212. https://doi.org/10.3390/languages8030212

Yeo, M. A. (2023). Academic integrity in the age of Artificial Intelligence (AI) authoring apps. *TESOL Journal*, *14*(3). https://doi.org/10.1002/tesj.716

Zou, M., & Huang, L. (2023). To use or not to use? Understanding doctoral students' acceptance of ChatGPT in writing through technology acceptance model. *Frontiers in Psychology*, *14*, 1259531–1259531. https://doi.org/10.3389/fpsyg.2023.1259531

4
Reconceptualising literacy as co-literacy in language education with AI

Antonie Alm

> **Pre-reading questions:**
>
> 1) What does literacy mean to you? How has your understanding of literacy been shaped by your own education and experiences?
> 2) How might the interactions between humans and AI technologies reshape our understanding of what it means to be literate?
> 3) What implications might a reconceptualisation of literacy that positions AI as a collaborative agent have for language education?

Introduction

In an era where artificial intelligence (AI) can generate human-like text, translate languages with increasing accuracy, and engage in meaningful dialogue, what does it mean to be literate? The conventional view of literacy as the ability to read and write, deeply embedded in our formal education systems, no longer fully reflects the skills required to comprehend and engage with contemporary communication. Literacy has traditionally been defined in relation to print-based reading and writing, a perspective still evident in assessment systems, as shown by the resurgence of in-person written exams (Klein, 2023). This attachment to traditional literacy highlights the need for a broader conceptualisation.

Language learning, arguably more than any other field of education, has a long history of technological integration and adaptation. From early behaviourist approaches using language labs in the 1960s and 1970s, through the emergence of Computer Assisted Language Learning (CALL) in the 1980s with its focus on interactive software, to the transformative impact of the internet in the 1990s enabling collaborative approaches, connecting language learners around the global, language education has continually evolved our understanding of how technology can support learning. As Kern (2021) documents in his 25-year retrospective of digital literacies in CALL, this evolution has been marked by continuous shifts in how we understand the relationship between technology and learning - from viewing digital technologies as tools for practice to recognising them as mediators of authentic communication and creative expression. The emergence of AI is both a continuation of this trajectory and, as Stickler (2024) puts it, a "sea change" moment that requires us to reconsider how knowledge and meaning are generated in language learning contexts.

AI applications such as Google Translate and ChatGPT, while not designed for language education, have shown great potential for supporting learners (Klimova et al., 2024). Their usefulness for language learning stems from their fundamentally multilingual nature, and their multimodal capabilities, enabling interaction through text, speech, and image, challenging language teachers to rethink pedagogical approaches to language teaching.

This chapter introduces the concept of co-literacy to address the opportunities and challenges posed by AI in language education. Co-literacy builds on the principles of multiliteracies (New London Group, 1996), emphasising the importance of multimodal communication, critical engagement, and learner agency. By viewing AI as a collaborative partner in meaning-making, co-literacy reframes literacy as a shared process that requires critical evaluation and creative negotiation of AI outputs. This framework reflects Kalantzis and Cope's (2025) vision for a revised multimodal grammar of literacy, integrating the affordances of AI while fostering critical awareness.

Through the lens of co-literacy, language learners become active participants in a co-creative process with AI, developing the skills to produce, evaluate and adapt AI-generated outputs. This approach prepares learners for the complexities of AI-mediated communication, enabling them to traverse the "AI wilderness" (Alm, 2024), a terrain marked by both immense possibilities and ethical challenges. By proposing co-literacy as a conceptual approach to human-AI interaction, this chapter aims to encourage educators to reimagine language education in the AI age.

Historical and theoretical foundations of literacy

Historical foundations

Historically, literacy was defined as the ability to read and write in standardised, print-based formats. This traditional perspective prioritised text-centric, monolingual, and linear communication, treating literacy as an individual cognitive process focused on decoding and producing text according to prescriptive norms. As Kern (2015) explains, this conceptualisation was tied to the technological and material conditions of its time, with the invention of the printing press embedding norms of uniformity, linearity, and standardisation into literacy practices. Kalantzis and Cope (2025) further suggest that this model reflected the priorities of industrial societies, emphasising efficiency and control over creative or diverse forms of communication.

In the latter half of the 20th century this view began to shift in response to social, cultural, and technological changes. Scholars such as Michael Halliday, Brian Street, and James Gee critiqued the limitations of this text-centred model of literacy, leading to more inclusive and dynamic perspectives. Halliday's notion of "language as social semiotic" emphasised that literacy is anchored in cultural systems, highlighting how meaning-making is defined by social context and purpose (Halliday, 1978). Similarly, Street's (1984) distinction between autonomous literacy, which treats literacy as an isolated set of skills, and ideological literacy, which considers its cultural and contextual dimensions, reframed literacy as a socially situated practice (Barton & Hamilton, 2000). These shifts reflected broader recognition of the ways in which individuals engage with texts, media, and cultural artifacts in different social and technological settings.

The multiliteracies framework

The New London Group (NLG), a collective of literacy scholars argued in 1996 that literacy could no longer be limited to text-based modes of communication, given the increasing prominence of multimodal communication and cultural diversity. They introduced the concept of *multiliteracies*, which expanded the scope of literacy by including visual, auditory, gestural, spatial, and digital resources, reflecting the plurality of literacy practices influenced by social and technological contexts (Kalantzis & Cope, 2025).

Central to this framework is the *Design Concept*, which defines literacy as an active, iterative process in which learners use and transform multimodal resources to generate new meanings. The process involves three interconnected dimensions:

- *Available Designs*: The semiotic resources learners draw upon, including linguistic, visual, auditory, and cultural elements.
- *Designing*: The active process of meaning-making, where learners interpret, synthesise, and reconfigure available designs in contextually meaningful ways to construct and convey new understandings.

- *The Redesigned:* The outcome of this process, where learners generate novel meanings that reflect their intentions and the specific communicative contexts in which they operate.

Each stage builds upon the previous one, with the Redesigned becoming a new Available Design for further exploration. This iterative process enables learners to progressively refine their communicative practices through authentic engagement with multimodal resources. Reflection and feedback play a central role in this cycle, helping learners develop their strategies to engage in diverse communicative events.

In their review of multiliteracies in language learning, Paesani and Allen (2020) explore how linguistic and cultural competencies develop through the use of multimodal resources. They illustrate this through tasks such as analysing multilingual advertisements or creating digital stories, which combine textual interpretation with creative production. These examples demonstrate the framework's potential to integrate language and cultural learning while enhancing practical communication skills. Paesani and Allen situate these examples within broader discussions on incorporating multimodal elements—such as visual and auditory modes—into language education, emphasising their role in fostering cultural awareness and real-world relevance. However, despite its potential, implementing the multiliteracies framework can be challenging for educators. Paesani and Allen (2020) observed that applying multiliteracies principles in communicative language teaching is challenging as they can conflict with established teaching methods. Teachers also reported a lack of confidence in adapting these principles to their teaching practices, reinforcing the need for ongoing professional development as literacy practices evolve with technological and societal shifts - especially amid the rapid changes currently driven by AI.

The multiliteracies framework offered a forward-looking approach to literacy. Introduced in the late 1990s, it laid the groundwork for rethinking pedagogy to address the multimodal nature of communication and the sociocultural diversity of globalised societies. While the multiliteracies manifesto emerged before digital technologies became widespread, its principles anticipated many of the challenges and opportunities now associated with digital literacies. By focusing on learner agency, transformative meaning-making, and multimodal resources, it remains central to literacy in both traditional and digital contexts. As the internet, social media, and multimodal platforms gained prominence, they introduced new tools and affordances, giving rise to digital literacies frameworks.

Digital literacies

Building on the NLG's multiliteracies framework, Dudeney, Hockly, and Pegrum introduced the initial *Framework of Digital Literacies* in 2013. The updated 2022 version, now referred to as *Digital Literacies 3.0*, refines these literacies to reflect emerging digital practices. The framework defines digital literacies as "the individual and social skills needed to effectively manage meaning in an era of digitally networked, often blended, communication" (Pegrum et al., 2022, p. 5). Rather than being limited to technical proficiency, digital literacies involve the ability to engage critically with digital tools and platforms in communicative contexts. The framework organises digital literacies into four interconnected dimensions that parallel key elements of the multiliteracies framework.

- *Communicating* (print literacy, texting literacy, and multimodal literacy, focusing on effective engagement across textual, spoken, and visual communication modes)
- *Informing* (search literacy and information literacy, emphasising the ability to locate, filter, and critically evaluate information in a digitally saturated environment)
- *Collaborating* (participatory and network literacies, fostering the skills needed to engage with diverse online communities and work collaboratively across cultural contexts)
- *(Re)Designing* (remix literacy and code literacy, supporting creative reinterpretation of existing resources and ethical engagement with digital content)

This framework reinforces the NLG's emphasis on literacy as an active and socially situated process, recognising that digital literacies are not isolated skill sets but interconnected practices. For instance, participatory and remix literacies enable learners to interact with and transform digital content, fostering collective intelligence and cultural transformation. Meanwhile, attentional and critical literacies address the growing challenges of managing digital distractions and evaluating the ethical implications of technology use.

Impact on language learning

Digital technologies have introduced innovative approaches to language education, transforming how learners engage with language and communication. Kern (2021) identifies three critical contributions of digital tools to language learning: agency and autonomy, creativity, and sociality. These dimensions reflect the ways learners interact with, adapt to, and transform the digital tools at their disposal, offering opportunities for language learning and intercultural engagement.

Agency and autonomy

Kern conceptualises agency as the ability of learners to act purposefully, determined by the dynamic relationship between individual intentions and the social, cultural, and technological contexts in which they operate. Autonomy represents learners' capacity to make informed and reflective decisions about their language learning processes. Kern provides the example of learner-generated YouTube channels, where students assume the role of content creators, showcasing their language skills to a global audience. These activities empower learners to take ownership of their learning, demonstrating agency by integrating their linguistic, cultural, and personal experiences into their creations. Such practices illustrate how learners actively participate in the design and dissemination of knowledge, reinforcing their roles as autonomous agents within a globally connected communicative network.

Creativity

The multimodal affordances of digital tools enable learners to explore new forms of expression, combining text, visuals, and audio to create innovative outputs. Kern (2021) describes creativity in digital language learning as a process of experimentation and re-design, where learners reimagine "available designs" to produce contextually relevant, meaningful texts. Projects such as digital storytelling and fan fiction exemplify this process, encouraging learners to engage in creative activities while using their second language (L2). For instance, a language learner might create a multimedia presentation that combines narrative writing with video and audio elements, using their linguistic and cultural knowledge in imaginative ways. Such activities use digital tools to create an environment where learners can experiment with linguistic forms, cultural representations, and multimodal communication.

Kern also underlines the importance of fostering creativity as a collaborative process. By working together on projects, learners develop not only their linguistic skills but also their abilities to construct meaning with others, balancing individual expression with collective goals.

Sociality

Digital technologies have expanded the social dimensions of language learning by facilitating collaboration within the classroom, beyond it, and on a global scale. Kern discusses how platforms such as language exchange apps, social media groups, and virtual classrooms enable learners to engage in authentic interactions with other L2 and L1 speakers. These interactions support the development of communicative competence while exposing learners to diverse linguistic and cultural perspectives.

However, Kern also acknowledges the challenges of digital sociality, such as the difficulty of interpreting tone in written messages or the stereotypes that may arise in intercultural exchanges. These complexities require learners to develop intercultural literacy and critical awareness to address the challenges of online communication.

Kern emphasises that sociality is not limited to peer-to-peer interaction but also includes participation in wider discourse communities. By contributing to projects, discussions, and digital content creation, learners can position themselves as active participants in social networks. This interconnectedness exemplifies how digital tools not only mediate communication but also create opportunities for learners to build meaningful relationships and participate in collective meaning-making processes.

While these contributions illustrate the transformative potential of digital tools, Kern underlines the important critical digital literacies' skills to address the challenges they pose. Issues such as algorithmic filtering, embedded biases, and unequal access to technology highlight the need for educators to guide learners in addressing the complexities of digital language learning environments. By integrating digital tools into language education, educators can foster engagement, creativity, and meaningful communication while preparing learners to analyse and respond to the ever-changing demands of digital contexts.

Multiliteracies of the future

While digital literacies have expanded the scope of literacy, they remain fundamentally human-centric, emphasising the agency and creativity of individual learners. As Kalantzis and Cope (2025) argue, the emergence of Generative AI (GenAI) signals a shift in the nature of meaning-making, where digital tools evolve from instruments of human creativity to active collaborators in the communicative process.

GenAI tools such as ChatGPT (text), Midjourney (images), Synthesia (video and animation), and Suno (music and soundscapes) challenge traditional notions of authorship, agency, and creativity by introducing new possibilities for collaboration and creation that were previously unattainable. These tools create diverse multimodal content, introducing new "available designs" that learners can adapt and transform. At the same time, they demand new forms of critical thinking skills, particularly to evaluate biases, manage misinformation, and ensure cultural relevance in AI outputs.

This shift necessitates a re-evaluation of digital literacies to include collaborative dynamics between humans and AI. By extending the principles of digital literacies to address these complexities, educators can prepare learners to work within the increasingly blurred boundaries between human and machine agency. Critical digital literacies becomes vital for preparing learners to question, interpret, and engage with AI technologies through a process of critical experimentation.

The literacy of machines

As Kalantzis and Cope (2025) provocatively ask, "If a machine can write, what is literacy?" The emergence of Large Language Models (LLMs), which operate GenAI systems like ChatGPT, has introduced new dimensions to literacy practices, challenging conventional notions of human literacy. While human literacy entails critical evaluation, ethical reasoning, and contextual awareness, LLMs operate through pattern recognition and data synthesis. The juxtaposition of these literacies reveals their distinct yet complementary strengths and limitations.

A defining feature of "AI literacy" is the ability to generate vast quantities of textual content. However, it is devoid of genuine understanding or intent (Kalantzis & Cope, 2025; Bender et al., 2021). In addition, LLMs, while text-based, operate across modalities, excelling at synthesising text, images, and speech to enable scalable multimodal content creation (Cope & Kalantzis, 2024). These features illustrate the technical strengths of LLMs, but also highlight their fundamental limitations: their output is limited by the quality of their training data and lacks lived experience or emotional depth, relying on statistical probabilities (Mishra et al., 2024).

Challenges and limitations of AI literacy

Before proposing AI as a co-agent in literacy, I want to acknowledge and address the inherent challenges and limitations posed by GenAI systems. These concerns are central to critical digital literacies (CDL), which examine the biases and non-neutrality of digital tools. Scholars such as Darvin (2017) and Jones (2021) argue that these systems influence user behaviour, reflect entrenched biases, and reinforce systemic inequities. GenAI introduces additional complexities that call for a critical educational response.

A major challenge is the lack of transparency in how GenAI generates its outputs. Many systems do not disclose the origins of their data, making it difficult for users to verify credibility or trace sources. Mishra et al. (2024) describe this opacity as intrinsic to the design of GenAI, likening it to a "black box", whose operations remain elusive even to its creators. Chapelle et al. (2024) stress that fostering systematic questioning and verification of AI outputs is vital to overcoming the challenges posed by these opaque systems.

Bias, equity, and agency are equally critical concerns. GenAI reflects biases in its training data, reinforcing inequities. Darvin (2017) emphasises that digital technologies mirror the sociocultural power structures of their contexts, subtly guiding user behaviour and limiting agency. This concept relates to what Jones (2021) refers to as "algorithmic authority", where users often trust AI systems to make objective decisions, overlooking the biases embedded in their design. This misplaced trust can reinforce societal inequalities and perpetuate stereotypes in AI outputs. More recently, Jones (2024) has characterised AI systems as "culture machines" that embed dominant cultural narratives while marginalising alternative voices and perspectives. Kalantzis and Cope (2025) extend these critiques, arguing that equitable outcomes can only be achieved by teaching learners the critical skills needed to interrogate the socio-political implications of AI-generated outputs and carefully managing AI's potential for multimodal and intercultural communication to prevent reinforcing existing hegemonies.

Uncritical acceptance of GenAI output risks diminishing learners' role as active participants in meaning-making. In my work with Watanabe (Alm & Watanabe, 2023), I discussed how ChatGPT's data processing resembles the 'banking model' of education criticised by Freire (1970). We argued that while ChatGPT excels at reciting information, it cannot engage in the emancipatory dialogue central to critical pedagogy, and reliance on its outputs may reduce opportunities for meaningful teacher-student interaction and knowledge co-creation. To counter this risk, we proposed strategies to ensure AI serves goals of equity and critical awareness rather than just efficiency, including developing students' critical AI literacy and promoting learner agency through problem-posing approaches. Collaborative tasks that require learners to discuss, compare, and evaluate AI-generated content can help them develop the critical skills needed to assess its reliability and limitations while maintaining their agency in digital interactions. These challenges underline the importance of critical AI literacy, enabling learners to assess AI's limitations and societal impacts while making informed and ethical decisions (Kalantzis & Cope, 2025).

In addition to these challenges, generative AI systems impose environmental and social costs. Mishra et al. (2024) highlight the enormous computational resources required to develop and maintain these systems, contributing to substantial environmental impacts. Furthermore, the human labour involved in fine-tuning these systems – often low-paid – raises ethical concerns about equity and exploitation in the AI development pipeline. Another issue is the large-scale appropriation of intellectual property without permission, as GenAI models are trained on vast amounts of copyrighted content. These ethical and environmental concerns necessitate a critical evaluation of AI's broader implications, ensuring that its benefits do not come at an unsustainable or inequitable price.

Contrasting human literacy and AI literacy

AI and humans contribute differently to the construction of knowledge, each with distinct strengths and limitations. AI's computational power enables it to rapidly process vast amounts of data, sustain attention, and perform multimodal transformations, making it highly efficient for large-scale tasks (Zhang, 2024). However, while AI excels in information synthesis and organisation, it lacks contextual awareness and ethical judgement, requiring human input to verify its output (Zhang, 2024; Kalantzis & Cope, 2025).

Meanwhile, humans excel in creativity, flexibility in adapting to new situations, and ethical reasoning. However, they also face challenges such as information overload, working memory constraints, and susceptibility to systematic errors in reasoning, which can affect decision-making and learning processes (Morris, 2017). While education can support the development of digital literacies and critical thinking, certain cognitive limitations, such as susceptibility to misinformation and difficulties handling large-scale data synthesis, remain fundamental to human cognition (Morris, 2017).

AI's strengths in semantic search, automated content generation, and data analysis enable it to support human decision-making by efficiently retrieving and structuring large volumes of information. However, human contextualisation remains essential to validate and interpret these outputs (Mishra et al., 2024; Kalantzis & Cope, 2025).

Furthermore, AI facilitates multilingual communication and multimodal synthesis, transforming how meaning is constructed. But again, human adaptability, the ability to navigate new contexts, apply cultural and situational awareness, and interpret content critically, remains essential for accurate interpretation and meaningful application. These differences in strengths and limitations are summarised in Table 1.

This comparison illustrates the potential for a complementary relationship, where generative AI tools enhance human capabilities while requiring human oversight for critical evaluation and ethical reasoning - a concept often referred to as 'the human in the loop' (Godwin-Jones, 2024) to emphasise active human participation in managing AI outputs. For example, AI's semantic search capabilities can support human

Insights into AI and Language Teaching and Learning

Table 4.1 *Human vs AI strength and limitations*

Dimension	Human Strengths	AI Strengths	Human Limitations	AI Limitations
Communicating	Contextual awareness; emotional depth; ethical reasoning	Multimodal scalability; rapid data processing	Limited capacity to process high volumes of multimodal data quickly	Lacks deep cultural understanding
Informing	Critical thinking; source evaluation; ethical reasoning	Rapid aggregation; efficient data synthesis; semantic search	Cognitive biases; difficulty handling large-scale information processing	Prone to generating plausible but inaccurate information
Collaborating	Empathy; adaptability; interpretation of complex social interactions	Multilingual and multimodal communication; real-time data processing	May need to develop intercultural literacy, learn prompting skills to guide AI interactions	Lacks lived experience and cultural understanding, leading to misinterpretation of social and cultural cues
(Re)designing	Creativity; innovation; ethical content transformation	Efficient multimodal and textual transformation	Requires time to develop original outputs	Outputs may lack originality, ethical awareness, or contextual depth

critical evaluation in research tasks by quickly providing relevant data, which humans can then assess for credibility and context. Similarly, AI's ability to transform content across modalities can streamline creative projects, enabling educators to focus on refining ethical and cultural dimensions in the outputs.

By juxtaposing human critical thinking, creativity, and ethical awareness with AI's ability to process vast datasets and generate multimodal content, the potential emerges for a transformative partnership that integrates technology while maintaining and enhancing human agency.

Theoretical foundations

As AI becomes increasingly embedded in communicative practices, literacy can no longer be understood as an exclusively human practice. The relationship between human and AI literacies suggests the need for an integrated perspective - one that accounts for both human meaning-making processes and AI's computational contributions. Co-literacy proposes that literacy in an AI-mediated world is neither purely human nor entirely machinic but co-constructed. To ground this concept, I draw on four key theoretical perspectives that present different facets of human-AI collaboration and examine how communication, cognition, and creativity are transformed when humans and AI interact, providing the foundation for a more comprehensive model of literacy for language education in the age of AI.

Cyber-social literacy learning

Kalantzis and Cope's (2025) concept of cyber-social literacy learning addresses the dialogic relationship between humans and machines in meaning-making processes. Expanding on their foundational work with the New London Group, they integrate the multiliteracies framework into human-AI collaboration, recognising AI as an active participant in literacy development. Central to this vision is their adaptation of the design framework into three key dimensions:

- *Found Designs* refer to the semiotic resources learners draw upon, now expanded to include AI-generated content alongside traditional linguistic, visual, auditory, and cultural elements.
- *Transposition* involves shifting meaning across different modes and contexts, such as adapting written drafts into multimodal formats. This highlights a key aspect of cyber-social literacy: the ability to engage critically with AI-generated outputs and adapt them to meet specific communicative needs.
- *Transformation* goes beyond transposition by requiring learners to fundamentally change the meaning, purpose, or impact of content. This involves critiquing AI-generated outputs, integrating new perspectives, and producing original, contextually appropriate meanings—developing higher-order thinking skills in digital environments.

While conceived as a broader framework for AI-mediated literacy, cyber-social literacy has particular relevance for language learning. By creating and engaging with AI-generated content, language learners participate in an iterative process of meaning-making that reflects real-world communication, where language develops through interaction, feedback, and adaptation to different contexts. This approach encourages learners to continuously evaluate, adapt, and transform AI-generated text to fit specific linguistic and cultural contexts, fostering engagement with multimodal and multilingual literacy practices.

Cybersapien literacy

Gee and Zhang's (2024) concept of cybersapien literacy explores how LLMs transform writing practices. Rather than viewing AI as a threat to traditional skills, they highlight its potential to make writing more participatory and engaging. They draw parallels between writing with LLMs and "affinity spaces" (Gee, 2004)—environments where people collaborate informally around shared interests, creating social, multimodal, and purposeful texts driven by intrinsic motivation. The authors suggest that writing with LLMs could replicate this dynamic by making writing more participatory and engaging. AI tools can function as interactive writing partners, helping learners refine ideas, develop arguments, and experiment with rhetorical strategies in ways that mirror the collaborative nature of affinity spaces. This shift moves writing away from a mechanical exercise toward a more dynamic and personally meaningful process.

Another useful concept discussed by Gee and Zhang is the distinction between frozen and flexible writing, which they draw from Lemke (1990). Frozen writing refers to standardised, rigid text, often found in formal documents and AI-generated content. While useful for clarity, it can lack adaptability and creativity. AI-generated text typically defaults to frozen structures - formulaic phrasing and predictable patterns that prioritise efficiency (tellingly, 'efficiency' itself appears with notable frequency in LLM outputs, reinforcing this very prioritisation) over personal voice. In contrast, flexible writing is adaptive and personal, allowing for interpretation and modification. Gee and Zhang emphasise that writing with AI should involve an iterative process where learners transform frozen text into flexible writing by reshaping AI-generated outputs to reflect their own voice.

Gee and Zhang propose that interactions between humans and generative AIs should enable "both parties [to] learn and get smarter (and more ethical)" without diminishing human skills (p. 35). This dynamic process fosters skill development—enhancing human adaptability and critical engagement while also improving AI's ability to support meaningful and context-sensitive writing. However, Gee and Zhang emphasise that human writers must actively direct AI through iterative refinements, ensuring that the final output embodies human intent, creativity, and ethical considerations rather than defaulting to AI-generated patterns.

In the context of language learning, cybersapien literacy provides a useful lens for understanding how generative AI transforms writing into a collaborative and iterative process. Cybersapien literacy positions AI as a co-creator in the writing process, fostering critical engagement, creativity, and adaptability in learners. The distinction between frozen and flexible writing is particularly relevant, as language learners need to develop the ability to transform generic AI-generated text into writing that genuinely reflects their own voice and communicative goals.

Co-intelligence

Co-intelligence, as conceptualised by Ethan Mollick (2024), describes a form of human-AI collaboration where AI acts as a cognitive partner, complementing human creativity, reasoning, and expertise.

Mollick (2024) presents the centaur and cyborg metaphors to illustrate two modes of human-AI collaboration. The centaur metaphor represents a strategic division of labour, where humans and AI each contribute based on their respective strengths. Humans retain decision-making control, while delegating specific tasks – such as data analysis or content summarisation – to AI. This allows individuals to focus on higher-order thinking while using AI for efficiency. The cyborg metaphor, in contrast, describes a deeper integration of human and AI efforts. Cyborg interactions involve constant, dynamic interplay between human and machine. For instance, a writer, might co-develop text with an AI by iteratively refining its suggestions, using AI as an active collaborator throughout the process. This model reflects the fluidity of human-AI engagement, where AI extends human capabilities rather than assisting in predefined tasks.

These metaphors illustrate how co-intelligence adapts to different contexts. The centaur model is well suited for structured tasks requiring precision, while the cyborg model enhances creative and exploratory processes. By shifting between these approaches, learners and educators can take advantage of AI's capabilities while maintaining active control over meaning-making.

For language learners, co-intelligence provides a framework for incorporating AI into various aspects of language learning. The centaur metaphor applies when learners use AI to enhance their learning experience by delegating specific tasks to AI while maintaining control over the overall process. For example, AI can assist in essay writing by providing outlines or summarising key points, enabling learners to focus on refining their ideas and arguments. The centaur model enables learners to take an active role in their learning, using AI as a supportive tool that allows them to concentrate on interpretation, critical thinking, and creativity. In contrast, the cyborg model supports a more integrated engagement with AI, where learners collaborate with AI to explore and refine their writing iteratively. For example, learners might co-write a text by continuously modifying AI-generated text to reflect their personal voice and experimenting with stylistic variations.

Co-creativity

Co-creativity, as described by Wingström et al. (2024), occurs when AI functions as a creative partner or tool that enhances human creativity. Although their study predates the rise of generative AI, it provides a useful perspective on how co-creativity can redefine creative processes. The authors point out that while AI can generate novel outputs and detect patterns, it lacks independent intention, self-awareness, and the ability to assign meaning. However, its ability to synthesise large amounts of data and identify connections at scale allows it to contribute to creative processes in ways that differ from human cognition. AI serves as a catalyst for human creativity, offering suggestions that require human interpretation, adaptation, and contextualisation to be relevant and meaningful.

Interestingly, Wingström et al. observed differences in the ways computer scientists and new media artists engaged with AI. Scientists approached AI as a tool for hypothesis testing, data analysis, and optimisation, associating creativity with problem-solving. In contrast, artists treated AI as a collaborative partner, using its unpredictable outputs for experimentation and artistic exploration. This duality - AI as a tool for optimisation and as a partner for innovation - shows its versatility in supporting different creative needs and purposes.

For language learners, co-creativity highlights AI's role in fostering both divergent and convergent thinking, as discussed by Wingström et al. (2024). AI can encourage creative language use by generating varied linguistic expressions (divergent thinking) while also refining writing through iterative feedback and stylistic enhancement (convergent thinking). Creativity scholar Abraham (2024) emphasises that both cognitive engagement and affective satisfaction are central to creativity, suggesting that AI can support learners by facilitating experimentation, self-expression, and structured refinement. In addition to enhancing confidence and proficiency, AI-mediated projects provide opportunities for external validation, enabling learners to share work, collaborate, and receive feedback—reinforcing creativity as both a personal and social process.

These four frameworks illustrate how AI is redefining literacy as a collaborative process between humans and machines. Cyber-social literacy learning and cybersapien literacy, grounded in the multiliteracies framework, highlight the role of AI in meaning-making and the transformation of writing into a dynamic, participatory practice. Co-intelligence and co-creativity add further dimensions, showing how AI can support problem-solving and creative exploration. These perspectives point to the need for a new conceptualisation of literacy—one that recognises the shared agency of humans and AI. Co-literacy emerges from this shift, offering a way to understand literacy in an AI-mediated world.

Making the case for co-literacy

What is co-literacy?

Co-literacy responds to the need to redefine concepts of literacy at a time when AI can generate human-like text, translate between languages with increasing accuracy, and engage in meaningful dialogue. This is particularly relevant for language learning, where AI's multilingual and multimodal affordances create new possibilities for communication, comprehension, and meaning-making. Co-literacy is predicated on the notion that humans and AI can collaborate to produce, interpret, and refine language in ways that were unimaginable before GenAI emerged. While co-literacy represents a shift in how we conceptualise literacy, it builds on the foundational principles of multiliteracies, which emphasise multimodal, multicultural and dynamic approaches to literacy. The multiliteracies framework, highlights the need for literacy education that supports learners in navigating diverse cultural and communicative contexts through multimodal engagement. Digital literacies, particularly in the context of language learning, extend this foundation by addressing the complexities of a superdiverse era, fostering collaboration, critical thinking, and creativity (Pegrum et al., 2022). GenAI further expands multilingual and multimodal literacy opportunities, allowing learners to interact with text, speech, and images across languages and formats in increasingly dynamic ways.

The rise of GenAI has led scholars like Kalantzis and Cope (2025) and Gee and Zhang (2024) to call for a redefinition of literacy that integrates human-AI collaboration. Co-literacy embraces this shift, recognising that AI-mediated language use is inherently multimodal, incorporating text, speech, visuals, and interactive media. It reframes language learning as an interactive and participatory process where learners use AI to develop communication skills, enhance comprehension, and refine linguistic expression.

Drawing from the theoretical perspectives outlined above, co-literacy can be understood as: (1) a collaborative process where humans and AI each contribute distinct capabilities—humans with contextual awareness and ethical reasoning, AI with computational power and pattern recognition; (2) an iterative approach to meaning-making that involves continuous evaluation and transformation of AI-generated content, (3) a critical practice that encourages awareness of AI's limitations and biases, enabling informed choices about engagement with AI tools; and (4) a multimodal engagement that integrates AI to facilitate interactions across languages and modalities.

In co-literacy, language learners become designers, adapting "found designs" into outputs by drawing on their own creativity alongside the computational power of AI. Building on Mollick's (2024) concept of co-intelligence and Wingström et al.'s (2024) notion of co-creativity, co-literacy fosters shared agency in developing, evaluating, and refining linguistic and communicative competence.

Core principles of co-literacy

Co-literacy builds on Kern's (2021) dimensions of digital literacies: agency, creativity, and sociality by reinterpreting these dimensions through the lens of human-AI collaboration. This perspective positions AI as an active participant in literacy practices, defining how learners engage with language, develop meaning, and interact with digital tools.

Co-agency

In Kern's (2021) framework, agency is understood as the capacity of learners to act purposefully and reflectively, within their social, cultural, and technological contexts. Co-literacy extends this idea by embedding agency within an AI-mediated environment, where learners' intentions intersect with AI affordances. This integration creates new opportunities for learners to experiment with, adapt, and reflect on multimodal expressions.

Godwin-Jones' (2024) discussion on the concept of distributed agency reframes agency as a co-constructed process emerging from the interplay between human actors and technological systems. Distributed agency shifts the focus from agency as an individual attribute to one that recognises the collaborative nature of human-AI interactions, where both contribute to designing, refining, and critiquing language outputs. This collaborative dynamic reflects the iterative and reflective nature of co-literacy.

In a recent study on learner autonomy (Alm, 2024) I explored how intermediate learners of German engaged with AI as part of a four-week Language Challenge. Learners pursued self-selected language goals, documented their progress using AI tools and traditional resources, and reflected on their experiences. This process supported autonomy by encouraging critical engagement with AI tools. Learners moved from initial exploration to deliberate integration of these tools, refining their strategies to meet personalised goals, such as improving grammatical accuracy or conversational fluency. Importantly, learners engaged constructively with AI outputs to maintain their personal voice and intentions while benefiting from computational feedback, demonstrating both control and creativity.

Jacob et al. (2024) describe the case of Kailing, a learner who used AI to simulate workplace communication tasks. By generating and evaluating responses, Kailing illustrated how learners can apply AI to practical contexts while exercising autonomy. Similarly, Zhang (2024) emphasises that learners critically assess and adapt AI outputs to suit their goals, reflecting the importance of questioning and revising available designs in diverse sociocultural contexts.

Co-literacy fosters a reflective and collaborative approach to agency, advancing the multiliteracies principle of learners as designers of meaning while incorporating Kalantzis and Cope's (2025) vision of AI as a transformative force in literacy education. Learners engage critically with AI tools, navigating complex digital environments with intentionality, adaptability, and creativity while maintaining in charge of their learning goals.

Co-creativity

Kern (2021) conceptualises creativity as a core dimension of language learning as the ability to transform resources into meaningful and contextually appropriate outputs. Co-literacy extends this to co-creativity, where human intuition and AI-generated possibilities interact dynamically.

Wingström et al. (2024) define co-creativity as the interactive blending of human and AI contributions, where AI generates novel ideas through data synthesis, and humans provide the interpretive depth and contextual understanding needed to meaningful outcomes. This broadens Kern's notion of learners as designers to include collaboration with AI, inviting them to co-create and refine outputs in multimodal and multilingual contexts. As discussed in the previous section, co-creativity emerges in multimodal contexts, such as using AI to create visual, auditory, or textual narratives.

Practical applications of co-creativity demonstrate its transformative potential in language learning. For example, learners engage in digital storytelling by collaborating with AI to generate narrative prompts, develop stories, and integrate multimodal elements such as images and audio. This fosters divergent thinking as learners explore various narrative possibilities, while convergent thinking emerges as they refine AI-generated suggestions for coherence, tone, and cultural relevance.

In cultural exploration projects, learners use AI tools to create multimedia presentations on cultural themes or practices. These projects might involve designing infographics that compare idiomatic expressions across languages, enriched with AI-generated visuals and textual content, which enhances both linguistic creativity and intercultural competence.

Another example includes social media-based projects, where learners produce Instagram posts, YouTube videos, or TikToks in their L2.

AI tools assist by generating captions, subtitles, or visual themes, allowing learners to express themselves creatively while engaging interactively with their audiences.

Abraham (2024) discusses creativity as involving both cognitive engagement and hands-on engagement, emphasising the importance of internal satisfaction in the creative process. She describes creativity as having both a personal, affective dimension and an external validation component linked to public recognition. From a co-literacy perspective, AI-mediated projects can foster curiosity-driven exploration while also providing opportunities for external validation through digital content creation and collaborative engagement.

Co-sociality

Kern (2021) situates sociality as an essential dimension of language learning, focusing on the ways learners interact within sociocultural contexts to construct meaning. In the multiliteracies framework, sociality transcends individual efforts, emphasising the collaborative and intercultural dynamics of communication. Co-literacy extends these ideas by embedding AI as a participant in social interaction, redefining how learners engage with peers, communities, and diverse cultural perspectives.

Co-literacy redefines sociality by positioning AI as a collaborator. Mishra et al. (2024) highlight how learners perceive AI as both a cognitive and affective partner, capable of providing iterative feedback, suggesting ideas, and engaging in dialogue. This partnership cultivates trust and reinforces the learner's agency and creativity in language learning.

For L2 speakers, AI alleviates linguistic challenges by offering integrated, context-sensitive support. Tseng and Warschauer (2023) note that AI tools enable feedback on grammar, paraphrasing, and usage, creating an environment where language learners in both formal and informal learning contexts, can refine their skills without fear of judgement.

Jeon and Lee (2024) conceptualise chatbots as "novel interlocutors," combining human-like conversational abilities with machine-like patience and reliability. Chatbots can engage learners in extended interactions, offering personalised, non-judgemental feedback and allowing repeated practice, an important component in language development. By reducing performance anxiety often associated with human interlocutors, chatbots offer flexibility in conversational practice.

While AI enhances sociality in co-literacy, it also necessitates critical reflection. Kosinski (2024) predicts that AI's increasing ability to simulate Theory of Mind-like behaviours will make its role as a conversational partner even more compelling and engaging for learners.

However, this enhanced capability raises concerns about anthropomorphism—where learners attribute human-like qualities to AI—potentially affecting how they interact with technology and peers.

Sociality in co-literacy transcends individual interactions, extending into collaborative and intercultural spaces. AI facilitates global collaborations, enabling learners to co-author multilingual texts and connect with peers from diverse cultural backgrounds.

Addressing challenges

While co-literacy offers transformative potential, its integration into education presents challenges that must be addressed to ensure meaningful engagement. These challenges do not simply arise from AI itself, but from the ways AI is integrated into learning environments.

One concern is over-reliance on AI, where learners disengage from the creative and critical aspects of literacy. Kern (2024) warns that unchecked dependence on AI-generated outputs risks reducing learners to passive users, undermining the iterative refinement processes described in cyber-social literacy learning. To counter this, educators must design activities that foster intentionality, ensuring that AI functions as a cognitive and dialogic partner rather than a substitute for independent thought.

Bias and ethics also present critical concerns, particularly when learners engage with AI-generated content uncritically. The frameworks of cybersapien literacy and co-creativity emphasise the adaptive and iterative transformation of meaning, suggesting that AI-generated content should not be treated as fixed knowledge (or "frozen language") but as material for critical re-evaluation and redesign. Tseng and Warschauer (2023) emphasise the importance of developing AI literacy through explicit instruction on recognising bias, enabling learners to challenge and modify AI-generated representations.

Lastly, accessibility remains an important issue. While AI can facilitate inclusivity by supporting diverse linguistic and multimodal engagement, access to AI technologies is not equitably distributed. If co-literacy is to fulfil its promise of shared agency, educators must advocate for policies that prioritise access to AI technologies while ensuring that human agency remains central to learning.

Co-literacy in action

Bringing co-literacy into language learning helps students develop the skills needed to engage critically and creatively with AI in real-world communication. Literacy frameworks, such as multiliteracies and digital literacies, highlight the importance of multimodal and networked communication. Co-literacy builds on these ideas by focusing on how learners and AI interact to enhance language comprehension, and production skills across different language settings and communicative situations. As learners increasingly engage with AI in their personal lives—whether using translation apps, AI chatbots for casual conversation, or AI-generated media for entertainment, they become increasingly familiar with AI as a communicative tool. Co-literacy encourages educators to acknowledge and bring AI-mediated social practices into formal language learning, helping students bridge the gap between informal and academic language use. By engaging with the AI tools they already use with a critical mindset, learners develop the skills to assess AI's affordances for language learning. At the same time, using AI for language learning fosters the development of AI literacy skills, creating a reciprocal process where AI literacy and language proficiency reinforce one another.

Co-literacy redefines what it means to be literate in the age of AI. As AI continues to transform knowledge production and communication, educators must move beyond static views of AI as a tool and instead recognise the dialogic and collaborative dimension of meaning-making. By fostering shared agency between humans and AI, co-literacy empowers learners to use, critique, and co-create in a world where AI is increasingly embedded in everyday communication.

Post-reading questions:

1) In what ways does "co-literacy" expand traditional literacy models, and how can it be implemented in the language classroom?
2) How does AI influence learner agency in language education? What strategies can educators use to help learners maintain control over their language development while working with AI?
3) In what ways can AI act as a collaborator in language learning, helping learners engage in creative linguistic experimentation and play?

References

Abraham, A. (2024). *The creative brain: Myths and truths*. MIT Press.

Alm, A. (2024). Exploring autonomy in the AI wilderness: Learner challenges and choices. *Education Sciences*, *14*(12), 16pp. https://doi.org/10.3390/educsci14121369

Alm, A., & Watanabe, Y. (2023). Integrating ChatGPT in language education: A Freirean perspective. *Iranian Journal of Language Teaching Research*, *11*(3 (Special Issue), 19–30. https://doi/10.30466/ijltr.2023.121404

Barton, D., & Hamilton, M. (2000). Literacy practices. In D. Barton, M. Hamilton, & R. Ivanic (Eds.), *Situated literacies: Reading and writing in context* (pp. 7–15). Routledge.

Bender, E. M., Gebru, T., McMillan-Major, A., & Shmitchell, S. (2021, March). On the dangers of stochastic parrots: Can language models be too big? In *Proceedings of the 2021 ACM conference on fairness, accountability, and transparency* (pp. 610–623).

Chapelle, C. A., Beckett, G. H., & Ranalli, J. (2024). Paths for exploring AI in applied linguistics. In C. A. Chapelle, G. H. Beckett, & J. Ranalli (Eds.), *Exploring artificial intelligence in applied linguistics* (pp. 262–274). Iowa State University Digital Press. https://doi.org/10.31274/isudp.2024.154.15

Cope, B., & Kalantzis, M. (2024). On cyber-social learning: A critique of artificial intelligence in education. In *Trust and inclusion in AI-mediated education: Where human learning meets learning machines* (pp. 3–34). Springer Nature Switzerland.

Darvin, R. (2017). Language, ideology, and critical digital literacy. In: Thorne, S., May, S. (eds) *Language, education and technology. Encyclopedia of language and education*. Springer. https://doi.org/10.1007/978-3-319-02328-1_35-2

Freire, P. (1970). *Pedagogy of the oppressed*. Bloomsbury Publishing USA.

Gee, J. P. (2004). *Situated language and learning: A critique of traditional schooling*. Routledge.

Gee, J. P., & Zhang, Q. A. (2024). Cybersapien literacy: Integrating AI and human. *Phi Delta Kappan*, *106*(3), 32–38. https://doi.org/10.1177/00317217241295428

Godwin-Jones, R. (2024). Distributed agency in language learning and teaching through generative AI. *Language Learning & Technology*, *28*(2), 5–31. https://hdl.handle.net/10125/73570

Halliday, M. A. K. (1978). *Language as social semiotic: The social interpretation of language and meaning*. Edward Arnold.

Jacob, S., Tate, T. & Warschauer, M. (2024). Emergent AI-assisted discourse: A case study of a second language writer authoring with ChatGPT. *Journal of China Computer-Assisted Language Learning*. https://doi.org/10.1515/jccall-2024-0011

Jeon, J., & Lee, S. (2024). Can learners benefit from chatbots instead of humans? A systematic review of human-chatbot comparison research in language education. *Education and Information Technologies*, 1–32. https://doi.org/10.1007/s10639-024-12725-9

Jones, R. H. (2021). The text is reading you: Teaching language in the age of the algorithm. *Linguistics and Education*, *62*, https://doi.org/10.1016/j.linged.2019.100750

Jones, R. H. (2024). Culture machines. *Applied Linguistics Review* 1–10. https://doi.org/10.1515/applirev-2024-0188

Kalantzis, M., & Cope, B. (2025). Literacy in the time of artificial intelligence. *Reading Research Quarterly*, *60*(1), e591. https://doi.org/10.1002/rrq.591

Kern, R. (2015). *Language, literacy, and technology*. Cambridge University Press.

Kern, R. (2021). Twenty-five years of digital literacies in CALL. *Language Learning & Technology*, *25*(3), 132–150. http://hdl.handle.net/10125/73453

Kern, R. (2024). Twenty-first century technologies and language education: Charting a path forward. *The Modern Language Journal*. https://doi.org/10.1111/modl.12924

Klein, A. (2023, October 2). Teachers turn to pen and paper amid AI cheating fears, survey finds. *Education Week*. https://www.edweek.org/technology/teachers-turn-to-pen-and-paper-amid-ai-cheating-fears-survey-finds/2023/10

Klimova, B., Pikhart, M., & Al-Obaydi, L. H. (2024). Exploring the potential of ChatGPT for foreign language education at the university level. *Frontiers in Psychology*, *15*, https://doi.org/10.3389/fpsyg.2024.1269319

Kosinski, M. (2024). Evaluating large language models in theory of mind tasks. *Proceedings of the National Academy of Sciences*, *121*(45), e2405460121. https://doi.org/10.1073/pnas.2405460121

Kress, G., & van Leeuwen, T. (1996). *Reading images: The grammar of visual design*. Routledge.

Lemke, J. L. (1990). *Talking science: Language, learning, and values*. Ablex Publishing.

Mollick, E. (2024). *Co-Intelligence: Living and working with AI*. Portfolio/Penguin.

Morris, A. (2017). Human cognitive limitations. Broad, consistent, clinical application of physiological principles will require decision support. *Annals of the American Thoracic Society* *15*(1), S53–S56. https://doi.org/10.1513/AnnalsATS.201706-449KV

New London Group. (1996). A pedagogy of multiliteracies: Designing social futures. *Harvard Educational Review*, *66*(1), 60–92. https://doi.org/10.17763/haer.66.1.17370n67v22j160u

Paesani, K., & Allen, H. W. (2020). Teacher development and multiliteracies pedagogy: Challenges and opportunities for postsecondary language programs. *Second Language Research & Practice*, *1*(1), 124–138. http://hdl.handle.net/10125/69844

Pegrum, M., Hockly, N., & Dudeney, G. (2022). *Digital literacies.* Routledge. https://doi.org/10.4324/9781003262541

Mishra, P., Warr, M. & Rezwana I. (2023). TPACK in the age of ChatGPT and generative AI. *Journal of Digital Learning in Teacher Education, 39*(4), 235–251. https://doi.org/10.1080/21532974.2023.2247480

Stickler, U. (2024). Online language teaching in times of change: A CALL to action for language teachers and educators. *Journal of China Computer-Assisted Language Learning.* https://doi.org/10.1515/jccall-2024-0010

Street, B. V. (1984). *Literacy in theory and practice.* Cambridge University Press.

Tseng, W., & Warschauer, M. (2023). AI-writing tools in education: If you can't beat them, join them. *Journal of China Computer-Assisted Language Learning, 3*(2), 258–262. https://doi.org/10.1515/jccall-2023-0008

Wingström, R., Hautala, J., & Lundman, R. (2024). Redefining creativity in the era of AI? Perspectives of computer scientists and new media artists. *Creativity Research Journal, 36*(2), 177–193. https://doi.org/10.1080/10400419.2022.2107850

Zhang, J. (2024). Artificial intelligence vs. human intelligence: Which excels where and what will never be matched. https://sbmi.uth.edu/blog/2024/artificial-intelligence-versus-human-intelligence.htm

Zhang, Z. (2024). ChatGPT: Enhancing learner agency and multilingual practices in English writing class. *Journal of Education, Humanities and Social Sciences, 26,* 1153–1160.

5
AI and language assessment

Peter Crosthwaite

Qing Ma

> **Pre-reading questions:**
>
> 1) What are the main AI technologies commonly used in L2 language assessment, and why?
> 2) Will the advent of generative AI and large language models render human L2 language assessment obsolete?

Introduction

Artificial intelligence (AI) has already played a major role in language assessment over the past few decades, taking on roles traditionally undertaken by humans including the evaluation and scoring of written assessment (also known as Automated Essay Scoring, AES), provision of feedback (also known as Automated Writing Evaluation, AWE), spoken assessments (e.g., automated speech recognition, ASR, spoken dialogue systems) and plagiarism detection. AI in language assessment is used in preparing for and administering high-stakes, large-scale proficiency tests (e.g. Duolingo) where human ratings are both costly and time-consuming. AI-assisted language assessment typically utilizes natural language processing (NLP) technologies in tandem with either rule-based (knowledge-based) or predictive (iterative) AI models. These systems analyze natural language input to generate relevant outputs when attempting to assess language use and proficiency. The recent advent of generative AI and large language models now marks a period of transition in how the language assessment field works with AI, and vice versa, in that the very nature of preparing for, administering, grading and providing feedback on language assessment is potentially set for radical change for language educators.

This chapter provides a brief overview of the history of language assessment and AI, covering established applications before outlining the affordances of (and potential risks posed by) the incorporation of generative AI (GenAI) and large language models into the language assessment space. We also present relevant examples from Australian, Chinese and Hong Kong SAR language assessment contexts.

Assessment and AI

AI in language assessment has been applied across a diverse range of use cases for the assessment of both receptive and productive language skills. For speaking, automated speech recognition (ASR) employs AI and machine learning / deep learning techniques to serve as a bridge for improved human-human and human-machine collaboration (Yu & Deng, 2016). Users' speech is converted into an audio signal which is converted to an acoustic model, the features of which (e.g. intonation, stress, pauses, etc.) are then extracted and compared with an AI language model trained on a reference corpus. Within the context of language assessment, ASR together with a scoring model whereby the extracted acoustic and linguistic features are used in a model predictive of human ratings of those features, covering the scoring of both what was said and how it was said (Van Moere & Downey, 2016). Automated speaking assessment can be used to augment or replace human raters for large scale tests, as human raters are costly while human ratings are time consuming (Evanini & Zechner, 2020).

More recently, the incorporation of spoken dialogue systems into language testing has allowed for a shift from the assessment of single, one-way responses to the assessment of interactional competence in authentic two-way dialogue (Mitchell et al., 2014), as well as providing opportunities for the assessment of L2 listening. For example, Ayedoun et al. (2019) created a conversational agent aimed at enhancing communication skills. This agent was designed using communication strategies and affective feedback. Learners were able to engage in conversations with the AI by asking questions, which the agent would then respond to, helping them practice and improve their conversation abilities.

For writing, Automated Essay Scoring (AES) has a long history of use in high stakes assessment, dating back to software created by language testing companies such as Educational Testing Service (ETS) in the 1990s (*E-Rater*, Burnstein et al., 2013; *Pearson Intelligent Essay Evaluator*, Folz et al., 2013). AES employs NLP to derive the linguistic features of a text, which can be classified under statistical measures (e.g. word/sentence length, average word/sentence length), style measures (e.g. part of speech, punctuation, lexis) or content measures (e.g., cohesion, semantic role). Traditional AES adopted a frequency-based regression approach to the analysis of these measures against established norms for quality without necessarily learning from the texts themselves, while later AES methods employed AI techniques of machine learning (e.g. classification models) and neural networks/deep learning to both learn and then assess the language, coherence and content of actual texts. However, issues remain with the commonly used NLP systems (e.g. Natural Language Toolkit, NLTK, Wang & Hu, 2021) employed to the derive the linguistic features of texts, as well as the generic nature of datasets used for benchmarking, causing issues for assessment of domain-specific texts (Ramesh & Sanampudi, 2022).

There is comparatively less research on AI for the assessment of reading. However, the development of AI-based Intelligent tutoring systems has been shown to help provide learners with hints and feedback regarding text structures, with the AI used to organize textual information (Wijekumar et al., 2017). AI feedback has been used in dynamic assessment situations, providing corrective feedback in response to learner input to gauge learners' reading and listening comprehension (e.g. Poehner & Lantolf, 2013). This has also been applied to the assessment of writing as AI-based AWE systems (e.g. *Criterion*) have evolved to incorporate NLP techniques allowing for the addition of form and content-based automated feedback in assessment contexts (e.g., Zhu et al., 2020).

Arguably one of the most ambitious attempts to integrate AI into assessment practice across all four skills is the use of NLP and machine learning in the construction of the Duolingo English Test (Settles et al., 2020). Specifically, the authors "propose the use of test item formats that can be automatically created, graded, and psychometrically analyzed using ML/NLP techniques" (p. 247), reducing the need for human pilot testing of assessment items. Items are aligned to the Common European Framework Reference (CEFR) through the combination of a CEFR-aligned training corpus and the Simple English Wikipedia which is subject to ranking, scaling and validation through machine learning techniques, automatically generating an item bank of 25,000 test items with strong criterion validity and test reliability. This is one of the largest attempts to generate a large-scale, high-stakes language test entirely through artificial intelligence techniques.

AI is now also being used to enhance the validity of language assessment from its current focus on construct validity, i.e. "determining the competencies that underlie performance on a set of test tasks" to form a language model accounting for variance in test scores (Buck, 2001, p. 106). Rather, AI in the form of deep learning has the potential to better account for domain-specific language use, in effect "enabling the field to conduct 'testing' without using tests" (Aryadoust, 2023, p.13). This can potentially be achieved through the analysis and creation of large language models formed from the mass collection of natural language data, to which we now turn our attention in the next section on GenAI.

Generative AI and assessment

The advent of GenAI applications and the large language models underpinning them has already impacted much research in assessment generally and language assessment in particular, with educators wrestling with threats to assessment integrity and ethical consideration on the one hand (Kutbi et al., 2024) while trying to understand how to harness its affordances to enhance (language) assessment on the other (e.g., Mizumoto et al, 2024). For the former, Lodge et al. (2023a, p.3) suggest that "the barriers to engaging in cheating behavior (in terms of effort and risk) have been lowered significantly, and the ability to detect cheating has become significantly more difficult, if not impossible". This suggests assessment redesign to prevent integrity concerns may be a priority in the short term. ChatGPT 4.0 has already been shown to perform excellently on standardized tests of English reading comprehension (e.g., de Winter, 2023), potentially necessitating a rethink of such assessment formats. Moorhouse et al. (2023) recommend using ChatGPT to evaluate assessments before they are launched, determining whether and how the tool might complete them. However, the integration of AI in assessment practice needs serious consideration in the medium term as educators and students prepare for AI to become ubiquitous for work and life in the real world (Lodge et al, 2023a; Moorhouse et al., 2023), although questions remain around how to achieve this equitably and ethically (Foung et al., 2024). For example, uploading students' work to third-party generative AI applications e.g. ChatGPT was seen as a potentially sackable offence by Australian F-10 teachers in a study by Crosthwaite et al. (2024). A potential workaround to this involves the training of LLMs and creation of custom GPTs on local systems, although the degree of technical expertise and computing power required to do so would (at the time of writing) limit the applicability of this solution in most language teaching contexts (Li et al., 2023).

GenAI can make a significant contribution to existing AI-driven methods for language assessment. ChatGPT, for example, has already been applied to the task of automated essay scoring (Mizumoto & Eguchi, 2023; Pfau et al., 2023; Mizumoto et al, 2024; Poole & Coss, 2024; Kim et al., 2024). Mizumoto and Eguchi (2023) used GPT3.5 to score 12,500 essays from the ETS Corpus of Non-Native Written English, providing the IELTS Task 2 rubric within the prompt used and comparing the derived scores with those of professional human ratings. A range of syntactic and lexical complexity features were also derived from the corpus using a suite of NLP tools[1] (e.g. Kyle & Crossley, 2018), with ChatGPT provided with these features in the prompt as additional support for the rating of a stratified sample of 1,250 essays. It was found that GPT3.5 could accurately predict essay scores using the IELTS rubric across the larger dataset, with improvements in the accuracy of its predictions across the smaller dataset when the prompt was supplemented with information about the linguistic features of the texts. Taking this one step further, Mizumoto et al. (2024) tested ChatGPT's potential for assessing error and accuracy rates across a sample 232 written L2 texts taken from the Cambridge Learner Corpus First Certificate in English (CLC FCE) corpus, again finding a strong correlation between professional human analysis and that of ChatGPT. Similarly, Pfau et al. (2023) used ChatGPT to assess 100 L2 essays across five proficiency levels while coding for precision and recall of L2 errors, finding that while ChatGPT rarely misidentifies errors, it often underestimates the total error count.

However, later research in Xu et al. (2024) reveals that prompt engineering including consideration of temperature settings in the supplied prompt can improve accuracy and recall of L2 errors. Poole and Coss (2024) used ChatGPT to assess 144 Chinese L2 English written essays taken from a corpus of texts with pre-assigned human rated grades of between 4-7 on the ACTFL proficiency scale. It was found that the correlation between human grades and those of ChatGPT depended significantly on the prompt provided for each party. Specifically, providing two examples within the prompt (also known as two-shot prompting) was found to be advantageous over other single-shot prompts, providing the complete rubric, or asking ChatGPT to apply ACTFL grades from its own knowledge base. The writing task was found to predict grading outcomes in ChatGPT, but not with human ratings. Additionally, the order of tasks affected the reliability of assessments using ChatGPT compared to human raters. Finally, Kim et al. (2024) compared human ratings from the Iowa State University English Placement Test Corpus of Learner Writing with ChatGPT 4 yet finding "ChatGPT's reliability was moderate to low" (p. 73).

While less numerous than studies on writing, a number of studies have already employed ChatGPT for the assessment of speaking. However, the results are (to date) less positive for those of writing. Similarly to Mizumoto et al. (2024) for writing, Uchida (2024) compared ChatGPT's assessment with those of human raters, using of a corpus of human-assessed spoken monologues sourced from the International Corpus Network of Asian Learners of English (ICNALE, Ishikawa, 2020). However, ChatGPT's assessment of the spoken data was found

---

[1] https://www.linguisticanalysistools.org/

to be considerably less reliable than that of written data overall. Sakai (2023) explored the potential for ChatGPT to be used for practising the Test of English for International Communication (TOEIC) with L1 Japanese L2 English learners, particularly focusing on how ChatGPT deals with errors from these L2 English speakers. While ChatGPT had no issues comprehending error-filled L2 discourse, it was unable to clearly differentiate speakers of different proficiency levels. More experimental work needs to be done in this area before firmer conclusions can be drawn. Finally, Gao et al. (2024) trained two generative AI classifiers (one a feature-based LLM and one using a BERT pre-trained LLM) on aberrant L2 oral responses in data from the Linguaskill Business Speaking test across 6 CEFR levels, finding improved performance in the feature-based model.

Recently, the two authors of this chapter raised a novel concept, ChatGPT literacy, to guide language teachers how to use ChatGPT to facilitate their language teaching, including conducting language assessment (Ma et al., 2024). ChatGPT literacy comprises "the competencies involved in leveraging ChatGPT's educational potential and mitigating its limitations while critically appraising its response, designing effective prompts, adopting it for assessment, and ensuring its ethical use" (Ma et al., 2024, p. 4). Specially, it includes six constructs, benefits, limitations, prompts, evaluation (of ChatGPT responses), assessment (assisted by ChatGPT), and ethics. This six-construct ChatGPT literacy was validated with the survey data from 492 language teachers. While the majority of language teachers self-perceived to have a relatively high competence in benefits, limitations, evaluation and ethics, they are relatively weaker in prompts and assessment. This indicates that language teachers need additional support and resources in integrating GenAI as useful assessment tools. Teacher professional development that focusing on developing teachers' ChatGPT literacy, especially how to turn GenAI into effective assessment tools, would be a solution.

Examples of assessment involving GenAI from the australian context

Despite the vast potential for generative AI to improve the teaching, learning and assessment of language in education, the current situation for many is to revise assessment practices to protect assessment integrity. For some, this has already involved a switch to in-person, invigilated pen and paper assessment practices, although we and others (e.g., Lodge et al, 2023a) argue this is a considerable step backwards for (language) education. Rather, it is important for policymakers at the local and national levels to recognize the opportunities posed by the integration of AI technologies into practice, creating guiding frameworks for the ethical and responsible use of AI in schools, including language education. The Australian Framework for GenAI in Schools (Figure 1, Australian Department of Education, 2023) is one such example of a coherent national approach, calling for critical engagement with generative AI technologies from the perspective of their impact on instruction, teacher expertise, student critical thinking, learning design (including assessment), and academic integrity.

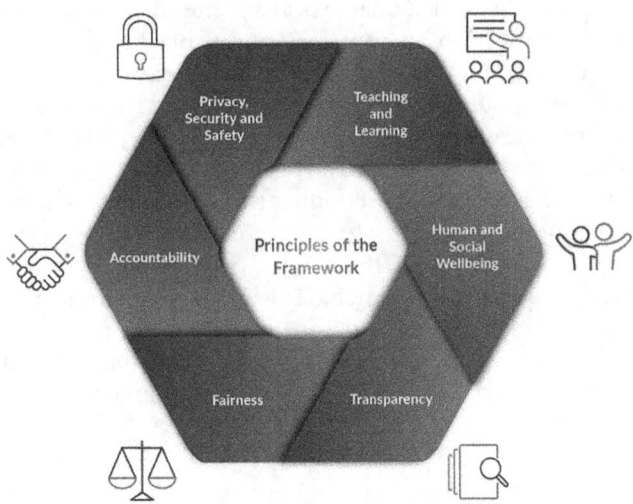

Figure 5.1 *Australian framework for generative AI in schools.*

Specifically regarding assessment, a 2023 Australian Tertiary Education Quality and Standards Agency white paper on assessment reform in the age of artificial intelligence (Lodge et al., 2023b) proposes two guiding principles, namely that "Assessment and learning experiences equip students to participate ethically and actively in a society where AI is ubiquitous" and "Forming trustworthy judgements about student learning in a time of AI requires multiple, inclusive and contextualized approaches to assessment" (p. 1–2). Proposed strategies to achieve these aims for (language) assessment include appropriate, authentic engagement with AI for assessment, a systemic approach to assessment aligned with disciplines/qualifications, and opportunities for students to work appropriately with each other and AI.

While we acknowledge that the incorporation of GenAI into teachers' or even students' self-language assessment practice is arguably still a medium-term ambition at the time of writing, modifying assessment practices to acknowledge – and critique – the quality of GenAI produced texts is certainly possible in the short term. By way of example, the first author of this chapter coordinates a large (300+ student) undergraduate academic writing course at a leading Australian tertiary institution. The course curriculum primarily focuses on the research skills, language and rhetorical structures of the academic essay, including citation and referencing practice, the use of meta discourse for academic argumentation, evaluating academic sources, and the use of academic language corpora. Course assessment prior to the advent of GenAI involved the production of a structured essay plan earlier in the semester, a complete essay based on that same plan later in the semester, and the production of a final text in a genre of the students' choice together with a reflection on how the text was produced with reference to the course materials at the end of the semester.

Obviously, the potential threat posed by GenAI to the assessment integrity of this academic writing course was severe, given ChatGPT's ability to produce academic essays of the required length and tone at the touch of a button. To counter this, the final assessment was revised to request to students to revise an academic essay produced using ChatGPT (version 4), the design of which involved prompting ChatGPT to *intentionally* include sections containing poor APA citation/referencing practice, non-academic tone (in certain places), overly strong claims (e.g., 'the data obviously prove that…') and several English language errors. An example is shown in Figure 2.

Introduction

Social media has cast a malevolent shadow over the lives of today's youth, inflicting them with a host of distressing consequences. This essay explores the dark side of social media influence on youth, shedding light on its detrimental effects on mental health, self-esteem, and personal relationships. From spiraling anxiety to a distorted sense of self-worth, the impact of social media has ensnared young minds in a web of despair and disillusionment.

Body Paragraphs

Firstly, social media has become a breeding ground for mental health issues among youth. The constant exposure to unrealistic beauty standards, curated lifestyles, and peer comparison has fueled a rise in anxiety, depression, and body dissatisfaction. The carefully crafted personas and highlight reels presented on social media create an illusion of perfection, leaving young individuals feeling inadequate and unworthy. The pursuit of likes, followers, and validation on these platforms perpetuates a toxic cycle of seeking external validation and constant self-comparison, leading to a deteriorating mental well-being.

Secondly, social media platforms have dealt a severe blow to self-esteem and self-perception among young users. The relentless pressure to conform to societal norms and fit into narrow beauty ideals portrayed on social media exacerbates feelings of inadequacy and self-doubt. The incessant scrutiny of one's appearance, lifestyle choices, and popularity metrics can cause a distorted self-image and a diminished sense of self-worth. Youth are left grappling with a fragmented identity as they struggle to meet the unattainable standards set by the digital world.

Lastly, social media has transformed personal relationships, leading to a decline in authentic connections and genuine human interactions. The rise of virtual communication has replaced face-to-face interactions, leading to a deterioration in social skills and empathy. Online interactions lack the depth and intimacy of real-life connections, perpetuating a sense of loneliness and isolation. The excessive time spent on social media detracts from meaningful relationships and hinders the development of strong interpersonal bonds.

Conclusion

In conclusion, social media's influence on youth has cast a dark and troubling shadow over their lives, impacting mental health, self-esteem, and personal relationships. The pursuit of perfection, fueled by the curated content on social media platforms, has given rise to a mental health crisis among young individuals. The erosion of self-esteem and the distorted self-perception fostered by these platforms perpetuate feelings of inadequacy and self-doubt. Furthermore, the virtual nature of social media communication has eroded authentic connections, leaving youth feeling lonely and isolated. It is crucial to raise awareness about the harmful effects of social media, promote digital well-being, and foster a culture that values real-life connections and genuine self-acceptance. Only then can we mitigate the dark side of social media and restore the well-being and happiness of our youth.

Figure 5.2 *Generative-AI produced essay for revision.*

Students would then revise this GPT-produced passage 'to appropriate tertiary academic standards' including improvements across citation, research and language areas, before submitting a reflective video response (doubling as an identity verification procedure) explaining how they drew upon course content to a) recognize the issues within the GPT-produced essay, b) revise those issues, and c) consider how reliance on GenAI software for academic writing may negatively influence the quality of the final work.

Another initiative created by the first author at the same institution tackles the issue of assessment for AI from a teacher-focused perspective. A 5-hour online staff training module, *"Working with Linguistically Diverse Writers"*, covers the topic of *differentiation* (Tomlinson et al, 2003; Taplin, 2017), which involves tailoring teaching to meet the diverse needs of students. Course content covers differentiation of instruction, feedback and assessment and feedback, and is designed to allow teaching staff to address English proficiency gaps, promote better engagement and improve academic achievement. Regarding assessment, differentiation involves providing clarity through precise assessment instructions and scaffolded task components, offering language support by allowing reasonable adjustments to conditions, using examples and illustrations by providing assessment exemplars and discussing examples of good practice, and using multiple modes by explaining assessment tasks in multiple ways and providing students with a choice of output type. Importantly, GenAI is introduced as a key method for achieving differentiated assessment practice for linguistically diverse learners, as shown in Figure 3.

After students have exhausted any support, workshops and past exams provided by the University, you could suggest they experiment with ChatGPT in the following ways. Generative AI can provide instant, tailored assistance with exam preparation, potentially leading to increased academic achievement if managed effectively (Lo, 2023). Before you do this though, make sure your students have done the Digital Essentials: Artifical intelligence module and read the UQ Library's information on ChatGPT.

Practice exams: ChatGPT can provide learners with practice exams or interactive exercises that simulate exam conditions that are specifically designed to assess their English language proficiency, and give feedback on areas that need improvement.

Language support: ChatGPT can provide learners with support for understanding complex exam questions and instructions, and provide assistance in interpreting and responding to them appropriately. ChatGPT can help learners improve their vocabulary and grammar by providing targeted exercises and examples that are specific to the types of questions that will be on the exam.

Subject-specific support: ChatGPT can provide learners with subject-specific support, such as explanations of key concepts, examples of past exam questions, and practice exercises that are specific to their field of study.

Figure 5.3 *Achieving differentiated assessment.*

A final set of examples of GenAI within Australian assessment practices is sourced from Australian F-10 teachers (Crosthwaite et al, 2024). In this study, 38 teachers submitted 252 GenAI prompts they considered to be 'pedagogically useful' and 19 that were deemed 'pedagogically poor' through an online form. They also completed semi-structured interviews where they discussed how they incorporate GenAI into their daily teaching practices.

Analysis of the prompt data shows that teachers use GenAI for various purposes including developing instructional tasks, fostering creativity, defining, explaining, or summarizing concepts and texts, differentiating instructional materials for students with different proficiency levels, and handling assessment-related, administrative, and organizational tasks. Thematic analysis of the interview data highlighted teachers' views on using GenAI to expand ideas and approaches, design assessment-related tasks, and to model students' use of generative AI. Specifically regarding assessment, teachers' GenAI prompts were categorized as per Figure 4.

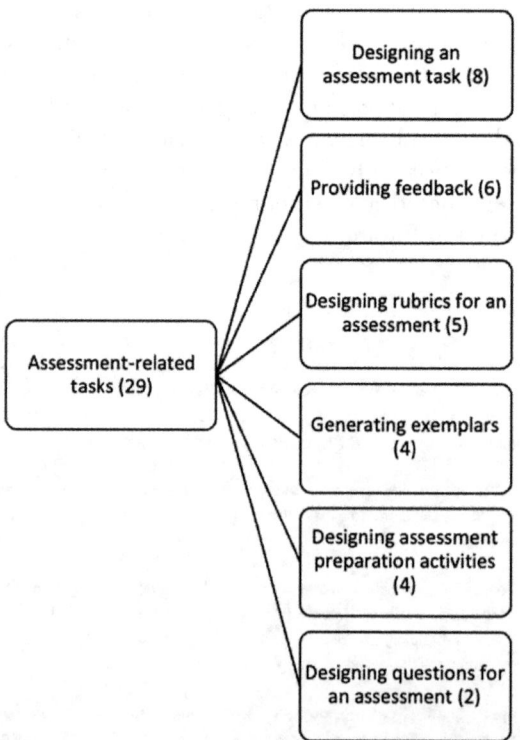

Figure 5.4 *Australian F-10 teachers' generative AI prompts for assessment (Crosthwaite et al., 2024).*

Teachers frequently prompted ChatGPT to generate assessment tasks or test items, e.g.

"Create an assessment task for Y7 students to introduce themselves to a Japanese person for the first time."

Generating exemplar assessment responses for learners' modelling purposes was also a feature of the assessment-related prompts provided, e.g. (where ACARA standards for the Australian Curriculum),

"Prepare exemplar responses in language of a Year 7 ACARA standard."

The generation of assessment rubrics was also a feature of the teachers provided prompts, e.g.

"Can you make me a rubric based on the initial ACARA content descriptors as well as communication skills?"

In the interview data, the teachers discussed how they leveraged generative AI tools to design and refine a variety of assessment resources, including student assessments, rubrics, and grading guides aligned with curriculum standards. ChatGPT was used to assist with crafting model responses, developing rubrics tailored to different curriculum versions, and generating differentiated assessment tasks suitable for students at various levels of proficiency.

Examples of assessment involving GenAI in Hong Kong and elsewhere

The Australian Framework for GenAI in Schools provides valuable policy direction for appropriate and ethical use of GenAI in assessment. However, translating these policy guidelines into concrete, pedagogically sound assessment tasks requires further exploration. To address this need, the Education University of Hong Kong has developed the 6-P pedagogy (plan, prompt, preview, produce, peer-review, portfolio-tracking) for integrating GenAI into academic essay writing at the tertiary level (Kong et al., 2024). This Gen-AI assisted assessment pedagogy, grounded in the principles of self-regulated learning (SRL) (Zimmerman, 2002) and the authoring cycle (Short et al., 1996), aims to promote students' critical thinking skills. SRL encourages students to take ownership of their learning through three phases: forethought (planning), performance (monitoring), and self-reflection (Zimmerman, 2002), and hence fostering critical thinking (Anwar & Muti'ah, 2022;

Kusmaharti & Yusttia, 2022). Similarly, the authoring cycle, with its iterative stages of engagement, research, writing, and reflection, guides students through a deep learning process that enhances critical thinking (Kong et al., 2024). By aligning assessment tasks with these learning theories, the 6-P assessment pedagogy provides a practical framework for leveraging GenAI to foster critical thinking in language education. See Figure 5 for this model.

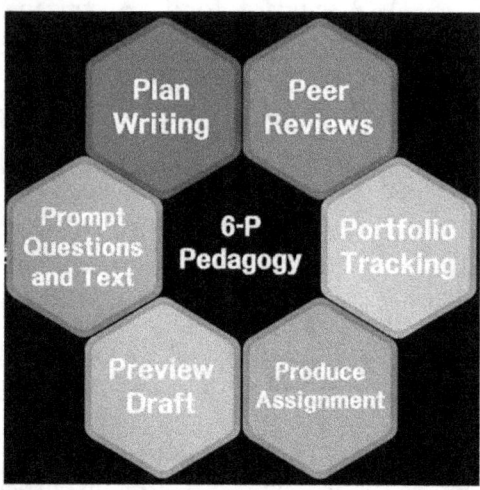

Figure 5.5 *6-P pedagogy for GenAI-assisted assessment.*

The 6-P pedagogy fosters deep learning by guiding students through a structured process of utilizing GenAI for academic writing, specifically essay assignments. The first step, planning, encourages students to define the writing's scope and structure, reflecting a problem-solving approach (Flower et al., 1989) and aligning with the forethought phase of self-regulated learning (SRL) (Zimmerman, 2002). Subsequently, students engage in prompt engineering (Reynolds & McDonell, 2021) to retrieve relevant information, followed by critically evaluating, revising and supplementing AI-generated content (preview). The fourth step emphasizes producing original work by integrating AI insights with writer's research and personal perspectives. Like scholarly peer review before journal article publication, students then engage in peer feedback to enhance writing quality and identify areas for improvement. These steps (prompt, preview, produce, and peer-review) correspond to the performance phase of SRL. Finally, students reflect on their writing process and strategize for future writing tasks in portfolio-tracking, aligning with SRL's self-reflection phase. This structured and iterative approach empowers students to leverage GenAI effectively while fostering critical thinking and self-regulated learning.

The 6-P pedagogy offers a practical framework for integrating GenAI into language-oriented courses. Take, for example, an introductory linguistics course where students collaborate to develop a chapter covering various linguistic aspects such as phonology, vocabulary, grammar, discourse, etc. Following the 6-P model, groups would first plan their chapter structure, utilizing ChatGPT for brainstorming. Next, students would individually formulate prompts to generate content on the part allocated to them in the group project. Crucially, they would then critically evaluate and refine the AI-generated information, ensuring accuracy and minimizing bias. The writing process would then commence, followed by peer review for quality enhancement and language error detection. Finally, students would reflect on their collaborative process, documenting their GenAI interactions and suggesting improvements for future tasks. To ensure engagement and collect evidence of learning, teachers could require students to document each step in a shared digital space, providing valuable insights into their learning journey.

While the previous examples illustrated summative assessment tasks usually conducted at the end of a course, GenAI's application can also extend to various formative assessment tasks throughout a course. A recent study charting ChatGPT literacy among nearly 500 language teachers globally (Ma et al., 2024) revealed its widespread use for formative assessment both inside and outside the classroom. Teachers reported utilizing ChatGPT to generate engaging learning activities, such as creating reading comprehension questions, designing fill-in-the-blank exercises, and formulating writing prompts. Furthermore, ChatGPT's role as a useful feedback tool emerged, with teachers encouraging students to utilize it for self-assessment of their writing, grammar, and vocabulary. This practice is exemplified by one teacher's statement: "I am encouraging my students to use ChatGPT as a learning buddy outside the classroom." These findings highlight the versatility of GenAI in facilitating dynamic and personalized language learning experiences through diverse formative assessment practices.

Conclusion

This chapter has briefly outlined the history of AI in language assessment, together with commentary on the limitations of the state-of-the-art, and the risks and opportunities of what may come in the (near) future. The arrival of ChatGPT demands a reimagination of language assessment, moving away from static, traditional methods towards dynamic evaluation embedded in real-world communication (Moqbel & Al-Kadi, 2023; Shaikh et al., 2023). The capacity of GenAI to engage in interactive dialogue opens doors for authentic assessments that mirror real-life language use. Language teachers are exploring its use in both formative assessments, providing ongoing feedback to guide student learning, and summative assessments, evaluating their overall learning outcomes, as well as encouraging students to use GenAI as self-assessment tool outside classroom learning. This signifies a shift towards a more comprehensive and authentic evaluation of learner language proficiency.

Encouragingly, despite all the claims around assessment integrity and security now posed by generative AI, debate is also turning towards generative AI's potential role in increasing equity for language test takers. For example, discussion in Voss et al. (2023) notes the language test preparation industry "perpetuates a "hidden" cost that serves as a barrier for under-privileged and under-resourced students" (p. 526). Generative AI may serve as a more affordable method, with tools such as TalkPal (https://talkpal.ai/) now available for a nominal fee and with ChatGPT still free at the time of writing. In addition, incorporating Generative AI allows for scalable assessment previously considered expensive or overly time-consuming in the case of large student populations, e.g., conducting spoken assessment in contexts such as China or Saudi Arabia (e.g. Zheng et al., 2024).

Of course, much of the discussion in this article has been on the assessment of English. It must be said that several review articles of AI for education (including language assessment) (e.g., Huang et al., 2023) do not mention languages other than English (LOTE). Notable exceptions include Luo et. al. (2022) who used AI for automating the creation of vocabulary test items for L2 Chinese. Students piloting both the AI and human-produced materials reported several differences between them, including discrimination of proficiency and the knowledge/linguistic constructs being tested by the items. Very few studies have explored the use of generative AI applications for assessment of LOTE, e.g. Ma (2024) discusses the potential for using ChatGPT for L2 Mandarin oral assessment, although this is not an experimental study.

That said, generative AI does have the potential to drastically improve this situation, with ChatGPT 4, for example, claiming to have mastered "approximately 95 languages" when prompted with the question of how many languages it knows. However, recent research suggests that overall, ChatGPT's performance on LOTE (particularly languages of the Global South) is poor given how the training data underpinning ChatGPT's and similar LLMs was collected through internet-scraping software (Choudhury, 2023). Studies have also shown that even for relatively well-documented languages (e.g., Mandarin, Vietnamese), ChatGPT struggles with regional dialect-specific lexis, potentially reinforcing hegemonic dominance of standardized 'central' dialects (e.g., Putonghua, Northern Vietnamese, see Tran & Stell, 2024).

Teacher education in AI assessment literacy will also prove crucial in the short term. For example, Xu (2024) investigated the AI assessment literacy of Chinese high school EFL teachers using the Chinese AI-powered chatbot, ERNIE Bot. Teachers demonstrated a notable degree of practical and conceptual knowledge around AI yet were found to lack the degree of technical proficiency required to achieve competence in AI assessment literacy. While the GenAI tools hold immense potential for creating dynamic and authentic assessment, language teachers require adequate support and training to improve their GenAI literacy and capabilities. Traditional assessment methods must evolve to align with the interactive and communicative nature of GenAI. As Moqbel and Al-Kadi (2023) suggest, a shift towards performance-based assessments, self and peer evaluations, portfolio assessments, and teacher observations is necessary, all of which can be enhanced through the strategic use of ChatGPT. To facilitate this transition, dedicated professional development programs are crucial for language teachers (Kong et al., 2024; Ma et al., 2024). These programs should focus on equipping teachers with the knowledge and skills to effectively integrate ChatGPT into various aspects of assessment. This includes learning how to design assessments that leverage ChatGPT's capabilities, designing personalized tasks that reflect real-world communication scenarios. Importantly, these programs should also empower teachers to promote learner autonomy by guiding students in leveraging GenAI tools for self-assessment and reflection on their language learning progress. Teachers' improved ChatGPT literacy ultimately leads to more engaging and effective learning experiences for students, ushering in a new era of language learning empowered by GenAI.

To conclude, we must prepare for the future of language assessment in the (generative) AI era by recognizing the affordances of this technology in terms of reliability, scalability and equality, while also recognizing its shortcomings in terms of performance and threats to assessment integrity and security. We are keen to stress that the worst-case scenario for language assessment is the submission of written/spoken language data produced using generative AI for subsequent assessment using generative AI-produced rubrics and generative AI raters, with accompanying generative AI-produced scores and feedback. While AI can help reduce cost and increase equity for test-takers, there must still be a place for authentic human L2 production combined with human judgement on assessment performance, lest test-takers begin to prepare only to beat the AI rather than attempt to communicate in a second language.

Post-reading questions:

1) How will AI shape the field of L2 language assessment over the next five years?
2) What are some of the limitations of (generative) AI for language assessment, and how might they be overcome?

Further reading

1. Aryadoust, V. (2023). The vexing problem of validity and the future of second language assessment. *Language Testing, 40*(1), 8–14.
   This forward-thinking article explores how AI can help overcome the key issue of construct validity in L2 language assessment, which is crucial if the field is to develop.
2. Chappelle et al. (2024). AI in applied linguistics. Iowa State University Digital Press. https://www.iastatedigitalpress.com/plugins/books/154/
   This state-of-the-art overview of AI in applied linguistics has several excellent chapters devoted to the use of AI for second language assessment.
3. Koraishi, O. (2023). Teaching English in the age of AI: Embracing ChatGPT to optimize EFL materials and assessment. *Language Education & Technology (LET Journal), 3*(1), 55–72. This work explores how ChatGPT can personalize language learning and assessment by facilitating tailored material development and providing real-time, individualized feedback on learner performance.

References

Anwar, Y. A. S., & Muti'ah, M. (2022). Exploration of critical thinking and self-regulated learning in online learning during the COVID-19 pandemic. *Biochemistry and Molecular Biology Education, 50*(5), 502–509. https://doi.org/10.1002/bmb.21655

Aryadoust, V. (2023). The vexing problem of validity and the future of second language assessment. *Language Testing, 40*(1), 8–14.

Ayedoun, E., Hayashi, Y., & Seta, K. (2019). Adding communicative and affective strategies to an embodied conversational agent to enhance second language learners' willingness to communicate. *International Journal of Artificial Intelligence in Education, 29*(1), 29–57.

Burstein, J., Tetreault, J., & Madnani, N. (2013). The e-rater® automated essay scoring system. In M. Shermis & J. Bursten (Eds.) *Handbook of automated essay evaluation* (pp. 55–67). Routledge.

Choudhury, M. (2023). Generative AI has a language problem. *Nature Human Behaviour*, 7(11), 1802–1803.

Crosthwaite, P., Smala, S., & Spinelli, F. (2024). Prompting for pedagogy? Australian F-10 teachers' generative AI prompting use cases. *The Australian Educational Researcher*, online ahead of print. https://doi.org/10.1007/s13384-024-00787-0

de Winter, J. C. (2023). Can ChatGPT pass high school exams on English language comprehension? *International Journal of Artificial Intelligence in Education*, 1–16.

Evanini, K. & Zechner, K. (2020). Overview of Automated Speech Scoring. In K. Zechner & K. Evanini, (eds). *Automated speaking assessment* (pp. 3–21). Routledge.

Flower, L., Schriver, K. A., Carey, L., Haas, C., & Hayes, J. R. (1989). Planning in writing: The cognition of a constructive process. Center for the Study of Writing. https://files.eric.ed.gov/fulltext/ED313701.pdf

Foltz, P. W., Streeter, L. A., Lochbaum, K. E., & Landauer, T. K. (2013). Implementation and applications of the intelligent essay assessor. In *Handbook of automated essay evaluation* (pp. 68–88). Routledge.

Foung, D., Lin, L., & Chen, J. (2024). Reinventing assessments with ChatGPT and other online tools: Opportunities for GenAI-empowered assessment practices. Computers and Education: Artificial Intelligence, 100250.

Gao, S., Gales, M., & Xu, J. (2024). Detecting aberrant responses in automated L2 spoken English assessment. In C. A. Chapelle, G. H. Beckett, & J. Ranalli (Eds.), Exploring artificial intelligence in applied linguistics (pp. 96–117). Iowa State University Digital Press. https://doi.org/10.31274/isudp.2024.154.07

Huang, X., Zou, D., Cheng, G., Chen, X., & Xie, H. (2023). Trends, research issues and applications of artificial intelligence in language education. *Educational Technology & Society*, 26(1), 112–131.

Ishikawa, S. (2020). Aim of the ICNALE GRA project: Global collaboration to collect ratings of Asian learners' L2 English essays and speeches from an ELF perspective. *Learner Corpus Studies in Asia and the World*, 5, 121–144.

Kim, H., Baghestani, Sh., Yin, Sh., Karatay, Y., Kurt, S., Beck, J., & Karatay, L. (2024). ChatGPT for writing evaluation: Examining the accuracy and reliability of AI-generated scores compared to human raters. In C. A. Chapelle, G. H. Beckett, & J. Ranalli (Eds.), Exploring artificial intelligence in applied linguistics (pp. 73–95). Iowa State University Digital Press. https://doi.org/10.31274/isudp.2024.154.06

Kong, S.-C., Lee, J. C.-K., & Tsang, O. (2024). A pedagogical design for self-regulated learning in academic writing using text-based generative artificial intelligence tools: 6-P pedagogy of plan, prompt, preview, produce, peer-review, portfolio-tracking. *Research and Practice in Technology Enhanced Learning, 19*(030). https://doi.org/10.58459/rptel.2024.19030

Kusmaharti, D, Yustitia, V. (2022). Self-regulated learning-based digital module development to improve students' critical thinking skills. *Al-Jabar: Jurnal Pendidikan, 13*(1), 211–220.

Kutbi, M., Al-Hoorie, A. H., & Al-Shammari, A. H. (2024). Detecting contract cheating through linguistic fingerprint. *Humanities and Social Sciences Communications, 11*(1), 1–9.

Kyle, K., & Crossley, S. A. (2018). Measuring syntactic complexity in L2 writing using fine-grained clausal and phrasal indices. *The Modern Language Journal,* 102(2), 333–349.

Li, X., Yao, Y., Jiang, X., Fang, X., Meng, X., Fan, S., ... & Wang, Y. (2023). Flm-101b: An open llm and how to train it with $100 k budget. arXiv preprint arXiv:2309.03852

Lodge, J. M., Thompson, K., & Corrin, L. (2023a). Mapping out a research agenda for generative artificial intelligence in tertiary education. Australasian Journal of Educational Technology, 39(1), 1–8.

Lodge, J.M., Howard, S & Bearman, M. (2023). Assessment reform for the age of artificial intelligence. Australian Tertiary Education Quality and Standards Agency (TEQSA). Available https://www.teqsa.gov.au/sites/default/files/2023-09/assessment-reform-age-artificial-intelligence-discussion-paper.pdf Retrieved August 5, 24.

Luo, Y., Wei, W., & Zheng, Y. (2022). Artificial intelligence-generated and human expert-designed vocabulary tests: A comparative study. *SAGE* Open, 12. https://doi.org/10.1177/21582440221082130

Ma, L. (2024). Research on oral teaching of international Chinese language education assisted by ChatGPT. *Journal of Higher Vocational Education, 1*(2), 129–134

Ma, Q., Crosthwatie, P., Sun, D., & Zou, D. (In press). Exploring and constructing ChatGPT literacy in language education: A global perspective and comprehensive approach. *Computers & Education: Artificial Intelligence.*

Mitchell, C. M., Evanini, K., & Zechner, K. (2014). A trialogue-based spoken dialogue system for assessment of English language learners. In Proceedings International Workshop on Spoken Dialogue Systems.

Mizumoto, A., & Eguchi, M. (2023). Exploring the potential of using an AI language model for automated essay scoring. *Research Methods in Applied Linguistics, 2*(2), 100050.

Mizumoto, A., Shintani, N., Sasaki, M., & Teng, M. F. (2024). Testing the viability of ChatGPT as a companion in L2 writing accuracy assessment. *Research Methods in Applied Linguistics, 3*(2), 100116.

Moorhouse, B. L., Yeo, M. A., & Wan, Y. (2023). Generative AI tools and assessment: Guidelines of the world's top-ranking universities. *Computers and Education Open*, 5, 100151.

Moqbel, M. S. S., & Al-Kadi, A. M. T. (2023). Foreign language learning assessment in the age of ChatGPT: A theoretical account. *Journal of English Studies in Arabia Felix*, 2(1), 71–84.

Pfau, A., Polio, C., & Xu, Y. (2023). Exploring the potential of ChatGPT in assessing L2 writing accuracy for research purposes. Research Methods in Applied Linguistics, 2(3), 100083.

Poehner, M. E. & Lantolf, J. P. (2013) Bringing the ZPD into the equation: Capturing L2 development during computerized dynamic assessment. *Language Teaching Research*, 1ˆ7(3): 323–342. https://doi.org/10.1177/1362168813482935

Poole, F. J., & Coss, M. D. (2024). Can ChatGPT reliably and accurately apply a rubric to L2 writing assessments? The devil is in the prompt (s). *Journal of Technology & Chinese Language Teaching*, 15(1).

Ramesh, D., & Sanampudi, S. K. (2022). An automated essay scoring systems: A systematic literature review. *Artificial Intelligence Review*, 55(3), 2495–2527.

Reynolds, L., & McDonell, K. (2021). Prompt programming for large language models: Beyond the few-shot paradigm. In Y. Kitamura, A. Quigley, K. Isbister & T. Igarashi (Eds.), Extended Abstracts of the 2021 CHI Conference on Human Factors in Computing Systems (pp. 314, 1–7). Association for Computing Machinery. https://doi.org/10.1145/3411763.3451760

Sakai, N. (2023, March 31). Native, non-native, or bilingual? A concise assessment of ChatGPT's suitability for second-language instruction as a native or non-native pedagogue. https://doi.org/10.31219/osf.io/hy9ju

Settles, B., T. LaFlair, G., & Hagiwara, M. (2020). Machine learning–driven language assessment. *Transactions of the Association for computational Linguistics*, 8, 247–263.

Shaikh, S., Yayilgan, S. Y., Klimova, B., & Pikhart, M. (2023). Assessing the usability of ChatGPT for formal English language learning. *European Journal of Investigation in Health, Psychology and Education*, 13(9), 1937–1960.

Taplin, A. (2017). Accounting for the needs of EAL/D students in the mainstream classroom. *Metaphor*, (1), 48.

Tomlinson, C. A., Brighton, C., Hertberg, H., Callahan, C. M., Moon, T. R., Brimijoin, K., Conover, L. A. & Reynolds, T. (2003). Differentiating instruction in response to student readiness, interest, and learning profile in academically diverse classrooms: A review of literature. *Journal for the Education of the Gifted*, 27(2/3), 119–145. https://doi.org/10.1177/016235320302700203

Tran, H. & Stell, A. (2024). Beyond borders or building new walls? The potential for Generative AI in recolonising the learning of Vietnamese dialects and Mandarin varieties. *Australian Review of Applied Linguistics*, online ahead of print.

Uchida, S. (2024). Evaluating the accuracy of ChatGPT in assessing writing and speaking: A verification study using ICNALE GRA. *Learner Corpus Studies in Asia and the World*, 6, 1–12.

Van Moere, A., & Downey, R. (2016). 21. Technology and artificial intelligence in language assessment. *Handbook of second language assessment*, 341–358.

Voss, E., Cushing, S. T., Ockey, G. J., & Yan, X. (2023). The use of assistive technologies including generative AI by test takers in language assessment: A debate of theory and practice. *Language Assessment Quarterly*, 20(4-5), 520–532.

Wang, M., & Hu, F. (2021). The application of NLTK library for python natural language processing in corpus research. *Theory and Practice in Language Studies*, 11(9), 1041–1049.

Wijekumar, K. K., Meyer, B. J., & Lei, P. (2017). Web-based text structure strategy instruction improves seventh graders' content area reading comprehension. *Journal of Educational Psychology*, 109(6), 741–760.

Xu, Y., Polio, Ch., & Pfau, A. (2024). Optimizing AI for assessing L2 writing accuracy: An exploration of temperatures and prompts. In C. A. Chapelle, G. H. Beckett, & J. Ranalli (Eds.), Exploring artificial intelligence in applied linguistics (pp. 151–174). Iowa State University Digital Press. https://doi.org/10.31274/isudp.2024.154.10

Yu, D., & Deng, L. (2016). *Automatic speech recognition (Vol. 1)*. Springer.

Zheng, C., Zhang, T., Chen, X., Zhang, H., Wan, J., & Wu, B. (2024). Assessing learners' English public speaking anxiety with multimodal deep learning technologies. *Computer Assisted Language Learning*, Online ahead of print, https://doi.org/10.1080/09588221.2024.2351129

Zhu, M., Liu, O. L. & Lee, H.-S. (2020) The effect of automated feedback on revision behavior and learning gains in formative assessment of scientific argument writing. *Computers & Education*, 143: Article 103668. https://doi.org/10.1016/j.compedu.2019.103668

Zimmerman, B. J. (2002). Becoming a self-regulated learner: An overview. *Theory into Practice*, 4^1(2), 64–70. https://doi.org/10.1207/s15430421tip4102_2

6
Ethical considerations of AI
Gilbert Dizon

Pre-reading questions:

1) How do you feel about the integration (or lack thereof) of artificial intelligence in your institution or classroom?
2) What role should second language educators play in supporting the development of students' digital literacy?
3) What kinds of ethical challenges have you faced regarding the use of artificial intelligence in your institution or classroom?

Introduction

The past several years have seen a rapid increase in research related to artificial intelligence (AI) and language learning. A Google Scholar search of the keywords *artificial intelligence* and *language learning* between 2020 and 2022 produces 20,000 results, while the same query for the single year of 2023 results in nearly the same number of articles (N = 18,400). Although much of this attention has been attributed to the rise of generative AI (GenAI) and large language models (LLMs), most notably, Open AI's ChatGPT, the use of AI in language teaching and learning dates back to the early 1980's (Underwood, 1982).

Considering the widespread use of AI in language education, several systemic review papers on the topic have been published to highlight relevant trends and research gaps in the literature. Recent examples include Huang et al.'s (2023) bibliometric analysis of AI in language education, Zhai and Wibowo's (2023) review on AI dialogue systems and second language (L2) students' interactional competence, Shi and Aryadoust's (2024) review study on AI-based automated writing evaluation (AWE), and Law's (2024) scoping review of GenAI in language teaching and learning. While these review studies provide insight into the current state of AI-assisted language learning, ethics is still an under-addressed topic in the literature. Notable exceptions include

Pack and Maloney, who discuss issues such as ethical teaching with AI, questions regarding ownership, and the potential of AI to increase educational gaps in society, as well as Hockly (2023), who raises concerns related to AI data collection and privacy. Due to the research gap concerning ethics, the primary aim of this chapter is to provide a theory synthesis of three widely used AI technologies in the context of language learning and teaching: automatic speech recognition (ASR), machine translation (MT), and GenAI. The chapter is guided by the following question: *What ethical issues and concerns have been raised in the context of AI-assisted language learning?*

Theory synthesis

A theory synthesis is a conceptual work that aims to "contribute by summarizing and integrating extant knowledge of a concept or phenomenon" (Jaakkola, 2020, p. 21). While systematic reviews serve a similar purpose, Jaakkola notes that there are key differences between systematic review papers and theory syntheses. Specifically, systematic reviews are more suitable for mature fields and for papers where one of the primary goals is to identify gaps in the research. In contrast, theory syntheses aim to provide a macro perspective of a specific phenomenon to develop a novel conceptualization of a topic. Another major difference between systematic reviews and theory syntheses is the function of the literature review. In the former, the literature review functions as the ultimate objective, seeking insight into the development and future of a particular research area. Whereas in the latter, the literature review is just one aspect of an analytical process that ultimately seeks to reveal the most significant components of a concept. As such, researchers may minimize or exclude certain findings to highlight the areas most pertinent to the aims of the theory synthesis.

Although the framework of theory synthesis has been sparsely used in L2 literature, it has been more widely adopted in the broader domain of education. For instance, Cai and Leask (2024) utilized theory synthesis to better understand the implications of recent societal shifts within the under-researched area of internationalization in higher education. In the same vein, this chapter adopts a theory synthesis approach to highlight the relatively nascent field of AI-assisted language learning. Specifically, the author will review how specific AI technologies have been used in L2 literature and draw attention to ethical concerns addressed in these studies. Through this theory synthesis, researchers and practitioners in L2 teaching may be able to better address these ethical issues in their research and teaching practices.

Automatic speech recognition

Automatic speech recognition or ASR is "the process and the related technology for converting [a] speech signal into its corresponding sequence of words or other linguistic entities by means of algorithms implemented in a device, a computer, or computer clusters" (Li et al., 2015, p. 1). In other words, ASR analyzes aural language and creates a corresponding output, most often in written form. ASR has been implemented in popular systems, most notably, intelligent personal assistants (IPAs) such as Alexa, Google Assistant, and Siri.

Although IPAs were not created with non-native speakers in mind, they have been utilized for L2 learning purposes in various contexts (e.g., Dizon et al., 2022; Moussalli & Cardoso, 2020; Tai & Chen, 2022). Results from these studies indicate that these ASR-based systems can support speaking improvements in the L2 while simultaneously providing an engaging learning environment. However, the same research also demonstrates that these ASR-based systems have difficulties understanding L2 speech. Consequently, L2 learners may give up when faced with communication breakdowns rather than utilizing strategies (i.e., repeat or rephrase) that might alleviate these communication issues.

Other ASR systems have been developed explicitly for L2 learning purposes, for example, NovoLearning (Bashori et al., 2022; 2024), Japañol (Tejedor-García et al., 2021), and ELSA Speak (Rad & Roohani, 2024). Findings from these studies show that ASR systems developed specifically for L2 learners can positively influence both language skills and affective factors. For instance, Bashori et al. investigated two ASR websites (NovoLearning & I Love Indonesia) in two studies and found that they enhanced vocabulary knowledge and pronunciation among L2 English students. In a study involving L2 Spanish learners, Tejedor-García et al. examined the efficacy of two ASR systems on students' pronunciation of minimal pairs. The students who used ASR were able to make significant improvements in Spanish pronunciation that were on par with students who received in-class pronunciation instruction. Rad and Roohani's study focused on ELSA Speak, a mobile ASR-based app that incorporates AI to provide English pronunciation feedback. Not only did the L2 English students who used the app make greater pronunciation improvements than the control group, which received traditional face-to-face instruction, but they also had more positive attitudes toward the tool as a method for English pronunciation instruction. Specifically, students who used ELSA Speak stated that it provided instant feedback and promoted language-learning motivation.

Ethical issues concerning ASR

The ASR studies outlined above show that the technology offers various benefits for L2 learning. However, key ethical issues remain regarding its use in the L2 context. One of these concerns is the reliability of ASR in understanding L2 speech. In particular, the L2 speech intelligibility of an ASR system should be equivalent to that of a human listener. If there is a mismatch between what an ASR system transcribes and what an L1 or advanced L2 speaker deems intelligible, then any feedback provided by the ASR-based system would be erroneous. According to Rogerson-Revell (2021), this is a common issue among ASR systems, which in turn, can frustrate and demotivate language learners. Earlier research on ASR by Derwing et al. (2000) highlights the disparity between the L2 speech intelligibility of ASR systems and human raters. The researchers assessed the reliability of a popular ASR system (Dragon Naturally Speaking) in understanding L2 speech and compared the system's judgments to those of human listeners. The ASR system accurately understood 24-26% less L2 speech than the human evaluators; thus, suggesting that there was a large gap between what ASR systems could comprehend compared to human raters.

While more recent research by McCrocklin and Edalatishams (2020) indicates that modern ASR systems have made significant improvements in understanding L2 speech, approaching that of human raters, Inceoglu et al.'s (2023) study only partially supports the notion that ASR understands L2 speech to a similar degree as human listeners. Their study compared Google's ASR system to the intelligibility judgments of human evaluators. Although the overall word recognition rates were similar between the ASR system and the human listeners, there were discrepancies between which speakers the Google ASR and the human listeners found most intelligible. That is, the two L2 participants who received the highest intelligibility ratings by the ASR system had the lowest intelligibility scores according to the human evaluators. Moreover, positive correlations between the ASR and human listener judgments were only found between two out of the four L2 learners. Similar results were found in terms of the sentence-level recognition rates, i.e., ASR and human evaluators' scores were correlated for only two L2 participants. According to Inceoglu et al., the conflicting results between their study and the findings of McCrocklin and Edalatishams may be due to proficiency level. Namely, the participants in Inceoglu et al. had a beginner to intermediate level of L2 proficiency while those in McCrocklin and Edalatishams were more advanced L2 learners. In short, the contradictory results found in these two studies suggest that current ASR systems cannot be used as a replacement for feedback from teachers as the L2 intelligibility rates of ASR systems may not consistently align with that of human evaluators.

Another ethical concern involving ASR is bias. Although there is a dearth of research focusing on bias and ASR in the context of L2 speech, a growing number of L1 studies point to significant biases in the performance of ASR systems when it comes to factors such as age, gender, ethnicity, and regional dialect. Research by Koenecke et al. (2020) demonstrated that ASR systems from Apple, Amazon, Google, and Microsoft performed significantly better when it came to the speech of White Americans when compared to African Americans. In a study involving ethically-related dialects, Wassink et al. (2022) found that three L1 English ethnic groups–Native Americans, African Americans, and ChicanX–had significantly higher ASR error rates when compared to Caucasian Americans. Feng et al. (2024) conducted a study involving two ASR systems and two target languages (Dutch and Mandarin). Their results showed major differences between the two languages. That is, Dutch performance showed ASR biases related to gender, age, and L2 speech, while Mandarin performance indicated that the ASR systems were biased against certain regional accents. Importantly, only a small number of these identified biases were attributed to pronunciation differences between the different speakers. Thus, the researchers concluded that other factors such as biases in the ASR systems' acoustic models were likely to blame. Taken together, the results from these studies have implications for L2 learning. Specifically, because ASR systems struggle to recognize speech that differs significantly from the training data (Feng et al.), L2 speakers may also encounter difficulties being recognized by these systems. Consequently, as Feng et al. point out, it is imperative "to create inclusive ASR, i.e., ASR for everyone, irrespective of how one speaker or the language one speaks" (p. 2).

Machine translation

Machine translation tools such as Google Translate and DeepL are one of the most used digital language-learning resources (Vinall et al., 2023). Compared to earlier versions of MT which relied on statistical machine translation, and thus translated in a phrase-based manner, modern MT utilizes neural machine translation (NMT) in which a neural network directly translates the source language into the target language (Stahlberg, 2020). As a result, NMT can produce much more accurate translations (Shin & Chon, 2023).

Many MT studies have been conducted in the L2 context. In a mixed-methods study, Lee (2020) found that L2 English students were able to make significant improvements in grammatical and lexical accuracy using MT. The students also had positive views of MT. Namely, they thought it was a superior tool for finding contextually appropriate vocabulary compared to a dictionary. Shin and Chon (2023) focused on the post-editing strategies of L2 English learners when using MT. Although advanced L2 learners were able to successfully utilize MT to post-edit their writing, intermediate learners often resorted to negative overcorrection as the MT output was far more advanced than what the learners could comprehend. Chung and Ahn (2022) examined the effects of MT on L2 English learners' writing complexity, accuracy, and fluency (CAF). While positive results were found in relation to accuracy, there were mixed results concerning syntactic and lexical complexity, and no improvements in terms of fluency. In short, these studies demonstrate that MT can support L2 learners' writing, particularly when it comes to accuracy. However, it may not be as successful in terms of other CAF measures, and the efficacy of MT may ultimately depend on the language ability of the learner.

Ethical issues concerning MT

Academic integrity is the primary ethical issue that appears in language learning literature on MT. Even though many language instructors do not approve of the use of MT, L2 students tend to have more favorable perceptions (Paterson, 2023). This gap between teachers' and students' views regarding MT is exemplified in a study by Clifford et al. (2013). While 88% of the L2 students reported using MT, 77% of language instructors disapproved of its use. Due to these negative views, some advocate a detect and prevent approach to L2 student use of MT (Jolley & Maimone, 2022). For example, Harris (2010) states that MT use among L2 students is "unacceptable and will have a detrimental effect on the learning process" (p. 28). Consequently, he suggests that students take part in an awareness-raising activity that highlights the limitations of MT, and that any students suspected of using MT should re-submit assignments. Correa (2014) takes a less severe approach to MT in the L2 classroom as she believes it could play a supplementary role in the language learning process. Still, she stresses utilizing MT as a means to raise metalinguistic awareness to discourage academic dishonesty.

Others have adopted a more favorable attitude when it comes to L2 students' use of MT. Instead of implementing a detect and prevent approach, these educators opt for an integrate and educate model (Jolley & Maimone, 2022). For example, Ducar and Schocket (2018) stress that MT use is an essential 21st-century skill and that L2 instructors should incorporate MT activities in the classroom to highlight the strengths and limitations of the digital resource. However, they make it clear that simply translating language with MT and representing that output as one's own work without modification is academic misconduct. Thus, Ducar and Schocket recommend that the ethical and effective use of MT be emphasized in the classroom. Patterson (2023) states that MT can be used as a pedagogical tool to support L2 learner autonomy and writing development. She claims that restrictions on student use of MT are ineffective and may lead to L2 students using it more irresponsibly or uncritically. Similarly, Stapleton and Kin (2019) state that the ubiquity of MT makes it virtually impossible to eliminate its use among L2 students. Consequently, they believe L2 instructors must reconsider L2 writing pedagogy and adopt MT as an instructional tool. Based on the results of their study, Grieve et al. (2024) conclude that many L2 students do not blindly use MT, but rather, deeply reflect on its use from both a philosophical and ethical perspective. As such, they view student MT use through the lens of translanguaging, i.e., MT can be an educational resource for L2 students similar to other skills and knowledge they possess in their linguistic repertoire. In short, the body of work detailed in this paragraph emphasizes MT as a pedagogical tool instead of a pedagogical threat, while also encouraging responsible use of the digital resource.

Generative AI

While ASR and MT are examples of narrow AI, i.e., AI designed for a specific task, GenAI is an example of general-purpose AI, systems that can perform a wide variety of tasks even though they were not specifically designed for those purposes (Triguero et al., 2024). GenAI technologies such as Gemini, Copilot, and ChatGPT are chatbots that are trained on large amounts of data called LLMs, thereby allowing them to produce text and images in a natural, human-like manner. One machine learning technique that enables GenAI to produce accurate output that approaches human naturalness is reinforcement learning with human feedback (RLHF). RLHF incorporates human feedback into the LLM training process, which allows GenAI chatbots to understand what humans value, thus empowering them to go beyond simple imitation of human behavior (Liu, 2024).

Due to their versatility and accessibility, GenAI tools have been increasingly utilized in L2 settings, particularly in the context of automated writing evaluation (AWE). Mizumoto and Eguchi (2023) were one of the first to tackle this issue. In their study, the researchers used ChatGPT 3.5 to automatically score a corpus of Test of English as a Foreign Language (TOEFL) essays. Based on their findings, they concluded that ChatGPT could be used as an effective tool for automated essay scoring (AES). Pfau et al. (2023) examined the potential of ChatGPT 4.0 to accurately measure L2 students' writing accuracy. One hundred L2 English essays were coded for errors using ChatGPT and these ratings were compared to that of human coders. Although there was a high correlation between ChatGPT and the human raters when it came to L2 writing accuracy, the GenAI tool was less consistent in its ability to assess the L2 writing of novice learners. Wang and Gayed (2024) also examined the capacity of ChatGPT to automatically score L2 students' writing. However, unlike Mizumoto and Eguchi and Pfau et al, Wang and Gayed utilized finetuning to improve the performance of the GenAI tool for AES. In other words, the researchers trained the LLM using different types of input (i.e., scoring rubrics, essays, and essay scores) to enhance ChatGPT's scoring accuracy and reliability. Three finetuned models and one base (non-finetuned) model were used to score the TOEFL essays. Results showed that the finetuned models outperformed the base model in both accuracy and reliability. Taken together, the results from these three studies demonstrate the potential of GenAI for AES of L2 writing, which is significant given the taxing and time-consuming nature of human scoring.

A growing body of L2 literature has also been devoted to L2 teachers' and students' perspectives toward GenAI. Jeon and Lee (2023) interviewed language teachers in China to explore their beliefs regarding the use of LLMs in L2 education. Based on these interviews, the researchers identified four roles concerning GenAI and L2 teaching: interlocutor, content provider, teaching assistant, and evaluator. The teacher-participants in their study also stressed ethical awareness when it came to the use of LLMs for L2 learning. Specifically, the language instructors believed that transparency and rule-setting were key to the ethical use of GenAI. In another study in the Chinese context, Gao et al. (2023) conducted mixed-methods research to investigate the views of EFL university instructors toward LLMs in language teaching. Quantaitively, the teachers perceived LLMs could serve as effective pedagogical tools, improve student achievement, and increase L2 engagement. However, they also doubted the feasibility of using LLMs to teach an L2 and expressed concern that GenAI could replace traditional yet proven learning resources. The qualitative results from Gao et al. also highlighted some of the other concerns shared by the teachers such as academic integrity, accuracy of information, and privacy. These ethical concerns were also shared by the L2 students in Yan's (2023) study. That is, while the L2 English learners were impressed by the quality of the text produced by ChatGPT, they also worried about its effects on educational equity.

Ethical issues concerning GenAI

Academic integrity is a recurring theme in literature focused on GenAI and L2 learning. As noted in the previous section, the participants in both Gao et al. (2023) and Yan (2023) stressed the impact of ChatGPT and other GenAI tools on academic dishonesty. Academic integrity was also mentioned as a major concern among the L2 participants in Liu et al.'s (2024) study. Pack and Maloney (2024) delve into the issue of academic integrity further in their GenAI-focused article on ethical and pedagogical considerations in L2 teaching. They note that issues involving misuse of GenAI not only pertain to L2 students, but also L2 teachers as plagiarism and transparency are equally relevant to both. Therefore, L2 teachers and students must be deliberate in their use of GenAI to ensure their AI practices are aligned with L2 learning theory and institutional guidelines regarding academic integrity.

Another critical ethical issue related to GenAI is the accuracy of its output. Even newer LLMs such as ChatGPT-4 can still hallucinate, i.e., they are prone to inaccurate or unreliable output (UNESCO, 2023). Given this, accuracy is a common concern raised in both conceptual papers related to GenAI and L2 teaching (Pack & Maloney, 2024; Topal, 2024) as well as L2 research on these technologies (Gao et al., 2024; Mohamed, 2024). Although there is evidence that GenAI can be trained or finetuned to accurately perform specific L2 assessment tasks (e.g., Wang & Gayed, 2024), its reliability outside of the context of AWE is still untested. And even when issues related to GenAI accuracy are identified, it is impossible to determine the underlying reasons for these issues given the black box nature of LLMs. That is, the developers of LLMs are unable to identify why GenAI systems make certain decisions, which makes it difficult to impossible to prevent undesirable outcomes (Rawashdeh, 2023).

A final ethical consideration concerning GenAI that cannot be overlooked is its impact on the environment. Specifically, the development and usage of LLMs have led to immense amounts of energy consumption. For example, the final training run of a single transformer with over 200 million parameters produces emissions equal to that of 125 round-trip flights between New York and Beijing, and this amount does not factor in the estimated 5,000 models that need to be pre-trained before the final training run (Jiang et al., 2024). Even a single interaction with an LLM consumes a non-trivial amount of energy—approximately the equivalent of leaving an LED lightbulb on an hour (Wells, 2023).

Although the connection between GenAI's environmental impact and language learning may not be readily apparent, Goulah (2017) asserts that the development of an eco-ethical consciousness among the stakeholders in L2 education is necessary for sociocultural reasons. That is, the discourse around climate change has transformed the topic from an evidenced-based discussion to one that more strongly relates to ideology and culture. Results from Goulah's study demonstrate that L2 instruction centered on climate change not only supports students' language acquisition, but also encourages students to think critically about environmental ethics. A recent study by Porto (2024) reinforces the notion that an eco-centered approach to L2 teaching fosters both language learning and critical student engagement. In short, GenAI has a tremendous impact on the environment, and work by Goulah and Porto suggests that L2 teachers should play an active role in raising awareness about these types of environmental issues to enrich students' ecological citizenship, intercultural awareness, and critical thinking skills.

Conclusion

The goal of this chapter was to discuss ethical issues in the context of three AI-assisted language learning technologies. Two ethical concerns stood out from the identified literature: the reliability of AI and academic integrity in the age of AI. The ability of AI to consistently recognize L2 student speech in a similar way to humans has been extensively studied in ASR research (Derwing et al., 2000; Inceoglu et al., 2023; McCrocklin & Edalatishams, 2020) as false feedback can cause affective issues among L2 learners (Rogerson-Revell, 2021). The reliability of GenAI has also been questioned in L2 literature given that LLMs are prone to hallucinations which generate inaccurate output (Pack & Maloney, 2024; Topal, 2024; UNESCO, 2023), thus contributing to the spread of misinformation. From the perspective of MT use in the L2 classroom, academic integrity has been a central ethical concern, often resulting in a divide between language teachers and students (Clifford et al., 2013). Although some L2 educators have adopted a punitive stance toward student MT use (Harris, 2010), others have advocated for an approach that promotes the ethical and critical use of online translation (Ducar & Schocket, 2018; Patterson, 2023). Similarly, academic integrity is a core issue in many L2 works on the topic of GenAI (Gao et al., 2023; Liu et al., 2024; Pack & Maloney, 2024; Yan, 2023). Thus, language instructors should inform students of the affordances and limitations of GenAI tools so that they can develop learning strategies that encourage the effective use of these AI resources.

In light of these ethical concerns, the author recommends that stakeholders in the field of L2 learning take a proactive role in training and guidance when implementing AI tools in the classroom. In this regard,

UNESCO (2023) has developed a list of strategies that institutions, researchers, and teachers can use to promote the ethical and effective use of AI in education. An abbreviated list of these recommendations has been provided below (pp. 24–28):

- Develop institutional principles regarding the ethical and critical use of AI
- Provide sufficient training and continued support to teachers to promote the understanding of AI-related ethical issues
- Ensure that AI does not undermine learner autonomy so that students continue to develop their intellectual skills
- Avoid the use of AI in situations where it would limit students' opportunities to interact with others in the real world
- Inform teachers and students about the data that is collected from AI services
- Encourage teachers and learners to critique the accuracy of the output of AI tools
- Promote universal connectivity to AI by identifying students who do not or cannot afford the internet connectivity to use these tools, and take steps to provide them with access

In addition to these suggestions, Chiu et al.'s (2024) AI literacy and competency framework may be a valuable resource for L2 teachers looking to incorporate AI in their language teaching. Along with 30 middle school teachers with experience in AI education, Chiu et al. developed revised definitions of both AI literacy and AI competency. They defined AI literacy as "an individual's ability to clearly explain how AI technologies work and impact society, as well as to use them in an ethical and responsible manner and to effectively communicate and collaborate with them in any setting" and AI competency as "an individual's confidence and ability to clearly explain how AI technologies work and impact society, as well as to use them in an ethical and responsible manner and to effectively communicate and collaborate with them in any setting" (p. 4). In response to these definitions, Chiu et al. proposed a comprehensive framework to help support AI-mediated education. The five components of the framework are as follows: technology, impact, ethics, collaboration, and self-reflection (see Figure 1). Technology refers to core knowledge relating to AI, namely, the basic components, perception, and applications. Impact describes the influence that AI has on social good, risks, and the future of work. The third component, ethics, relates to ethical issues concerning AI including accountability, biases, privacy, social benefit, and trust. Next in the framework is collaboration, which is students' confidence and ability to communicate with AI tools in various settings. The final component, self-reflection, refers to students' capacity to evaluate their own knowledge of AI. Together, these five components may help students gain a fundamental understanding of AI and how it can support or possibly inhibit their language learning journeys.

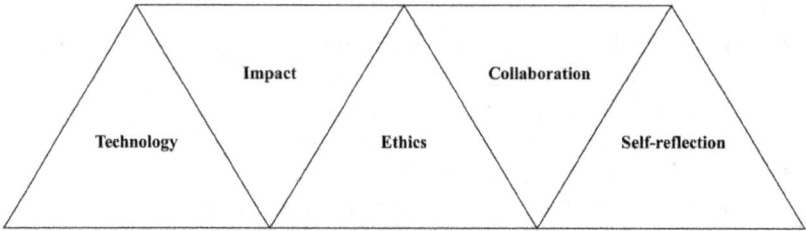

Figure 6.1 *AI literacy and competency framework by Chiu et al. (2024).*

Chiu et al.'s (2024) framework can be used to guide educators' design of AI-assisted tasks in the language classroom, which in turn, may minimize the impact of the ethical issues addressed in this chapter. However, as noted by the researchers, the framework has yet to be thoroughly examined in actual teaching practice. Therefore, future research should address the effectiveness of the framework and how it might be used to overcome ethical challenges related to AI-assisted language learning and teaching.

> **Post-reading questions:**
>
> 1) What are your views on L2 students using AI tools in the context of academic integrity?
> 2) How can teachers encourage L2 learners to critique the accuracy of GenAI output?
> 3) How transparent should L2 teachers be regarding the use of AI in their language teaching practices?

Further reading

Ingley, S. J., & Pack, A. (2023). Leveraging AI tools to develop the writer rather than the writing. *Trends in Ecology & Evolution, 38*(9), 785–787. https://doi.org/10.1016/j.tree.2023.05.007
   Informed by second language theories and principles, the authors explain an AI framework that aims to develop L2 writers instead of

only their written output. They offer three specific ways AI can support the writing of academic texts: brainstorming, structuring articles, and drafting/revising papers.

Liu, K., Kwok, H. L., Liu, J., & Cheung, A. K. (2022). Sustainability and influence of machine translation: Perceptions and attitudes of translation instructors and learners in Hong Kong. *Sustainability*, *14*(11), Article 6399. https://doi.org/10.3390/su14116399

This empirical study examines the beliefs of translation teachers and learners regarding the use of MT in the classroom. Based on the results, the authors propose a definition of MT literacy that revolves around the understanding of MT technologies, critical evaluation of MT output, and the ability to edit MT output to enhance readability and accuracy.

Payne, A. L., Austin, T., & Clemons, A. M. (2024). Beyond the front yard: The dehumanizing message of accent-altering technology. *Applied Linguistics*, *45*(3), 553–560. https://doi.org/10.1093/applin/amae002

In this article, the authors push back against linguistic prescriptivism and AI systems that seek to reduce L2 students' accents. Instead, they call on L2 stakeholders to take a firm stance against accent-altering technologies and encourage the promotion of linguistic diversity.

References

Bashori, M., van Hout, R., Strik, S., & Cucchiarini, C. (2022). 'Look, I can speak correctly': learning vocabulary and pronunciation through websites equipped with automatic speech recognition technology. *Computer Assisted Language Learning*. Advance online publication. https://doi.org/10.1080/09588221.2022.2080230

Bashori, M., van Hout, R., Strik, S., & Cucchiarini, C. (2024). I can speak: Improving English pronunciation through automatic speech recognition-based language learning systems. *Innovation in Language Learning & Teaching*. Advance online publication. https://doi.org/10.1080/17501229.2024.2315101

Cai, Y., & Leask, B. (2024). Rethinking internationalization of higher education for society from an outside-in perspective. *Journal of Asian Public Policy*. Advance online publication https://doi.org/10.1080/17516234.2024.2406093

Chiu, T. K., Ahmad, Z., Ismailov, M., & Sanusi, I. T. (2024). What are artificial intelligence literacy and competency? A comprehensive framework to support them. *Computers and Education Open*, *6*, Article 100171. https://doi.org/10.1016/j.caeo.2024.100171

Chung, E. S., & Ahn, S. (2022). The effect of using machine translation on linguistic features in L2 writing across proficiency levels and text genres. *Computer Assisted Language Learning*, *35*(9), 2239–2264. https://doi.org/10.1080/09588221.2020.1871029

Clifford, J., Merschel, L., & Reisinger, D. (2013). Meeting the challenges of machine translation. *The Language Educator*, *8*, 44–47.

Correa, M. (2014). Leaving the "peer" out of peer-editing: Online translators as a pedagogical tool in the Spanish as a second language classroom. *Latin American Journal of Content and Language Integrated Learning*, *7*, 1–20.

Derwing, T., Munro, M., & Carbonaro, M. (2000). Does popular speech recognition software work with ESL speech? *TESOL Quarterly*, *34*(3), 592–603. https://doi.org/10.2307/3587748

Dizon, G., Tang, D. & Yamamoto, Y. (2022). A case study of using Alexa for out-of-class, self-directed Japanese language learning. *Computers & Education: Artificial Intelligence*, Article 100088. https://doi.org/10.1016/j.caeai.2022.100088

Ducar, C., & Schocket, D. H. (2018). Machine translation and the L2 classroom: Pedagogical solutions for making peace with Google translate. *Foreign Language Annals*, *51*(4), 779–795. https://doi.org/10.1111/flan.12366

Feng, S., Halpern, B. M., Kudina, O., & Scharenborg, O. (2024). Towards inclusive automatic speech recognition. *Computer Speech & Language*, *84*, Article 101567. https://doi.org/10.1016/j.csl.2023.101567

Gao Y., Wang, W., & Wang, X. (2024). Exploring EFL university teachers' beliefs in integrating ChatGPT and other large language models in language education: A study in China. *Asia Pacific Journal of Education*. Advance online publication. https://doi.org/10.1080/02188791.2024.2305173

Goulah, J. (2017). Climate change and TESOL: Language, literacies, and the creation of eco-ethical consciousness. *TESOL Quarterly*, *51*(1), 90–114. https://doi.org/10.1002/tesq.277

Grieve, A., Rouhshad, A., Petraki, E., Bechaz, A., & Dai, D. W. (2024). Nursing and midwifery students' ethical views on the acceptability of using AI machine translation software to write university assignments: A deficit-oriented or translanguaging perspective? *Journal of English for Academic Purposes*, *70*, Article 101379. https://doi.org/10.1016/j.jeap.2024.101379

Harris, H. (2010). Machine translations revisited: Issues and treatment protocol. *The Language Teacher*, *34*(3), 25–29. https://doi.org/10.37546/JALTTLT34.3-5

Hockly, N. (2023). Artificial intelligence in English language teaching: The good, the bad and the ugly. *RELC Journal*, *54*(2), 445–451. https://doi.org/10.1177/00336882231168504

Huang, X., Zou, D., Cheng, G., Chen, X., & Xie, H. (2023). Trends, research issues and applications of artificial intelligence in language education. *Educational Technology & Society*, *26*(1), 11–131. https://doi.org/10.30191/ETS.202301_26(1).0009

Inceoglu, S., Chen, W.-H., & Lim, H. (2023). Assessment of L2 intelligibility: Comparing L1 listeners and automatic speech recognition. *ReCALL*, *35*(1), 89–104. https://doi.org/10.1017/s0958344022000192

Jaakkola, E. (2020). Designing conceptual articles: Four approaches. *AMS Review*, *10*(1–2), 18–26. https://doi.org/10.1007/s13162-020-00161-0

Jeon, J., & Lee, S. (2023). Large language models in education: A focus on the complementary relationship between human teachers and ChatGPT. *Education and Information Technologies*, *28*, 15873–15892. https://doi.org/10.1007/s10639-023-11834-1

Jiang, P., Sonne, C., Li, W., You, F., & You, S. (2024). Preventing the immense increase in the life-cycle energy and carbon footprints of LLM-powered intelligent chatbots. *Engineering*. Advance online publication. https://doi.org/10.1016/j.eng.2024.04.002

Jolley, J. R., & Maimone, L. (2022). Thirty years of machine translation in language teaching and learning: A review of the literature. *L2 Journal*, *14*(1), 26–44. https://doi.org/10.5070/L214151760

Koenecke, A., Nam, A., Lake, E., Nudell, J., Quartey, M., Mengesha, Z., Toups, C., Rickford, J. R., Jurafsky, D., & Goel, S. (2020). Racial disparities in automated speech recognition. *PNAS*, *117*(14), 7684–7689. https://doi.org/10.1073/pnas.1915768117

Kohnke, L., Moorhouse, B. L., & Zou, D. (2023). Exploring generative artificial intelligence preparedness among university language instructors: A case study. *Computer and Education: Artificial Intelligence*, Article 100156. https://doi.org/10.1016/j.caeai.2023.100156

Law, L. (2024). Application of generative artificial intelligence (GenAI) in language teaching and learning: A scoping literature review. *Computers and Education Open*, *6*, Article 100174. https://doi.org/10.1016/j.caeo.2024.100174

Li, J., Deng, L., Haeb-Umbach, R., & Gong, Y. (2015). *Robust automatic speech recognition: A bridge to practical applications*. Academic Press.

Liu, G. K.-M. (2023, February 28). *Transforming human interactions with AI via reinforcement learning with human feedback (RLHF)*. MIT. https://computing.mit.edu/wp-content/uploads/2023/06/Transforming-Human-Interactions-with-AI-via-Reinforcement-Learning-with-Human-Feedback-RLHF.pdf

Liu, Y., Park, J., & McMinn, S. (2024). Using generative artificial intelligence/ChatGPT for academic communication: Students' perspectives. *International Journal of Applied Linguistics*. Advance online publication. https://doi.org/10.1111/ijal.12574

McCrocklin, S., & Edalatishams, I. (2020). Revisiting popular speech recognition software for ESL speech. *TESOL Quarterly, 54*(4), 1086–1097. https://doi.org/10.1002/tesq.3006

Mizumoto, A., Eguchi, M. (2023). Exploring the potential of using an AI language model for automated essay scoring. *Research Methods in Applied Linguistics, 2*(2), Article 100050. https://doi.org/10.1016/j.rmal.2023.100050

Mohamed, A. M. (2024). Exploring the potential of an AI-based Chatbot (ChatGPT) in enhancing English as a foreign language (EFL) teaching: Perceptions of EFL faculty members. *Education and Information Technologies, 29*, 3195–3217. https://doi.org/10.1007/s10639-023-11917-z

Moussalli, S., & Cardoso, W. (2020). Intelligent personal assistants: Can they understand and be understood by accented L2 learners? *Computer Assisted Language Learning, 33* (8), 865–890. https://doi.org/10.1080/09588221.2019.1595664

Pack, A., & Maloney, J. (2024). Using artificial intelligence in TESOL: Some ethical and pedagogical considerations. *TESOL Quarterly, 58*(2), 1007–1018. https://doi.org/10.1002/tesq.3320

Paterson, K. (2023). Machine translation in higher education: Perceptions, policy, and pedagogy. *TESOL Journal, 14*(2), Article e690. https://doi.org/10.1002/tesj.690

Pfau, A. Polio, C., & Xu, Y. (2023). Exploring the potential of ChatGPT in assessing L2 writing accuracy for research purposes. *Research Methods in Applied Linguistics, 2*(3), Article 100083. https://doi.org/10.1016/j.rmal.2023.100083

Porto, M. (2024). How can language education contribute to securing a livable planet? *TESOL Quarterly*. Advance online publication. https://doi.org/10.1002/tesq.3321

Rad, H. S., & Roohani, A. (2024). Fostering L2 learners' pronunciation and motivation via affordances of artificial intelligence. *Computers in the Schools*. Advance online publication. https://doi.org/10.1080/07380569.2024.2330427

Rawashdeh, S. (2023, March 6). *AI's mysterious 'black box' problem, explained*. University of Michigan-Dearborn. https://umdearborn.edu/news/ais-mysterious-black-box-problem-explained

Rogerson-Revell, P. M. (2021). Computer-assisted pronunciation training (CAPT): Current issues and future directions. *RELC Journal, 52*(1), 189–205. https://doi.org/10.1177/0033688220977406

Shi, H., & Aryadoust, V. (2024). A systematic review of AI-based automated written feedback research. *ReCALL*. Advance online publication. https://doi.org/10.1017/S0958344023000265

Shin, D., & Chon, Y. V. (2023). Second language learners' post-editing strategies for machine translation errors. *Language Learning & Technology, 27*(1), 1–25. https://hdl.handle.net/10125/73523

Stahlberg, F. (2020). Neural machine translation: A review. *Journal of Artificial Intelligence Research, 69*, 343–418. https://doi.org/10.1613/jair.1.12007

Stapleton, P., & Kin, B. L. K. (2019). Assessing the accuracy and teacher's impressions of Google Translate: A study of primary L2 writers in Hong Kong. *English For Specific Purposes, 56*, 18–34. https://doi.org/10.1016/j.esp.2019.07.001

Tai, T.-Y., & Chen, H. H.-J. (2022). The impact of intelligent personal assistants on adolescent EFL learners' speaking proficiency. *Computer Assisted Language Learning*. Advance online publication. https://doi.org/10.1080/09588221.2022.2070219

Topal, I. H. (2024). ChatGPT: A critical evaluation. *TESOL Journal*. Advance online publication. https://doi.org/10.1002/tesj.810

Triguero, I., Molina, D., Poyatos, J., Del Ser, J., & Herrera, F. (2024). General purpose artificial intelligence systems (GPAIS): Properties, definition, taxonomy, societal implications and responsible governance. *Information Fusion, 103*, Article 102135. https://doi.org/10.1016/j.inffus.2023.102135

Underwood, J. H. (1982). Simulated conversation as a CAI strategy. *Foreign Language Annals, 15*(3), 209–212. https://doi.org/10.1111/j.1944-9720.1982.tb00248.x

UNESCO. (2023). *Guidance for generative AI in education and research*. United Nations Educational, Scientific and Cultural Organization (UNESCO). https://doi.org/10.54675/EWZM9535

Vinall, K., Wen, W., & Hellmich, E. A. (2023). Investigating L2 writers' uses of machine translation and other online tools. *Foreign Language Annals*. Advance online publication. https://doi.org/10.1111/flan.12733

Wang, Q., & Gayed, J. M. (2024). Effectiveness of large language models in automated evaluation of argumentative essays: finetuning vs. zero-shot prompting. *Computer Assisted Language Learning*. Advance online publication. https://doi.org/10.1080/09588221.2024.2371395

Wassink, A. B., Gansen, C., & Bartholomew, I. (2022). Uneven success: Automatic speech recognition and ethnicity-related dialects. *Speech Communication, 140*, 50–70. https://doi.org/10.1016/j.specom.2022.03.009

Wells, S. (2023, October 23). *Generative AI's energy problem today is foundational*. IEEE Spectrum. https://spectrum.ieee.org/ai-energy-consumption

Yan, D. (2023). Impact of ChatGPT on learners in a L2 writing practicum: An exploratory investigation. *Education and Information Technologies*. Advance online publication. https://doi.org/10.1007/s10639-023-11742-4

Zhai, C., & Wibowo, S. (2023). A systematic review on artificial intelligence dialogue systems for enhancing English as foreign language students' interactional competence in the university. *Computers and Education: Artificial Intelligence, 4,* Article 100134. https://doi.org/10.1016/j.caeai.2023.100134

7
Research methods and AI
Yijen Wang

> **Pre-reading questions:**
>
> 1) Why do we need to research AI in language teaching and learning?
> 2) What are the trends of research in AI in language education?
> 3) What are the methodological challenges in researching AI's impact on language education?

Introduction

AI has been a buzzword since the launch of ChatGPT by OpenAI in 2022, attracting the discussions and attention of technologists and educators alike with its potential to revolutionize various sectors, including language education. Most educators might think of AI in language education as another emerging technology; however, research into AI in the field is not without its precedents. The integration of AI into language teaching and learning has historical roots that are both deep and instructive, providing us with essential lessons on the promises and limitations of technology in educational settings (see Chapter 2 and Chapter 3).

The journey of AI in language education started long before the current era, with early studies like Bailin's 1988 work in the CALICO journal, which explores the potential of integrating AI into computer-assisted language instruction (CALI), focusing on natural language processing, problem-solving, language learning, and modelling teacher behaviour. Bailin's (1988) perspective was one of cautious optimism, recognizing AI's potential to significantly enhance personalized learning while also warning of the need for careful implementation and the crucial role of language teachers in its development. This early scholarship laid a foundation that helps us critically examine how modern AI tools like ChatGPT can be utilized responsibly and effectively in language education (see also Underwood, 1982; Stockwell, 2024).

Today, the need to critically evaluate AI's role in language education is driven by the technology's rapid evolution and its emergence into the core of pedagogical issues. Research in this area has rigorously assessed how AI tools influence teaching methodologies, learner engagement, and the dynamics of the classroom. As AI technologies become more integrated into educational settings, understanding their impact on pedagogical practices becomes imperative. Moreover, the exploration of AI in language education must address both the potential benefits and the inherent challenges. While AI can offer significant advantages, such as increased accessibility to language learning resources and real-time feedback, it also raises substantial ethical concerns. These include issues related to data privacy, the potential for bias in AI algorithms, and the digital divide that may exacerbate educational inequalities (see more in Chapter 6). Such challenges necessitate a robust research methodology that not only evaluates the effectiveness and efficiency of AI tools but also ensures that their alignment with educational values is equitable and ethical.

This chapter will thus provide an overview for conducting methodologically sound research in AI applications within language teaching. It will outline strategies to critically assess AI tools' pedagogical impacts, explore their operational implications, and evaluate their broader socio-educational effects. By doing so, it aims to equip educators, technologists, and policymakers with the insights needed to harness AI's potential responsibly and innovatively in language education contexts.

Research methods and trends in AI and language education

Understanding research trends in AI and language education is vital as the insights enable educators to adopt AI tools that significantly enhance teaching and learning efficiency. They also assist researchers in identifying fruitful areas for further investigation and innovation. For policymakers, such knowledge is crucial to formulating guidelines that support effective and equitable AI integration. This section outlines the current research trends by following a progression from exploring pedagogical potentials to assessing real-world applications and outcomes.

Exploring the affordances of AI

Early research on AI in language learning, or so-called Intelligent Computer-Assisted Language Learning (ICALL) or CALI-AI (Computer-Assisted Language Instruction using Artificial Intelligence), focused on developing systems that could replicate the cognitive processes and decision-making abilities of human language teachers (Bailin, 1988). While the ambitious goal of fully replicating human teaching abilities remains unrealized, recent studies continue to explore the evolving role of AI in language education.

Research on AI's affordances in language learning employs metaphors to conceptualize the relationship between AI, learners, and educators. Common metaphors describe AI as a *companion* that supports learners throughout their educational journey or as a *navigator* that guides them through the complex process of language acquisition. These metaphors offer useful frameworks for understanding the diverse roles AI can play and how it shapes interactions between learners, teachers, and technology. The concept of *affordance* was introduced by Gibson (1986) to describe the potential actions an environment or object offers a living being. In the context of technology-enhanced language learning, affordances refer to the ways specific functionalities of technology either enhance or hinder the learning experience (Anderson, 2015; van Lier, 2004). AI technologies offer unique affordances, and research aims to uncover both their positive contributions and limitations, particularly during their early stages of adoption (Dizon, 2021).

Researchers often employ diverse methods to investigate AI affordances in language learning. Case studies provide detailed insights into how AI is used in specific contexts, highlighting both its effectiveness and challenges (e.g., Annamalai et al., 2023). For example, Dizon (2017) conducted a mixed-methods case study examining the use of the intelligent personal assistant Alexa by Japanese learners of English. The study found that while Alexa could enhance learners' speaking skills, it had limitations in comprehending non-native (L2) speech. Other data collection methods, such as surveys and questionnaires, gather broad insights into users' perceptions and experiences with AI (e.g., Alm & Ohashi, 2024; Fu et al., 2020). In contrast, interviews and focus groups capture more nuanced feedback from learners, teachers, and other stakeholders. In Jeon's (2024) study, the findings from interviews revealed that the chatbot could be helpful for the learners to receive immediate feedback, focusing on pronunciation and further enhances learners' motivation. On the other hand, the chatbot was not without limitations, as the multilingual chatbot was unable to speak more than two languages at the same time. Although the technical issues may be solved someday, some students found they preferred talking with their peers rather than the chatbot.

It should be noted that the affordance theory is not without criticism, as the definition is vague and overly focused on environmental capabilities, as it heavily depends on the user's perception and interaction capabilities (Oliver, 2005). There is also a call for affordance theory to enhance its predictive power in practical applications. These criticisms suggest a need for more precise definitions and frameworks that incorporate a fuller understanding of the learner's context, aiming to make the theory more applicable and effective in real-world educational technology design and implementation.

Looking at perceptions of AI

While affordance research examines the objective capabilities of technology, perception research focuses on the subjective experiences and evaluations of AI by students and teachers. This understanding is crucial for integrating AI into language education curricula effectively. Studies in this domain explore users' attitudes toward AI, assessing its perceived benefits, potential drawbacks, and adoption barriers, thus identifying key factors that influence AI's acceptance and utilization in educational settings.

Empirical studies on perceptions typically employ surveys, interviews, and observational methods to collect data. These methods help researchers uncover not only the common attitudes toward AI but also the reasons behind resistance or enthusiasm. For example, a survey by Mustroph and Steinbock (2024) shows that pre-service teachers in Germany generally have positive attitudes towards using ChatGPT in EFL classrooms, although they are cautious about its potential to improve educational quality. Additionally, examining students' perceptions of AI in contrast to human teachers has long been a prominent research topic.

However, perception research has been critiqued for its focus on temporal attitudes, which may not accurately reflect long-term views or may not fully capture the dynamic nature of attitudes toward technology. Longitudinal studies are suggested to track changes in attitudes and motivation more effectively (Dörnyei & Csizér, 2002). Additionally, there is often a discrepancy between positive perceptions of AI tools and their actual usage, as demonstrated by Wang (2020), who found that despite favorable views of a certain educational technology, actual engagement was low. To bridge this gap, employing multiple research methods or data sources can enhance the reliability of findings, providing a more comprehensive understanding of AI's impact in language education.

Employing a multi-method approach and investigating perceptions from various angles—considering both teachers' and learners' views—can deepen understanding and improve AI's practical application in language learning environments (e.g., Neff et al., 2024). Furthermore, personal factors like familiarity with technology, perceived efficacy, and privacy concerns, along with broader interpersonal, institutional, sociocultural, and political influences within the educational context, shape these attitudes, underscoring the need for comprehensive research strategies (Wang, forthcoming a).

Looking at effectiveness of AI

The effectiveness of AI in language education represents a critical area of study, focusing on how these technologies influence language acquisition and overall learning outcomes. A variety of AI tools have been developed to enhance overall outcomes or specific language skills such as grammar, vocabulary (Liu & Chen, 2024), pronunciation (Jones, 2020), and writing proficiency (Godwin-Jones, 2022) and psychological impacts, like motivation, autonomy, anxiety, confidence (Zhou & Hou, 2024).

Research methodologies often involve experimental and quasi-experimental designs that involve control and experimental groups to measure the effectiveness of AI interventions, comparing student performance with and without AI support (see Xu & Wang, 2024). True-experimental studies are highly structured where participants are randomly assigned to either a control group, which uses so-called "traditional" learning methods, or an experimental group, which employs AI-assisted techniques. This randomization helps to eliminate biases and allows for the isolation of the effects of AI tools on learning outcomes. Measures typically include tests on language skills before and after the intervention to assess the impact of AI directly. For instance, research by Liu and Chen (2024) found that students using AI-based object-detected translation (ODT) applications demonstrated higher vocabulary test outcomes and quicker improvement in vocabulary acquisition compared to those using the Google Translate method.

However, researchers examining the effectiveness of AI should be aware of significant concerns, such as the short-term focus of many studies, which often concentrate on immediate learning outcomes rather than long-term retention and skill integration. Additionally, there is an over-reliance on quantitative data, such as test scores, which can overshadow qualitative aspects like student motivation, attitudes, and the broader educational context. It is crucial that not only the assessment methods but also the application of AI and the desired outcomes be consistent across studies. Some studies suggest that AI-generated translation tools can enhance learners' reading comprehension skills and reduce anxiety. This outcome is expected, as learners are reading in a language they are familiar with, which naturally reduces anxiety. However, claims about the "effectiveness" of AI in improving writing outcomes need careful examination to ensure that they are substantiated by robust research designs (see also Wang, forthcoming b).

Commonly used theoretical frameworks/models

Understanding the theoretical frameworks that underpin research in AI and language education is crucial for developing insights that are both deep and actionable. These frameworks guide the interpretation of data, the design of interventions, and the extrapolation of findings to broader contexts (Brown & Coombe, 2015). This section discusses various aspects of commonly used theoretical frameworks to conduct research into AI in language learning and teaching.

From a psychological perspective

A major of research looks into the impact of AI on learners' motivation, as motivation is a central theme in the psychological study of language learning. Theories such as self-determination theory (SDT) and expectancy-value theory (EVT) are commonly applied to understand how AI tools influence learners' motivation. SDT, for example, emphasizes the importance of supporting learners' autonomy, competence, and relatedness needs, which AI tools can be designed to address by providing personalized learning experiences and feedback (e.g., Annamalai, 2023; Du & Alm, 2024). EVT, on the other hand, assesses how learners' expectations of success and the value they attach to learning outcomes affect their motivation to engage with AI educational tools (e.g., Wang et al., 2023).

From learning theory

Numerous studies examine how AI integrates into the language learning process by applying language learning theories (see Gibson et al., 2023). For example, cognitive learning theories emphasize the mental processes involved in learning and the structures that support knowledge acquisition and application. In language education, AI often utilizes cognitive load theory to design content that optimally balances the information load for learners at any given time (Woo et al., 2024). Furthermore, metacognitive theories focus on learners' ability to understand and regulate their learning processes with AI, which is critical in the context of AI-enhanced education (Van Horn, 2024; Wang, 2024). These cognitive and metacognitive frameworks are essential for assessing the instructional design of AI language learning applications, ensuring that they complement and enhance human cognitive capabilities.

From technological perspective

The technological perspective on AI in language education involves frameworks that assess the interaction between technology and users. The Technology Acceptance Model (TAM) and the Unified Theory of Acceptance and Use of Technology (UTAUT) are two prominent models used in this domain. TAM (Davis, 1989) evaluates how perceived ease of use and usefulness influence the adoption of AI tools, while UTAUT provides a broader analysis, including factors such as social influence and facilitating conditions. These models are instrumental in understanding how the technological attributes of AI tools influence user acceptance and usage in educational settings (Xu & Thien, 2024; Zou et al., 2023). However, they have faced criticism for possibly oversimplifying the variables that impact technology adoption. It is suggested that future research should consider additional complexities, such as individual differences among users and the dynamic nature of technological environments, to provide a deeper understanding of these interactions.

From an ecological perspective: Sociocultural theories

Sociocultural theories provide a rich framework for understanding the ecological perspective of AI in language education. These theories emphasize the importance of social interaction and cultural context in learning processes. Vygotsky's sociocultural theory, for instance, underscores the role of social interactions in cognitive development and can be used to analyze how AI tools facilitate or hinder meaningful social engagement in language learning (Meihami, 2023). The other theories, such as situated learning theory (SLT) (Lave, 1991), are also pertinent as they look at how learners engage with communities of practice, potentially supported by AI environments that facilitate such communities (Poquet & de Laat, 2021).

Challenges in research methods

The exploration of AI in language education, while rich with potential, is fraught with methodological challenges that can complicate the interpretation and applicability of research findings. By acknowledging and tackling these methodological issues, the field can move towards more comprehensive and inclusive research that better captures the transformative potential of AI in language education.

Methodological limitations

Current research often disproportionately focuses on certain AI tools such as Automated Writing Evaluation (AWE) systems (e.g., Grammarly,

Ginger, Pigai) and chatbots (like ChatGPT) (Huang et al., 2023). This focus may inadvertently overlook emerging or specialized technologies that could offer unique benefits or meet particular educational needs. For example, newer AI-driven tools utilizing advanced machine learning models to adapt to individual learner needs might not be widely commercialized but could provide significant advantages in personalized learning settings. The predominant attention on a narrow range of tools can skew the understanding of AI's comprehensive capabilities and might lead to a skewed portrayal of its effectiveness in enhancing language education and receive less development and testing attention.

Another significant limitation is the control of variables in AI-related studies. Some studies seem to be experimental but fail to adequately control variables. Factors such as individual learner differences, the educational environment, and variations in AI tool implementation can significantly affect outcomes (see also Cerezo et al., 2013). For instance, a study might report positive results for AI use in a treatment group compared to a control group, but if the teaching methods and materials differ between groups, the results could be misleading. Furthermore, studies often confuse "real effectiveness" with "perceived effectiveness", where real effectiveness refers to objectively measured improvements in learning outcomes, while perceived effectiveness relates to learners' subjective evaluations of their experience and progress. Additionally, the preconceptions and attitudes of researchers–such as an inherent optimism about AI's capabilities–can bias the design, implementation, and interpretation of results. This optimistic bias suggests that researchers favourable toward AI might design studies that do not sufficiently challenge these technologies or neglect to rigorously evaluate potential negative outcomes.

Using AI to conduct research

AI technologies offer innovative approaches to data collection and analysis in the field of language learning research. These tools may enhance the efficiency and depth of research methodologies, though they also present challenges that must be carefully managed. For instance, natural language processing (NLP) tools can analyze vast amounts of textual data from student interactions, essays, and feedback forms to identify patterns in language use, grammar acquisition, or common errors. Similarly, speech recognition technologies can accurately capture spoken language inputs from learners, facilitating the analysis of pronunciation, fluency, and oral competencies. However, researchers should rigorously validate and verify AI tools to ensure their accuracy and reliability in data collection and analysis. This involves not only technical testing but also field testing in realistic educational settings.

While AI tools can enhance the research process, they also raise significant data privacy concerns. The collection and analysis of learner data must comply with stringent data protection regulations, such as the General Data Protection Regulation (GDPR) in the EU, which governs the storage and handling of personal data. AI tools involving the collection of biometric data, such as voice prints or video recordings, can be considered sensitive personal data. In such cases, researchers must ensure that all AI-driven data collection and analysis tools adhere to these legal frameworks to protect learner privacy.

Ethical considerations

Ethical considerations are crucial when integrating AI into language learning research, given the potential impacts on privacy, access, and equity. These considerations are not just academic; they affect how research is perceived and its real-world applicability and fairness.

Many scholarly journals are now requiring authors to declare their use of AI tools in conducting research or in the preparation of manuscripts. This requirement stems from the need for transparency in research methodologies, particularly regarding the use of AI that could influence research outcomes or the interpretation of data. For example, if AI tools are used to analyze textual data or generate content, disclosing these details helps reviewers and readers assess the validity and reliability of the findings. It also maintains the integrity of the academic record, ensuring that contributions made by AI are appropriately credited and scrutinized.

The digital divide–differential access to technology based on geographic, economic, or social factors–presents significant ethical challenges in the use of AI in research. Researchers must ensure that AI tools are accessible to all participants. If AI tools confer benefits in learning, ensuring equitable access to these technologies becomes an ethical imperative. In research settings, it is crucial to provide equivalent AI resources to control and experimental groups to uphold the integrity of the study and ensure fair treatment of all participants. Beyond research, the broader educational context also demands attention to equity (see Wang & Stockwell, 2024).

Future directions

As AI continues to evolve and integrate into language learning settings, the methodologies and approaches to research must also adapt to capture the full scope and impact of these technologies. Here are some future directions and suggestions for refining research methods in this dynamic field.

Replicated research

The rapid pace of technological development and the allure of novel findings often push researchers towards pioneering studies rather than replicating existing ones. This trend towards novelty over verification can undermine the scientific foundation of AI applications in language education. Most of the recent research merely focuses on short-term effects. Thus, replicated research may help to verify the effectiveness of AI tools across diverse environments and eliminate the risk of findings being an antique of specific conditions or biases inherent in a single study (Stockwell, 2019). For instance, an AI-based pronunciation tool might show positive results in one cultural context but might not be as effective in another due to linguistic diversity and teaching practices. Replicating such studies in varied settings allows researchers to identify and analyze these differences, contributing to a more nuanced understanding of how AI tools can be optimized for diverse educational contexts. Moreover, reliable replicated findings can serve as a strong foundation for educational policies and teaching practices (see Porte, 2021). Educators and policymakers can make informed decisions about integrating AI tools into language curricula based on replicated evidence of their effectiveness and limitations.

Longitudinal studies

Many of the current studies on AI in language education tend to focus on short-term outcomes, such as immediate improvements in language skills or learner engagement. This short-term perspective can provide misleading or incomplete insights into the effectiveness of AI tools, as such transient improvements might not translate into sustained enhancements, and initial enthusiasm for new AI tools could diminish over time–dynamics only revealed through extended study durations. Therefore, longitudinal studies are essential for understanding the sustained impacts of AI integration in language education, providing insights into long-term benefits and challenges associated with AI tools (see Loewen & Philp, 2011 for a discussion of longitudinal research in language learning). These studies track learning outcomes over extended periods, which is crucial for assessing enduring effects on language learning, such as skill retention, the development of learner autonomy, and long-term attitudes towards AI. Despite their importance, conducting longitudinal research in AI and language education presents significant challenges. The rapid pace of technological advancement means that AI tools and methods may become outdated or evolve significantly within the study period. This necessitates flexible research designs that allow for the integration of new technologies as they become available, ensuring that the studies remain relevant and reflective of current practices. Also, longitudinal studies are resource-intensive and require sustained funding, commitment, and participant engagement, which can be difficult to maintain over time. Securing consistent support and resources is essential for these studies to deliver meaningful, actionable insights.

Enhancing diversity

Diversity in research settings is crucial for understanding the full spectrum of AI's impact on language education. By broadening the diversity in research participants, the range of AI tools studied, and the language skills investigated, researchers can gain a more comprehensive and nuanced understanding of how AI can be effectively integrated into diverse educational contexts. Including participants from a variety of socioeconomic, cultural, and linguistic backgrounds is essential for ensuring that research findings are universally applicable and inclusive. Diversity among participants helps to identify how different groups uniquely interact with and benefit from AI technologies. Also, while popular AI tools like ChatGPT have demonstrated significant potential in language education, focusing exclusively on such tools can limit the scope of research findings. Expanding research to include a broader range of AI technologies, especially emerging tools that incorporate advanced machine learning and natural language processing capabilities, can uncover new possibilities for enhancing language learning. Lastly, current research often focuses predominantly on certain languages and specific skills like writing (Yang & Kyun, 2022). To fully harness AI's capabilities, studies should encompass a broader spectrum of languages and linguistic skills, including languages other than English, lesser-studied languages and dialects (Sauro, 2016). Additionally, expanding the focus to include all major language skills – speaking, listening, reading, and writing – provides a holistic view of how AI can support comprehensive language learning. For instance, AI might be used to simulate multimodal composition (Liu, Zhang, & Biebricher, 2024).

Practice-based research

Transitioning from perception studies to good practice, understanding teacher and learner perceptions provides foundational insights that help predict and shape their future engagement with AI tools. This shift is essential as it informs the methodologies used in practice-based research, which are crucial for bridging theoretical advancements with practical applications in AI-enhanced language education. Practice-based research methods such as action research and design-based research are instrumental in bridging the gap between theoretical advancements and practical applications of AI in language education.

Action research is a powerful approach that allows teachers to investigate the effectiveness of specific teaching practices or tools within their own classroom settings (Brown & Coombe, 2015). It involves a cyclical process of planning (identifying specific pedagogical challenges), acting (implementing interventions), observing (collecting and analyzing data), and reflecting on the outcomes. This method allows teachers to act as both educators and researchers, conducting systematic inquiries into how AI tools affect teaching and learning dynamics. By implementing AI technologies and observing their impacts, teachers can iteratively test, modify, and optimize their use. This process not only helps in adapting AI tools to specific classroom needs but also empowers teachers to make evidence-based decisions that enhance educational outcomes. On the other hand, design-based research is a systematic but flexible methodology aimed at improving educational practices through iterative analysis, design, development, and implementation, based on collaboration among teachers, designers, and researchers. It seeks to help refine AI tools in iterative cycles of design, implementation, evaluation, and redesign. This approach ensures that AI tools are effectively tailored to meet the evolving needs of educators and learners.

The need for developing new guidelines and revising theories

As AI technologies continue to evolve, our theoretical frameworks must adapt to ensure they remain relevant and effective in guiding both research and practice in the field of language education (Gibson et al., 2022). As mentioned in the previous section, it is crucial to develop guidelines that address these ethical implications to responsibly guide the deployment of AI technologies in educational settings. There is also a significant need to revise and expand existing educational theories to incorporate the dynamic introduced by AI. For example, the concept of Vygotsky's Zone of Proximal Development (ZPD) might be reinterpreted to consider AI as part of the social presence that supports the learner, acting as a 'more knowledgeable other' in a digital format.

Conclusion

Looking at the shifts in research into technology and language education, it is evident that while educational technologies evolve, sound research methods remain constant. This enduring stability in research methodology provides a reliable foundation for evaluating new technological tools in language education. As we adopt new technologies like generative AI, the core principles of rigorous research – such as validity, reliability, and replicability – continue to guide our assessments and ensure the credibility of our findings. As this chapter suggests, the journey of integrating AI into language education is ongoing. The insights we gain today will pave the way for future research, guiding us towards more sophisticated and refined applications of AI in teaching and learning. It is our hope that this chapter serves as both a reflection on our current understanding and a guide for future research, inspiring continued exploration and innovation in the field of language education. Through such sustained inquiry and application, we can utilize the full potential of AI to enrich language learning experiences and outcomes worldwide.

Post-reading questions:

1) Are you integrating AI into your teaching practices? If so, how could you design a research study to demonstrate the impact of your AI integrations on teaching and learning outcomes?
2) In what ways can the personal biases of researchers influence the outcomes of studies on AI in language education, and how can these biases be mitigated?
3) What ethical considerations should be prioritized by researchers when conducting studies involving AI tools in language education?

Further reading

1. Brown, J. D., & Coombe, C. (Eds.). (2015). *The Cambridge guide to research in language teaching and learning*. Cambridge University Press.

    This comprehensive guide provides an overview of various research methodologies applicable to language teaching and learning. It is recommended for readers seeking foundational knowledge in research practices and theoretical frameworks within the field of language education.

2. Huang, X., Zou, D., Cheng, G., Chen, X., & Xie, H. (2023). Trends, research issues and applications of artificial intelligence in language education. *Educational Technology & Society, 26*(1), 112–131. https://doi.org/10.30191/ETS.202301_26(1).0009

    This article offers an in-depth analysis of current trends and critical research areas in the application of artificial intelligence in language education. It is valuable for understanding recent advancements, challenges, and the potential future direction of AI in this field.

References

Alm, A., & Ohashi, L. (2024). A worldwide study on language educators' initial response to ChatGPT. *Technology in Language Teaching & Learning, 6*(1), 1141. https://doi.org/10.29140/tltl.v6n1.1141

Anderson, J. (2015). Affordance, learning opportunities, and the lesson plan pro forma. *ELT Journal, 69*(3). 228–238. https://doi.org/10.1093/elt/ccv008

Annamalai, N., Eltahir, M. E., Zyoud, S. H., Soundrarajan, D., Zakarneh, B., & Al Salhi, N. R. (2023). Exploring English language learning via Chabot: A case study from a self-determination theory perspective. *Computers and Education: Artificial Intelligence, 100148*. https://doi.org/10.1016/j.caeai.2023.100148

Bailin, A. (1988). Artificial intelligence and ccomputer-assisted language instruction: A perspective. *CALICO Journal, 5*(3), 25–45. https://doi.org/10.1558/cj.v5i3.25-45

Brown, J. D., & Coombe, C. (Eds.). (2015). *The Cambridge guide to research in language teaching and learning*. Cambridge University Press.

Cerezo, L., Baralt, M., Suh, B. R., & Leow, R. P. (2013). Does the medium really matter in L2 development? The validity of CALL research designs. *Computer Assisted Language Learning, 27*(4), 294–310. https://doi.org/10.1080/09588221.2013.839569

Davis, F. D. (1989). Perceived usefulness, perceived ease of use, and user acceptance of information technology. *MIS Quarterly, 13*, 318–339.

Dizon, G. (2017). Using intelligent personal assistants for second language learning: A case study of Alexa. *Tesol Journal, 8*(4), 811-830. https://doi.org/10.1002/tesj.353

Dizon, G. (2021). Affordances and constraints of intelligent personal assistants for second-language learning. *RELC Journal, 54*(3), 848–855. https://doi.org/10.1177/00336882211020548

Dörnyei, Z., & Csizér, K. (2002). Some dynamics of language attitudes and motivation: Results of a longitudinal nationwide survey. *Applied Linguistics, 23*(4), 421–462.

Du, J., & Alm, A. (2024). The impact of ChatGPT on English for academic purposes (EAP) students' language learning experience: A self-determination theory perspective. *Education Sciences, 14*(7), 726. https://doi.org/10.3390/educsci14070726

Fu, S., Gu, H., & Yang, B. (2020). The affordances of AI-enabled automatic scoring applications on learners' continuous learning intention: An empirical study in China. *British Journal of Educational Technology, 51*(5), 1674–1692. https://doi.org/10.1111/bjet.12995

Gibson, D., Kovanovic, V., Ifenthaler, D., Dexter, S., & Feng, S. (2023). Learning theories for artificial intelligence promoting learning processes. *British Journal of Educational Technology*, 54, 1125–1146. https://doi.org/10.1111/bjet.13341

Gibson, J. J. (1986). *The ecological approach to visual perception*. Lawrence Earlbaum.

Godwin-Jones, R. (2022). Partnering with AI: Intelligent writing assistance and instructed language learning. *Language Learning & Technology, 26*(2), 5–24. http://doi.org/10125/73474

Hwang, G. J., Xie, H., Wah, B. W., & Gaelic, D. (2020). Vision, challenges, roles and research issues of artificial intelligence in education. *Computers and Education: Artificial Intelligence, 1*(2020). https://doi.org/10.1016/j.caeai.2020.100001

Jeon, J. (2024). Exploring AI chatbot affordances in the EFL classroom: Young learners' experiences and perspectives. *Computer Assisted Language Learning, 37*(1–2), 1–26. https://doi.org/10.1080/09588221.2021.2021241

Lave, J., & Wenger, E. (1991). *Situated learning: Legitimate peripheral participation*. Cambridge University Press. https://doi.org/10.1017/CBO9780511815355

Levy, M., & Stockwell, G. (2013). *CALL dimensions: Options and issues in computer-assisted language learning*. Routledge. https://doi.org/10.4324/9780203708200

Liu, P. L., & Chen, C. J. (2023). Using an AI-based object detection translation application for English vocabulary learning. *Educational Technology & Society, 26*(3), 5–20. https://doi.org/10.30191/ETS.202307_26(3).0002

Loewen, S., & Philp, J. (2011). Instructed second language acquisition. In A. Mackey & S. M. Gass (Eds.), *Research methods in second language acquisition: A practical guide* (pp. 53–73). Wiley-Blackwell. https://doi.org/10.1002/9781444347340.ch4

Meihami, H. (2023). Situated learning in CALL teacher preparation programs: an ecological perspective to student-teachers' agency. *Computer Assisted Language Learning*, 1–27. https://doi.org/10.1080/09588221.2023.2173614

Mustroph, C., & Steinbock, J. (2024). ChatGPT in foreign language education – friend or foe? A quantitative study on pre-service teachers' beliefs. *Technology in Language Teaching & Learning, 6*(1), 1–17. https://doi.org/10.29140/tltl.v6n1.1133

Neff, J., Arciaga, K., & Burri, M. (2024). EFL students' and teachers' perceptions of the ethical uses of AI tools. *Technology in Language Teaching & Learning, 6*(3), 1–19. https://doi.org/10.29140/tltl.v6n3.1714

Oliver, M. (2005). The problem with affordance. *E-learning and Digital Media, 2*(4), 402–413. https://doi.org/10.2304/elea.2005.2.4.402

Poquet, O., & de Laat, M. (2021). Developing capabilities: Lifelong learning in the age of AI. *British Journal of Education Technology, 52.* 1695–1798. https://doi.org/10.1111/bjet.13123

Porte, G. (2022). *Replication research in applied linguistics.* Cambridge University Press.

Sauro, S. (2016). Does CALL have an English problem? *Language Learning & Technology, 20*(3), 1–8. http://dx.doi.org/10125/44474

Stockwell, G. (2019). Insights from replication on the factors affecting task engagement in mobile-based learning activities. *Technology in Language Teaching & Learning, 1*(1), 33–51. https://doi.org/10.29140/tltl.v1n1.152

Stockwell, G. (2024). ChatGPT in language teaching and learning: Exploring the road we're travelling. *Technology in Language Teaching & Learning, 6*(1), 2273. https://doi.org/10.29140/tltl.v6n1.2273

Underwood, J. H. (1982). Simulated conversation as CAI strategy. *Foreign Language Annals, 15*(3), 209–212. https://doi.org/10.1111/j.1944-9720.1982.tb00248.x

Van Horn, K. R. (2024). ChatGPT in English language learning: Exploring perceptions and promoting autonomy in a university EFL Context. *TESL-EJ, 28*(1). https://doi.org/10.55593/ej.28109a8

Van Lier, L. (2004). *The ecology and semiotics of language learning: A sociocultural perspective.* Kluwer Academic Publishers.

Wang, F., King, R. B., Chai, C. S., & Zhou, Y. (2023). University students' intentions to learn artificial intelligence: the roles of supportive environments and expectancy-value beliefs. *International Journal of Educational Technology in Higher Education, 20*(1), 51.

Wang, Y. (2024). Cognitive and sociocultural dynamics of self-regulated use of machine translation and generative AI tools in academic EFL writing. *System, 126,* 103505. https://doi.org/10.1016/j.system.2024.103505.

Wang, Y., & Stockwell, G. (2024). Social justice and technology in second language education. *Iranian Journal of Language Teaching Research.* https://doi.org/10.30466/ijltr.2023.121403

Wang, Y. (Forthcoming a). Overcoming teacher resistance. In G. Stockwell., & Y. Wang (Eds.), *The Cambridge handbook of technology in language teaching and learning.* Cambridge University Press.

Wang, Y. (Forthcoming b). Research shifts. In G. Stockwell., & Y. Wang (Eds.), *The Cambridge handbook of technology in language teaching and learning.* Cambridge University Press.

Wang, Y. (2020). Engagement in PC-based, smartphone-based, and paper-based materials: Learning vocabulary through Chinese Stories. *Technology in Language Teaching & Learning, 2*(1), 3–21. https://doi.org/10.29140/tltl.v2n1.319

Woo, D. J., Wang, D., Guo, K., & Susanto, K. (2024). Teaching EFL students to write with ChatGPT: Students' motivation to learn, cognitive load, and satisfaction with the learning process. *Education and Information Technologies*. https://doi.org/10.1007/s10639-024-12819-4

Xu, T., & Wang, H. (2024). The effectiveness of artificial intelligence on English language learning achievement, *System, 125*, 103428. https://doi.org/10.1016/j.system.2024.103428

Xu, X. & Thien, L. M. (2024). Unleashing the power of perceived enjoyment: exploring Chinese undergraduate EFL learners' intention to use ChatGPT for English learning. *Journal of Applied Research in Higher Education*. https://doi.org/10.1108/jarhe-12-2023-0555

Yang, H., & Kyun, S. (2022). The current research trend of artificial intelligence in language learning: A systematic empirical literature review from an activity theory perspective. *Australasian Journal of Educational Technology, 38*(5), 180–210. https://doi.org/10.14742/ajet.7492

Zhou, C., & Hou, F. (2024). Can AI empower L2 education? Exploring its influence on the behavioural, cognitive and emotional engagement of EFL teachers and language learners. *European Journal of Education*, e12750. https://doi.org/10.1111/ejed.12750

Zou, B., Lyu, Q., Han, Y., Li, Z., & Zhang, W. (2023). Exploring students' acceptance of an artificial intelligence speech evaluation program for EFL speaking practice: an application of the Integrated Model of Technology Acceptance. *Computer Assisted Language Learning*, 1–26. https://doi.org/10.1080/09588221.2023.2278608

Part Two

Establishing the foundations of good practice

8
Motivational issues in AI integration

Zhan Shi

Chun Lai

> **Pre-reading questions:**
>
> 1) What motivational factors are associated with students' intention of using AI?
> 2) How do these factors affect students' intention to use AI?
> 3) How can teachers foster students' intention to leverage the power of GenAI?

Introduction

Generative artificial intelligence (GenAI), such as ChatGPT, is renowned for using advanced Large Language Models (LLMs) to generate human-like text based on natural language inputs (Yan et al., 2024). With the capacity of generating and analysing textual content and impressive performance in language generation tasks across multiple languages, GenAI has sparked off heated discussions on both its transformative power on and imminent threat to the language education field (Chapelle, 2024; Kern, 2024). In response, scholars are arguing for active incorporation of GenAI in language teaching and learning but with a considered repositioning of the goals of language education. However, foreign to the educational ecosystem, like other digital tools, the introduction of GenAI to language teaching and learning is sure to arouse motivational issues.

One of the most beneficial uses of GenAI in education is to empower learners with customized learning pathways, individualized feedback and adaptive learning content and materials that fit their needs and preferences (Grover, 2024; Hsu & Ching, 2023; Kuhail et al., 2023). Albeit a promising learning technology, GenAI is still new to students and in its infancy, which may affect learners' intention to use it as a facilitative learning tool. Highly motivated learners tend to invest more efforts and take the initiative to seek learning opportunities through interacting with AI, while students that are less motivated may find it challenging to effectively utilize AI for language learning (Jeon, 2024). Therefore, teachers need to carefully consider several questions before integrating AI into language learning. For example, what motivational factors may influence students' intention of using AI? And how can teachers foster students' intention to leverage the power of GenAI? Insights into these questions will enable both educators and learners to better harness the potential of AI for language learning. To answer these questions, we will first examine major motivational theories for key motivational concepts that deserve attention. Based on the review of theories, we will discuss how the components in these motivational theories can be supported in language teaching practices.

Key motivational drivers of AI integration

Given that scant attention has been devoted to understanding the motivational mechanisms behind learners' decision-making around AI use, it is imperative to investigate different motivational frameworks for potential factors that may influence learners' motivation for AI integration.

Self-determination theory

Self-determination theory (SDT) is one of the prominent theories that outlines the relationship between human needs and motivation (Ryan & Deci, 2020). It posits that individuals tend to be self-determined and intrinsically motivated when their basic psychological needs for autonomy, competence and relatedness are fulfilled (Deci & Ryan, 1985). *Autonomy* refers to an individual's capacity to make independent decisions and take certain actions (Deci & Ryan, 1985). Fulfilment of the need for independence can become the driving force behind students' learning involvement (Skinner et al., 2008). *Competence* refers to the level of capability to effectively engage in problem-solving or a specific task (Deci & Ryan, 1985). A competent individual possesses the success-oriented abilities essential to the accomplishment of their objectives. *Relatedness* represents an individual's intention to build up connections with the surrounding world to satisfy their social needs (Deci & Ryan, 1985). It has been identified as a predictor of students' behavioral and emotional involvement (Ruzek et al., 2016). These three motivation drivers are robust predictors of learners' self-directed informal digital language learning (e.g., Fathali & Okada, 2017; Nikou & Economides, 2017). Recent studies have also shown that GenAI can provide digital support that satisfies learners' psychological needs for autonomy, competence, and relatedness (Chiu, 2024; Xia et al., 2022), which may potentially boost learners' integration of AI in learning.

GenAI can fulfill learners' needs for autonomy by offering them a sense of agency over their learning (Chiu, 2024). For example, students have the ownership to ask specific questions and elicit personalized ideas when interacting with GenAI (Gill et al., 2024). The time and space flexibility also enables students to access language learning materials at anytime, anywhere, encouraging students to become independent and self-regulated learners (Annamalai et al., 2023). Thus, perceiving the potential of AI in helping satisfy their psychological needs for autonomous action may strengthen students' motivation of using AI in learning.

AI tools, which can serve as an intelligent assistant that is always available at a click's distance and provides multimodal resources that facilitate comprehension (Annamalai et al., 2023), can enhance students' perceived competence in authentic language use. Through frequent exposure to the process of making queries and receiving tailored feedback, students are also likely to become proficient in using AI and develop enhanced self-efficacy (Gill et al., 2024). Such arguments are further supported by a recent study where the researcher utilized the Delphi method, which involves structurally gathering expert opinions through multiple rounds of consultation and found that ChatGPT-based learning activities are mainly considered effective in satisfying students' needs for competence (Chiu, 2024).

Compared to the other two psychological needs, relatedness does not appear to be easily achieved in the use of AI (Chiu, 2024). In a recent qualitative study guided by the SDT framework, the researchers explored EAP learners' language learning experience in using ChatGPT and found that even though some students developed a sense of companionship with AI, other students experienced a sense of isolation due to the lack of genuine connection with humans and social belonging when using AI (Du & Alm, 2024). Also, the interface of GenAI may not present a sense of real-world conversation that students may find warm and connected, and students may find it difficult to develop an emotional attachment with the systems and have their needs for relatedness fulfilled (Annamalai et al., 2023).

It has been found that perceived satisfaction of these three psychological needs not only directly predicted Chinese university learners' integration of GenAI for English as a foreign language learning but also moderated the influence of facilitating conditions on this behavioural intention (Zheng et al., 2024). Thus, the three sources of self-determined behaviours need to be considered when discussing motivational forces behind AI integration.

Expectancy-value theory

Expectancy-Value Theory (EVT) is another prominent framework used to understand students' learning motivation (Wigfield & Eccles, 2000). According to EVT, an individual's decision to engage in a specific task is shaped by two critical elements: expectancy and value. *Expectancy* refers to an individual's subjective belief about their competence to accomplish a task, and value denotes the perceived benefits associated with the task, which encompasses attainment value, intrinsic value, utility value, and cost (Wigfield & Eccles, 2000). *Attainment value* refers to one's belief that a particular behavior will lead to achievement of goal. *Utility value* refers to the belief that a behavior will result in practical benefits, such as enhanced skills or knowledge. *Intrinsic value* reflects one's satisfaction when engaging in a particular task. EVT has been updated by Eccles and Wigfield (2020), who postulated a more comprehensive framework: Situated Expectancy–Value Theory (SEVT). SEVT highlights the situated nature of expectancy and value beliefs and posits that learners' expectancy and value beliefs are shaped by supportive environments (Eccles & Wigfield, 2020).

In the context of using AI, expectancy belief can be operationalized as self-efficacy in using AI (Chai et al., 2021); in other words, learners' self-perceived competence in using AI. Previous research has indicated that learners' expectancy beliefs are positively related to their knowledge and familiarity with AI, in that learners who are more knowledgeable and familiar with AI tend to exhibit higher expectancy beliefs and are more likely to integrate AI into their learning routines (Chan & Zhou, 2023). In some AI-related research, learners' perceived value has also been operationalized as perceived usefulness of AI (Chai et al., 2021), and higher levels of perceived usefulness of AI has been found to lead to stronger intention to use AI (Ni & Cheung, 2023). Adopting SEVT as the theoretical framework, Wang et al. (2023) explored how supportive environments shaped university students' expectancy–value beliefs and their intention to learn about AI. In this study, 494 university students from China were recruited. The findings indicated that students with higher levels of expectancy-value beliefs who were exposed to a supportive environment were more inclined to leverage the potential of AI for learning.

Reason-oriented theories

The reason-oriented theories are a strand of theories extensively used to investigate user acceptance of technology (Pavlou & Fygenson, 2006). The origin can be traced back to Ajzen and Fishbein's (1980) theory for reasoned action (TRA), which is put forth to explain general human behavior in various domains. TRA posits that individuals' behavioral intention is shaped by their attitudes and subjective norm related to a specific behavior. Attitudes refer to a person's response to a particular behavior (Ajzen & Fishbein, 2005). Subjective norm denotes how an individual responds to social preferences toward a particular behavior (Cheon et al., 2012). These two components are deemed the predominant determinants of human's behavioral intention in TRA. The TRA framework was later extended by Ajzen (1991), who introduced theory of planned behavior (TPB), a refined model that takes factors associated with individuals' intention to use technology into account. The TPB model incorporates perceived behavioral control as a new element, in addition to attitudes and subjective norms. Perceived behavioral control refers to an individual's perception of the ease or difficulty of performing a particular behavior (Ajzen, 1991).

Given that TRA is a general theory "designed to explain virtually any human behavior" (Ajzen & Fishbein, 1980, p. 4), it has become the theoretical foundation for other reason-oriented frameworks that target human's behavioral intention pertaining to technology acceptance and adoption. One such framework is the Technology Acceptance Model (TAM) proposed by Davis (1989). The original TAM postulated that perceived ease of use and perceived usefulness are two critical antecedents to users' acceptance of technology (Davis, 1989). Perceived ease of use refers to an individual's perception toward the efforts required for utilizing a particular system, while perceived usefulness pertains to an individual's belief regarding whether employing a specific system will enhance their work performance (Davis, 1989). In the context of using AI for learning, perceived ease of use reflects learners' perceptions toward the difficulty of using AI systems, for instance, whether additional effort to learn to effectively interact with AI is required (Karacı et al., 2018). Perceived usefulness, on the other hand, indicates how strongly learners believe AI learning systems can improve their English learning performance.

The technology acceptance model (TAM) has been widely used to investigate learner's intention to use technology in learning (Scherer et al., 2018). Examining secondary students' intention to adopt AI-powered intelligent tutoring system for English learning, Ni and Cheung (2023) found that perceived usefulness was the most significant factor influencing students' intention to adopt AI learning systems for English learning. In contrast, the direct effect of perceived ease of use was not significant. Rather, its influence was mediated by perceived usefulness. They further found that technology anxiety contributed negatively to perceived usefulness and perceived enjoyment contributed positively to perceived usefulness. Thus, the more students believe that AI systems can enhance their learning, the more likely they will continue to adopt these systems for future learning (Kim et al.,

2020). Ivanov et al. (2024) further revealed that students' attitudes, subjective norms, and perceived behavioral control were positively associated with the perceived benefits of GenAI in the higher education context. In sum, the reason-oriented theories demonstrate the interplay between humans' perceptions and acceptance of technology, which helps to uncover the mechanisms affecting learners' intention to use AI for learning. Findings of the existing studies suggest that fostering a positive attitude toward AI and alleviating anxiety related to its use can enhance students' perceived usefulness of AI, which can subsequently increase their motivation to integrate AI into their language learning.

Unified theory of acceptance and use of technology (UTAUT)

While TAM has been frequently used to understand learners' intention of technology adoption, recent years have witnessed the research trend to extend TAM by incorporating environmental and motivational factors into the framework to gauge a more comprehensive understanding of learners' intention to adopt technology (Abdullah & Ward, 2016; Mousavinasab et al., 2021). The Unified Theory of Acceptance and Use of Technology (UTAUT) model is one of the prominent extended models, which draws upon the principal components from EVT, TAM and other contextual factors to account for the influences that might affect technology adoption (Venkatesh et al., 2003). The original UTAUT postulates that performance expectancy, effort expectancy, social influence, and facilitating conditions are four key constructs that have direct impact on technology adoption. *Performance expectancy* refers to the extent to which a person believes that making use of the system will be beneficial for performance improvement at work (Venkatesh et al., 2003). This construct partially derives from TAM, where perceived usefulness and perceived ease of use of a technology serve as the core elements (Davis, 1989). *Effort expectancy* shares similar definition with perceived ease of use from TAM, which refers to users' perception of the difficulty level of using a specific system (Venkatesh et al., 2003). *Social influence* refers to an individual's consideration of other people's opinions toward the importance of using a system. Like subjective norms from TRA and TAM, this construct highlights that people's behavior is shaped by others' perception. *Facilitating conditions*, such as teaching, services, and technological infrastructure, are essential environmental features that students believe may result in a more successful use of information and communication technologies (Venkatesh et al., 2003).

Even though UTAUT has been widely applied to understand users' technology adoption behaviors, it was mainly developed within the context of organizational settings. To extend the applicability of UTAUT in various research contexts, Venkatesh, Thong and Xu proposed UTAUT2, which addresses the role of behavioral and attitudinal determinants in non-organisational context (2012). As a refined model, UTAUT2 incorporates three additional components into the original UTAUT model, namely hedonic motivation (enjoyment), cost and habit (Venkatesh et al., 2012). In the UTAUT2 model, learners' emotional reactions toward technology are also considered as important determinants of technology acceptance and use (Venkatesh et al., 2012). *Hedonic motivation* that represents positive emotion can be a primary intrinsic motivator for technology adoption, as it can directly influence perceived ease of use, perceived usefulness and continuance intention to use technology (Li et al., 2021). Negative affect, such as technology anxiety, which usually derives from learners' unfamiliarity and apprehension with technology, can also impede students' motivation to adopt technology for learning, as it has been found to have negative influence on perceived usefulness and perceived ease of use (Zheng & Li, 2020). *Price value* reflects how individuals evaluate the trade-off between the benefits and costs of using a technology (Venkatesh et al., 2012). If learners consider the advantages of adopting a particular technology to be greater than its cost, they are more likely to use the technology. *Habit* is defined as the automatic performance of behaviors (Venkatesh et al., 2012). Unlike TRA and TPB that consider behavioral intention as the product of deliberate evaluations, habit is often deemed as unconscious behavior from the automaticity perspective (Kim et al., 2005).

Empirical studies have shown that these motivational constructs did shape adoption behaviors related to GenAI. An and colleagues (2023) explored secondary school students' intention to use AI for L2 learning in China. They found that these motivational variables had varying influence on junior and high school students' AI adoption. Performance expectancy was found to positively predict both groups of students' behavioral intention to use AI due to its wide range of affordances suitable for practicing language skills (Liang et al., 2021), but effort expectancy and facilitating conditions did not predict both groups of students' intention to use AI. Social influence was found to be a significant predictor of junior high school students' intention to use AI but not for senior high school students. Similarly, Wang et al. (2023) also found that junior high school students were more likely to be swayed by social influence than senior high school students. A possible explanation is that junior high school students with limited experience with technology may rely more on significant others' experiences and opinions, whereas senior students have gained more experience with technology and become more independent, and they would gradually become less susceptible to social influence (Venkatesh & Morris, 2000; Steinberg & Monahan, 2007). Regarding facilitating conditions, it has been found to positively influence learner's efficacy and perceived ease of use of technology for learning, thereby enhancing their continuance intention (Faqih & Jaradat, 2021; Wang et al., 2023; Ni & Cheung, 2023). Additionally, hedonic motivation has been identified as a crucial factor driving university language learners' self-directed use of GenAI for informal English learning (Liu et al., 2024; Zheng et al., 2024). Furthermore, price value is positively associated with perceived usefulness and adoption behavior in secondary school students' adoption of intelligent tutoring systems for English learning (Ni & Cheung, 2023).

Although the frameworks have different origins, some key motivational factors overlap across frameworks. Synthesizing these frameworks, we derive several key motivational dimensions that are critical to learners' intention to use AI for learning, including self-efficacy, perceived benefits, affective response, and supportive environment. In the section below, we will discuss how to build motivational mechanisms that support language learners' AI integration.

Constructing motivational mechanisms to support AI integration

Given that self-efficacy, perceived benefits, affective responses and supportive environment are motivational dimensions that are key to AI integration, motivational mechanisms that support AI integration need to target these dimensions (as shown in Figure 1). These dimensions suggest building in the following elements in students' learning

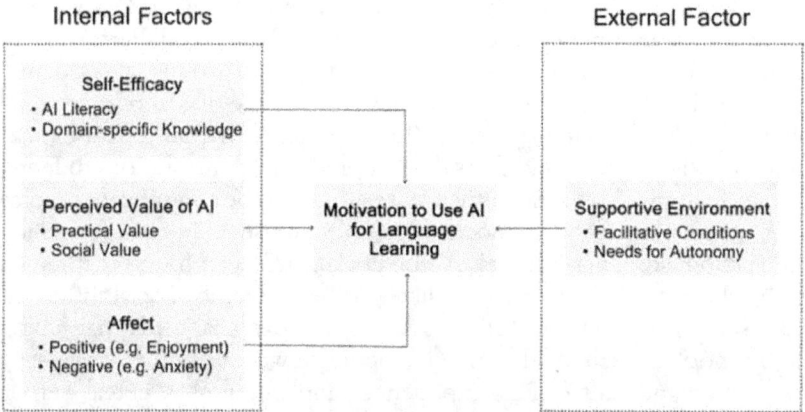

Figure 8.1 *Motivational mechanisms to support AI integration.*

experiences to promote their voluntary adoption of AI for learning: (1) boosting students' self-efficacy in interacting with AI; (2) strengthening students' perception of the value of AI; (3) promoting a sense of enjoyment and reducing anxiety when using AI; and (4) creating a supportive AI learning environment.

Boosting students' self-efficacy in interacting with AI

The importance of self-efficacy has been mentioned across all frameworks, which mainly concerns learners' perceived competence of using AI. This motivation source is highlighted in various motivational frameworks, using different terms such as competence, expectancy, perceived ease of use, perceived behavioral control and effort expectancy. The backbone of self-efficacy lies in not only AI literacy but also domain-specific knowledge on the use of AI for language learning (Xia et al., 2023). With better understanding of the affordances and limitations of AI, students will feel more competent using AI for effective language learning. With sufficient domain-specific knowledge, students are more likely to be able to comprehend and evaluate the learning content and feedback generated by AI, which will also boost their self-efficacy toward using AI. It is worth mentioning that disciplinary knowledge has been found more influential than technological knowledge when it comes to AI-assisted language learning (Xia et al., 2023). In this regard, teachers need to equip students with essential prior knowledge and skills regarding (1) how to effectively interact with AI; (2) how to use AI for language learning (e.g. explain the meaning of words and prepare notes for vocabulary learning; generate sample texts related to a specific topic to learn about the genre; generate questions to test reading comprehension, etc.; for more examples, please see Kohnke et al., 2023) to help students develop technology self-efficacy and subsequently enhance their motivation of using AI for language learning.

To foster self-efficacy, Bandura's (2001) four main sources of self-efficacy serve as a good starting point. According to Bandura, four sources interactively shape students' sense of self-efficacy:

1) Mastery experiences, i.e., learners' own personal experiences of success or failure. Mastery experience is the most influential source. Creating opportunities for students to experience different ways of using AI in language learning and guiding them to reflect critically on the experience may help boost students' self-efficacy. In the meantime, teachers also need to provide resources and step-by-step guidance in the form of workshops or presentations to illustrate specific examples of how to use AI, as well as how

to cope with the technical issues when using AI, to increase the likelihood that their personal experience would be a positive one (Hartnett, 2015).
2) Vicarious experiences, i.e., experience of seeing peers succeed through sustained effort. Seeing others succeed may boost learners' confidence in mastering comparable activities. Thus, it is equally important for teachers to organize peer sharing sessions or invite students to showcase their successful or creative experience of using AI for language learning.
3) Social persuasion, i.e., the experience of being persuaded of having the skills and capabilities to succeed. Verbal encouragement and positive feedback from significant others, including teachers, peers and parents, play an essential role in boosting self-efficacy.
4) Physiological and emotional states, such as anxiety and stress, may influence learners' judgment of their individual capacities and possibility of success. Thus, teachers need to attend to students' emotional responses when interacting with AI and take measures to foster positive states.

To help students understand how to use AI for language learning, teachers should also be aware that students at different language proficiency levels may require different forms of learning activities to enhance their competence (Xia et al., 2023). Fostering competence in the context of AI-assisted language learning entails allowing students to display their linguistic skills and offering appropriate learning activities (Annamalai et al., 2023). Students with limited language proficiency may not know what to ask and how to elicit meaningful content from AI. Therefore, for students at lower and intermediate proficiency level, tasks that concern using AI for knowledge consolidation would be considered more appropriate. In contrast, advanced students may be more likely to satisfy their needs through explorational tasks (Fryer et al., 2019).

Strengthening students' perception of the value of AI

All the motivational frameworks highlight the importance of perceived value, with some underscoring practical value (e.g., attainment and utility value, perceived usefulness, performance expectancy) and others featuring social value (e.g., relatedness, subjective norms, social influence). Thus, teachers may need to both work on changing individuals' perception of practical value and capitalize on the collective sources that influence social value.

Beliefs towards the value of AI are malleable and can be reshaped through interventions that help students understand the role AI plays for their future success (Rosenzweig et al., 2022). Highlighting the potential of AI in delivering personalized learning materials that cater to students' personal interests, needs and preference may help students internalize the value of AI for learning. Once students become aware of what GenAI can do, they are more inclined to improve their perceived usefulness and performance expectancy toward using AI.

To promote social values of AI integration, teachers may need to work on cultivating communities of inquiry that engage students in collaborative inquiry into the use of AI for language learning. Such communities can enhance relatedness and social influence. Given that learners of different age levels respond differently to social influences (An et al., 2023), schools and teachers need to adopt a differentiated approach. For younger students who are more easily influenced by social norms, schools and teachers may consider hosting workshops or setting up AI-related courses to encourage participation and peer collaboration. When younger students are given the opportunities to share their experiences with their teachers and peers and learn from the others, they are more likely to continue to use AI for learning purposes. For older students that pay less attention to other's opinions, teachers can consider giving them more autonomy to explore the topics and resources that align with their individual interests (An et al., 2023).

Promoting a sense of enjoyment and reducing anxiety when using AI

The motivational frameworks underscore the motivational forces of students' emotions (e.g., intrinsic value, attitudes, and hedonic motivation). Students' satisfaction and enjoyment of the experience can positively affect their willingness to adopt AI for learning (Ni & Cheung, 2023), whereas AI learning anxiety can negatively influence students' motivation (Wang et al., 2024). In this regard, attention should also be paid to fostering positive emotions and alleviating anxiety when students use AI.

Tan and colleagues (2024) identified four quality factors of GenAI that may affect university learners' satisfaction with GenAI:

1) system quality (the extent to which GenAI is considered user-friendly and can be navigated without much difficulty);
2) service quality (the extent to which GenAI is considered dependable, efficient and adaptable);
3) information quality (the extent to which GenAI-generated output is accurate, reliable and trustworthy);
4) conversational quality (the extent to which GenAI interaction is perceived as responsive and contextually relevant).

It is important to help learners develop the relevant capabilities to derive service, information and interaction experiences that are beneficial to learning. To achieve that, teachers should guide students to understand both the capabilities and limitations of GenAI. At the same time, teachers need to help learners develop the capacity to critically consume information acquired from GenAI through activities, such as engaging students to identify flaws in AI output and biases in the language used by AI. Additionally, teachers should provide guidance on critically interpreting information generated by AI. These measures can help enhance learners' satisfaction with their GenAI experience.

Encouraging students to create and share innovative and fun activities – such as generating multimodal learning resources to visualize concepts in the classroom, – can also boost positive emotions associated with AI experience/use. Success and achievement in these activities can strengthen students' confidence in using AI and reduce AI-related anxiety in learning (Wang et al., 2024).

Creating a supportive AI learning environment

A supportive AI learning environment is supposed to (1) enhance the facilitating conditions of GenAI, and (2) satisfy students' needs for autonomy.

Since facilitating conditions are a critical factor that shape students' intention to use AI (Wang et al., 2023), teachers should create mechanisms for easy access to support, such as high-quality prompt examples that illustrate effective ways to interact with AI. Teachers should also highlight the limitations of GenAI and establish ethical standards for responsible use of GenAI, to mitigate the negative effects of GenAI, such as plagiarism and fabricated information (Ivanov et al., 2024). To satisfy students' autonomy needs, teachers can provide learning resources (Chiu, 2021) and give students the freedom to choose the tools and materials tailored to their preferences and learning objectives for self-directed language learning. Equally important, is enhancing students' decision-making skills when using AI to foster personal empowerment and social transformation. This involves encouraging students to imagine different relations with AI and experiment with different ways to interact with AI. Finally, raising learners' metacognitive awareness of their AI behaviors through visualizing their interaction history and progress can further support their engagement (Annamalai et al., 2023).

Conclusion

In this chapter, we reviewed several major motivational frameworks to identify key motivational factors and mechanisms that are critical to students' integration of AI in learning. These mechanisms do not stand alone but rather interact with one another in shaping learners' AI behaviors. Teachers are hence encouraged to adopt a holistic approach in creating supportive infrastructure to motivate students' active incorporation of GenAI to transform their language learning experience. At the same time, it is essential for teachers to be aware of the ethical concerns related to the use of GenAI, such as students being tempted to use AI-generated content as their original work and committing plagiarism; or developing overreliance on GenAI which may diminish students' critical thinking skills and creativity. Pedagogical approaches that effectively address these ethical concerns can better enhance students' understanding of GenAI and ultimately lead to greater growth in AI literacy and language acquisition.

> **Post-reading questions:**
>
> 1) How might learners' engagement with AI reshape their motivation and agency in language learning?
> 2) How can the integration of AI in language learning foster a sense of community and collaboration among learners?

Further reading

Law, L. (2024). Application of generative artificial intelligence (GenAI) in language teaching and learning: A scoping literature review. *Computers and Education Open*, 100174. https://doi.org/10.1016/j.caeo.2024.100174

References

Abdullah, F., & Ward, R. (2016). Developing a general extended technology acceptance model for e-Learning (GETAMEL) by analyzing commonly used external factors. *Computers in Human Behavior*, 56, 238–256. https://doi.org/10.1016/j.chb.2015.11.036

Ajzen, I. (1991). The theory of planned behavior. *Organizational Behavior and Human Decision Processes*, 50(2), 179–211. https://doi.org/10.1016/0749-5978(91)90020-T

Ajzen, I., & Fishbein, M. (1980). *Understanding attitudes and predicting social behavior*. Prentice-Hall.

Ajzen, I., & Fishbein, M. (2005). The influence of attitudes on behavior. In D. Albarracin, B. T. Johnson, & M. P. Zanna (Eds.), *The handbook of attitudes* (pp. 173–221). Erlbaum.

An, X., Chai, C. S., Li, Y., Zhou, Y., & Yang, B. (2023). Modeling students' perceptions of artificial intelligence assisted language learning. *Computer Assisted Language Learning*, 1–22. https://doi.org/10.1080/09588221.2023.2246519

Annamalai, N., Eltahir, M. E., Zyoud, S. H., Soundrarajan, D., Zakarneh, B., & Al Salhi, N. R. (2023). Exploring English language learning via Chabot: A case study from a self determination theory perspective. *Computers and Education: Artificial Intelligence*, *5*, 100148. https://doi.org/10.1016/j.caeai.2023.100148

Bandura, A. (2001). Social cognitive theory: An agentic perspective. *Annual Review of Psychology*, *52*(1), 1–26. https://doi.org/10.1146/annurev.psych.52.1.1

Chai, C. S., Lin, P. Y., Jong, M. S. Y., Dai, Y., Chiu, T. K., & Qin, J. (2021). Perceptions of and behavioral intentions towards learning artificial intelligence in primary school students. *Educational Technology & Society*, *24*(3), 89–101. https://www.jstor.org/stable/27032858

Chan, C. K. Y., & Zhou, W. (2023). An expectancy value theory (EVT) based instrument for measuring student perceptions of generative AI. *Smart Learning Environments*, *10*(1), 64. https://doi.org/10.1186/s40561-023-00284-4

Chapelle, C. A. (2024). Open generative AI changes a lot, but not everything. *Modern Language Journal*, *108*, 534–540. https://doi.org/10.1111/modl.12927

Cheon, J., Lee, S., Crooks, S., & Song, J. (2012). An investigation of mobile learning readiness in higher education based on the theory of planned behavior. *Computers & Education*, *59*(3), 1054–1064. https://doi.org/10.1016/j.compedu.2012.04.015

Chiu, T. K. F. (2021). Digital support for student engagement in blended learning based on self-determination theory. *Computers in Human Behavior*, *124*, 106909. https://doi.org/10.1016/j.chb.2021.106909

Chiu, T. K. (2024). A classification tool to foster self-regulated learning with generative artificial intelligence by applying self-determination theory: A case of ChatGPT. *Educational Technology eResearch and Development*, 1–16. https://doi.org/10.1007/s11423-024-10366-w

Davis, F. D. (1989). Perceived usefulness, perceived ease of use and user acceptance of information technology. *MIS Quarterly*, *13*(3), 319–340. https://doi.org/10.2307/249008

Deci, E. L., & Ryan, R. M. (1985). *Intrinsic motivation and self-determination in human behavior*. Plenum.

Du, J., & Alm, A. (2024). The impact of ChatGPT on English for academic purposes (EAP) students' language learning experience: A self-determination theory perspective. *Education Sciences*, *14*(7), 726. https://doi.org/10.3390/educsci14070726

Eccles, J. S., & Wigfield, A. (2020). From expectancy-value theory to situated expectancy-value theory: A developmental, social cognitive, and sociocultural perspective on motivation. *Contemporary educational psychology*, *61*, 101859. https://doi.org/10.1016/j.cedpsych.2020.101859

Fathali, S., & Okada, T. (2017). A self-determination theory approach to technology-enhanced out-of-class language learning intention: A case of Japanese EFL learners. *International Journal of Research Studies in Language Learning*, *6*(4), 53–64. https://doi.org/10.5861/ijrsll.2016.1607

Faqih, K. M. S., & Jaradat, M. I. R. M. (2021). Integrating TTF and UTAUT2 theories to investigate the adoption of augmented reality technology in education: Perspective from a developing country. *Technology in Society*, *67*, 101787. https://doi.org/10.1016/j.techsoc.2021.101787

Fryer, L. K., Nakao, K., & Thompson, A. (2019). Chatbot learning partners: Connecting learning experiences, interest and competence. *Computers in Human Behavior*, *93*, 279–289. https://doi.org/10.1016/j.chb.2018.12.023

Gill, S. S., Xu, M., Patros, P., Wu, H., Kaur, R., Kaur, K., & Buyya, R. (2024). Transformative effects of ChatGPT on modern education: Emerging era of AI chatbots. *Internet of Things and Cyber-Physical Systems*, *4*, 19–23. https://doi.org/10.1016/j.iotcps.2023.06.002

Grover, V. (2024). Being informed by artificial intelligence. *Journal of Information Technology Case and Application Research*, *26*(1), 1–3. https://doi.org/10.1080/15228053.2023.2269714

Hartnett, M. K. (2015). Influences that undermine learners' perceptions of autonomy, competence and relatedness in an online context. *Australasian Journal of Educational Technology*, *31*(1), 86–99. https://doi.org/10.14742/ajet.1526

Hsu, Y. C., Ching, Y. H. (2023). Generative artificial intelligence in education, part two: International perspectives. *TechTrends*, *67*, 885–890. https://doi.org/10.1007/s11528-023-00913-2

Ivanov, S., Soliman, M., Tuomi, A., Alkathiri, N. A., & Al-Alawi, A. N. (2024). Drivers of generative AI adoption in higher education through the lens of the Theory of Planned Behavior. *Technology in Society*, *77*, 102521. https://doi.org/10.1016/j.techsoc.2024.102521

Jeon, J. (2024). Exploring AI chatbot affordances in the EFL classroom: Young learners' experiences and perspectives. *Computer Assisted Language Learning*, *37*, 1–26. https://doi.org/10.1080/09588221.2021.2021241

Karacı, A., Piri, Z., İbrahim, H., & Bilgici, G. (2018). Student perceptions of an intelligent tutoring system: A technology acceptance model perspective. *International Journal of Computer Applications*, *182*(22), 31–36. https://doi.org/10.5120/ijca2018918025

Kern, R. (2024). Twenty-first century technologies and language education: Charting a path forward. *Modern Language Journal*, *108*, 515–533. https://doi.org/10.1111/modl.12924

Kim, S. S., Malhotra, N. K., & Narasimhan, S. (2005). Research note – two competing perspectives on automatic use: A theoretical and empirical comparison. *Information Systems Research*, *16*(4), 418–432. https://doi.org/10.1287/isre.1050.0070

Kim, J., Merrill, K., Xu, K., & Sellnow, D. D. (2020). My teacher is a machine: Understanding students' perceptions of AI teaching assistants in online education. *International Journal of Human-Computer Interaction*, *36*(20), 1902–1911. https://doi.org/10.1080/10447318.2020.1801227

Kohnke, L., Moorhouse, B. L., & Zou, D. (2023). ChatGPT for language teaching and learning. *RELC Journal*, *54*(2), 537–550. https://doi.org/10.1177/00336882231162868

Kuhail, M. A., Alturki, N., Alramlawi, S., & Alhejori, K. (2023). Interacting with educational chatbots: A systematic review. *Education and Information Technologies*, *28*(1), 973–1018. https://doi.org/10.1007/s10639-022-11177-3

Li, C., He, L., & Wong, I. A. (2021). Determinants predicting undergraduates' intention to adopt e-learning for studying English in Chinese higher education context: A structural equation modelling approach. *Education and Information Technologies*, *26*(4), 4221–4239. https://doi.org/10.1007/s10639-021-10462-x

Liang, J. C., Hwang, G. J., Chen, M. R. A., & Darmawansah, D. (2021). Roles and research foci of artificial intelligence in language education: an integrated bibliographic analysis and systematic review approach. *Interactive Learning Environments*, *31*(7), 4270–4296. https://doi.org/10.1080/10494820.2021.1958348

Liu, G. L., Darvin, R., & Ma, C. (2024). Exploring AI-mediated informal digital learning of English (AI-IDLE): a mixed-method investigation of Chinese EFL learners' AI adoption and experiences. *Computer Assisted Language Learning*, 1–29. https://doi.org/10.1080/09588221.2024.2310288

Mousavinasab, E., Zarifsanaiey, N., Niakan Kalhori, R., Rakhshan, S., Keikha, M., & Ghazi Saeedi, M. (2021). Intelligent tutoring systems: A systematic review of characteristics, applications, and evaluation methods. *Interactive Learning Environments*, *29*(1), 142–163. https://doi.org/10.1080/10494 820.2018.1558257

Ni, A., & Cheung, A. (2023). Understanding secondary students' continuance intention to adopt AI-powered intelligent tutoring system for English learning. *Education and Information Technologies*, *28*(3), 3191–3216. https://doi.org/10.1007/s10639-022-11305-z

Nikou, S. A., & Economides, A. A. (2017). Mobile-based assessment: Investigating the factors that influence behavioral intention to use. *Computers & Education*, *109*, 56–73. https://doi.org/10.1016/j.compedu.2017.02.005

Pavlou, P. A., & Fygenson, M. (2006). Understanding and predicting electronic commerce adoption: An extension of the theory of planned behavior. *MIS Quarterly*, *30*(1), 115–143. https://doi.org/10.2307/25148720

Rosenzweig, E. Q., Wigfield, A., & Eccles, J. S. (2022). Beyond utility value interventions: The why, when, and how for next steps in expectancy–value intervention research. *Educational Psychologist*, *57*(1), 11–30. https://doi.org/10.1080/ 00461520.2021.1984242

Ruzek, E. A., Hafen, C. A., Allen, J. P., Gregory, A., Mikami, A. Y., & Pianta, R. C. (2016). How teacher emotional support motivates students: The mediating roles of perceived peer relatedness, autonomy support, and competence. *Learning and Instruction*, *42*, 95–103. https://doi.org/10.1016/j.learninstruc.2016.01.004

Ryan, R. M., & Deci, E. L. (2020). Intrinsic and extrinsic motivation from a self-determination theory perspective: Definitions, theory, practices, and future directions. *Contemporary Educational Psychology*, *61*, 101860. https://doi.org/10.1016/j.cedpsych.2020.101860

Scherer, R., Siddiq, F., & Tondeur, J. (2018). The technology acceptance model (TAM): A meta-analytic structural equation modeling approach to explaining teachers' adoption of digital technology in education. *Computers & Education*, *128*, 13–35. https://doi.org/10.1016/j.compedu.2018.09.009

Skinner, E., Furrer, C., Marchand, G., & Kindermann, T. (2008). Engagement and disaffection in the classroom: Part of a larger motivational dynamic? *Journal of Educational Psychology*, *100*(4), 765. https://doi.org/10.1037/a0012840

Steinberg, L., & Monahan, K. C. (2007). Age differences in resistance to peer influence. *Developmental Psychology*, *43*, 1531–1543. https://doi.org/10.1037/0012-1649.43.6.1531

Tan, C. N. L., Tee, M., & Koay, K. Y. (2024). Discovering students' continuous intentions to use ChatGPT in higher education: a tale of two theories. *Asian Education and Development Studies*. https://doi.org/10.1108/AEDS-04-2024-0096

Venkatesh, V., & Morris, M. G. (2000). Why don't men ever stop to ask for directions? Gender, social influence, and their role in technology acceptance and usage behavior. *MIS Quarterly*, *24*, 115–139. https://doi.org/10.2307/3250981

Venkatesh, V., Morris, M. G., Davis, G. B., & Davis, F. D. (2003). User acceptance of information technology: Toward a unified view. *MIS Quarterly*, *27*(3), 425. https://doi.org/10.2307/30036540

Venkatesh, V., Thong, J. Y. L., & Xu, X. (2012). Consumer acceptance and use of information technology: Extending the unified theory of acceptance and use of technology. *MIS Quarterly*, *36*(1), 157–178. https://doi.org/10.2307/41410412

Wang, F., King, R. B., Chai, C. S., & Zhou, Y. (2023). University students' intentions to learn artificial intelligence: The roles of supportive environments and expectancy–value beliefs. *International Journal of Educational Technology in Higher Education*, *20*(1), 51. https://doi.org/10.1186/s41239-023-00417-2

Wang, Y. M., Wei, C. L., Lin, H. H., Wang, S. C., & Wang, Y. S. (2024). What drives students' AI learning behavior: A perspective of AI anxiety. *Interactive Learning Environments*, *32*(6), 2584-2600. https://doi.org/10.1080/10494820.2022.2153147

Wigfield, A., & Eccles, J. S. (2000). Expectancy–value theory of achievement motivation. *Contemporary Educational Psychology*, *25*(1), 68–81. https://doi.org/10.1006/ceps.1999.1015

Xia, Q., Chiu, T. K. F., Lee, M., Temitayo, I., Dai, Y., & Chai, C. S. (2022). A self-determination theory design approach for inclusive and diverse artificial intelligence (AI) K-12 education. *Computers & Education*, *189*, 104582. https://doi.org/10.1016/j.compedu.2022.104582

Xia, Q., Chiu, T. K., Chai, C. S., & Xie, K. (2023). The mediating effects of needs satisfaction on the relationships between prior knowledge and self-regulated learning through artificial intelligence chatbot. *British Journal of Educational Technology*, *54*(4), 967–986. https://doi.org/10.1111/bjet.13305

Yan, L., Sha, L., Zhao, L., Li, Y., Martinez-Maldonado, R., Chen, G., ... & Gašević, D. (2024). Practical and ethical challenges of large language models in education: A systematic scoping review. *British Journal of Educational Technology*, *55*(1), 90–112. https://doi.org/10.1111/bjet.13370

Zheng, J., & Li, S. (2020). What drives students' intention to use tablet computers – An extended technology acceptance model. *International Journal of Educational Research*, *12*, 1–12. https://doi.org/10.1016/j.ijer.2020.101612

Zheng, Y., Wang, Y., Liu, K. S. X., & Jiang, M. Y. C. (2024). Examining the moderating effect of motivation on technology acceptance of generative AI for English as a foreign language learning. *Education and Information Technologies*, 1–29. https://doi.org/10.1007/s10639-024-12763-3

9
AI and teaching communities
Louise Ohashi

> **Pre-reading questions:**
>
> 1) What aspects of AI in language education are most important for you to learn about?
> 2) Which teacher communities do you belong to now? Do any others appeal to you?
> 3) What support do you need from teacher communities to integrate AI into your teaching?
> 4) How do you support other teachers? What support could you offer?

Introduction

Restrictions on face-to-face classes during the COVID-19 pandemic brought digital technology into language education at a scale that nobody could have imagined. Now we are back in classrooms, but advances in artificial intelligence (AI) have brought digital tools into sharp focus again. The release of ChatGPT in November, 2022, propelled chatbots and generative AI (GenAI) into the public eye, capturing the attention and imagination of the world. ChatGPT is a natural language processing (NLP) and natural language understanding (NLU) application that can simulate human-like multilingual conversations in written and spoken modes. Since ChatGPT's release, GenAI has experienced exponential growth, with many tools now capable of engaging with and/or producing content such as images, audio, videos, computer code, spreadsheets, and presentation slides. This technology is on the path to ubiquity, both due to its widespread adoption in business, government and other facets of society, as well as its growing integration into commonly-used tools. GenAI's multilingual NLP and NLU capabilities make it an obvious choice for exploration and exploitation in foreign/second (L2) language education. As readers will already be aware, AI can offer valuable benefits, but also poses substantial challenges and risks. This means the need for AI literacy, which involves knowing how "to critically evaluate AI technologies, communicate and collaborate effectively with AI, and use AI as a tool online, at home, and in the workplace" (Long & Magerko, 2020, p. 2), is more important than ever. And with recent developments, this can be narrowed further to GenAI literacy, which at a minimum includes sound knowledge of operational, ethical and privacy-related issues; the ability to effectively understand, use, and collaborate with GenAI across different modes to meet user objectives; and the capacity to critically assess AI-generated output.

Echoing the situation faced during the pandemic, there is an urgent need for educators to gain new skills with forms of technology that many of them are unfamiliar with, and they must consider the impact of this new technology on their courses. If you were a teacher during the pandemic, think back to 2020. Did you have the knowledge and skills required to teach online? How easy or hard was it for you to make the transition? Did you get help from peers or your employer? Did you support others? In my context in Japan, teachers who had already been integrating technology into their courses and early adopters of new tools like Zoom were very active in supporting peers. This was perhaps most strongly evidenced for me through the Facebook group *Online Teaching Japan*, which was created by and for L2 educators and quickly became a hub of information for those with different levels of tech-related experience to connect, seek help, and offer support. Teachers initially exchanged information via written posts, but this soon expanded to include videocalls, with members running training sessions, problem-solving together, and sharing their ideas and concerns. At a time when most institutions in Japan were moving classes online but offering minimal–if any–training, this teacher community was a lifeline to many L2 instructors. Alongside my anecdotal observations, research has shown these types of teacher communities can be meaningful spaces for educators. For example, Ito's (2023) study with an online community of L2 educators during the pandemic found that it offered a valuable space to access information and resources, as well as technical and emotional support.

The pandemic is behind us now, but the new AI era demands our attention. To me, teacher communities will be essential in dealing with this challenge too. This chapter uses the Communities of Practice (CoP) framework (Lave & Wenger, 1991) as a lens for examining and explaining the vital role teacher communities will play as L2 education adapts to the influx of GenAI technologies. This framework, which positions learning as socially situated, has three key elements: the domain, community, and practice. The *domain* is the area of interest that the community shares. The *community* is the people who engage with each other about the domain: people who "help each other, and share information. They build relationships that enable them to learn from each other" (Wenger-Trayner & Wenger-Trayner, 2015, para. 7). The *practice* is what they do together. This includes their shared experiences, interaction, time, and resources. In other words, a CoP is a group of people with a common interest who come together over time to share skills, knowledge and tools that facilitate learning within the community. This chapter focuses on the domain "AI in L2 education", introducing the domain, community and practice in turn. Throughout these sections, I share some personal experiences I have had within my teacher communities and encourage you to reflect on your own current and future roles.

The domain (What We Focus On)

The domain of AI in language education covers a wide range of tools and issues. For many teachers, interest in this domain began when ChatGPT was released, as it sparked a sense of urgency within education. Media reports told us of a new kind of chatbot technology that had universities "revamping how they teach" over concerns that students could use it to do their coursework (Huang, 2023). A global study I conducted with 367 L2 teachers shortly after ChatGPT's release revealed strong concerns about its potential use as a cheating aid (Alm & Ohashi, 2024; Ohashi & Alm, 2023), echoing earlier concerns I found in a study with 153 L2 educators in Japan on the use of machine translation (Ohashi, 2022). In extreme initial reactions to fears over cheating, the use of ChatGPT in public schools was banned by education boards in countries such as the U.S. and Australia (Johnson, 2023). However, it was impossible to monitor whether the ban was being respected outside of schools, and rules were soon reversed, with school boards ultimately opting to provide students with the skills needed to safely and effectively use this new technology (Henebery, 2023). This move towards ensuring safe use is warranted and has been recognised far beyond classrooms, resulting in new legislation such as the EU Artificial Intelligence Act (European Union Directorate-General for Communication, 2024). Given the issues mentioned above, some readers may have reservations about AI that make them feel it is better to keep it out of their classrooms. Undoubtedly, strong reservations are what forced ChatGPT out of U.S. and Australian schools at first. However, just like those school boards found, banning and ignoring this technology is not a viable option. Therefore, finding ways to deal with problems GenAI poses is central to this domain.

Another key part of this domain relates to understanding the benefits AI offers and learning how to maximise its potential. MIT sought to alleviate early fears educators held by proposing that ChatGPT would "change education, not destroy it" (Heaven, 2023). Since that time, a large number of studies on GenAI in L2 education have emerged. For example, when used productively, ChatGPT has been shown to facilitate gains in L2 writing (Kwon et al., 2023) and a study by Jia Min (2024) found students who used ChatGPT to learn synonyms made greater vocabulary gains than the those using traditional methods (worksheets, textbooks, teacher instruction). Furthermore, it can be used to give personalised feedback on writing to help learners understand their grammar errors, as shown through a study with Japanese learners of English who reported benefiting from ChatGPT's bilingual corrective feedback (Schmidt-Fajlik, 2023). GenAI also provides opportunities for one-to-one conversation practice, either through written chat or voice options. Research on this is still limited, but Turkish learners of English found ChatGPT beneficial for written dialogue practice, acknowledging some comprehension issues, but also noting that they received constructive feedback in level-appropriate language (Üstünbaş, 2024). ChatGPT has also been recommended for oral presentation and pronunciation practice, with Huang (2024) documenting a range of voice prompts that provided useful feedback when tested with ChatGPT. While GenAI has the potential to facilitate L2 learning, much guidance is needed. For example, studies have shown that learners may have difficulty creating appropriate prompts for chatbots and receive output that lacks specificity (Alrajhi, 2024; Pham et al., 2024) and there are concerns from teachers about student over-reliance (Alm & Ohashi, 2024; Ohashi & Alm, 2023). To increase effective and ethical use of AI among students, support from teachers is essential. For example, when students use AI for writing tasks, Tseng and Warschauer (2023) have suggested teachers provide guidance in five key areas: 1. understanding tools' capabilities and biases; 2. accessing the appropriate functionalities they need (understanding which tools offer them and how to use them); 3. prompting effectively; 4. corroborating the accuracy of output; 5. incorporating output into their work in a way that is accepted as appropriate and ethical in their learning context.

With sufficient knowledge and skills, teachers can guide students more effectively and use AI appropriately in their teaching roles, so this domain also extends to AI literacy, including GenAI literacy. While we do not need to (and cannot) become experts overnight, we have already entered an era in which educators need at least foundational AI knowledge and skills in order to guide students towards facilitative application and away from misuse. This technology is widely available to students, so even teachers who do not want to harness its affordances need to know about its capabilities. After all, without a basic understanding of GenAI, educators may find themselves making baseless assumptions and even high-stakes errors. An example of the latter went viral when a teacher failed students after asking ChatGPT if the students' work had been created by it, which is something ChatGPT cannot determine (D'Agostino, 2023). While some AI-detectors claim to be able to identify AI-generated content (with this capability widely contested), ChatGPT was not designed for such detection so the teacher's lack of knowledge led to him misusing ChatGPT and penalising innocent students. A lack of knowledge and skills will also mean that teachers cannot guide students towards optimal use of technology that exists all around them and uninformed teachers may not understand the ways that their students are augmenting their language development (or misusing AI for assignments) outside of class. They may also be unable to guide students away from overreliance or adequately equip them with the skills needed to understand ethical issues such as privacy concerns, data protection, in-built biases, and the possibility for output to contain misinformation (often referred to as "hallucinations"). For these reasons, AI literacy is essential for L2 educators and forms a central part of this domain.

The community (Who We Are)

In order to develop our own AI literacy and our students', teachers need to be supported and actively engaged. Educational institutions should play a central role in staff training, but this can only be done if there are people who have the skills and knowledge to run those sessions or if funding is available to outsource them. And for teachers to benefit from such training, it needs to be accessible and target their needs. At present, there is great disparity in what is being provided and teacher engagement also varies considerably. Whether training is provided by institutions or not, teachers can learn from and with each other and often do so even when institutional support is provided. Oakley and Pegrum (2015) demonstrated this through a study that tracked how lecturers at an Australian university learnt about digital technologies when participating in a workplace learning community, concluding that the formal professional development sessions offered were "only a trigger – much unplanned and unanticipated professional learning occurred through informal interaction, with lecturers co-learning with colleagues, and indeed with students, in an environment of enthusiastic experimentation" (p. 397). While teachers can and do learn through workplace programs, they are not simply passive recipients of formal training. Teachers have networks that extend beyond this, often seeking out opportunities to learn from others and guide best practices through their innovations and leadership. Teacher agency pushes teachers beyond employer-led professional development programs–which may be compulsory, optional, or non-existent–so the following sections focus on voluntary participation within teaching associations and more informal teaching communities.

Teaching associations

Throughout the world there are a large number of teaching associations for L2 educators, such as TESOL International (Teaching English to Speakers of Other Languages), EUROCALL (European Association for Computer Assisted Language Learning), and JALT (Japan Association for Language Teaching). These organisations aim to bring together language specialists over the common domain of L2 education. For example, TESOL International sees itself as a "global community for knowledge and expertise in English language teaching" (TESOL International Association, n.d.) and EUROCALL refers to itself as an organisation that "brings together researchers, practitioners and developers–both new and experienced– who feel passionate about the use of technology for the learning and teaching of languages and cultures" (EUROCALL, n.d.). Similarly, JALT's mission statement is to promote "excellence in language learning, teaching, and research by providing opportunities for those involved in language education to meet, share, and collaborate" (JALT, n.d.). Many teaching associations have Special Interest Groups (SIGs), some of which focus on CALL in general (such as JALTCALL) or AI more specifically. EUROCALL's AI SIG states that its domain encompasses "all areas that relate to AI and language learning/teaching" as "AI's impact on the field of second language acquisition is going to be of great interest to researchers and practitioners for many years to come" (EUROCALL AI SIG, n.d.).

Perhaps you are already a member of one or more of these organisations and may have already attended events or even taken on an active role as a volunteer. Or perhaps you are interested, but have hesitated to take the first step. You may feel you don't have enough AI expertise to belong in teaching associations like EUROCALL or JALTCALL, but nothing could be further from the truth. Whether you are new to AI or have extensive knowledge, there is a role for you in these types of teacher communities. Lave and Wenger's (1991) work on CoPs positions learning as a social act that is facilitated when we watch others and participate in activities in groups. To be successful, CoPs need people with different levels of experience, from novices to experts, to give those with less skills and knowledge the opportunity to observe community members at further stages of development. In other words, there are roles for all readers of this chapter. If you know how to use particular tools, understand how to exploit AI's affordances, or have other skills and knowledge that you could share, there are members who need your support. If you are lost and looking for guidance, there are members you can learn from. If you are between these ends of the spectrum, you can teach and learn. The challenge is bringing people at different stages of the journey together, and given the pace of change with GenAI, I would argue that we do not stay in the "expert" role for long and constantly have new opportunities to be the novice.

Informal communities

Teacher communities are not just officially sanctioned teaching associations, but also informal, naturally occurring communities. In workplaces, perhaps in casual settings like the lunch area, you may have colleagues you regularly talk to about teaching. And maybe the domain is L2 education and the role of AI is just a small part of that domain. Your discussions could be about anything from overcoming an institution-specific problem, such as dealing with AI-generated assignments, to enhancing each other's AI-competence so you can manage your roles more effectively. The important thing in a teacher community is teachers' shared desire to repeatedly collaborate. If you regularly meet these people and share your AI-related problems, ideas and expertise, this could be considered an informal AI teacher community.

Or perhaps a more familiar community for you is rooted in social media such as Facebook or Bluesky. Online communities can be found with people you actually know or those you have never met. In some cases, online communities may even transition into real-life bonds. For example, many teachers got to know each other during the pandemic in the Facebook group *Online Teaching Japan*, bonding through Facebook posts and video calls, and some decided to meet face-to-face when the pandemic ended. This group of 3,000 members has continued to thrive post-pandemic, with recent posts sharing AI-related resources, ideas, challenges, and questions. Perhaps you are already a member of an online community like this, or could seek out some options. On Facebook, I am part of numerous communities: Online Teaching Japan, EUROCALL's AI SIG, JALTCALL, Language Teaching with AI, and even Higher Ed Discussions of AI Writing & Use, which does not focus on L2 education but keeps me informed nonetheless. While my level of interaction with each groups varies greatly, I credit all of them with contributing to my AI literacy development.

The practice (What We Do)

The practice component of the CoP model is concerned with the actions that teachers undertake and different levels of participation that exist in these communities. There is no definitive list of what constitutes practice, but as noted by Stoll and Louis (2007) when attempting to define professional learning communities, "you will know that one exists when you can see a group of teachers sharing and critically interrogating their practice in an ongoing, reflective, collaborative, inclusive, learning-oriented, growth-promoting way" (p. 2). In this section, I outline some common practices within teacher communities, share personal experiences, and invite readers to consider their own practices and those they would like to adopt.

Practical action within teacher communities

Teaching organisations can help teachers raise their AI literacy in a multitude of ways. For example, in May, 2024, JALTCALL showed its strong commitment towards building AI-ready teacher communities by making "The Impact of AI in Language Education" the key theme of its annual three-day conference. This event, which I attended, brought together over 250 teachers for research presentations and workshops that aimed to build knowledge and skills within that teacher community. It also reached beyond the event itself, creating opportunities to learn for those who could not attend by making all abstracts publicly available[1]. Perhaps readers of this chapter have taken part in a similar event, either as an organiser or participant, within their own contexts. If so, were you already part of the community? If not, did it draw you in? While teachers may like to attend such events, some find it difficult or even impossible due to issues such as lack of funding, conflicts with work, health issues, and family responsibilities. To make learning opportunities more accessible, many teaching organisations host online events. For example, EUROCALL's AI SIG hosts interactive webinars every year. While not an exhaustive list, teaching associations provide opportunities to build AI-literacy skills though their face-to-face and online events, their online presence, research output, and the personal bonds they help members to make. Whether you are at the start of your AI-literacy journey or in a position to assist others, there is a valuable place for you in these teacher communities.

---

[1] Interested readers can access them at https://jaltcall.org/wp-content/uploads/2024/06/book-of-abstracts.pdf

Furthermore, informal communities have much to contribute. Many teachers spend time engaging with each other about AI within the workplace, which increases their collective knowledge and skills. Discussions with colleagues and peer guidance (on policies, tool operation, practical applications, etc.) are invaluable for discovering and implementing good teaching practices. Online groups like those introduced in the previous section can help us to raise awareness of tools and practices used outside of our immediate teaching context and provide a space for educators to broaden their knowledge at their own pace. One key practice in these informal communities is sharing resources. For example, members share links to AI tools, articles (research articles, news, blogs, etc.), or videos (demonstrations, presentations). Another central practice is recounting experiences, often with the aim of informing others or seeking advice. Members may also share information about events and teaching materials. At times, online communities can also be sources of heated debate, giving readers exposure to multiple perspectives.

Our role in collaborative learning and knowledge sharing

Whatever part of the AI novice-expert continuum you are at now, you can play a vital role in your teacher communities. The steps we take can impact others in important ways and this can have a ripple effect. For example, in recent years I have been asked to run workshops on AI within my JALT community and each invitation pushes me to learn more so I will have something valuable to deliver. In fact, questions in workshops pushed me to conduct a systematic literature review on machine translation in L2 education settings (Ohashi, 2024), extending an earlier review by Lee (2021) that I had drawn upon in presentations. A great deal of what I know about AI is directly attributable to things I have learnt through my teacher communities or been inspired by them to explore. And the stronger the community, the more I feel we can achieve. For example, I recently conducted research about ChatGPT with 2,522 L2 learners at Japanese universities (forthcoming). I could never have reached so many students without the support of my JALT community, who passed on my questionnaire to their students and colleagues. In the past, many teachers from the same community participated in my teacher-based studies on machine translation (Ohashi, 2022) and ChatGPT (Alm & Ohashi, 2024; Ohashi & Alm, 2023). To my mind, we are all important parts of the same chain, as I publish the data that teachers help me gather, and through that we all learn more. Their active support with data collection means we co-create knowledge. And my learning has been shaped over many years by others in the JALT community who were there to show me how to be a researcher. Reading *The JALT Journal* and *The Language Teacher*, attending JALT's annual international conference and smaller events, discussing my ideas, getting feedback: my JALT community nurtured me, and now I am doing what I can to nurture it back so we can continue growing together. Previous research has demonstrated growth in the self-efficacy of both novice and experienced teachers who engaged in collaborative tasks in a teaching community (Zonoubi et al., 2017), and my own experiences in teacher communities at different stages of my career support this. My self-efficacy has improved both when I have been supported and when I have taken supporting roles.

With AI still evolving, we all have much to learn. If you already have AI-related skills and knowledge, consider how you can share what you know with others. Your guidance in a workshop could help teachers to gain practical skills or your research ideas could lead to an interesting and valuable study that informs policy. Whether you are the keynote speaker at an international conference, run a workshop at a local event, teach a colleague how to use a new tool at lunchtime, or even just share your ideas though social media, you can make a positive impact. If you do not feel ready to guide, consider joining in when others take the lead. When teachers turn up to presentations, the organisers and presenters feel that the time they invested in preparing was worthwhile. Alternatively, consider helping with research. Gathering participants is challenging and your contribution will be appreciated more than you may realise. If you do not have time to participate yourself or are not part of the target sample, consider sharing the call for participants or read the researcher's article when it is published.

Do you see yourself in any of the roles described in this section? How could you support your teacher communities more? And how could teacher communities help you to further develop your AI literacy? Use the checklist below to see what you have already done and choose some tasks to target for the future:

- Join a teaching organisation
- Join an online community
- Connect with other teachers at work
- Participate in a face-to-face event (presenter or attendee)
- Participate in a webinar (presenter or attendee)
- Participate in AI-related discussions
- Share an AI-related article/video with others
- Comment on a social media post about AI in language education
- Show someone else how to use an AI tool or share your experience of using one
- Conduct some AI-related research (as a formal project or informally for yourself)
- Organise an event
- Extra: _____

Some readers may be looking for ideas on how to strengthen their teacher communities by taking on even more active roles. In the section below, I share community-building initiatives I have employed in my role as EUROCALL's AI SIG Chair (in conjunction with other community members) and pose questions to encourage readers to consider what might be appropriate in your own contexts.

1. **AI SIG Website**[2]: A static page for the AI SIG was created to share information about the SIG and provide links for the SIG's mailing list and Facebook group.
   Questions for readers: Does your teacher community have a website? If not, would it be useful? Who could set this up?
2. **Mailing List:** Messages are sent periodically to share information about up-coming SIG events, invite members to present at SIG events and share their articles, and provide links about the Facebook group, EUROCALL, membership, etc.
   Questions for readers: Would a mailing list be useful? Where could the contact list be stored? How frequently will messages be sent out? Who by?
3. **Webinars:** These are hosted by the AI SIG Chair and AI SIG Secretary, with presenters found through the mailing list, Facebook group, and personal connections. Slides for some sessions are shared via the mailing list to reach beyond the events.
   Questions for readers: Could you organise a webinar? Are community members likely to attend? Do you know what topics would be most useful? How could it be publicised?
4. **AI SIG Symposium:** This is held at EUROCALL's annual conference. It has been held in hybrid and face-to-face formats.
   Questions for readers: Would face-to-face events be possible/preferable in your community? Would hybrid options be useful and feasible?
5. **AI SIG Meeting:** This is held at the annual EUROCALL conference and is open to all. Participants have the opportunity to discuss a range of AI-related topics, share their institutional AI policies, and exchange contact details with each other. It has been held in hybrid and face-to-face formats. Volunteers are called for and SIG officers are elected.
   Questions for readers: Would formal/informal meetings be beneficial for your community? How often would be ideal? Who would organise them? Does your group need "officer" positions?

---

[2] Available at https://eurocall-languages.org/sigs/ai-sig/

6. **Facebook Group:** This group was created to share information, events and research, facilitate discussion, and provide a space for members to connect. Use the search term "EUROCALL AI SIG" if you would like to be part of this community.
   Questions for readers: Does your community have any social media accounts? Which type of social media is most beneficial for reaching members? Would a page or group be better? Should it be private or public? Who could moderate it?
7. **Research Archive:** A Google Doc, accessible to mailing list and Facebook group members, has been created for teachers to share their AI-related articles.
   Questions for readers: Would it be useful to have something like this in your community? Who would keep it updated and publicise it?

Wenger-Trayner (2011) identifies five levels of participation in CoPs: core group, active participants, occasional participants, peripheral participants, and transactional participants. Currently, the AI SIG officers are the core group, defined by as Wenger-Trayner (2011) as "a relatively small group of people whose passion and engagement energize and nurture the community" (para. 1). It is more difficult at this stage to identify the **active participants** who are "recognized as practitioners and define the community" (Wenger-Trayner, 2011, para. 1) because the community has had few opportunities to meet face-to-face and online interaction is still quite limited, but this will evolve in time. For now, it is encouraging to see a growing number of **occasional participants**, who "participate when the topic is of special interest, when they have [something] specific to contribute, or when they are involved in a project related to the domain of the community" (Wenger-Trayner, 2011, para. 1). Currently, the largest groups are **peripheral participants,** "who have a sustained connection to the community, but with less engagement and authority, either because they are still newcomers or because they do not have as much personal commitment to the practice" (Wenger-Trayner, 2011, para. 1) and **transactional participants** "who interact with the community occasionally without being members themselves, to receive or provide a service or to gain access to artifacts produced by the community, such as its publications, its website, or its tools" (Wenger-Trayner, 2011, para. 1).

Events are well-attended and breathe life into the AI SIG, but online interaction between members is still limited. Does this mean the online presence of this teacher community is not valuable to members? No, not necessarily. Community building takes time and even the quietest members may be benefiting. Years ago, I set up an independent learning group on Facebook to unite English language learners and when analysing participation, I categorised members into roles similar to those that Wenger-Treynor (2011) described. As with the AI SIG community, I found most members assumed less-active roles, but interviews showed that even just participating as a reader, without posting, had value (Ohashi, 2016). Therefore, if you are attempting to strengthen a teacher community and do not "see" it flourishing, keep going. It is doubtlessly more meaningful to some of the invisible members than you realise. Nevertheless, a community will not stay strong without engagement, so I encourage all readers to think about their roles in their teacher communities and take more steps to make their presence felt. Your post, "like", comment, email, presentation or attendance at events will add value to your community, either as a new source of knowledge or an act that motivates contributors to feel their efforts were worthwhile. And the more you give to your community, the more it will give back to you. Teacher agency is essential as we navigate the evolving educational landscape. Together, united, teacher communities can lead the way to responsible and effective integration of AI into L2 education.

Conclusion

This chapter stressed the importance of AI literacy development among L2 educators and presented teacher communities as valuable spaces for the development of an AI-ready workforce. By sharing my personal experiences and the work of others, I aimed to ignite a flame within readers to engage more fully in teacher communities within and beyond their workplaces. Reading this chapter was a step. If it inspired you, plan your next step and take it.

Post-reading questions:

1) Return to the pre-reading questions. Would you answer anything differently after reading this chapter?
2) Think of someone in your teacher communities that you think has more GenAI skills and knowledge than you. What would you like to learn from them? Reach out to ask.
3) How can you support people in your teacher communities? Take action, no matter how small.
4) Go back to the checklist in this chapter. Choose something to do this week, month and year.

Further reading

Long, D., & Magerko, B. (2020, April). What is AI literacy? Competencies and design considerations. In CHI '20: Proceedings of the 2020 CHI Conference on Human Factors in Computing Systems (pp. 1–16). Association for Computing Machinery, New York, US. https://doi.org/10.1145/3313831.3376727

Pratschke, M. B. (2024). *Generative AI and education: Digital pedagogies, teaching innovation and learning design.* Springer.

UNESCO. (2022). Recommendation on the ethics of artificial intelligence. *UNESCO.* https://www.unesco.org/en/articles/recommendation-ethics-artificial-intelligence

References

Alm, A., & Ohashi, L. (2024). A worldwide study on language educators' initial response to ChatGPT. *Technology in Language Teaching & Learning, 6*(1), 1–23 https://doi.org/10.29140/tltl.v6n1.1141

Alrajhi, A. S. (2024). Artificial intelligence pedagogical chatbots as L2 conversational agents. *Cogent Education, 11*(1). https://doi.org/10.1080/2331186X.2024.2327789

D'Agostino, S. (2023, Sept 15). Professor to students: ChatGPT told me to fail you. *Inside Higher Ed.* https://www.insidehighered.com/news/quick-takes/2023/05/19/professor-students-chatgpt-told-me-fail-you

EUROCALL. (n.d.). *Home.* Retrieved January 22, 2025, from https://eurocall-languages.org/

EUROCALL AI SIG. (n.d.). Retrieved January 22, 2025, from https://eurocall-languages.org/sigs/ai-sig/

European Union Directorate-General for Communication. (2024, August 1). AI Act enters into force. *European Union News.* https://commission.europa.eu/news/ai-act-enters-force-2024-08-01_en

Heaven, W. D. (2023, April 6). ChatGPT is going to change education, not destroy it. *MIT Technology Review.* https://www.technologyreview.com/2023/04/06/1071059/chatgpt-change-not-destroy-education-openai/

Henebery, B. (2023, July 13). Why the ChatGPT ban in public schools is being reversed. *The Educator Australia.* https://www.theeducatoronline.com/k12/news/why-the-chatgpt-ban-in-public-schools-is-being-reversed/282834

Huang, J. (2024). Enhancing EFL speaking feedback with ChatGPT's voice prompts. *International Journal of TESOL Studies, 6*(3), 4–23. https://doi.org/10.58304/ijts.20240302

Huang, K. (2023, January 16). Alarmed by A.I. chatbots, universities start revamping how they teach. *The New York Times*. https://www.nytimes.com/2023/01/16/technology/chatgpt-artificial-intelligence-universities.html

Ito, Y. Examining a technology-focused language teacher community on Facebook during a crisis situation. *Asian-Pacific Journal of Second and Foreign Language Education, 8*(1), 2023. https://doi.org/10.1186/s40862-022-00159-0

JALT. (n.d.). *NPO The Japan Association for Language Teaching (JALT): Learning to Teach, Teaching to Learn*. Retrieved January 22, 2025, from https://jalt.org/

Jia Min, C. (2024). The use of AI and ChatGPT in teaching synonyms to EFL students. *Research Studies in English Language Teaching and Learning, 2*(4), 187–207. https://doi.org/10.62583/rseltl.v2i4.53

Johnson, A. (2023, January 31). ChatGPT in schools: Here's where it's banned–and how it could potentially help students. *Forbes*. https://www.forbes.com/sites/ariannajohnson/2023/01/18/chatgpt-in-schools-heres-where-its-banned-and-how-it-could-potentially-help-students

Kwon, S. K., Shin, D., & Lee, Y. (2023). The application of chatbot as an L2 writing practice tool. *Language Learning & Technology, 27*(1), 1–19. https://doi.org/10125/73541

Lave, J., & Wenger, E. (1991). *Situated learning: Legitimate peripheral participation*. Cambridge University Press.

Lee, S. M. (2021). The effectiveness of machine translation in foreign language education: A systematic review and meta-analysis. *Computer Assisted Language Learning, 36*(1–2), 103–125. https://doi.org/10.1080/09588221.2021.1901745

Long, D., & Magerko, B. (2020). What is AI literacy? Competencies and design considerations. In *Proceedings of the 2020 CHI conference on human factors in computing systems* (pp. 1–16). Association for Computing Machinery. https://doi.org/10.1145/3313831.3376727

Oakley, G., & Pegrum, M. (2015). Engaging in networked learning: Innovating at the intersection of technology and pedagogy. *Education Research and Perspectives, 42*, 397–428. https://doi.org/10.70953/ERPv42.15012

Ohashi, L. (2016). Taking English outside of the classroom through social networking: Reflections on a two-year project. In S. Papadima-Sophocleous, L. Bradley & S. Thouësny (Eds), *CALL communities and culture – Short papers from EUROCALL 2016* (pp. 345–350). Research-publishing.net. https://doi.org/10.14705/rpnet.2016.eurocall2016.586

Ohashi, L. (2022). The use of machine translation in L2 education: Japanese university teachers' views and practices. In B. Arnbjörnsdóttir, B. Bédi, L. Bradley, K. Friðriksdóttir, H. Garðarsdóttir, S. Thouësny, & M. J. Whelpton (Eds), *Intelligent CALL, granular systems, and learner data: Short papers from EUROCALL 2022* (pp. 308–314). Research-publishing.net. https://doi.org/10.14705/rpnet.2022.61.1476

Ohashi, L. (2024). Machine translation in language education: A systematic review of open access articles. *Kenkyu Nenpou: The Annual Collection of Essays and Studies, 70*, 105–125. https://www.gakushuin.ac.jp/univ/let/top/publication/KE_70/KE_70_008.pdf

Ohashi, L., & Alm, A. (2023). ChatGPT and language learning: University educators' initial response. In B. Bédi, Y. Choubsaz, K. Friðriksdóttir, A. Gimeno-Sanz, S. Björg Vilhjálmsdóttir, & S. Zahova (Eds.), *CALL for all languages – EUROCALL 2023 short papers* (pp. 31–36). University of Iceland, Reykjavik. https://doi.org/10.4995/EuroCALL2023.2023.16917

Pham, T. T., Nguyen, L. A. D., Dang, H. M., & Le, T. T. P. (2024). Exploring tertiary Vietnamese EFL students' engagement in vocabulary learning through the use of an AI tool. *Proceedings of the AsiaCALL International Conference, 4*, 129–149. https://doi.org/10.54855/paic.23410

Schmidt-Fajlik, R. (2023). ChatGPT as a grammar checker for Japanese English language learners: A comparison with Grammarly and ProWritingAid. *AsiaCALL Online Journal, 14*(1), 105–119. https://doi.org/10.54855/acoj.231417

Stoll, L., & Louis, K. S. (2007). Professional learning communities: Elaborating new approaches. In L. Stoll & K. S. Louise (Eds.), *Professional learning communities: divergence, depth and dilemmas* (pp. 1–13). Open University Press.

TESOL International Association. (n.d.). *About TESOL*. Retrieved January 22, 2025, from https://www.tesol.org/about/

Tseng, W., & Warschauer, M. (2023). AI-writing tools in education: If you can't beat them, join them. *Journal of China Computer-Assisted Language Learning, 3*(2), 258–262. https://doi.org/10.1515/jccall-2023-0008

Üstünbaş, Ü. (2024). Hey, GPT, can we have a chat? A case study on EFL learners' AI speaking practice. *International Journal of Modern Education Studies, 8*(1), 91–107. https://doi.org/10.51383/ijonmes.2024.318

Wenger-Trayner, B. (2011). Slides: Levels of participation. *Wenger-Trayner*. https://www.wenger-trayner.com/slide-forms-of-participation/

Wenger-Trayner, E. & Wenger-Trayner, B (2015). Introduction to communities of practice: A brief overview of the concept and its uses. *Wenger-Trayner.* https://www.wenger-trayner.com/introduction-to-communities-of-practice/

Zonoubi, R., Rasekh, A. E., & Tavakoli, M. (2017). EFL teacher self-efficacy development in professional learning communities. *System, 66*, 1–12. https://doi.org/10.1016/j.system.2017.03.003

10
Critical TPACK as a foundation for teaching with AI

Jaeho Jeon

Seongyong Lee

> **Pre-reading questions:**
>
> 1) How does the ability of GenAI to generate human-like language affect your approaches to language teaching and assessment?
> 2) What challenges might arise from its presence or integration into language teaching, and what knowledge or competencies do you believe teachers need to navigate these challenges?

TPACK in the age of GenAI

Generative Artificial Intelligence (GenAI) is rapidly developing and permeating content generation in many areas of people's lives, including language teaching and learning practices (Jeon & Lee, 2023). In accordance with this technological change, there has been extensive discussion about how AI supports various areas of language education, including, but not limited to, writing (Guo et al., 2024), speaking (Moorhouse et al., 2024), reading (Lee et al., 2023), and assessment (Shin & Lee, 2023). However, as noted by Jeon et al. (2024), the use of AI, including GenAI, is not always beneficial for language learning. Specifically, Jeon et al. found that students' prolonged use of an AI language training app led them to view language as a fixed subject to master rather than a tool that could be flexibly used for communication. Bender et al. (2021) and Chomsky et al. (2021) also point out that GenAI is designed to produce what is statistically probable based on its training data, which can further facilitate language standardization. Collectively, research highlights the need for a balanced approach to integrating GenAI in language teaching, particularly one that considers both its benefits and constraints (e.g., Handley, 2024). In response to this need and given the difference between non-generative technologies and GenAI, we draw on the TPACK framework as a theoretical foundation to guide teachers' effective integration of GenAI and emphasize the importance of including critical thinking as an explicit dimension in TPACK exploration.

How teachers use technology for teaching should not simply be about knowing how to use technology itself. As noted by Mishra and Koehler (2006), teachers need not only to have technological knowledge but also know how to apply it to a specific content's instructional situation in a manner that is most appropriate. This is also echoed by Tseng (2018), who noted, "simply adding a new piece of technology to existing teaching procedures and structures does not necessarily lead to technology integration that enhances student learning" (p. 391), highlighting a limitation of many existing teacher technology training programs for professional development, which have generally focused only on technological skill development as a separate knowledge domain rather than in the context of pedagogical application.

In this context, the TPACK framework that Mishra and Koehler (2006) developed based on Shulman's (1986) PCK (Pedagogical Content Knowledge) framework was introduced, adding technology as a major component of the full spectrum of knowledge that teachers need to integrate technology effectively into teaching specific subject content. In the original TPACK framework, three main knowledge types are included (Bostancıoğlu & Handley, 2018; Mishra & Koehler, 2006): Technology Knowledge (TK), Pedagogy Knowledge (PK), and Content Knowledge (CK). TK refers to teachers' knowledge of how specific technologies operate and how to use them; PK refers to teachers' general knowledge of how learning takes place and commonly used approaches to teaching; CK refers to teachers' knowledge of subject matter. Mishra and Koehler argued that teachers need to be sufficiently knowledgeable about the overlap of the three types, emphasizing that their lack of either PK or CK would likely limit their instructional use of technology, whatever their level of technical expertise. In other words, what is more important than teachers simply having TK is learning and using TK in relation to the other two types of knowledge, that is, knowledge of how to use technology in a specific content's instructional situation (i.e., TPACK).

Since its introduction, the TPACK framework has been widely applied by many researchers, particularly in the field of Computer-Assisted Language Learning (CALL; e.g., Bostancıoğlu & Handley, 2018; Crosthwaite et al., 2021; Nami, 2022; Tseng, 2018; Tseng et al., 2022). The literature focusing on language teachers' practical use of TPACK in classroom settings has identified and focused on three dimensions of the framework: (1) the conceptual dimension, which addresses how each knowledge type is understood and interpreted by teachers in the context of language teaching (e.g., Liu et al., 2019); (2) the design dimension, which examines how the TPACK framework can help teachers create a technology-supported language teaching environment (e.g., Jeon et al., 2022); and (3) the application dimension, which considers how the TPACK framework helps teachers use existing technological materials to enrich language teaching practices (e.g., Crosthwaite et al., 2021; Tseng, 2018). These dimensions illustrate how the framework can be interpreted, applied, and utilized differently by language teachers as they integrate technology into their classrooms, creating a space for each teacher to use the framework in their own creative and effective manner.

When developing the TPACK framework, Mishra and Koehler (2006) acknowledged that the digital technologies prevalent in the 21st century were only beginning to emerge in Shulman's (1986) time and thus had not been accounted for in his PCK framework. However, given the accelerated development of digital technologies over the subsequent two decades, they have attracted extensive attention from TPACK researchers (e.g., Koehler & Mishra, 2009). Similarly, as GenAI becomes increasingly ubiquitous (Mishra et al., 2023), we need to reflect on how to integrate this fundamentally different technology into teaching. However, as will be detailed in the subsequent section, we believe that what distinguishes GenAI from earlier digital technologies demands another dimension in the use of TPACK for teaching, particularly language teaching. We therefore argue for the need to address critical thinking as an explicit, additional dimension of TPACK exploration, alongside the conceptual, design, and application dimensions.

In this chapter, based on the TPACK framework and its four dimensions for its exploration, we provide guidelines for integrating GenAI into language education. Given our focus on GenAI, we address only the technology-related components: TK, TPK, TCK, and TPACK (see Figure 1), rather than all seven components of the original framework.

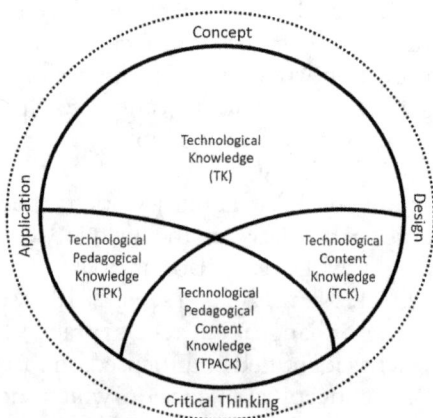

Figure 10.1 *TPACK for GenAI.*

In what follows, building on Mishra et al.'s (2023) conceptual work, we first explain why critical thinking needs to be included as a fundamental dimension of the framework.

Critical thinking as a fundamental dimension of GenAI integration in education

To understand why critical thinking needs to be an integral dimension of the TPACK framework when using GenAI, we believe that understanding the "value-laden" characteristic of GenAI, along with GenAI's "generative" and "social" characteristics (Mishra et al., 2023), is necessary. In a recent conceptual analysis, Mishra et al., one of TPACK's original creators, argued that GenAI's qualitatively different nature requires modifications to TPACK. They identify two key characteristics that distinguish GenAI from previous digital technologies: GenAI is "generative" and "social." By "generative," they referred to the technology's capability to produce original (but not always novel) content. For example, unlike a Google search, which leads users to existing pieces of information that they must then synthesize to produce new content, GenAI generates responses by combining data according to user input. If requested, some platforms, such as ChatGPT, can provide citations of original sources used for generation, but it is of note that they do not directly display original sources in their responses. By "social," they referred to the user's tendency to anthropomorphize AI and to consider GenAI's output as plausible human thought, given its credible interaction with a human in natural language. Research also supports Mishra et al.'s observation of its social nature, providing evidence that some users perceive AI as having human-like characteristics (Bender & Koller, 2020; Lee & Jeon, 2022; Xu et al., 2021).

Building on their characterization of GenAI as generative and social, we suggest a third characteristic: GenAI is inherently "value-laden". This characteristic has implications for education and necessitates the inclusion of critical thinking as a fundamental dimension of the TPACK framework. As the term itself implies, GenAI is designed to produce a response that is inevitably value-laden, which makes it important for students to be able to critically engage with the response. To further explain this, we must first examine how GenAI works.

While many GenAI models exist, with varying capabilities, we use ChatGPT as a representative example. Simply put, ChatGPT operates on statistical models. Chomsky et al. (2023) describe this operation by stating,

"… they [GenAI models] take huge amounts of data, search for patterns in it, and become increasingly proficient at generating statistically probable outputs – such as seemingly humanlike language and thought" (p. 2).

When prompted by user input, GenAI produces responses through a process that Mishra et al. (2023) characterize as "a concise and refined amalgamation of the information learned from those [training] texts, formulating responses based on its recollection and patterns interwoven within the training data …" (p. 3). The resulting content can be original or replicated from existing information, although its newness does not guarantee novelty.

The "generative" characteristic operates through algorithmic decisions that involve value-based choices and behaving similarly to a human social agent (Tanksley, 2024). This makes GenAI inherently value-laden, as it fabricates/creates content in ways that are not fully transparent to users but in ways that follow certain statistical logic set by its developers, and it is therefore exceptionally important for users to be critical of its output. When prompted, the system generates responses from a partial corpus of possible views typically favoring the most prevalent patterns in its training data.

The combination of the value-laden nature and the "social" characteristic of GenAI makes critical thinking even more essential. The conversational format in which these AI systems typically operate tends to make users experience the exchange as if they were interacting with someone (Lee & Jeon, 2024). In other words, to some extent, what GenAI generates by combining different pieces of information can be perceived as human-generated. In human-to-human discourse, participants generally attribute meaning to language based on the assumption that it was produced by someone with whom they share a common communicative intent (Bender et al., 2021). The social nature of GenAI, to which this assumption only seemingly applies, makes it tempting for users to accept what it produces at face value (Mishra et al., 2023). All of these factors make the explicit inclusion of critical thinking in TPACK exploration necessary.

Before examining how critical thinking interacts with TPACK components in language teaching, we need to understand both micro- and macro-level issues that affect teachers' TK of GenAI. With regard to micro issues, users should be aware of different sources of bias in natural language processing, such as types of data collected for training a model and how the data are labeled and annotated in the training process (Hovy & Prabhumoye, 2020). They should also understand how AI research and development is conceptualized so as to critically assess results (Navigli et al., 2023). Questions related to macro issues may include questioning who benefits the most and the least from GenAI, how the technology can be made broadly accessible worldwide, and how individual safety can be assured in the collection and management of private data (Bender et al., 2021). Taking such critical approaches to TK is needed to pave the way for responsible and effective integration of GenAI into education. These questions also serve as a starting point for teachers to delve deeper into TPACK for GenAI in language teaching.

TPACK for GenAI in language teaching

The TPACK framework highlights the pivotal role of teachers in using technology when selecting and teaching the content knowledge of a given domain in a manner that is effective for learners (Mishra and Koehler, 2006). Similarly, the transformative power of GenAI forces educators to rethink core educational issues, including what to teach (i.e., content) and how to teach (i.e., pedagogy). Accordingly, language educators need to consider the technological features of GenAI as well as the significance of these features in configuring language pedagogy and language content when they plan to integrate GenAI into their classrooms. To be more specific, the value-laden aspect of GenAI, together with the generative and social characteristics, necessitates that language teachers reconsider how the critical dimension of TK affects decisions regarding how language practice (CK) is represented and how language pedagogy (PK) is developed and implemented.

In GenAI-powered language education, one question related to TCK can be: "How does the use of GenAI affect the approach to and our understanding of language practice?" The field broadly encompasses speaking, writing, listening, and reading for different purposes across various communicative contexts of language use, which were considered uniquely human before the advent of advanced versions of GenAI capable of natural human-machine interaction. In this context, it is important to pose critical questions about how GenAI affects our understanding of the productive and receptive nature of human language practice. Taking language production as an example, the traditional standards of organization and accuracy of human language production might play a diminished role in the age of GenAI, as these standards are easily achievable with its use. Similarly, as far as language reception is concerned, basic comprehension of a given text or information will still be as important, but critical engagement with its value-laden characteristic–such as detecting possible biases in texts and information–might also be important content knowledge to learn, given that GenAI is designed in such a way that it might produce bias.

In addition, questions need to be posed regarding its value-laden aspect and its influence on language practice. As mentioned, while the generative nature of GenAI's language abilities will enable us to have some qualities of language, such as organization and accuracy, more easily, areas that cannot be covered by this nature, such as experimentation, criticality, and creativity in language as a fluid process rather than a standardized prescription, will emerge as more important language-related content to learn as well (Lee et al., 2024; Stornaiuolo et al., 2024).

On a similar note, the unique characteristics of GenAI also affect how language pedagogy is understood and implemented (TPK), which leads us to ask, "How does the use of GenAI affect language teaching pedagogy?" Given that GenAI, such as ChatGPT, can generate almost any content that users require in a conversational format, it can simultaneously serve many of the roles typically expected of human language teachers. For example, Jeon and Lee (2023) found that ChatGPT can serve as an interlocutor, content provider, teaching assistant, and evaluator, roles typically assumed by human teachers, but in a manner that supplements rather than replaces them. Specifically, it was reported that language teachers designed conversational activities in which ChatGPT played the role of one of the interlocutors alongside other human peers, produced and customized language materials using the technology, collaborated with it to create a more active learning environment, and first asked it to evaluate the student assignment before providing their own more in-depth assessment of the assignment.

Similarly, Mishra et al. (2023) also envisioned a new TPK scenario taking the use of GenAI for a writing lesson as an example and demonstrated how the technology can facilitate deep, meta-level learning:

> "In a writing assignment the teacher may ask a student to use GenAI to create a first draft [and] then annotate the draft to identify the strengths and weaknesses of GenAI's response This allows learners to think more about the deeper ideas of composition, meaning-making, rhetoric, argumentation, and flow" (p. 8).

How the use of GenAI affects our understanding of language pedagogy is an important consideration that warrants continued investigation. However, such inquiry must not omit reflection on its value-laden aspect and how it affects language pedagogy. In other words, it is important for teachers to be aware that, as another agent in the classroom, GenAI is different from humans in that it is designed to operate within the realm of statistical probability, following a certain statistical logic. Uncritically endorsing the probability outcomes of GenAI in teaching practices may lead to the standardization of what is already prevalent in society, marginalizing minority voices, particularly those unrepresented in the training data (Jeon et al., 2024).

GenAI's human-like capabilities also influence how students' language performance should be assessed. Plagiarism has always been a concern for educators, but ChatGPT's increasing prevalence has greatly complicated the issue. For fair assessment, students now have additional responsibilities, such as ensuring that their content is their own rather than AI-generated and proving that their content is original. Moreover, the fact that GenAI follows statistical standards makes it critical to pose questions regarding its use in assessment. Educators need to consider whether using foundational models that operate in the realm of probability can guarantee a fair assessment of linguistically diverse students, as most GenAI developers who work in commercial sectors might not prioritize the public good and education as much as they prioritize profit.

In sum, critical understandings of TPK and TCK in relation to GenAI's value-laden aspect demonstrate the need for a modified conceptualization and exploration of TPACK suitable for the age of GenAI. Thus, we introduced critical thinking as an explicit dimension to help teachers implement it more effectively in the classroom. As a generic framework, TPACK is a theoretical foundation designed to help teachers come up with their own creative and effective technology integration solutions for their teaching practices (Mishra & Koehler, 2006). Therefore, it is up to individual teachers to decide how to apply TPACK to meet the unique needs of their learners in their educational contexts.

However, to provide a space where language teachers can gain an initial understanding of how to apply TPACK when using GenAI and navigate their own future endeavors, in what follows, we explain each component of the TPACK framework in terms of four complementary dimensions, of which three (i.e., concept, design, and application) are established in the existing TPACK literature (e.g., Crosthwaite et al., 2021; Jeon et al., 2023; Nami, 2022), and the fourth (i.e., critical thinking) is newly added as another important dimension of the framework in the age of GenAI.

Concept, design, application, and critical thinking in TPACK for GenAI

As mentioned in the section "TPACK in the age of GenAI," CALL researchers have focused so far on three dimensions of TPACK: concept, design, and application. Collectively, these dimensions indicate how the framework can be interpreted and utilized differently by language teachers when they aim to integrate technology into their classrooms. However, compared to previous digital technologies, GenAI is not only generative and social (Mishra et al., 2023) but also value-laden, as it performs algorithmic value selections to produce responses. Teachers, therefore, need a deep understanding of how these technical characteristics influence the TPACK components for their instructional planning.

By focusing on the four interpretive dimensions–concept, design, application, and critical thinking–we distinguish and elaborate on each component of the TPACK framework (i.e., TK, TPK, TCK, and TPACK) so that individual teachers can creatively and effectively apply the framework when designing GenAI-assisted language classrooms in their unique teaching environments (Mishra & Koehler, 2006). We provide these examples merely for illustrative purposes, along with descriptions of the four dimensions of the TPACK framework, to inspire each language teacher's creative application along with new developments in GenAI. Table 1 summarizes how each TPACK component functions within each of the four dimensions in the context of language teaching involving GenAI (Bostancıoğlu & Handley, 2018; Islam & Mishra, 2024).

Table 10.1 *TPACK for GenAI in language teaching*

Dimension	TK	TCK	TPK	TPACK
Concept	Understanding how GenAI operates.	Understanding how GenAI transforms language content and practice.	Understanding how GenAI affects language teaching methods and assessment.	Understanding how to integrate GenAI's capabilities with language teaching methods to enhance learning outcomes.
Design	Designing effective prompts and customized GenAI systems.	Designing effective prompts and customized GenAI systems to support language practice.	Designing effective GenAI-powered language learning experiences.	Designing comprehensive GenAI-powered language learning experiences that integrate learning goals, pedagogical approaches, and technological affordances.
Application	Selecting and implementing appropriate GenAI applications for specific tasks.	Selecting and implementing appropriate GenAI applications for language content and practice.	Selecting and implementing appropriate GenAI applications to support language teaching methods and assessment.	Selecting and implementing GenAI applications that create optimal conditions for language learning through the integration of content, pedagogy, and technology.
Critical thinking	Understanding the value-laden aspect of how GenAI produces biases.	Analyzing how GenAI's biases and limitations affect language content representation and authenticity.	Evaluating how GenAI's value-laden nature influences teaching methods and assessment validity.	Developing critical awareness of GenAI's impacts on language content, pedagogy, and learning to make informed decisions about technology integration.

Conceptual dimensions involve developing a fundamental, cognitive understanding of each knowledge domain. For example, it includes understanding how GenAI works and how it influences pedagogical performance as well as language practices in a language teaching context. This conceptual foundation underpins the other dimensions of TPACK, that is, design, application, and critical thinking, by providing the essential knowledge base required for more active and informed instructional knowing.

Design dimensions include teachers' knowledge about the design requirements of GenAI, such as how to create effective prompts (Jeon & Lee, 2023; Sahoo et al., 2024) and how to develop personalized AI systems to facilitate the language teaching process. Note that while design knowledge itself (e.g., effective prompt design and personalized AI development) falls under TK, the pedagogical application of that knowledge (e.g., how to apply prompt engineering skills effectively to language practice for teaching purposes) belongs to TPACK.

For example, teachers need to learn how to use and adapt existing prompt engineering frameworks, such as the CO-STAR framework (AI Advisory Boards, 2024), for language teaching and learning purposes. That is, the focus of TPACK should be on experimenting with how this type of framework can be adapted to support language practice and exploring how it can be applied in language teaching. Meanwhile, some platforms now allow teachers to use natural language (without advanced coding skills) to design customized AI chatbots. For example, OpenAI has recently released MyGPTs, a platform in which teachers can create customized chatbots using natural language to support their teaching. These platforms help bridge the gap between the conceptual understanding of GenAI and the design dimensions of the TPACK framework, enabling teachers to focus on the overlap of the three components rather than excessively emphasizing technical skills (e.g., coding skills).

Application dimensions relate to leveraging existing GenAI-powered applications to maximize GenAI's educational benefits for language teaching. For example, teachers need to start by learning various characteristics of GenAI technologies, such as image, text, video, sound generation, and each application's particular characteristics. This knowledge should be explored in close relation to language practice and teaching purposes. To illustrate, when teachers decide to use text-based GenAI, they need to consider the types of text they aim to teach for their teaching purposes and choose an appropriate application. For example, if creative writing is the aim of language teaching, hallucination effects (i.e., AI-generated content that appears coherent but is not necessarily factual) might be effective in order to leverage GenAI to maximize students' creativity (Mishra et al., 2023). For this purpose, teachers can consider platforms that leverage this effect and encourage users to use GenAI's propensity to hallucinate to produce creative prompts and fictional stories (e.g., https://character.ai/; see Stornaiuolo et al., 2024 for an application example). Meanwhile, if the accuracy of text needs to be prioritized, AI platforms that are equipped with fact-checking and thus produce content based on actual citations can be employed (e.g., https://consensus.app/search/) to help students focus on the factuality of the text.

Finally, it is critical to understand how the technological aspects of GenAI produce bias and perpetuate existing prejudices by under-representing minority voices (Benjamin, 2021; Tanksley, 2024). The fact that GenAI operates within the realm of statistical probability (Bender et al., 2021; Payne et al., 2024) must be considered with regard to the use of its generated content in language classes powered by GenAI. As GenAI operates within the boundaries of standardization (Bender et al., 2021), students' acceptance of GenAI-produced content at face value as agreed-upon human thought will contribute to the perpetuation of prevalent trends in society at the expense of diverse views. This narrowing of perspectives stifles exposure to the full variety of voices in language practice, tasks, and pedagogy (Lee et al., 2024). These limitations indicate the need for critical thinking as a fundamental aspect of TPACK for GenAI. It is important for teachers to have knowledge of how AI produces bias, at least to the extent that they recognize its impact on language practice used for teaching purposes.

Conclusion

GenAI has already become a reality in society and continues to be developed with significant investments from both the private and public sectors. In this rapidly changing environment, how this widely applicable and increasingly ubiquitous technology can be integrated into language education as a teaching tool remains an open question, one that calls for creative solutions from diverse perspectives. In response to this call, we have suggested that such inquiries begin with an accurate understanding of what GenAI is, alongside a solid educational theoretical foundation. Specifically, this chapter used TPACK as a theoretical foundation and newly introduced the value-laden characteristics of GenAI, while also describing its generative and social aspects (Mishra et al., 2023). Drawing on these characteristics, we emphasized the importance of critical thinking when integrating GenAI into language teaching, identifying it as one of the four essential dimensions to consider: concept, design, application, and critical thinking.

It must be acknowledged that GenAI may assume and replace some of the responsibilities teachers have traditionally carried out. However, as we have demonstrated in this chapter, its introduction also creates a new level of responsibility for teachers to ensure that GenAI is used in an effective and responsible manner. Among these new responsibilities, as we argued, the most salient is the inclusion of critical thinking as a foundational dimension for integrating GenAI into language teaching. We discussed that this necessity arises from the value-laden nature of GenAI, which significantly differentiates it from non-generative technologies. It is our hope that the generic nature of "TPACK for GenAI" we propose provides guidelines that can lead individual teachers to navigate their own creative and effective TPACK exploration that can support their teaching practices. We also hope that this chapter serves as an initial reference, supporting the idea that, as agents in their classrooms, teachers can find strategic ways to integrate technology into their instruction so as to maximize the values pursued by both individuals and society.

> **Post-reading questions:**
>
> 1) What are the differences between the original TPACK and critical TPACK? Explain why critical thinking needs to be considered an indispensable aspect of TPACK in the age of GenAI.
> 2) Using a language lesson that you recently taught and considering the components and aspects of TPACK for GenAI, elaborate on how GenAI can be integrated into the lesson.

Further reading

1. For a theoretical understanding of TPACK: Mishra & Koehler (2006). https://doi.org/10.1111/j.1467-9620.2006.0068
2. For theoretical discussion on TPACK in the age of GenAI: Mishra et al. (2023). https://doi.org/10.1080/21532974.2023.2247480
3. For an elaborated understanding of teacher roles when teaching with ChatGPT: Jeon & Lee (2023). https://link.springer.com/article/10.1007/s10639-023-11834-1
4. For detailed information about prompt engineering: Sahoo et al. (2024). https://arxiv.org/html/2402.07927v1

References

AI Advisory Boards (2024, January 30). *CO-STAR Framework*. https://aiadvisoryboards.wordpress.com/2024/01/30/co-star-framework/

Bender, E. M., & Koller, A. (2020). Climbing towards NLU: On meaning, form, and understanding in the age of data. *In Proceedings of the 58th Annual Meeting of the Association for Computational Linguistics*, 5185-5198.

Bender, E. M., Gebru, T., McMillan-Major, A., & Shmitchell, S. (2021). On the dangers of stochastic parrots: Can language models be too big? *Proceedings of the 2021 ACM Conference on Fairness, Accountability, and Transparency, Canada* (pp. 610–623). ACM.

Benjamin, R. (2021). *Race after technology*. Polity Press.

Bostancıoglu, A., & Handley, Z. (2018). Developing and validating a questionnaire for evaluating the EFL 'Total PACKage': Technological Pedagogical Content Knowledge (TPACK) for English as a Foreign Language (EFL). *Computer Assisted Language Learning, 31*(5-6), 572–598.

Chomsky, N., Roberts, I., & Watumull, J. (2023, March 8). The false promise of ChatGPT. *The New York Times*. https://www.nytimes.com/2023/03/08/opinion/noam-chomsky-chatgpt-ai.html

Crosthwaite, P., Luciana, & Wijaya, D. (2021). Exploring language teachers' lesson planning for corpus-based language teaching: A focus on developing TPACK for corpora and DDL. *Computer Assisted Language Learning*. Advance online publication. https://doi.org/10.1080/09588221.2021.1995001

Guo, K., Li, Y., Li, Y., & Chu, S. K. W. (2024). Understanding EFL students' chatbot-assisted argumentative writing: An activity theory perspective. *Education and Information Technologies, 29*(1), 1–20.

Handley, Z. L. (2024). Has artificial intelligence rendered language teaching obsolete? *The Modern Language Journal, 108*(2), 548–555. https://doi.org/10.1111/modl.12929

Hovy, D., & Prabhumoye, S. (2021). Five sources of bias in natural language processing. *Language and Linguistics compass, 15*(8), e12432.

Islam, R., & Mishra, P. (2024, March). The design of a TPACK survey for Gen AI: A preliminary study. In *Society for Information Technology & Teacher Education International Conference* (pp. 2415–2420). Association for the Advancement of Computing in Education (AACE).

Jeon, J., & Lee, S. (2023). Large language models in education: A focus on the complementary relationship between human teachers and ChatGPT. *Education and Information Technologies, 28*(12), 15873–15892.

Jeon, J., & Lee, S. (2024). Can learners benefit from chatbots instead of humans? A systematic review of human-chatbot comparison research in language education. *Education and Information Technologies*. Advance online publication. https://doi.org/10.1007/s10639-024-12725-9

Jeon, J., Lee, S., & Choe, H. (2022). Enhancing EFL pre-service teachers' affordance noticing and utilizing with the Synthesis of Qualitative Evidence strategies: An exploratory study of a customizable virtual environment platform. *Computers & Education, 190*, Article 104620.

Koehler, M., & Mishra, P. (2009). What is technological pedagogical content knowledge (TPACK)? *Contemporary issues in technology and teacher education, 9*(1), 60–70.

Lee, J. H., Shin, D., & Noh, W. (2023). Artificial intelligence-based content generator technology for young English-as-a-foreign-language learners' reading enjoyment. *RELC Journal, 54*(2), 508–516.

Lee, S., & Jeon, J. (2024). Visualizing a disembodied agent: Young EFL learners' perceptions of voice-controlled conversational agents as language partners. *Computer Assisted Language Learning, 37*(5-6), 1048–1073.

Lee, S., Jeon, J., & Choe, H. (2024). Enhancing pre-service teachers' global Englishes awareness with technology: A focus on AI chatbots in 3D metaverse environments. *TESOL Quarterly*. Advance online publication. https://doi.org/10.1002/tesq.3300

Liu, H. X., Wang, L. N., & Koehler, M. J. (2019). Exploring the intention-behavior gap in the technology acceptance model: A mixed-methods study in the context of foreign- language teaching in China. *British Journal of Educational Technology, 50*(5), 2536–2556.

Mishra, P., & Koehler, M. J. (2006). Technological pedagogical content knowledge: A framework for teacher knowledge. *Teachers College Record, 108*(6), 1017–1054.

Mishra, P., Warr, M., & Islam, R. (2023). TPACK in the age of ChatGPT and generative AI. *Journal of Digital Learning in Teacher Education, 39*(4), 235–251.

Moorhouse, B. L. (2024). Generative artificial intelligence and ELT. *ELT Journal, 78*(4), 378–392.

Nami, F. (2022). Developing in-service teachers' pedagogical knowledge of CALL through project-oriented tasks: The case of an online professional development course. *ReCALL, 34*(1), 110–125. https://doi.org/10.1017/S0958344021000148

Navigli, R., Conia, S., & Ross, B. (2023). Biases in large language models: origins, inventory, and discussion. *ACM Journal of Data and Information Quality, 15*(2), 1–21.

OpenAI. (2023, December 15). *Introducing GPTs*. OpenAI. https://openai.com/blog/introducing-gpts

Payne, A. L., Austin, T., & Clemons, A. M. (2024). Beyond the front yard: The dehumanizing message of accent-altering technology. *Applied Linguistics, 45*(3), 553–560.

Shin, D., & Lee, J. H. (2023). Can ChatGPT make reading comprehension testing items on par with human experts? *Language Learning & Technology, 27*(3), 27–40. https://hdl.handle.net/10125/73530

Shulman, L. (1986). Those who understand: Knowledge growth in teaching. *Educational Researcher, 15*(2), 4–14.

Stornaiuolo, A., Higgs, J., Nichols, T. P., Leblanc, R. J., & de Roock, R. S. (2024). The platformization of writing instruction: considering educational equity in new learning ecologies. *Review of Research in Education, 47*(1), 311–359.

Tanksley, T. C. (2024). "We're changing the system with this one": Black students using critical race algorithmic literacies to subvert and survive AI-mediated racism in school. *English Teaching: Practice & Critique, 23*(1), 36–56.

Tseng, J. J. (2018). Exploring TPACK-SLA interface: Insights from the computer-enhanced classroom. *Computer Assisted Language Learning, 31*(4), 390–412. https://doi.org/10.1080/09588221.2017.1412324

Tseng, J. J., Chai, C. S., Tan, L., & Park, M. (2022). A critical review of research on technological pedagogical and content knowledge (TPACK) in language teaching. *Computer Assisted Language Learning, 35*(4), 948–971.

11
Teacher's practical pedagogical knowledge

Zoe Handley

> **Pre-reading questions:**
>
> This chapter explores English for Academic Purposes (EAP) tutors' understanding of generative Artificial Intelligence (AI), and beliefs and practices about its use for learning, teaching, and assessment through an interview study. Before reading the chapter, it would be helpful to reflect on your own position concerning the main questions that were posed in the interviews, namely:
>
> 1) How would you explain what generative AI is?
> 2) What is the role of generative AI in education?
> 3) How did you develop your understanding of generative AI and its role in education?

Introduction

Since its release in November 2022, ChatGPT has generated considerable debate in higher education institutions. Enabling users to generate texts, generative AI, of which ChatGPT is an example, has reinvigorated discussions about academic integrity and the potential for students, and international students in particular, to cheat by using

ChatGPT to generate essays and other assessments. Even before Scarfe et al. (2024) demonstrated that AI-generated essays are not detectable and may achieve higher grades than student-produced essays, Higher Education (HE) institutions in the UK were deliberating and developing policies on the acceptable use of these tools (Russell Group, 2023). While this has resulted in a consensus on some principles among leading research institutions in the UK (Russell Group, 2023), there remains considerable variation across and within institutions, with some institutions and departments focusing on developing students' AI literacy and associated academic skills, while others are implementing outright bans or placing considerable restrictions on the use of generative AI (Young et al., 2024).

Guided by the following research questions, this chapter explores what English for Academic Practice (EAP) tutors working with international students for whom English is not their first language (L1) know about these technologies, how they think these technologies might be used to support learning and teaching, and what they think the implications are for assessment.

1. How do EAP tutors working in HE in the UK conceive of (generative) AI?
2. What are EAP tutors' beliefs and practices about (generative) AI and teaching?
3. What are EAP tutors' beliefs and practices about (generative) AI and assessment?
4. How are EAP tutors developing their practical pedagogical knowledge for the use of (generative) AI?

(Generative) AI in HE

To contextualize the study, this section reviews the current debate surrounding AI in HE with a focus on the UK context. Surveys of the general public conducted before the release of ChatGPT suggest that most knew very little about AI and that their conceptions were limited to "*plausible* basic understandings" (Selwyn et al., 2021, p. 1645), that is definitions "involving computers (or other artefacts) engaging in cognitive feats (such as decision-making, thinking or learning)" (Selwyn et al., 2021, p. 1647) that demonstrate an awareness of the general purpose of AI, namely to enable computers to carry out tasks that normally require human intelligence. It is therefore critical to clarify what we understand by AI, and generative AI more specifically, in this study. This discussion will also provide a benchmark against which to evaluate the conceptions of AI reported by the EAP tutors.

AI

For most tutors in HE, AI has become synonymous with generative AI, a technology that allows users to generate texts from a prompt that outlines the scope of the text to be produced. AI is, however, a much broader concept that has been around since the 1950s when researchers began working on the development of "thinking machines" (Turing, 1950). AI refers to a range of technologies that enable computers to perceive, learn, abstract, and reason (Launchbury, 2017) including speech and language technologies such as generative AI, chatbots, and machine translation.

Large Language Models (LLM) have also become synonymous with AI. LLMs are statistical models of the patterns and connections between the words of a language which enable speech and language technologies to recognize and produce human language. These general purpose or foundational models are developed by training a complex statistical model referred to as an Artificial Neural Network (ANN) on a large corpus of un-tagged text (Kolides et al., 2023; Rodman, 1999). As such, as Kern (2024) highlights, generative AI and other speech and language technologies "do[n't] really "know" anything about language--or the world--rather, it predicts sequences of characters (and then larger chunks of language) based on their statistical likelihood of occurrence within the corpora on which it has been trained" (p. 519).

AI and assessment

According to an article recently 'co-authored'[3] with ChatGPT itself, the debate surrounding the impact of AI on HE has tended to focus on the possibility that students might use it to generate assignments (Cotton et al., 2024; see also Budhathoki et al., 2024, Perkins, 2023, and The Russell Group, 2023). Several studies validate concerns about cheating. While students in the UK are anxious about using AI due to their awareness of policies on academic misconduct, the ease with which they could use the technology to complete their assignments appears to outweigh those concerns (Budhathoki et al., 2024). Moreover, several studies have demonstrated that students could use these tools to generate essays better than they could produce themselves and that tutors are unable to distinguish such automatically generated essays from student-produced essays (Klyshbekova & Abbott, 2024; Scarfe et al., 2024). Many universities have therefore sought to put in place policies on the use of these technologies in assessments. A survey of

---

[3] Although Cotton et al. (2024) do not actually credit ChatGPT for a number of reasons including, in particular, the fact that it cannot take responsibility for the article, they explain how the article was generated using the tool.

university websites in the UK reveals that while some institutions have attempted to ban AI completely, others have developed more nuanced policies that attempt to explicate how generative AI and other AI tools such as paraphrasers and machine translation may be used, and others are actively supporting students to develop the skills to use these tools to support their academic studies and assignment writing.

Where policies are in place, these tend to have developed from policies about plagiarism, "misrepresenting the effort that has been carried out by the author of a written document" (Perkins et al., 2019, p. 5), and the use of proofreaders. AI use has been conceptualized as "second generation" plagiarism (Malesky et al., 2016) because while the text has not been copied directly from a published text, it has been automatically generated from a body of previous texts. The debate has therefore shifted from plagiarism to authorship (see for example Anson, 2022), that is "who produced or wrote the assessment" (Gribble & Waldrop, 2024, p. 268).

Many tutors believe that they can identify AI-generated assignments. Some corpus research suggests that AI-generated essays differ from student-authored essays along several linguistic dimensions, including lexical density and syntactic complexity (Nkhobo & Chaka, 2023). It is, however, widely acknowledged that it is difficult to prove students have used AI tools, and, as such, policies are difficult to enforce (Perkins, 2023). Another predominant theme of discussion has therefore been AI-proofing assessment by modifying or completely changing assessment formats (Perkins, 2023; Cotton et al., 2024).

EAP tutors play a significant role in the implementation of policies in HE institutions with high numbers of international students. This study therefore sought to understand EAP tutors' knowledge, beliefs, and practices about the use of AI in assessment and teaching.

Method

To investigate EAP tutors' practical pedagogical knowledge for AI in assessment and teaching, EAP tutors currently working in universities in the UK and partner institutions offering pre-sessionals were invited to participate in a one-hour semi-structured interview. Ethical approval was obtained from the researcher's departmental ethics committee. All tutors were given a £5 Amazon voucher as compensation for their time.

Eleven EAP tutors (nine male, two female) participated in the interviews. Some were employed to run pre-sessionals within universities or partner institutions, others were employed to run in-sessionals, and others as personal tutors. Five of the tutors reported completing a master's and PhD programme in applied linguistics. As such the participants demonstrated strong pedagogical and theoretical knowledge, often citing specific theories in applied linguistics and learning and development more broadly. One tutor (Participant 22) also had experience as a learning technologist, and another was developing his own consultancy in this area (Participant 21). All tutors reported adopting student-centred and communicative approaches focused on academic skills development including speaking as well as writing (see Table 1 for a summary of the key characteristics of the participating EAP tutors. Note: CELTA refers to the Certificate in Teaching English to Speakers of Other Languages issued by Cambridge English).

The semi-structured interviews, which were carried out online during April and May 2024, explored tutors' understanding of AI as well as their knowledge, beliefs and practices about teaching and assessment (see Table 2). Reflecting Borg's (2003) model of teacher cognition for language teaching and insights from Attia (2011) into teacher cognition for CALL, tutors were also asked about their language teaching background, any training they had received in the use of AI, and any personal use of the technology. The interviews which took place on zoom, lasted around forty-five minutes each and were recorded and transcribed verbatim.

Having transcribed the data, they were coded inductively following Braun and Clarke's (2006) approach to thematic analysis. Themes (axial coding) were then identified using the 'one sheet of paper' (OSOP) technique (Ziebland & McPherson, 2006), before reviewing and naming them. OSOP is a mind-mapping approach to qualitative data analysis in which all codes related to a specific topic are organised on a single sheet of paper with a view to facilitating the identification of patterns, connections and common themes in the data.

Table 11.1 *Key characteristics of the sample of participating EAP tutors*

Participant	Age	Gender	Years Teaching	CELTA	Level of Education	Role
6	55–64	Male	20+	Yes		Pre-sessional
17	35–44	Male	6–10			In-sessional
18	35–44	Male	6–10	Yes		In-sessional
20	55–64	Female	16–20		PhD	Pre-sessional
21	45–54	Male	16–20			Personal tutor
22	45–54	Male	20+		PhD	
23	45–54	Male	20+	Yes	PhD	
29	45–54	Male	20+		PhD	In-sessional
80	35–44	Male	16–20		PhD	Pre-sessional
86	35–44	Male	20+			Pre-sessional
98	55–64	Female	20+			Pre-sessional

Note: Where cells are left blank, this information was not provided.

Table 11.2 *Interview schedule*

Theme	Interview questions
Warm-up and background information	Could you tell me a little about yourself and your experience of English language teaching?
Conceptions and impact of AI	Could you tell me what AI means to you. What is it? What are the implications for your profession? For language learning? For language teaching?
Use of generative AI and related tools	Do you use it for teaching? How? Why? How successful are these activities? How do you know?
	Repeated for: Generative AI, text generation, text summarisation, paraphrasing, machine translation, and spelling and grammar checking.
AI and assessment	Should students be permitted to use AI in their assessments? Why? / Why not? Are there any circumstances when you think students should be able to use AI tools?
Student use of AI	What do you think AI means to your students? How are they using it?
Institutional context	What is your institution's policy on AI? Does your institution provide access to any AI tools?
Training related to AI	Have you received any training in AI?
Personal use of AI	Have you used AI for the purposes of (language) learning? Do you use AI outside your teaching in your wider personal life?

Findings

This section summarises the main themes the tutors raised about the use of AI in assessment and for teaching and learning.

Engagement with AI: From colleagues with their "head in the sand" to "tech bros"

Most of the EAP tutors in this study were male and had advanced degrees in applied linguistics (see Table 1 above). They reported a range of attitudes towards AI among their colleagues, from colleagues who "stick their head in the sand" (Participant 6) and see it as a threat to their jobs (Participant 20), through colleagues who fear they might be "losing something because the tool's doing it for [them]" (Participant 18), to "tech bro[s]" (Participant 22) who believe that AI marks a "fundamental shift" (Participant 22) in practices in the field. Most of the participants were, however, inherently "curious" (Participant 6) about the technology. As well as attending webinars by "gurus" on the topic, tutors had often spent a considerable amount of time exploring the capabilities of different tools for themselves.

Conceptions of AI: From ChatGPT and "robot brain[s]" to "self-trained algorithms"

Despite the interest the EAP tutors showed for AI, they tended to conceive of AI in terms of specific tools and functions, with ChatGPT and other examples of generative AI (i.e. Microsoft Copilot and Google Gemini) the most oft-cited, and machine translation (i.e. Google Translate and DeepL) a close second. Some tutors were, however, aware of a wider range of tools and applications of AI, with some even attempting to create chatbots, software applications that can converse with users in natural language, using ChatGPT. Prompts, natural language descriptions of the task to be performed or the desired output (Nazary et al., 2023), were widely recognized as a key feature of interacting with generative AI which some believed might be considered a new genre of writing (Ranade et al., 2024):

> *we've got a particular type of language that we use for prompts so you often start prompt with you are a what you say you assign a role to the large language model ... and then you add context and you can work with these sort of syntactic frameworks to slot in lexis (Participant 80)*

While some tutors also mentioned more technical terms associated with generative AI such as Large Language Models (LLMs), few attempted to define AI. Where some equated LLMs with a "robot brain" (Participant 21), others were able to provide more detailed explanations that demonstrated an understanding of how the technology works and the difference between different generations of AI, namely human-programmed intelligence versus machine learning (Scarfe et al., 2024):

> *I think it's a concept which originally was almost designed to mimic or replicate intelligence and I think over time maybe it's becoming accepted that that's not what it's trying to do I think there's more understanding it's very much about data processing huge amounts of data processing beyond possibly what you can really easily comprehend (Participant 18)*

In other words, most of the tutors' understandings were limited to plausible basic understandings of AI (Selwyn, 2021).

Quality of AI generated texts: "dumbed down" texts "which could get a passing grade"

In terms of the quality produced by generative AI and machine translation tools, many expressed amazement reporting that they believed it could produce better texts than the students themselves and "could get a passing grade at master's" (Participant 17). Limits on the quality of the output produced by generative AI with respect to writing academic assignments were, however, also noted including its capacity to "hallucinate", i.e. fabricate, and the fact that it is not able to "write something evaluative" and engage in "higher order thinking" (Participant 20).

Similarly, it was noted that while machine translation had improved significantly in recent years to the extent that it is much less noticeable when machine translation has been used to draft a text, automatically translated texts were perceived to be "dumbed down" and "have a much simpler level of English than the original" (Participant 6), lack nuance and as such would lead to "very superficial understanding" (Participant 17) if students rely on them too heavily.

Impact of AI: A "radical change" with assessment "blocking the door" to pedagogical change

Despite these limitations, machine translation was perceived to be having as much, if not more, impact on HE, with students openly using a combination of automatic speech recognition, i.e. speech-to-text conversion, and machine translation to support their engagement in lectures:

> they're starting to use translation apps in conversation and seminars so they've got a device which is translating things in real time they also seem to be using a lot better tech to help them with the writing and with their translation so it's almost as if the actual ChatGPT functions have receded into the background slightly so translation is in the foreground but AI ChatGPT is slightly kind of overshadowed by all of that (Participant 21)

While some EAP tutors believed that AI could provide a "way into the reading" for students who were struggling via automatically generated summaries (Participant 18) and taking on the role of "a sort of personal tutor" (Participant 17), most perceived machine translation to pose "just as much a threat as generative AI" (Participant 29). Coupled with the possibilities generative AI offers to produce assessments, it was felt that machine translation would lead to a "radical change"

(Participant 98) in EAP teaching practices. Assessment was, however, viewed as a "massive elephant ... blocking the door" (Participant 22) to using AI to support teaching and learning.

Due to the impact of AI on written assessments, the development and clarification of assessment policy was seen as a priority. It was, however, clear from the EAP tutors' different views that generative AI and machine translation raise some fundamental questions about what it means to study for a degree in the UK that need to be addressed before a consensus on assessment policy can be achieved. For example, while some tutors were of the view that it was a "tacit assumption that if you've come and done a master's degree in the UK then you'll come back with a reasonable level of spoken English ability" (Participant 17), others felt that "we shouldn't really be penalizing that [English] anyway" (Participant 29). Still others recognized that students "are going to be using it in their real life" (Participant 18), and, as such, the use of AI tools should not be prohibited during their studies.

Assessment policies: Their "own work" that "demonstrate[s] their knowledge or abilities"

Reflecting the acknowledgement that students will have access to these technologies when they graduate, policies have "gone from no use of generative AI to no unauthorised use of generative AI" (Participant 29). With respect to authorised use, the concept of authorship tended to guide policies, with authorship typically defined as the students' "own work" (Participant 80) that "demonstrate[s] their knowledge or abilities" (Participant 86). Reflecting the debate about what it means to graduate from a UK HE institution discussed above, authorship was associated with ownership of the ideas and to a lesser extent the language:

> *so in the end she had an essay which I think was about forty percent ChatGPT's language and then ... about twenty percent er refined so like kind of paraphrasing what ChatGPT had said and making it fit and it was about forty percent her own because ... she had to introduce it she had to conclude it properly so she still owned quite a lot of the language she owned all of the ideas in it and she still retained control of what was in the essay (Participant 29)*

Authoring texts: From "gather[ing] and summaris[ing] texts" through reading and writing to proofreading

Concerning academic reading and writing, the EAP tutors demonstrated an awareness of a wide range of different ways in which AI tools might be used to support assignment preparation, from facilitating the identification of literature that relates to the topic of their assignment, through scaffolding reading via interaction with a chatbot and automatically generating summaries of articles, to proofreading the final text (see Table 3). The EAP tutors in this study tended to agree that it was acceptable to use these tools to support some of the earlier and later stages of the writing process, namely brainstorming and proofreading, but not to generate text for inclusion in their assignment.

Concerning proofreading, as noted regarding the purpose of studying for a degree in the UK, there were differences in tutors' views

Table 11.3 *AI use during the reading and writing process*

Phase	Quote
Literature search	*I've been teaching students how to do literature searches recently and there are various tools like Elicit and Perplexity which use AI to gather text and summarise them this is a great way to find literature especially because you can search using your research questions rather than find search terms something I've noticed with my students is that they always struggle to come up with like clear search terms (Participant 17)*
Brainstorming	*based on the module leaders identification of how they would like to them to use it was very much their suggestion to the students was that the most helpful thing for them was to use it in the generation of ideas around the topic of brainstorming (Participant 18)*
Reading	*then have a ton of uses for ChatGPT that aren't gonna create problems you know like scaffolding complex like journal articles scaffolding journal articles (Participant 21)*
Summarising sources	*they should be allowed to use the tools for example if it's part of the study skills and they want to get a quick summary of an article to understand it better or generate ideas that's fine (Participant 06)*
Evaluating sources	*you can use it AI to produce a descriptive text but if you're gonna to actually write something evaluative where you're you know thinking higher order thinking levels it's not capable of doing that yet (Participant 20)*
Planning	*there's one called Jenni AI which helps you plot like structure and plan an academic writing source I haven't shared this with my students because I think this is I don't think there are any benefits of it which aren't academic misconduct (Participant 17)*
Writing	*where do you draw the line to make them realise that "write me the answer" is not is not the solution (Participant 98)*
Proofreading	*checking the spelling and grammar would be good so the same sort of language required things that a proofreader could do not anything but proofreading and yeah basically that's where I put it (Participant 18)*
Referencing	*the more responsible students use it as a straightforward proofreader and especially for APA 7th because everyone hates getting the style right (Participant 23)*

about the importance of producing 'polished' writing (Participant 18). Attitudes towards the use of AI tools to plan an assignment, however, differed - while Participant 17 believed that this constitutes academic misconduct (see Table 2), Participant 18 felt that this was an acceptable use of the technology:

> based on the module leaders identification of how they would like them to use it was very much their suggestion ... that the most helpful thing for them was to use it in the generation of ideas around the topic of brainstorming and to provide maybe to provide them ... a bit of an idea of structure which they would then develop into their own structure (Participant 18)

It is, however, notable that the tutor who suggested that it was acceptable to use AI for planning suggested that the AI-generated plan should be a starting point for their *own* structure.

Enforcing assessment policies: "toothless" policies with "no bright line" between acceptable use and overreliance that rely on "students' honesty"

With respect to the enforcement of policies on the use of AI, although tutors cited a range of indicators that they believe signalled that a text was likely to have been automatically generated, it was generally agreed that policies regarding the use of AI to prepare assessments were 'toothless' because offences were impossible to prove (Participant 29). While plagiarism and "ghost references" (Participant 06) can be proven, other indicators text has been written using AI (e.g. "perfect and polished" texts (Participant 20), overuse of "delve" (Participant 06), "bland academic voice" (Participant 29) or "overly flowery language" (Participant 29)) cannot be proven unless you have a benchmark of students' linguistic ability obtained for example through "some kind of supervised writing" (Participant 22). As such, tutors reported that cases they had referred to academic misconduct committees were often not upheld, even though they were aware from working with the students that they could not have produced them given their language ability and the fact that they had admitted using AI tools to write their assignments.

It was also widely acknowledged that, in the same way that it is difficult to draw the line between proofreading and editing, it is difficult to draw the line between acceptable and unacceptable use of AI tools to support assignment preparation:

> obviously translating individual phrases and words that's very useful the problem comes when it's whole scale translation and the dividing line between translating one word two words a phrase a sentence a paragraph there's no clear division (Participant 6)

The future of assessment: "AI-proofing" assessment by "taking summative written assignments off the table"

Considering the difficulties enforcing policies on the use of AI in assignment preparation and the difficulty drawing the line between acceptable use and over-reliance, most tutors reported that they believed it was no longer possible to assess students using traditional written assignments. As such institutions were exploring alternative formats of assessment which it was believed were AI proof, "sit down exams" and oral assessments (Participant 21) being the most popular suggestions. It was, however, noted that the latter were not feasible if working with large cohorts of students. Submitting drafts (Participant 29), continuous assessment (Participant 6), and reflective assignments based on in-class group work (Participant 29) were also among the suggestions. Some, however, suggested that this approach is misguided because there is always some way in which AI tools might be used to make assessment tasks easier for students:

> *I sit in meetings and people say oh we're gonna get them to do this because that will avoid them using AI and I think well no you just copy the transcript get them to translate it get them to summarise it it's done you could always think of a way to use AI to make that task easy (Participant 6).*

Discussion and conclusion

Key findings

This study is one of the first studies to explore EAP tutors' conceptions of (generative) AI and practical pedagogical knowledge for its use in teaching and assessment. Eleven EAP tutors participated in the study, which explored their knowledge, beliefs and practices about the use of AI for teaching and assessment. Most of the tutors who participated in the study demonstrated a strong curiosity for AI and had spent considerable time 'playing' with it. Insights from the tutors suggested that fundamental questions about what it means to graduate with a degree from a UK HE institution need to be addressed before any policy on AI use can be articulated, and this policy in turn needs to be developed before tutors can explore the use of AI to support learning. They reported that existing policies tended to focus on the concept of authorship. While there was a certain level of agreement among tutors on acceptable tool use, differences suggest tutors vary in terms of their understanding of authorship. Beyond assessment policy, tutors also often cited the potential for AI to enable students to bypass learning opportunities. Tutors, nevertheless, also recognized the potential for AI to support learning.

Situating the findings

EAP tutors might be expected to have a more in-depth understanding of AI technologies, given their proximity to opportunities to engage with experts (Morss & Murray, 2005). It is, however, not unsurprising that their understanding of AI, like that of the public (Selwyn et al., 2021), does not go far beyond a basic understanding of the aim to mimic human intelligence. Almost any software application that automates a human task might be considered AI, even if it is based on human programmed intelligence rather than more recent machine learning technique (Scarfe et al., 2024). Moreover, AI is also currently used to refer to technologies that go beyond mimicking human intelligence and enable computers to complete tasks that are more complex and require the processing of more data than is humanly possible. In other words, AI is now also associated with extended intelligence.

That assessment policy is driving EAP tutors' practices is also unsurprising, given that it is commonly accepted that learning and teaching should align with assessment. Differences in what tutors believe constitute academic misconduct and in particular differences in tutors' emphasis on whether the language, as well as the ideas, should be the students' own might be explained by the tutors' primary role. Tutors who provide pre-sessional and in-sessional language support might naturally be concerned with developing students' language proficiency to meet the threshold levels required to engage with the demands of their academic programmes, while personal tutors might be more concerned with their mastery of the subject matter. Differences in attitudes towards the extent to which different uses of AI during the process of preparing an assignment constitute academic misconduct reflect previous debates about proofreading in which there can be substantial disagreement among some tutors about what is acceptable (Harwood, 2023) with some going beyond minor amendments to spelling, punctuation, grammar and sentence structure.

With an in-depth understanding of theories of (language) learning and development, it is also unsurprising that the EAP tutors were conscious of the dangers of bypassing opportunities to learn by avoiding putting in the cognitive effort required to develop (language) skills and understanding for themselves. This in-depth understanding, however, at the same time explains their ability to see the potential affordances of the technology and the potential positive applications of the technology to support learning. Previous research demonstrates that a lack of pedagogical knowledge can be as much a barrier to the effective use of technology to support learning and teaching as a lack of technical knowledge (Chai et al., 2010).

Limitations of the study

Caution should, however, be exercised in interpreting the findings of this study. The current sample appears to be biased towards colleagues with an inherent interest in AI and its potential use in HE and EAP. EAP tutors more broadly may not have the breadth of awareness of AI tools nor the depth of understanding of their capabilities and limitations. Many of the tutors who volunteered to participate in this study had clearly spent a lot of time exploring how the tools might be used by students to complete assignments as well as in their role as tutors to develop materials and support learning and teaching, time which other tutors may not be afforded due to their workload or other commitments in their lives.

Implications for teacher education

Nevertheless, the results of the study provide some insights into the professional development needs of EAP tutors with respect to AI as well as how best to deliver any training. First and foremost, the results highlight the need to develop EAP tutors' AI literacy. Even though many of the tutors in this study had an active interest in AI, most equated AI with specific applications and demonstrated little insight into the technology itself beyond its functions and the quality of the output it can currently produce. While some tutors reported joining webinars and consulting articles on the topic, those with the most well-developed conceptual understanding of AI, its functions, and limitations, had spent considerable time independently exploring its capabilities. As such, it is recommended any training work from tools to a conceptual understanding via experiential learning, i.e. 'playing' with the different tools. Acknowledging that most EAP tutors will not have as much time as our participants to dedicate to upskilling themselves in this area, such experiential learning ought to be scaffolded, to enable tutors to relatively quickly come to understand the capabilities and limitations of these technologies, in particular with respect to completing summative written assignments. In other words, having experimented with the tools themselves, tutors should be provided with tried and tested prompts that demonstrate the capabilities and limitations of the tools.

With respect to developing teachers' practical pedagogical knowledge for AI for assessment and learning and teaching, any training ought to explore tutors assumptions about the relative importance of the ability to express oneself in the language of instruction as well as demonstrate an understanding of the subject, before moving on to explore the concept of authorship and the extent to which students should retain ownership of different stages in the process of preparing an assignment - Participant 29's description of how they worked as a personal tutor with a student to prepare an assignment with AI support might provide a useful stimulus for these discussions along with the extracts in Table 3:

> *I did this in my EAP module last maybe a year ago now where I actually showed them I said if you you know they came up with an essay title for their for their module and one of them was from Nigeria and she wanted to compare 2 aspects of the Nigerian healthcare system and I said okay put that into just put the title into ChatGPT and let's see what it gives you as an introduction to that essay and I knew that it would give something very banal not very helpful and it did although she thought it was great you know so I had to go through and say well this is why it doesn't really work what do you want this essay to really be about? and then say that you want the essay to be about these things and that you want to make this argument and then put that into ChatGPT and see what it produces and it produced something a bit better and then they said okay now go and find some resources which you think really make your argument stronger? some citations which you would like to include which really make your point for you and put that into ChatGPT and ask them to use that in support of the argument and it got better not brilliant but better and we kind of carried out that that process for most of the essay as in she gave it increasingly specific detailed prompts it gave her work and it again I I presume you must have used it yourself quite a bit at this point it goes off in tangents that you never ask it to it You know I mean one of the things that started going on was along with UN sustainable goals like sustainable development goals which we just I don't know It threw that in and thought we might like it but she had to take that back out because that wasn't part of what she wanted to be the essay the essay to be about so in the end she had an essay which I think was about forty per cent ChatGPT's language and then about oh I forget I gave a presentation about this last year but I forgot it was about twenty percent er refined so like kind of paraphrasing what ChatGPT had said and making it fit and it was about forty per cent her own because she had to add in bits she had to introduce it she had to conclude it properly so she still owned quite a lot of the language she owned all of the ideas in it and she still retained control of what was in the essay (Participant 29).*

Given the general view that AI "tak[es] summative written assignments off the table", tutors should then be encouraged to explore alternative approaches to assessment (see The Future of Assessment and Meakin 2023 for some alternatives to summative written assessments that are being considered) and consider how students might use AI tools to help them complete those assessments. Again, reflection on the extent to which those uses constitute "false authorship" is advised.

In conclusion, even the most curious EAP tutors do not fully grasp the capabilities of the latest generation of AI technologies and their implications for learning, teaching and assessment. Moreover, those capabilities are continually improving and expanding. As such, it is essential for EAP tutors to engage in continuous professional development and establish communities of practice to keep abreast of developments in AI in HE.

Post-reading:

Before focusing in on the specific questions raised by this study, it would be helpful to revisit the pre-reading questions and ask yourself:

- Has your position on the role of generative AI in education changed? If so, how?

Focusing in on the issues raised by the participants in this study, it would also be helpful to ask yourself:

- What principles underpin policies on (generative) AI use in your context?
- What is the relative importance of language and content in your context?
- In your opinion, what does it mean to author a text?
- To what extent do you think the examples of students' use of AI described in this chapter are acceptable (see Table 3 and section 5.4)?

Further reading

1. For a discussion of policies on (generative) AI use:
   Perkins, M., & Roe, J. (2024). Decoding academic integrity policies: A corpus linguistics investigation of AI and other technological threats. *Higher Education Policy*, *37*(3), 633–653.
2. For a discussion of authorship:
   Cheung, K. Y. F., Elander, J., Stupple, E. J. N., & Flay, M. (2018). Academics' understandings of the authorial academic writer: A qualitative analysis of authorial identity. *Studies in Higher Education*, *43*(8), 1468–1483.
   Cheung, K. Y. F., Stupple, E. J. N., & Elander, J. (2017). Development and validation of the Student Attitudes and Beliefs about Authorship Scale: a psychometrically robust measure of authorial identity. *Studies in Higher Education*, *42*(1), 97–114.

References

Anson, C. M. (2022). AI-based text generation and the social construction of "fraudulent authorship": A revisitation. *Composition Studies*, 50, 37–46. https://compositionstudiesjournal.files.wordpress.com/2022/07/anson.pdf

Attia, M. (2011). *Teacher cognition and the use of technology in teaching Arabic to speakers of other languages.* [Unpublished doctoral dissertation. The University of Manchester].

Borg, S. (2003). Teacher cognition in language teaching: A review of research on what language teachers think, know, believe, and do. *Language Teaching*, 36(2), 81–109.

Braun, V., & Clarke, V. (2006). Using thematic analysis in psychology. *Qualitative Research in Psychology*, 3(2), 77–101.

Budhathoki, T., Zirar, A., Njoya, E. T., & Timsina, A. (2024). ChatGPT adoption and anxiety: A cross-country analysis utilising the unified theory of acceptance and use of technology (UTAUT). *Studies in Higher Education*, 1–16.

Chai, C. S., Koh, J. H. L., & Tsai, C. C. (2010). Facilitating preservice teachers' development of technological, pedagogical, and content knowledge (TPACK). *Journal of Educational Technology & Society*, 13(4), 63–73. https://www.jstor.org/stable/jeductechsoci.

Cotton, D. R., Cotton, P. A., & Shipway, J. R. (2024). Chatting and cheating: Ensuring academic integrity in the era of ChatGPT. *Innovations in Education and Teaching International*, 61(2), 228–239.

Gribble, L. C. & Waldrop, J. E. (2024). Empowering students from assumptions to knowledge: Making integrity everyone's business (pp. 263 - 280). In Mahmud, S. (Ed.). (2024). *Academic integrity in the age of artificial intelligence*. IGI Global.

Harwood, N. (2023). Lecturer, language tutor, and student perspectives on the ethics of the proofreading of student writing. *Written Communication*, 40(2), 651–719.

Klyshbekova, M., & Abbott, P. (2024). ChatGPT and assessment in higher education: A magic wand or a disruptor? *Electronic Journal of e-Learning*, 22(2), 30–45.

Kolides, A., Nawaz, A., Rathor, A., Beeman, D., Hashmi, M., Fatima, S., ... & Jararweh, Y. (2023). Artificial intelligence foundation and pre-trained models: Fundamentals, applications, opportunities, and social impacts. *Simulation Modelling Practice and Theory*, 126, 102754.

Launchbury, J. (2017). A DARPA perspective on artificial intelligence. *DARPA*. https://www.darpa.mil/attachments/AIFull.pdf

Lee, S. M. (2023). The effectiveness of machine translation in foreign language education: A systematic review and meta-analysis. *Computer Assisted Language Learning*, 36(1-2), 103–125.

Malesky, L. A., Baley, J., & Crow, R. (2016). Academic dishonesty: Assessing the threat of cheating companies to online education. *College Teaching, 64*(4), 178–183. https://doi.org/10.1080/87567555.2015.1133558

Morss, K. & Murray, R. (2005). *Teaching at university*. Sage.

Nazary, F., Deldjoo, Y., & Di Noia, T. (2023, September). ChatGPT-healthprompt. Harnessing the power of XAI in prompt-based healthcare decision support using ChatGPT. In *European Conference on artificial intelligence* (pp. 382–397). Springer Nature Switzerland.

Perkins, M. (2023). Academic integrity considerations of AI large language models in the post-pandemic era: ChatGPT and beyond. *Journal of University Teaching and Learning Practice, 20*(2).

Perkins, M., Basar Gezgin, U., & Gordon, R. (2019). Plagiarism in higher education: Classification, causes and controls. *Pan-Pacific Management Science, 2*, 3–21. https://doi.org/10.13140/RG.2.2.20694.11841

Ranade, N., Saravia, M., & Johri, A. (2024). Using rhetorical strategies to design prompts: A human-in-the-loop approach to make AI useful. *AI & SOCIETY*, 1–22.

Russell Group (2023). *Russell Group principles on the use of generative AI tools in education*. Russell Group, July 2023. https://russellgroup.ac.uk/news/new-principles-on-use-of-ai-in-education/

Scarfe, P., Watcham, K., Clarke, A., & Roesch, E. (2024). A real-world test of artificial intelligence infiltration of a university examinations system: a "Turing Test" case study. PloS one, *19*(6), e0305354.

Selwyn, N., & Gallo Cordoba, B. (2022). Australian public understandings of artificial intelligence. *AI & SOCIETY, 37*(4), 1645–1662.

Turing, A. M. (1950). Computer machinery and intelligence. *Mind,* 59, 433–460

Young, A., Chandler, J., Norris, C., & Prevatt-Goldstein, A. (2024). Generative AI and academic skills support at UCL: An institutional approach. *Journal of EAHIL, 20*(2), 16–19.

Ziebland, S., & McPherson, A. (2006). Making sense of qualitative data analysis: An introduction with illustrations from DIPEx (personal experiences of health and illness). *Medical Education, 40*(5), 405–414.

12
Professional development and learner training for AI

Glenn Stockwell

> **Pre-reading questions:**
>
> 1) What AI tools are you using (or plan to use) in your teaching? How did you hear about these tools?
> 2) Do you feel that the guidelines about using AI in your classes are clear? Are these different from teacher to teacher? Does the teacher give reasons for the guidelines?
> 3) Do you remember receiving training in using any technology for your language learning? Do you think that type of training also applies to using AI?

Introduction

The rapid integration of artificial intelligence (AI) into language teaching and learning has had a significant impact on educational practices, transforming not only the tools that are available for instruction but also the roles of both teachers and learners. As AI systems have evolved, they have increasing potential to offer a range of adaptive, personalised experiences for learners, but at the same time, they are also reshaping the skills and knowledge required by teachers to effectively integrate these technologies. In this evolving landscape, professional development and learner training emerge as essential pillars. Teachers find that they must adapt to new pedagogical approaches, develop an understanding of AI-driven systems, and acquire skills that can facilitate meaningful learning experiences. Similarly, learners can benefit from training that enables them to navigate and make the most of AI tools effectively, ensuring that they become active participants in their language learning pathways.

This chapter examines both the professional development of teachers and the preparation of learners within AI-driven learning environments. It outlines the essential skills that teachers must develop to use AI ethically and innovatively, focusing on areas like data literacy, ethical responsibility, and adaptable teaching methods. Additionally, it discusses strategies for training learners to become independent and proficient in AI-enhanced learning, highlighting the importance of digital literacy and critical thinking in technologically advanced settings. As education continues to evolve, the integration of professional development that includes learner training as a central becomes even more imperative, emphasising the need for collaborative and reflective approaches allow both teachers and learners to make the most of these emerging tools.

Development of AI tools

While earlier renditions of generative AI have been around for several years, it has really been tools based on OpenAI's GPT-3.5 that have brought about the most profound changes to education. The appearance of ChatGPT in 2022 dramatically changed the face of many aspects of our daily lives, ranging from finance and media through to marketing and, of course, education. Just weeks after GPT-3.5 became publicly available, media reports were conveying voices of those that were impressed by the technology ("quite simply, the best artificial intelligence chatbot ever released to the general public"), and at the same time, fears over its negative implications for education, such as marking the "death of the college essay" (Roose, 2022). This article included a statement that likely echoed the fears of many teachers at the time, when considering the potential of the yet-to-be-released GPT-4: "We are not ready." In light of the massive advances in AI technologies since then, there is no doubt many that feel that even now.

Over two years have passed since this article was published at the time of writing this chapter, and GPT-4o is now a reality and has found its way into classrooms and educational research (e.g., Fincham & Arronte Alvarez, 2024). The variety of tools that have appeared following the release of OpenAI's GPT-3.5 LLM in 2022 has continued to expand, as illustrated in Table 1. The tools listed in the table have been categorised according to function, namely research, content creation, visual media, web development, audio production, or workflow automation. This list is far from exhaustive, and the range of tools will continue to evolve as new applications appear and older ones either establish their place in the market or disappear.

Table 12.1 *Examples of generative AI categories and tools*

Category	Tools
Research and academic writing support	ChatGPT, Claude, Consensus, Copilot, Elicit, Grammarly, Jasper, Paperpile, Poe, Research Rabbit, Scite, Writefull, Zotero
Writing and content creation	Anyword, Beautiful.ai, Shortwave, Tome
AI image and video generation	Adobe Photoshop, DALL·E 3, Midjourney, Runway, Wondershare Filmora
Website and app development	Framer, Microsoft Power Apps, Pico, Wix
Audio and voice generation	ElevenLabs, Suno
Marketing and automation	Jasper, Zapier Central, Zapier Chatbots
Automation and productivity tools	Microsoft Power Apps, Zapier Central

The functions of AI-based tools will no doubt evolve over time, and the variety of applications is expected to keep expanding as technological advances continue. Furthermore, tools that are not based on OpenAI's LLM models, such as Google Gemini, have begun to emerge and have demonstrated different but comparable results in tasks such as creating lesson plans (Baytak, 2024). A broader range of technologies can afford teachers more options, it also makes it harder to stay updated with the latest developments. For teachers who are not well-versed in these technologies, distinguishing between tools–especially those with similar functionalities–can be both time-consuming and resource-intensive. To many, maintaining relevance in this rapid change is a highly traumatic experience, as they feel high levels of "techno-stress" with the abundance of new tools that they feel compelled to use (see Vendramin, Nardelli, & Ipsen, 2021). Much of this stress is derived from the view of these tools as a perceived threat, and this means that these teachers need to find ways to cope with this threat. Needless to say, stress in the workplace is far from new, and there have been multiple theories proposed over time that have direct relevance to understanding how teachers can better understand and deal with the rapid changes taking place, which are described below.

Positioning professional development in theory

Artificial intelligence may be viewed as an ambivalent technology, something that is neither inherently good nor bad but rather is dependent upon the context and the way in which is it used. This perspective aligns with the *Transactional Theory of Stress and Coping* (Lazarus &

Folkman, 1987; see also Obbarius et al., 2021), which argues that stress is not just a product of the stressor (i.e., new AI tools), but also how it is interpreted. The theory posits that when people are exposed to a stressor, they conduct an initial appraisal to evaluate whether it is relevant to them, and if so, the degree to which they find it potentially threatening or harmful. This is then followed by a second appraisal of whether they have the resources and coping strategies to deal with the stressor. There are two possible strategies that a person may then choose to adopt: *problem-focused*, where they see how to directly solve the problem or threat; or *emotion-focused*, where they manage their emotional response to the situation rather than the threat itself.

The choice of strategy is often dependent upon the degree of control that people feel that they have over the outcomes when placed in situations that are stressful or threatening to them. Rothbaum et al. (1982) proposed the *Two-process Theory of Perceived Control* as a two-tier response comprised of two distinct processes, primary and secondary control. Primary control refers to an individual's attempts using direct action to change the environment to align with their own desires or goals, whereas secondary control refers to their attempts to adapt themselves to the environment when they are unable to directly control it, including acceptance, adjustment, or reinterpretation of situations. Thus, in broad terms, teachers may choose to either alter the environment in which they find themselves or to alter themselves. Sometimes when the larger environment (i.e., the existence of these tools in society or education at large) cannot be altered, teachers may choose to adopt a coping strategy where they decide to exclude the technologies altogether from their own teaching contexts, by not learning more about them and/or completely banning students from using them.

Bridging the gap between individual coping mechanisms and the broader implications for professional development, the *Theory of Planned Behavior* (TPB) offers a valuable lens through which to examine teachers' responses to AI integration in education. TPB suggests that an individual's intention to perform a specific behaviour, such as adopting or resisting AI tools, is shaped by their attitude towards the behaviour, subjective norms (perceived social pressure), and perceived behavioural control (belief in their ability to engage in the behaviour) (Mnguni et al., 2024). Considering AI in education, teachers' attitudes towards AI tools, influenced by their perceived benefits and risks, alongside the social norms within their educational environment and their perceived control over AI implementation, collectively contribute to their intention to use or resist these technologies. This theoretical framework underscores the importance of addressing not only individual concerns but also the social and control-related factors that influence teachers' decisions regarding AI adoption. Evidence exists to show that the view posited by TPB has empirical validity, where Ivanov et al. (2024) suggested that understanding both the positive *and* negative aspects of generative AI can indeed lead to both a more positive attitude and a higher intention to use it.

In an environment where AI tools being referred to as either a threat or a reformation in higher education (Yusuf et al., 2024), seen together, these theories allude to two important points that have direct relevance for professional development. Firstly, teachers need to take an objective look at these tools to see the extent to which they are in fact a "threat" to them, and secondly to employ a combination of both problem-focused and emotion-focused strategies to assist them in coping rationally. This can only be achieved by adequate understanding the available AI technologies, identifying where support can be found to learn more about them, and exploring how the range of tools can be used to facilitate or support learners in achieving specific pedagogical goals.

Professional development in context

A significant challenge facing many teachers and students is the lack of clear and consistent AI policies across universities. A recent study of the top 100 universities in the United States by H. Wang et al. (2024) found that while outright bans are rare, over a third lack definitive guidelines on AI usage, with more than half (55%) leaving it up to teachers to decide whether to allow students to use AI. This ambiguity often leaves the decision-making power to individual instructors, leading to inconsistencies and a potential mismatch between faculty approaches and institutional expectations. When instructors are granted discretion, a majority (51%) fail to clearly state their position on AI usage and nearly half (47%) prohibit its use, with only 2% of teachers explicitly permitting it.

This not only suggests a prevailing cautiousness towards AI that may not only potentially hinder students' ability to develop critical skills in utilising AI tools, but it also can result in confusion among learners about what they should and shouldn't do (see Y. Wang, 2024, for a discussion). The lack of a clear policy by many institutions clearly highlights the difficulties in conducting meaningful training programs for teachers by institutions – as long as institutions remain uncommitted to their perspectives on the use of AI, professional development programs are unlikely to be provide concrete instruction and/or assistance for teachers, which ultimately has a knock-on effect for learners.

Given this situation, professional development initiatives ultimately fall on the shoulders of teachers, who are looking for ways of coping with the rapid advancements in technology, particularly AI, and at the same time being as effective as they can as teachers. This constant state of flux necessitates a dynamic and adaptable approach to professional development. The following section outlines a framework for professional development that builds on Stockwell's (2008, 2024) work on teacher change and professional growth. This framework aims to empower teachers to navigate the complexities of AI integration in education by focusing on how teachers can develop the necessary knowledge and skills to effectively integrate AI tools into their teaching practices, while simultaneously fostering a culture of critical reflection and continuous learning.

A framework for professional development

1. *Critical examination of the teaching and learning environment*
   Effective professional development begins with a thorough understanding of the existing learning environment. Key considerations include identifying the specific characteristics of the learners, the tools they currently utilise, and their existing engagement with AI technologies. It is crucial to investigate any institutional regulations or guidelines governing the use of AI within the educational context. Furthermore, exploring institutionally recommended or supported AI tools can provide valuable insights into best practices and available resources. While it has been around for several decades, the *Task-Technology Fit* model (Goodhue et al., 1995) is of relevance here, where it is important to understand the characteristics of the task, the technology, and the individual characteristics of users (in this case teachers and learners) to determine whether the technology fits the task and vice versa. This also involves exploring the impact of the technology and task on performance.
2. *Seeking sources of information and support*
   To effectively integrate AI into their teaching practices, language teachers must actively seek relevant information and support. This may involve exploring academic resources such as journals and conferences that focus on the intersection of technology and language education. Engaging with online communities and social media groups dedicated to these topics can provide valuable insights and opportunities for collaboration with other teachers (Ito, 2023). Additionally, investigating any available institutional support mechanisms, such as workshops or mentorship programs, can significantly enhance professional growth.
3. *Keeping up with necessary technological developments*
   As was alluded to at the beginning of the chapter, the field of AI is constantly evolving, necessitating ongoing professional

development for language teachers. Advances have taken place in not only the processing power of AI but also its expanding range of multimodal capabilities (Shadiev et al., 2024). This requires a commitment to staying abreast of the latest advancements through a diverse range of sources, including both academic (i.e., journals and books) and non-academic (books, technical websites, etc.) publications. Regular discussions with colleagues about their experiences with technology in the classroom can provide valuable insights and alternative perspectives.

4. *Attending conferences, webinars, and other professional development opportunities*

   Participating in conferences, webinars, and other professional development events dedicated to technology in language education provides valuable opportunities for learning and networking (Stockwell, 2009). While focusing on developments within the specific field of language teaching is essential, exploring how technology is being used in other disciplines can offer valuable cross-disciplinary insights. It is crucial to critically examine the relationship between technology and pedagogical goals, ensuring that the integration of technology aligns with and supports desired learning outcomes.

5. *Understanding the implications of technology on learner training*

   The effective integration of AI in language teaching requires a comprehensive understanding of learner needs and skills. This necessitates assessing learners' existing technological proficiency and identifying any necessary training or support. To do this, however, teachers must possess sufficient technological skills to effectively guide and support learners in their use of AI tools. Developing and implementing clear guidelines for the appropriate and ethical use of AI technologies within the classroom is key to both student success and responsible technology integration (Beckingham et al., 2024). This is an absolutely essential element of professional development, particularly where technology is involved. While learners may be proficient users of technology in certain domains, this rarely extends to educational uses, where learners will depend very heavily on teachers to provide guidance on when, how, and why to use technology.

6. *Tracking progress with a professional development portfolio*

   Maintaining a professional development portfolio provides a valuable record of growth and accomplishments (see Farrell, 2022). This portfolio should include documentation of relevant training undertaken, both technical and pedagogical. Evidence of teaching evaluations, including student feedback, can provide valuable insights into the impact of technology integration on student learning. The portfolio should also document any changes made to teaching practices based on professional development experiences and reflect on the factors that influenced these changes. Finally, documenting collaborative efforts with other teachers can showcase the value of peer learning and support within the professional community.

This framework provides a comprehensive guide for language teachers to navigate the constantly shifting landscape of AI in education. By continuously engaging in critical self-reflection, seeking out relevant resources, and actively participating in professional development opportunities, language teachers can effectively integrate AI tools into their teaching practices, enhancing student learning and fostering a dynamic and engaging learning environment.

Shifting needs for language teaching professionals

The speed and scope of the advancements in AI mean that a significant shift in the skillset and knowledge base is required of language teachers. As alluded to earlier in this chapter, while the emergence of AI-powered tools such as language translation models, chatbot tutors, and AI-generated content presents various opportunities, they bring with them significant challenges for teachers. To effectively navigate this evolving terrain, language teachers must adapt their pedagogical approaches, embrace new technologies, and cultivate a deep understanding of how AI can be used to enhance language learning while mitigating potential risks.

Knowing how to "communicate" with AI to generate desired results is a necessary point of departure. A field that has emerged over the past few years is that of prompt engineering, which looks at how to use human language to provide commands for AI to complete tasks, ranging from simple through to highly complex. It has been predicted to become a major part of many jobs in the future (see Smith, 2023, for a discussion), and there are already books specifically dedicated to it (e.g., Phoenix & Taylor, 2024). Naturally, language teachers are also finding themselves in a position where they need to be able to learn how to use these tools, requiring prompt engineering skills (Isemonger, 2023). This necessitates a shift in professional development for language teachers, moving beyond traditional pedagogical training. This necessitates not only learning how to write effective prompts for AI models but also understanding the underlying principles of natural language processing and the limitations of AI-generated content. Professional development programs must therefore incorporate training on prompt engineering techniques, such as how to formulate clear and concise instructions, how to provide specific examples, and how to refine prompts to achieve desired outcomes. Furthermore, teachers need to develop a critical understanding of the strengths and weaknesses of different AI models, enabling them to select and utilise the most appropriate tools for specific language learning tasks.

Beyond prompt engineering, developing a strong foundation in AI literacy is like to become a fundamental requirement for language teaching professionals. This encompasses a broad range of skills and knowledge. Firstly, there is a need to understand the ethical implications of AI, including awareness of potential biases in AI algorithms, data privacy concerns, and the responsible use of AI in educational settings. Teachers must be equipped to critically evaluate AI-generated content, identify potential biases, and devise ways to ensure that AI is used equitably and ethically in their classrooms. Secondly, teachers need to develop critical thinking and evaluation skills regarding AI (see Mulvihill & Martin, 2024). As the amount of AI-generated content increases, learners also need to develop critical thinking skills to evaluate the accuracy, reliability, and appropriateness of AI-generated information. Teachers can play a vital role in fostering these skills by designing learning activities that encourage students to critically analyse and evaluate information from various sources, including AI-generated content. Next, teachers need to try to cultivate creativity and innovation in their teaching environments that build on the "humanity" of teachers and even language learning itself.

It should be pointed out, however, that the successful integration of AI in language education requires a significant shift in the skillset and knowledge base of language teachers. At the same time, ensuring that learners become competent with AI tools is paramount to leading them to not only successfully *use* AI but also to *learn* from using it.

Learner training

Using AI in language teaching and learning environments demands a multifaceted approach that considers both teacher professional development and learner training, necessitating a nuanced understanding of the interconnectedness between these two crucial aspects. These two facets are not independent entities but rather mutually influential components of a complex system. The section below does not aim to provide specific training in using AI technologies as these technologies are shifting at a speed that makes this difficult. Rather, it seeks to point out the various considerations that should be kept in mind when carrying out effective learner training regarding AI.

1. *Mutual dependency*
    There has been research which shows a relationship between professional development and positive learner outcomes (Ventista & Brown, 2023) as well as studies which suggest that equipping learners with the necessary skills and knowledge leads to greater success in language learning (Stockwell, 2019). This implies that both teachers and learners can benefit from guidance, and this is compounded even further when AI enters the equation. This is typically a top-down approach, where teachers need to learn how to use AI themselves to be able to train learners. This relationship between teacher professional development and learner training is symbiotic. Teachers must possess a foundational understanding of AI tools and their pedagogical applications to effectively guide learners, and learners need to express their concerns about knowing when it is and isn't appropriate to use these tools. Open dialogue enables teachers to design meaningful learning activities that leverage AI in a supportive and engaging manner. Effective learner training relies heavily on the teacher's ability to provide appropriate scaffolding and guidance, and without a clear understanding of learner needs and the potential of AI tools, teachers may struggle to design and implement effective learning experiences that maximize the benefits of AI while reducing potential risks.
2. *Alignment of goals*
    Both teacher professional development and learner training should prioritize the development of autonomy and critical digital literacy. Teachers require training to critically evaluate and select appropriate AI tools based on pedagogical needs and ethical considerations. This includes developing the skills to identify potential biases in AI algorithms and to understand the implications of data privacy (Y. Wang & Stockwell, 2024). Concurrently, learner training should focus on empowering students to use AI tools responsibly and effectively. This involves developing critical thinking skills to evaluate information generated by AI, understand the ethical implications of AI use, and apply AI tools creatively and ethically in their learning. This entails a need for both teachers and learners to develop their critical literacy skills and to share mutual perspectives on appropriate use of AI in achieving learning outcomes.
3. *Skills transfer*
    Related to the first point above, effective teacher professional development plays a crucial role in facilitating knowledge transfer to learners. When teachers gain expertise in specific AI-enhanced teaching strategies, they are better equipped to guide learners in the effective use of these tools (Paşa et al., 2022). For example, teachers trained in the use of AI-powered language feedback tools

can effectively demonstrate how to use these tools for self-assessment and identify areas for improvement. This transfer of skills empowers learners to become independent users of AI tools, fostering a deeper understanding of learning processes and enhancing their metacognitive abilities.

4. *Collaborative approach*

   A collaborative approach to AI integration in education fosters a dynamic and engaging learning environment. Teachers can model the effective use of AI tools, demonstrating best practices and critical thinking skills. Learners, in turn, can experiment with AI tools, discover new applications, and share their insights with their peers and teachers. This collaborative process encourages a two-way exchange of knowledge, where both teachers and learners contribute to the development of effective AI-enhanced learning strategies. This approach not only enhances student learning outcomes but also provides valuable professional development opportunities for teachers as they learn from their students' innovative uses of AI.

5. *Ethical considerations*

   Addressing ethical concerns related to AI is paramount in both teacher professional development and learner training. Teacher training programs must explicitly address ethical issues to equip them to identify and mitigate potential ethical challenges and to instil a sense of ethical responsibility in their learners (Beckingham et al., 2024). Learner training should emphasise the importance of critical evaluation of AI-generated information, the responsible use of data, and the potential societal impacts of AI technologies (see Khogali & Mekid, 2023). By fostering a culture of ethical AI use, teachers can ensure that AI is used to enhance learning and promote equitable and just outcomes for all students. This includes making students aware of the potential legal implications of misuse of AI tools (see Stockwell, 2024), which can also help to instil a more responsible attitude towards them.

6. *Focus on lifelong learning*

   The rapid evolution of AI technologies not only necessitates a commitment to lifelong learning for both teachers and learners, but also has the potential to support it. Teacher professional development programs should foster a growth mindset and encourage continuous exploration of new AI tools and pedagogical approaches. This emphasis on lifelong learning aligns with the skills and dispositions that teachers aim to cultivate in their students (see Stockwell, 2022, for a discussion), but learners need to be equipped with the necessary skills to be able to continue seeking out learning opportunities even after formal education is completed.

Moving forward with AI and professional development

The integration of AI within professional development itself is an area that is undergoing constant change that has the potential to view AI not only as a subject of professional development, but also as an active agent in the developmental process (Tammets & Ley, 2023). AI has the potential to move beyond traditional models to revolutionise how teachers engage with professional growth opportunities. By making the most of AI-powered tools and platforms, professional development can become more personalised, efficient, and engaging, ultimately enhancing teacher effectiveness and fostering a culture of continuous learning. As mentioned above, doing this requires a thorough understanding of the role of AI in achieving learning outcomes (see also Chiu, 2024). This means ensuring that AI is used purposefully with learning goals in mind rather than just a means to an end. In the midst of discussions of Education 4.0–the equipping of students with technology skills for the future–we need to see where AI can be used to meaningfully link to both productive competency and receptive competency (Sridhivya et al., 2024), as well as how it can lead to complex thinking (see Ramírez-Montoya et al., 2024) rather than simply using AI as a means of completing assigned tasks with minimal cognitive effort. Part of this also requires teachers to develop their assessment practices, where technology can be used as a tool for continual, formative assessment (Holmes et al., 2019) rather than one-off summative assessment which is susceptible to (ab)use of AI technologies.

A future area of inquiry regarding AI and professional development is the role that AI itself can play in the professional development process itself. Furthermore, AI can transform the delivery of professional development by automating time-consuming tasks and creating more engaging and interactive learning experiences. AI-powered chatbots and virtual assistants can be trained to provide on-demand support, answer questions, and offer guidance throughout the learning journey. AI can also be used to create immersive and interactive simulations that allow teachers to practice new skills and make decisions in a safe and controlled environment. For example, AI-powered simulations can replicate real-world classroom scenarios, enabling teachers to experiment with different teaching strategies, receive immediate feedback, and refine their practice without the risks associated with real-world implementation (Bondie & City, 2024). These innovative applications of AI have the potential to transform professional development into a more dynamic, engaging, and effective process, helping teachers to continuously learn and grow in their careers.

Conclusion

The implications of the content in this chapter are far-reaching and necessitate a shift in the approach to both professional development and learner training. In the evolving landscape of AI in language teaching and learning, the roles of both teachers and learners are being redefined. For professional development, the emphasis is on equipping teachers with the knowledge and skills to navigate the complexities of AI. This includes a deep understanding of AI tools, their pedagogical applications, and ethical implications. It also necessitates fostering critical thinking skills to evaluate AI-generated content and address potential biases. Learner training, on the other hand, needs to focus on empowering students to use AI tools effectively and responsibly. This involves developing critical thinking to evaluate AI-generated information, understanding the ethical implications of AI use, and fostering creativity and innovation in AI-enhanced learning environments. Furthermore, both teachers and learners need to be prepared to adapt to the evolving nature of AI, embracing lifelong learning as a means of staying up to date with the latest advancements and their implications for language teaching and learning.

> **Post-reading questions**
>
> 1) What specific skills do you think teachers need to effectively and ethically use AI in their teaching practices?
> 2) In what ways can learner training be designed to promote critical thinking and digital literacy in AI-enhanced environments?
> 3) How might aligning professional development for teachers with learner training impact the overall effectiveness of AI integration in teaching and learning?

References

Baytak, A. (2024). The content analysis of lesson plans created by ChatGPT and Google Gemini. *Research in the Social Sciences, 9*(1), 329–350. https://doi.org/10.46303/ressat.2024.19

Beckingham, S., Lawrence, J., Powell, S., & Hartley, P. (Eds.). (2024). *Using generative AI effectively in higher education: Sustainable and ethical practices for learning, teaching and assessment.* Routledge. https://doi.org/10.4324/9781003482918

Bondie, R., City, E. (2024). AI-powered simulation drives teacher learning. *The Learning Professional, 45*(2), 48–51. Retrieved from http://www.learningforward.org/

Chiu, T. K. F. (2024). Future research recommendations for transforming higher education with generative AI. *Computers and Education: Artificial Intelligence, 6*, 100197. https://doi.org/10.1016/j.caeai.2023.100197

Farrell, T. S. C. (2022). *Insights into professional development in second language teaching.* Castledown.

Fincham, N. X., & Arronte Alvarez, A. (2024). Using Large Language Models (LLMs) to facilitate L2 proficiency development through personalized feedback and scaffolding: An empirical study. In Y. Wang & M. S. Cardenas Claros (Eds.), *Proceedings of the International CALL Research Conference, 2024*, 59–64. https://doi.org/10.29140/9780648184485-09

Goodhue, D. L., & Thompson, R. L. (1995). Task-technology fit and individual performance. *Management Information Systems Quarterly, 19*(2), 213–235. https://doi.org/10.2307/249689

Holmes, W., Bialik, M., & Fadel, C. (2019). Artificial intelligence in education. In C. Stückelberger & P. Duggal (Eds.), *Data ethics: Building trust: How digital technologies can serve humanity* (pp. 621–653). Globalethics. http://dx.doi.org/10.58863/20.500.12424/4276068

Isemonger, I. (2023). Generative language models in education: Foreign language learning and the teacher as prompt engineer. *TESL Practice, 2*, 3–17. https://doi.org/10.5281/zenodo.10402411

Ito, Y. (2023). Why do teachers participate in technology-focused online language teacher communities on Facebook? *Journal of Research on Technology in Education*, 1–14. Advance online publication. https://doi.org/10.1080/15391523.2023.2224593

Ivanov, S., Soliman, M., Tuomi, A., Alhamar Alkathiri, N., & Al-Alawi, A. N. (2024). Drivers of generative AI adoption in higher education through the lens of the Theory of Planned Behaviour. *Technology in Society, 77*, 102521. https://doi.org/10.1016/j.techsoc.2024.102521

Khogali, H. O., & Mekid, S. (2023). The blended future of automation and AI: Examining some long-term societal and ethical impact features. *Technology in Society, 73*, 102232. https://doi.org/10.1016/j.techsoc.2023.102232

Lazarus, R. S., & Folkman, S. (1987). Transactional theory and research on emotions and coping. *European Journal of Personality, 1*(3), 141–169. https://doi.org/10.1002/per.2410010304

Mnguni, L., Nuangchalerm, P., El Islami, R. A. Z., Sibanda, D., Sari, I. J., & Ramulumo, M. (2024). The behavioral intentions for integrating artificial intelligence in science teaching among pre-service science teachers in South Africa and Thailand. *Computers and Education: Artificial Intelligence, 7*, 100334. https://doi.org/10.1016/j.caeai.2024.100334

Mulvihill, T. M., & Martin, L. E. (2024). Voices in education: Artificial intelligence (AI) and teacher education: What key points do teacher educators and policy makers need to consider related to AI? *The Teacher Educator, 59*(3), 279–281. https://doi.org/10.1080/08878730.2024.2353441

Obbarius, N., Fischer, F., Liegl, G., Obbarius, A., & Rose, M. (2021). A modified version of the transactional stress concept according to Lazarus and Folkman was confirmed in a psychosomatic inpatient sample. *Frontiers in Psychology, 12*, 584333. https://doi.org/10.3389/fpsyg.2021.584333

Paşa, D., Hursen, C., & Keser, H. Determining teacher candidates' levels of twenty-first century learner and teacher skills use. *Education and Information Technologies, 27*, 11537–11563. https://doi.org/10.1007/s10639-022-11100-w

Phoenix, J., & Taylor, M. (2024). *Prompt engineering for generative AI* (2nd ed.). O'Reilly Media, Inc.

Ramírez-Montoya, M. S., Castillo-Martínez, I. M., Sanabria-Z, J., & Miranda, J. (2022). Complex thinking in the framework of Education 4.0 and open innovation–A systematic literature review. *Journal of Open Innovation: Technology, Market, and Complexity, 8*(1), Article 4. https://doi.org/10.3390/joitmc8010004

Roose, K. (2022, December 5). The brilliance and weirdness of ChatGPT. *The New York Times*. Retrieved from https://www.nytimes.com/2022/12/05/technology/chatgpt-ai-twitter.html

Rothbaum, F., Weisz, J. R., & Snyder, S. S. (1982). Changing the world and changing the self: A two-process model of perceived control. *Journal of Personality and Social Psychology, 42*(1), 5–37. https://doi.org/10.1037/0022-3514.42.1.5

Shadiev, R., Chen, X., & Altinay, F. (2024). A review of research on computer-aided translation technologies and their applications to assist learning and instruction. *Journal of Computer Assisted Learning, 40*(6), 3290–3323. https://doi.org/10.1111/jcal.13072

Smith, C. S. (2023, April 6). Mom, Dad, I want to be a prompt engineer. *Forbes*. Retrieved from https://www.forbes.com/sites/craigsmith/2023/04/05/mom-dad-i-want-to-be-a-prompt-engineer

Sridhivya, D., Gurusamy, K., & Balamurali, E. (2024). Utilizing ELSA Speak and Busuu apps to enhance English for professional purposes among Indian students: An Education 4.0 approach. *Australian Journal of Applied Linguistics, 7*(3), 1717. https://doi.org/10.29140/ajal.v7n3.1717

Stockwell, G. (2009). Teacher education in CALL: Teaching teachers to educate themselves. *International Journal of Innovation in Language Learning and Teaching, 3*(1), 99–112. https://doi.org/10.1080/17501220802655524

Stockwell, G. (2022). *Mobile assisted language learning: Concepts, contexts and challenges*. Cambridge University Press.
Stockwell, G. (2024). ChatGPT in language teaching and learning: Exploring the road we're travelling. *Technology in Language Teaching & Learning, 6*(1), 2273. https://doi.org/10.29140/tltl.v6n3.2273
Stockwell, G. (2024). Self-directed professional development in CALL education. In L. McCallum & D. Tafazoli (Eds.), *The Palgrave encyclopedia of computer-assisted language learning*. Palgrave Macmillan. https://doi.org/10.1007/978-3-031-51447-0
Tammets, K., & Ley, T. (2023). Integrating AI tools in teacher professional learning: A conceptual model and illustrative case. *Frontiers in Artificial Intelligence, 6*. https://doi.org/10.3389/frai.2023.1255089
Vendramin, N., Nardelli, G., & Ipsen, C. (2021). Task-technology fit theory: An approach for mitigating technostress. In R. Appel-Meulenbroek & V. Danivska (Eds.), *A handbook of theories on designing alignment between people and the office environment* (pp. 39–53). Routledge. https://doi.org/10.1201/9781003128830-4
Ventista, O. M., & Brown, C. (2023). Teachers' professional learning and its impact on students' learning outcomes: Findings from a systematic review. *Social Sciences & Humanities Open, 8*(1), 100565. https://doi.org/10.1016/j.ssaho.2023.100565
Wang, H., Dang, A., Wu, Z., & Mac, S. (2024). Generative AI in higher education: Seeing ChatGPT through universities' policies, resources, and guidelines. *Computers and Education: Artificial Intelligence, 7*, 100326. https://doi.org/10.1016/j.caeai.2024.100326
Wang, Y. (2024). Cognitive and sociocultural dynamics of self-regulated use of machine translation and generative AI tools in academic EFL writing. *System, 126*, 103505. https://doi.org/10.1016/j.system.2024.103505
Wang, Y., & Stockwell, G. (2024). Social justice and technology in second language education. *Iranian Journal of Language Teaching & Research, 11*(3), 1–18. https://doi.org/10.30466/ijltr.2023.121403
Yusuf, A., Pervin, N., & Román-González, M. (2024). Generative AI and the future of higher education: A threat to academic integrity or reformation? Evidence from multicultural perspectives. *International Journal of Educational Technology in Higher Education, 21*, Article 21. https://doi.org/10.1186/s41239-024-00453-6

Part Three

AI in practice

13
Machine translation and writing

Sangmin Michelle Lee

Nayeon Kang

> **Pre-reading questions:**
>
> 1) What obstacles do EFL secondary students face in L2 writing?
> 2) What learner variables may influence students' L2 writing processes and outcomes?
> 3) What are the potential advantages and disadvantages of MT use in L2 writing classrooms?

Introduction

Writing in a second language (L2) is challenging for L2 learners because it requires not only generating ideas, but also articulating them effectively in a non-native language. Myles (2002) argues, "to write well is not a naturally acquired skill; nevertheless, it is usually learned or culturally transmitted as a set of practices in formal instructional settings or other environments. Therefore, writing skills must be practiced and learned through experience" (p. 1). This task is particularly daunting for beginner students, who often struggle to express their thoughts clearly and accurately. In this context, machine translation (MT) is emerging as a valuable pedagogical tool that provides immediate, multilingual feedback that is both convenient and cost-effective (Lee, 2023). Moreover, recent advances in machine learning have significantly improved the accuracy of

MT, reducing common errors such as literal translations, contextual misunderstandings, and various errors in vocabulary, grammar, and meaning (Jolley & Maimone, 2023, Shin & Chon, 2023; Tsai, 2022). Thus, despite ongoing debates over the past decade about the appropriateness of MT in educational settings (Briggs, 2018; Jolley & Maimone, 2015), its use among L2 learners has continued to grow, reflecting a broader acceptance and integration of this technology into language learning.

Accordingly, a significant number of studies have investigated the use of MT in L2 classrooms, particularly in L2 writing, and have reported overall positive results. Previous studies have argued that MT can improve the quality of L2 writing by reducing lexico-grammatical errors, presenting alternative language options, and increasing linguistic awareness (Chen et al., 2015; Chon et al., 2021; Chung & Ahn, 2022; Lee, 2022a; 2023; Tsai, 2019, 2022). In addition, MT supports learners by allowing them to focus on content rather than form and helps them to refine their revisions (Briggs, 2018; Chandra & Yuyun, 2018; Valijärvi & Tarsoly 2019). From the affective perspective, MT can increase motivation to write in L2, enhance L2 confidence, and lower L2 writing anxiety (Chon et al., 2021; Fredholm, 2021; Lee, 2022b; Tsai, 2022). Prior studies on learner perceptions have shown that learners have generally positive attitudes toward the use of MT in L2 writing, and as MT accuracy has improved in recent years, more students have come to view the use of MT positively (Chon et al., 2021; Niño, 2020; Lee, 2022a, 2023; Shin & Chon, 2023; Tsai, 2022).

However, the use of MT in language learning is not without its problems. Key considerations include the long-term effects of MT on language acquisition, the impact of MT on learner variables such as age and language proficiency, and ethical issues (Chon et al., 2021; Lee, 2022b; Loock et al., 2022). As MT becomes increasingly prevalent among a diverse population of L2 learners, it is crucial to explore these aspects from different perspectives and in different learning contexts. Previous studies have emphasized the role of learner variables in MT use, particularly language proficiency and confidence, but how learner variables affect students' MT use remains understudied. In addition, despite the growing number of MT studies, research on younger learners remains scarce; therefore, this study examined middle school students' MT use, perceptions of MT, and learner factors affecting their MT use. The current research addressed the following questions:

RQ1. How do Korean EFL middle school students perceive the use of MT in L2 writing?
RQ2. Does students' L2 writing ability influence their MT use and perceptions of MT use in L2 writing? What other factors influence students' MT use?

Literature review
Influence of machine translation on L2 writing
Over the last two decades, there have been remarkable advances in the field of MT, which have led to a significant improvement in the accuracy and quality of translated texts (Bowker & Ciro, 2019). Due to the continuous improvement in its quality and accessibility, MT is currently used by a significant number of users for various purposes, and in particular, the incorporation of MT has had a significant impact on the field of L2 learning (Reinhardt & Oskoz, 2021). While the literature has reported both favorable and unfavorable outcomes of the use of MT within and beyond the L2 educational setting (Muñoz-Basols et.al, 2023), systematic reviews have shown overall positive outcomes of the use of MT in the L2 classroom. According to Klimova et. al. (2023) and Lee (2023), the use of MT helps students develop lexical and grammatical structures, improve reading comprehension, and enhance students' language proficiency.

L2 writing is the domain where MT has been most widely used and researched. Numerous studies have confirmed that MT can help L2 students improve their writing skills by providing immediate feedback and suggestions for lexico-grammatical options (Chung & Ahn 2022; Lee & Briggs 2021; Shin & Chon, 2023; Tsai, 2022). Chang et.al (2022) found that MT is a valuable tool for error correction, enabling students to identify and correct their errors. From a revision perspective, MT mediates students' L2 revision process and helps them improve the quality of their writing (Chang et al., 2022; O'Neill, 2016; Stapleton & Leung, 2019; Tsai, 2019, 2022; Yang et al., 2023). MT serves as an effective aid in the writing process by assisting in the planning and drafting stages of writing and providing immediate linguistic suggestions that improve the quality of initial drafts (Lee, 2021). MT also provides individualized written corrective feedback to students by suggesting better lexical choices and reformulating sentences for the given context (Lee, 2022b). Considering the L2 classroom situation where the teacher cannot provide individualized feedback to each student, MT can serve as an alternative pedagogical tool to support students' L2 writing and revision. Finally, as MT helps students with language, it reduces their cognitive load and allows them to use their cognitive resources more for content and focus more on meaning (Chung & Ahn, 2022; Lee, 2023).

Factors affecting the use of machine translation
Although MT serves as a writing aid to facilitate L2 writing and revision, the results may vary depending on learner variables such as language proficiency, affective factors, and writing and revision strategies.

In terms of language proficiency, Chung and Ahn (2022) found that high proficiency learners used MT mainly for vocabulary search, being aware of MT's limitations such as word choice and grammatical accuracy, while low proficiency learners used MT mainly for grammar checking, focusing on improving syntactic accuracy. In Lee's (2022a) study, high-level students used MT strategically based on their linguistic knowledge and other resources and did not rely solely on MT in their writing process, while low-level students found the use of MT challenging, suggesting that they may have struggled to understand or effectively apply MT outputs in their writing tasks. Lee and Briggs (2021) also highlighted that high-level students use MT to refine their error correction strategies, focusing on reducing errors in their L2 texts, but low-level students tend to show a higher acceptance rate of MT suggestions, indicating a reliance on the tool for language correction. Despite the inconsistent results of previous studies regarding learners' proficiency levels and the effectiveness of using MT (Garcia & Pena, 2011, Niño, 2009, Tsai, 2019), recent studies have shown that high-level learners use more diverse strategies when revising their writing and rely less on MT than low-level learners (Chung & Ahn., 2022; Lee, 2022a; Lee & Briggs., 2021). On the other hand, studies have also shown that MT, if not used correctly, can hinder the growth of language skills and potentially encourage a reliance on technology rather than language learning (Rico & Pastor, 2022).

Previous studies have also investigated students' perceptions and attitudes toward the use of MT. According to Lee's (2023) meta-analysis, despite the frequent inaccurate results of MT, most L2 learners view MT as a useful tool to support writing. However, learners expressed mixed feelings about the use of MT (Chandra & Yuyun, 2018; Lee, 2023). That is, on the one hand, learners appreciated the benefits of using MT, but on the other hand, they distrusted MT because of its inaccuracy. Furthermore, they found MT useful for vocabulary, but not so much for grammar. In addition, Lee (2022a, b) found that learners' affective variables, such as confidence or anxiety in language skills and self-perception as a learner, influenced the use and perception of MT. According to Jolley and Maimone (2022), low-level students often have low confidence in their L2 writing abilities, and their lack of confidence often leads them to rely more on MT. Niño (2020) and Lee (2022a) also argued that low-level students rely more on MT, and this reliance stems from their limited ability to self-correct; therefore, low-level students often have difficulty making decisions between their writing and MT output. In addition, low-level students may rely too much on MT because they lack the confidence to engage directly with the language, which may hinder their ability to notice and learn from their mistakes (Deng & Yu, 2022; Lo, 2023).

Motivation is another important factor in the use of MT because it directly affects a learner's desire and effort to learn a new language, which shows a direct relationship with learning outcomes (Bower, 2019). While highly motivated learners may actively use MT as an L2 learning tool, students with low motivation may use MT less frequently because they may not be able to see the value of using MT for L2 improvement (Bower, 2019). In fact, Mostafa et.al. (2021) explored the motivational aspects behind corrective feedback preferences, such as language mindset and performance goals. They found that learners who aim to improve their language skills (development-approach goal) prefer explicit feedback types that provide clear corrections and learning opportunities, whereas learners who aim to maintain their skills (development-avoidance goal) prefer more implicit feedback that is less direct and focuses on maintaining current skill levels without overt correction. This suggests that learners with low motivation to learn a foreign language, may be unwilling to actively engage with MT as a revision tool. Students' use of MT also influences their motivation to write; when students can receive aids from MT in L2 writing, their motivation enhances, and they view the use of MT positively (Lee, 2020). Despite a significant amount of research on MT, most studies have still focused on the effectiveness of using MT in L2 writing. Various learner variables that may influence students' learning outcomes have not been sufficiently investigated. In addition, the research contexts are mostly limited to university, and other school contexts need to be further investigated.

Method

Participants and task descriptions

The current study involved 59 second grade Korean EFL middle school students. The students' English proficiency was mostly at beginner level (A1 on the CEFR or below) based on their pre-test scores. The writing activities included in the current study were their usual writing activities embedded in the English classroom, following the general process writing procedures. In the pretest, the students were given 20 minutes to write a 120-word essay in English on the topic, "The person I respect," without access to any external resources. The teacher encouraged the students to write in English as much as possible. While the students were encouraged to write the essay entirely in English, they were allowed to use Korean for unfamiliar words or phrases. They were then given one week to use MT to identify appropriate English words and phrases to match unfamiliar Korean words and phrases. During this time, they compared their initial drafts (pretest) with the MT-generated results and revised their essays accordingly. After completing the revisions, the students submitted the updated version of their essays. Two weeks later, they were asked to rewrite the essay without MT assistance (posttest). Based on Fredholm's (2019) observation that MT may not have a lasting impact on L2 writing skills, the two-week gap between the MT-assisted revision and the posttest in this study was expected to provide an opportunity to examine the longer-term effects of MT on the students' L2 writing development.

During the writing tasks, students were allowed to use MT to address any challenges they encountered in refining their initial drafts. Intermediate and advanced students were encouraged to use MT only to identify appropriate English words and phrases for their native language (Korean). However, for lower-level students who struggled to produce initial drafts in English, MT was allowed to translate entire Korean sentences. Given the students' previous experience with translation tools, no formal training was provided. However, to address the linguistic differences between Korean and English, participants were instructed on the correct use of Korean sentence structure. This included guidelines on how to avoid omitting the subject and how to use only one verb per sentence. Additionally, it should be noted that most of the students were not able to articulate their ideas in English, so in previous years they took fill-in-the-blank tests or wrote the essay after memorizing the given scripts for performance tests. However, with the help of MT, they were able to express their ideas in English. Both essays collected in the present study were scored using a holistic writing rubric on a five-point scale (see Appendix) by two trained educators who also served as researchers for this study. The interrater reliability for scoring was calculated to be 0.89, indicating high interrater agreement.

Data collection and analysis

The current study employed a quantitative research method, including the students' writing scores and the post survey. The survey was developed based on previous studies (Briggs, 2028; Jolley & Maimone; Lee, 2022b) and included 24 items related to perceived English proficiency in reading and writing, motivation to learn English, confidence and anxiety in English writing, strategies for using MT, and perceived usefulness for English writing (see Table 3). The survey used a five-point Likert scale except for their perceived English proficiency (high, medium, low). The reliability of the survey was .84 (Cronbach's Alpha), which proved reliable.

For the students' writing scores, inferential statistics were used; paired t-tests to compare the pretest and posttest writing scores, and ANOVA to compare the results according to the students' English writing proficiency levels. Descriptive and inferential statistics were used to examine the students' perceptions, the factors influencing the students' perceptions of using MT, and the relationships among the factors. SPSS 28 was used for all statistical analyses in this study.

Results

The t-test results showed that the students' writing scores increased significantly in the posttest ($p < .001$) as shown in Table 1. Based on the pretest scores, the students were categorized into three groups, high (point 5), intermediate (points 3 and 4), and low (points 1 and 2). The high group was able to express their ideas in English without many major language errors, which hindered understanding of the text. The intermediate group produced text with frequent major language errors, but generally delivered the intended meaning. The low group produced many major language errors, which hindered overall understanding of the text. The number of low-level students (N = 35) greatly exceeded the number of the intermediate-level students (N = 14) and the high-level students (N = 10). ANOVA confirmed that the difference between the groups was significant ($p = .007$). The paired t-test results for each group also showed that the writing of all three groups improved significantly in the posttest. The intermediate-level group improved the most, followed by the low-level group and the high-level group (Table 2).

Table 13.1 *Pretest and posttest results*

	Mean	Std.	t	p
Pre	1.64	.950	9.517	< .001
Post	3.64	1.662		

Table 13.2 *Pretest and posttest results of each group*

Group	N	Tests	Mean	Std.	t	p
Low	35	Pre	1.00	.000	−6.900	<.001
		Post	3.09	1.788		
Intermediate	14	Pre	2.07	.267	−8.341	<.001
		Post	4.40	1.092		
High	10	Pre	3.40	.699	−3.161	.006
		Post	4.60	.000		

The study examined the students' perceptions of their English, affective factors, strategies for using MT in English writing, and perceived usefulness of using MT (Table 3). In terms of language proficiency, the students rated their English reading proficiency higher than their English writing proficiency and rated both proficiencies as quite low. The present study specifically asked about their perceived proficiency in Korean (L1) to investigate whether their perceived L1 writing proficiency would affect their strategies or performance in using MT, and most students considered their L1 writing proficiency to be a medium level. From the affective perspective, the students showed a high level of motivation to learn and write well in English, but their confidence level was low, and their anxiety level was moderate. Regarding the perceived usefulness of using MT, they felt that MT helped them write English essays and find words and expressions,

Table 13.3 *Survey results*

Category	Item	Mean	SD
Perceived language proficiency	Korean Writing Proficiency	2.27	1.168
	English Reading Proficiency	2.09	.611
	English Writing Proficiency	1.79	.624
Affective and motivational factors	I want to speak English well	4.57	.850
	I want to write English well	4.41	.930
	I am trying hard to write English well.	3.71	1.074
	I am anxious about writing English.	3.21	1.366
	I am confident in English writing.	2.55	1.220
MT use and strategies	I use MT for English writing.	3.61	1.090
	Using MT can help me improve my English writing.	3.93	.988
	I write my own English writing before using MT.	3.39	1.289
	I read MT output before incorporating it into my writing.	3.87	1.129
	I compare MT output with my English writing.	3.39	1.275
Perceived usefulness of MT use	MT is useful for using appropriate words in English writing.	3.73	1.036
	MT is useful for using appropriate expressions in English writing.	3.75	.995
	MT is useful for using correct grammar in English writing.	3.14	1.069
	MT helps me improve my English.	3.20	1.017
	MT helps me learn English vocabulary.	3.59	.968
	MT helps me learn English grammar.	3.09	.996

but the perceived usefulness of using MT to help with grammar was lower than in other areas. Similarly, not only in L2 writing but also in L2 learning in general, the students perceived MT as more useful for learning vocabulary but less useful for learning grammar. In terms of the strategies, more than half of them wrote their essays without the support of MT (67.3%). Other strategies, such as reading MT output and comparing MT output with their own writing, also scored moderately high, indicating that more than half of the students used these strategies while using MT.

The results showed that the students responded differently to certain survey items depending on their writing ability. Most notably, the low-level students used MT more frequently than the other groups, and the intermediate-level group tended to find MT most helpful for English composition, followed by the low-level group, for English essay writing. For grammar, however, the low- (M = 3.94) and the intermediate-level (M = 4.17) groups found MT more helpful, while the high-level group found it less helpful (M = 3.60). In terms of strategies for using MT, the students' responses also varied by level. Most significantly, the high-level group wrote English essays without MT support more often before using MT, followed by the intermediate-level group, and the low-level group wrote essays on their own least often. On other items for strategies for using MT, the intermediate- and high-level groups used the strategies more often than the low-level group, such as reading the MT output carefully and comparing their output with the MT output. In terms of language areas, the low-level groups tended to find MT useful for vocabulary and expression, but not for grammar, but they still tended to be more dependent on MT for grammar than the other groups The results of the ANOVA showed that only three items, "frequent use of MT," "writing own's texts," and "perceived improved outcomes of L2 writing," showed significant differences between the groups (Table 4); while the low-level groups used MT more frequently and found it more useful, they wrote less frequently than the high-level group. Although differences were found for other items, they were not statistically significant.

Table 13.4 *Differences between the proficiency levels: ANOVA*

Item	Sum of Squares	F	Sig.	Rank
Use of MT	11.208	5.485	.007	1>2>3>
Writing their own	20.105	7.478	.001	3>2>1
Perceived outcomes	25.169	5.343	.008	1>2>3>

*1 = low; 2 = intermediate; 3 = high.

Table 13.5 *Influence of perceived language proficiencies on MT use: Regression*

Item	Unstandardized Coefficients		Standardized Coefficients	t	Sig.
	B	Std. Error	Beta		
Actual writing score	−.576	.172	−.414	−3.341	.002
English Reading	−.128	.232	−.072	−.552	.584
English Writing	−.939	.229	−.537	−4.100	<.001
Korean	.137	.106	.147	1.300	.199

Table 13.6 *Influence of affective factors on MT use: Regression*

Item	Unstandardized Coefficients		Standardized Coefficients	t	Sig.
	B	Std. Error	Beta		
Confidence	−.597	.091	−.668	−6.588	<.001
Anxiety	.468	.088	.587	5.324	<.001
Motivation	.160	.163	.112	.983	.330

In terms of perceived language proficiency, the students' perceived English writing proficiency influenced their use of MT. That is, the lower their perceived writing proficiency, the more MT they used. Their perceived English reading proficiency and Korean writing proficiency did not influence their MT use (Table 5). Other variables, the students' confidence and anxiety also significantly affected their MT use; the students with less confidence and more anxiety about English writing used MT more often (Table 6). The students' motivation did not affect the frequency of MT use, but it significantly affected their strategies of MT use; the students with higher motivation used more diverse strategies while using MT ($t = 5.509$, $p < .001$).

Discussion

The present study showed that the Korean middle school EFL students generally considered their Korean writing proficiency and English reading and writing proficiency to be low, and their confidence in English writing also to be low. However, they wanted to do well in learning and writing English. Regarding the first research question, the study found that the students had moderately positive views about using MT in L2 writing overall. In this study, most of them used MT frequently in L2 writing and they perceived that using MT helped to improve their L2 writing (M = 3.93). This finding was consistent with previous studies on students' perceptions of MT use in L2 writing, which showed more positive views of MT use (Chon et al., 2021; Niño, 2009, 2020; Lee, 2022a, 2023; Tsai, 2019, 2022). While participants in earlier MT studies showed mixed perceptions, sometimes even negative feelings, about MT use and usefulness (Briggs, 2018; Groves & Mundt, 2015), participants in more recent studies showed more positive perceptions and attitudes (Niño, 2020; Lee, 2023; Shin & Chon, 2023; Tsai, 2022). This shift in students' perceptions is largely attributed to improvements in the accuracy of MT in recent years. That is, when MT is used in L2 writing, its accuracy is a critical element that affects students' L2 writing, and their perceptions of the usefulness of MT in L2 writing depend on MT accuracy. Thus, as MT accuracy improves, students' perceptions of MT use become more positive.

More specifically, the students in the current study found the use of MT more useful for vocabulary and expressions than grammar in L2 writing. According to Niño (2009, 2020), Chon et al. (2021) and Lee (2022a, b), finding and correcting grammatical errors is more difficult than correcting lexical errors in their L2 writing. Since MT does not provide one-to-one feedback on students' lexico-grammatical errors, but often provides reformulated sentences for the intended meaning, comparing their writing with the MT output and correcting their errors is often challenging for L2 students, especially beginners, who do not have enough L2 linguistic knowledge and resources. Since the English proficiency of the participants in the current study was at the beginner level, they felt that MT was less useful for grammar. In particular, the low-level students were more likely to believe that MT was useful for grammar, and this finding is attributed to their low L2 proficiency and lack of confidence in making language judgments.

Regarding the second research question, this study showed the students' writing ability influenced their perceptions of MT use, such as confidence and language anxiety, which, in turn, affected their use of MT. L2 writing is a complex interplay of linguistic, cognitive, and affective learner factors. Previous L2 writing studies have emphasized that various learner variables, such as L2 proficiency, motivation, anxiety, and confidence, influence students' writing and revision behaviors, which ultimately affect the quality of L2 writing outcomes (Chen et al., 2015; Tang & Liu, 2018; Valijärvi & Tarsoly, 2019; Zhang & Cheng, 2021). Similarly, when using MT, these learner variables played a crucial role in shaping the students' perceptions and behaviors in the current study, and the students' language proficiency was one of the most important factors influencing their use of MT and its effectiveness. Regarding learners' language proficiency, there has been disagreement among previous studies. While Garcia and Pena (2011), Niño (2009), and Briggs (2018) claimed that beginners benefit more from MT, Lee (2022a), Chung (2020) and Shin and Chon (2023) argued that advanced students benefit more. A closer look at the studies reveals different reasons for the results of each study. The main reason why beginner students benefit from MT is that MT can help them express their ideas in the L2 that they might otherwise have difficulty articulating. However, although they can express their ideas in the L2 with the help of MT, it does not necessarily mean that they learn the L2 from the process of working with the L2. Due to their lack of L2 linguistic knowledge, they may simply copy or adopt the MT output instead of critically evaluating and comparing their errors and MT output. Conversely, advanced students, with their richer linguistic repertoire, can critically adopt MT output and strategically incorporate it into their writing. In the present study, the low-level students showed the greater gains on the posttest, but this may be partly because the high-level students had less room for improvement because their pretest scores were already higher than those of the other groups.

Previous studies have confirmed that not only students' L2 proficiency, but also other learner factors influence students' perceptions of MT use and actual MT use. Students' confidence in their L2 affects their perceptions and MT use. Polakova and Klimova (2023) found that learners' perceptions and experiences with MT tools may vary depending on individual characteristics, including L2 confidence. More specifically, since students with lower L2 confidence are likely to experience more difficulties in L2 writing, they tend to rely more on MT as a means of compensating for their lack of L2 knowledge (Niño, 2009; Lee, 2023). Interestingly, the students in Lee's study (2022a) showed mixed behaviors in their use of MT. In her study, while students with lower proficiency and confidence relied more on MT, they also showed hesitation in selecting and adopting output because they were not sure which options between MT output and their own writing were correct. Similarly, in the current study, the students with low L2 writing proficiency, low confidence, and high anxiety used MT most often, which is consistent with prior studies (Fredholm, 2019, 2021; Lee, 2023). Conversely, motivation did not affect how often the students used MT, but it did affect their strategies for using MT, that is, highly motivated students read MT output, compared their own writing to the MT output and wrote their own English writing before using MT more often. Zhang and Cheng (2021) argued that highly motivated students use multiple strategies in writing and revising, such as self-monitoring, drafting and redrafting, reflecting their writing, and using diverse technology tools to support their writing, and this tendency was also reflected in the students' use of MT in the current study.

Implications

Based on the results of the study, the present study suggests several pedagogical implications of using MT in the L2 writing classroom. In this study, MT improved students' writing scores. While this result indicates the potential benefit of MT as a pedagogical tool to support L2 writing, the benefit may not be permanent. Fredholm (2019) showed that students' L2 writing, especially lexical items, increased with the use of MT, but when MT was not available, the effect of MT disappeared. This means that increased L2 writing scores with MT do not guarantee students' L2 learning in the long run, but the effect may only be immediate and short-term. Therefore, to extend the positive effect of MT on L2 learning, it is essential to integrate various instructional strategies. For example, training sessions on effective MT use and post-writing workshops can help students develop a critical and reflective approach to MT, enabling them to better evaluate, assess, and adapt MT outcomes (O'Neill, 2019). In addition, language teachers can explicitly teach students how to use MT effectively and strategically for their L2 writing and learning. Depending on students' needs and instructional purposes, different strategies for using MT, such as pre-editing (editing the source language before using MT), post-editing (editing the MT output), comparing students' own writing with the MT output, and back-translating (translating the MT output back into the source language to check the accuracy of the MT output), can be used to further improve the quality of L2 writing outcomes. Moreover, as shown in the current study, students engage in different strategies and behaviors when using MT during writing and revision, and learner variables influence the interaction between students and MT in complex ways, which can either support or hinder students' language learning. Therefore, teachers should consider different learner variables in their instructional design of L2 writing. Students with low proficiency may not be able to benefit from MT, so teachers should consider their needs when using MT. Teachers also need to find ways to prevent students from over-relying on MT due to their lack of confidence in L2 writing.

Conclusion

As MT becomes more prevalent in L2 classrooms, it is imperative to conduct diverse research in different contexts to maximize its pedagogical benefits. This study focused on the use and perceptions of MT among Korean EFL middle school students in L2 writing contexts. The findings indicated that although MT use improved L2 writing scores and was perceived as beneficial by most students, the effectiveness of MT was strongly influenced by learner variables such as language proficiency and confidence in their L2 knowledge. Significantly, this research highlighted how these variables influence both MT use and perceptions of MT use. The findings suggest that the mere use of MT does not guarantee language learning; rather, educators need to implement guided and well-designed instructional strategies tailored to the diverse needs and characteristics of students to optimize the benefits of MT in educational settings.

Limitations

The scope of this study was limited to a small cohort from a single school, suggesting that the findings should be interpreted with caution and not overgeneralized. In addition, the study's reliance on quantitative data without the support of qualitative findings, such as student interviews or reflective essays, may limit the depth of understanding of students' true experiences and perceptions. Given that this was a short-term experiment, the long-term effects of MT on L2 writing remain unclear. Future research should aim to address these limitations by including more comprehensive qualitative analyses and increasing the sample size to improve the generalizability of the findings. In addition, it is important to examine the long-term effectiveness of MT use and to further investigate how MT interacts with various learner variables across linguistic, cognitive, and affective domains. This continued research will help refine the integration of MT tools into language learning curricula to ensure that they effectively meet learners' needs.

> **Post-reading questions:**
>
> 1) How can teachers guide secondary students' MT use in L2 writing?
> 2) What are the long-term effects of MT use on L2 writing and learning?

Further reading

1. Chung, E. S., & Ahn, S. (2022). The effect of using machine translation on linguistic features in L2 writing across proficiency levels and text genres. *Computer Assisted Language Learning, 35*(9), 2239–2264. https://doi.org/10.1080/09588221.2020.1871029

    This study investigated how learners' use of MT affects linguistic features (complexity, accuracy, lexical density and fluency measures) in L2 writing and whether proficiency level and text genre affect learners' use of MT.

2. Lee, S-M. (2022). L2 learners' strategies for using machine translation as a personalized writing assisting tool. In J. Colpaert &

G. Stockwell (Eds.) *Personalization, contextualization, and socialization* (pp. 184–206). Castledown Publishers. http://doi.org/10.29140/978191429101

This study investigated Korean EFL middle school students' strategies for using MT in L2 writing and showed how learner variables affected L2 writing outcomes based on the analysis of video recordings.

References

Bower, K. (2019). Explaining motivation in language learning: A framework for evaluation and research. *Language Learning Journal, 47*(5), 558–574. https://doi.org/10.1080/09571736.2017.1321035

Bowker, L. C., & Ciro, J. B. (2019). *Machine translation and global research: Towards improved machine translation literacy in the scholarly community.* Emerald Group Publishing. https://doi.org/10.1108/9781787567214

Briggs, N. (2018). Neural machine translation tools in the language learning classroom: Students' use, perceptions, and analyses. *JALT CALL Journal, 14*(1), 2–24. http://dx.doi.org/10.29140/jaltcall.v14n1.221

Chandra, S. O., & Yuyun, I. (2018). The use of Google Translate in EFL essay writing. *LLT Journal: A Journal on Language and Language Teaching, 21*(2), 228–238. https://doi.org/10.24071/llt.v21i2.1539

Chang, P., Chen, P. J., & Lai, L. L. (2022). Recursive editing with Google Translate: The impact on writing and error correction. *Computer Assisted Language Learning*, 1–26. https://doi.org/10.1080/09588221.2022.2147192

Chen, M.-H., Huang, S.-T., Chang, J. S., & Liou, H.-C. (2015). Developing a corpus-based paraphrase tool to improve EFL learners' writing skills. *Computer Assisted Language Learning, 28*(1), 22–40. https://doi.org/10.1080/09588221.2013.783873

Chon, Y. V., Shin, D., & Kim, G. E. (2021). Comparing L2 learners' writing against parallel machine-translated texts: Raters' assessment, linguistic complexity, and errors. *System, 96,* 1–12. https://doi.10.1016/j.system.2020.102408

Chung, E. S. (2020). The effect of L2 proficiency on post-editing machine translated texts. *The Journal of Asia TEFL, 17*(1), 182–193. http://dx.doi.org/10.18823/asiatefl.2020.17.1.11.182

Chung, E. S., & Ahn, S. (2022). The effect of using machine translation on linguistic features in L2 writing across proficiency levels and text genres. *Computer Assisted Language Learning, 35*(9), 2239–2264. https://doi.org/10.1080/09588221.2020.1871029

Deng, X., & Yu, Z. (2022). A systematic review of machine-translation-assisted language learning for sustainable education. *Sustainability, 14*(13), 7598. https://doi.org/10.3390/su14137598

Fredholm, K. (2019). Effects of Google Translate on lexical diversity: Vocabulary development among learners of Spanish as a foreign language. *Revista Nebrija de Lingüística Aplicada a la Enseñanza de las Lenguas, 13*, 98–117. http://doi.org/10.26378/rnlael1326300

Fredholm, K. (2021). Google Translate search strategies among learners of Spanish L3: A complex lexico-morpho-syntactic weave of trial-and-error. *Estudios de Lingüística Aplicada, 39*(72), 9–48. http://doi:10.26378/rnlael918248

Garcia, I., & Peña, M. (2011). Machine translation-assisted language learning: Writing for beginners. *Computer Assisted Language Learning, 24*(5), 471–487. http://doi:10.22201/enallt.01852647p.2021.72.926

Groves, M., & Mundt, K. (2015). Friend or foe? Google Translate in language for academic purposes. *English for Specific Purposes, 37*, 112–121. https://doi.org/10.1016/j.esp.2014.09.001

Jolley, J., & Maimone, L. (2015). Free online machine translation: Use and perceptions by Spanish students and instructors. In A. Moeller (Ed.) *Learn language, explore cultures, transform lives.* (pp. 181–200). Richmond, VA: Robert M. Terry.

Jolley, J. & Maimone, L. (2022). Thirty years of machine translation in language teaching and learning: A review of the literature. *L2 Journal, 14*(1), 26 –44. https://doi.org/10.5070/L214151760

Klimova, B., Pikhart, M., Polakova, P., Cerna, M., Yayilgan, S. Y., & Shaikh, S. (2023). A Systematic review on the use of emerging technologies in teaching English as an applied language at the university level. *Systems, 11*(1), 42. https://doi.org/10.3390/systems11010042

Lee, S-M. (2020). The impact of using machine translation on EFL students' writing. *Computer Assisted Language Learning, 33*(3), 157 –175. https://doi.org/10.1080/09588221.2018.1553186

Lee, S-M. (2022a). Different effects of machine translation on L2 revisions across students' L2 writing proficiency levels. *Language Learning & Technology, 26*(1), 1–21. https://hdl.handle.net/10125/73490

Lee, S-M. (2022b). L2 learners' strategies for using machine translation as a personalized writing assisting tool. In J. Colpaert & G. Stockwell (Eds.) *Personalization, contextualization, and socialization* (pp. 184–206). Castledown Publishers. http://doi.org/ 10.29140/978191429101

Lee, S-M. (2023). The effectiveness of machine translation in foreign language education: A systematic review and meta-Analysis. *Computer Assisted Language Learning, 36*(1–2), 103–125. https://doi.org/10.1080/09588221.2021.1901745

Lee, S.-M., & Briggs, N. (2021). Effects of using machine translation to mediate the revision process of Korean university students' academic writing. *ReCALL*, *33*(1), 18–33. https://doi.org/10.1017/S0958344020000191

Lee, Y. J. (2021). Still taboo? Using machine translation for low-level EFL writers. *ELT Journal*, *75*(4), 432–441. http://dx.doi.org/10.1093/elt/ccab018

Lo, S. (2023). Neural machine translation in EFL classrooms: Learners' vocabulary improvement, immediate vocabulary retention and delayed vocabulary retention. *Computer Assisted Language Learning*, *FirstView*. https://doi.org/10.1080/09588221.2023.2207603

Loock, R., Lechauguette, S., & Holt, B. (2022). Dealing with the elephant in the classroom: Developing language students' machine translation literacy. *Australian Journal of Applied Linguistics*, *5*(3), 118–134. http://doi.10.29140/ajal.v5n3.53si2

Maimone, L., & Jolley, J. (2023). Looks like Google to me: Instructor ability to detect machine translation in L2 Spanish writing. *Foreign Language Annals*, *56*(3), 627–644. https://doi.org/10.1111/flan.12690

Mostafa, P., Dominik, D., Wolff, D., Nakatsukasa, K., & Bellwoar, E. (2021). Motivational factors underlying learner preferences for corrective feedback: Language mindsets and achievement goals. *Language Teaching Research*, *25*(6), 858–877. https://doi.org/10.1177/13621688211018808

Muñoz-Basols, J., Neville, C., Lafford, B. A., & Godev, C. (2023). Potentialities of applied translation for language learning in the era of artificial intelligence. *Hispania*, *106*(2), 171–194. http://dx.doi.org/10.1353/hpn.2023.a899427

Myles, J. (2002). The writing process and error analysis in student texts. *Second Language Writing and Research*, *6*(2), 1–20.

Niño, A. (2009). Machine translation in foreign language learning: Language learners' and tutors' perceptions of its advantages and disadvantages. *ReCALL*, *21*(2), 241–258. http://doi.org/10.1017/S0958344009000172

Niño, A. (2020). Exploring the use of online machine translation for independent language learning. *Research in Learning Technology*, *28*, 2402. https://dx.doi.org/10.25304/rlt.v28.2402

O'Neill, E. M. (2016). Measuring the impact of online translation on FL writing scores. *The IALLT Journal of Language Learning Technologies*, *46*(2), 1–39. https://doi.org/10.17161/iallt.v46i2.8560

O'Neill, E. M. (2019). Online translator, dictionary, and search engine use among L2 students. *Computer-Assisted Language Learning*, *20*(1), 154–177.

Polakova, P., & Klimova, B. (2023). Using DeepL translator in learning English as an applied foreign language: An empirical pilot study. *Heliyon, 9*(8), e18595. https://doi.org/10.1016/j.heliyon.2023.e18595

Reinhardt, J., & Oskoz, A. (2021). Twenty-five years of emerging technologies. *Language Learning & Technology, 25*(3), 1–5. https://doi.org/10125/73442

Rico, C., & González Pastor, D. (2022). The role of machine translation in translation education: A thematic analysis of translator educators' beliefs. *Translation & Interpreting: The International Journal of Translation and Interpreting Research, 14*(1), 177–197. http://dx.doi.org/10.12807/ti.114201.2022.a010

Shin, D., & Chon, Y. V. (2023). Second language learners' post-editing strategies for machine translation errors. *Language Learning & Technology, 27*(1), 1–25. https://hdl.handle.net/10125/73523

Stapleton, P., & Leung, B. (2019). Assessing the accuracy and teachers' impressions of Google Translate: A study of primary L2 writers in Hong Kong. *English for Specific Purposes, 56*, 18–34. https://doi.org/10.1016/j.esp.2019.07.001

Tang, C., & Liu, Y. (2018). Effects of indirect coded corrective feedback with and without short affective teacher comments on L2 writing performance, learner uptake, and motivation. *Assessing Writing, 35*, 26–40. https://doi.org/10.1016/j.asw.2017.12.002

Tsai, S.-C. (2019). Using Google Translate in EFL drafts: A preliminary investigation. *Computer Assisted Language Learning, 32*(5–6), 510–526. https://doi.org/10.1080/09588221.2018.1527361

Tsai, S.-C. (2022). Chinese students' perceptions of using Google Translate as a translingual CALL tool in EFL writing. *Computer Assisted Language Learning, 35*(5–6), 1250–1272. https://doi.org/10.1080/09588221.2020.1799412

Valijärvi, R.-L., & Tarsoly, E. (2019). Language students as critical users of Google Translate: Pitfalls and possibilities. *Practitioner Research in Higher Education, 12*(1), 61–74.

Yang, Y., Wei, X., Li, P., & Zhai, X. (2023). Assessing the effectiveness of machine translation in the Chinese EFL writing context: A replication of Lee (2020). *ReCALL, 35*(2), 211–224. https://doi.org/10.1017/S0958344023000022

Zhang, L., & Cheng, X. (2021). Examining the effects of comprehensive written corrective feedback on L2 EAP students' linguistic performance: A mixed-methods study. *Journal of English for Academic Purposes, 52*, 101043. https://doi.org/10.1016/j.jeap.2021.101043

Appendix

Rubric for writing assessment
1 – The student could barely write the essay in English.
2 – The essay contained many major errors, which seriously undermined the meaning and overall quality of writing, including many incomprehensible sentences.
3 – The essay contained many serious major errors, but delivered the overall meaning.
4 – The essay contained several major errors with many minor errors, but delivered the overall meaning.
5 – The essay contained a few major and minor errors, which did not damage the meaning of the sentence.

14
Generative AI and chatbots

Curtis Green-Eneix

Lucas Kohnke

> **Pre-reading questions:**
>
> 1) To what extent should ChatGPT have a role in students' additional language learning journey?
> 2) How have you engaged with ChatGPT, and to what extent has (or would) ChatGPT reshape your relationship with certain academic tasks (e.g., reading and writing) after using it?
> 3) How, in your opinion, can ChatGPT have a sustainable role in the (language) classroom?

Introduction

Artificial intelligence in education (AIED) allows this technology to reach teachers, learners and institutions (Hwang et al., 2020; Nemorin et al., 2023) and play a vital role in enhancing learning, teaching, assessment and administrative processes (Chiu et al., 2023; Kohnke et al., 2023a; Zhang & Aslan, 2021). For example, adaptive learning platforms and chatbots can personalize learning, automate assessment and provide students with detailed feedback (Kohnke et al., 2023b; Zawacki-Richter et al., 2019). Moreover, since the introduction of ChatGPT in 2022, generative AI (GenAI) has begun to revolutionize education. Using its training data (Barret & Pack, 2023), GenAI tools can create original content – including text, images, music, code and synthetic data (Kohnke, in-press) – assess student performance, tailor learning experiences to individual needs and enhance overall educational outcomes (Stöhr et al., 2024). Of the various applications of GenAI, chatbots have emerged as a particularly promising option for transforming education and providing tailored learning for students.

As GenAI chatbots like ChatGPT, Claude, and Gemini provide new avenues for innovative and interactive pedagogies and data-driven insights, scholars have made a concerted effort to explore the implications of GenAI chatbots for education (Dempere et al., 2023). Research has illustrated how these tools can serve as self-study aids, facilitate personalized learning experiences, enhance engagement, and provide real-time feedback that supports academic growth that can benefit students' learning (Chen et al., 2023; Kohnke et al., 2023a). Other recent investigations have also illustrated that they can produce educational content (e.g., practice exercises, quizzes, and reading materials) that is tailored to individual students' needs and proficiency levels (Law, 2024) and assist teachers with grading assignments, providing real-time feedback and facilitating online discussions, thereby freeing up time for high-value activities such as lesson planning and providing one-to-one student support (Kohnke & Zou, in-press). As these studies provide insight into how education can utilize artificial intelligence, these studies do not provide the field insight into how language learners view these resources. This is especially needed to understand their view of GenAI as conversations revolving around the tool have focused on ethical issues related to academic integrity, bias, and equitable access (Mahmud, 2024).

While these insights on how the tool can support both teachers and students, there is a need to understand the perceptions that revolve around using GenAI tools. As indicated by prior studies focusing on non-GenAI tools (Alm & Nkomo, 2020; Sydorenko et al., 2017), students' perception of a tool or teaching approach can impact their motivation and the extent to which they use these and GenAI tools for their learning (e.g., Chan & Hu, 2023). Although the role of beliefs has begun to be investigated concerning pre-and in-service teachers' use of GenAI tools within the classroom (e.g., Barret & Pack, 2023; Moorhouse & Kohnke, 2024; Wang & Cheng, 2021), research focusing on learners' beliefs toward these tools still needs to be further investigated (e.g., Chan & Hu, 2023; Gallacher et al., 2018), especially within a context where English is used to teach academic subjects where the first language of a majority of the population is not English (Kwok et al., 2024). In addition, there is a need to understand how students identify and perceive the ethical challenges revolving around GenAI, as concerns about untraceable copying and cheating by students using GenAI have also arisen and led to the reevaluation of some established assessment practices (Farazouli et al., 2023; Kong et al., 2024).

In identifying a need to understand further students' perceptions toward GenAI and the ethical issues they associate with these tools, this chapter addresses this need by investigating university students' perception of using GenAI within an English for Academic Purposes (EAP) course at a higher education institution in Hong Kong, exploring its potential and challenges in enhancing learning experiences.

This chapter also discusses and explores strategies that address ethical issues, privacy and bias, thereby enhancing learning and improving educational outcomes. Given the transformative potential and the challenges associated with integrating ChatGPT into educational settings, it is crucial to understand its impact on students' learning experiences and their views toward the tool. Before going into the study, we expand our points in the introduction to discuss what GenAI chatbots are and how they have been applied within education contexts. We also discuss the limitations and concerns of this tool and then present the role students' beliefs play in implementing this tool within the classroom.

Literature review
GenAI chatbots and applications within education

Over the past two decades, educators have been building chatbots on user-friendly platforms such as Google's Dialogflow (e.g. Kim et al., 2022; Kohnke, 2023a; Lee & Jeon, 2022). Using Dialogflow, they can design chatbots that perform specific tasks (e.g., answering common grammar questions and providing vocabulary practice) so learners can engage in purposeful and targeted communication. Dialogflow requires no programming knowledge. Educators can simply consider their students' needs and proficiency levels to determine the functions and contextualize them using the platform (Kim et al., 2022; Kohnke, 2023a). However, the release of ChatGPT showcased and introduced the world to the significant advancements in natural language processing, machine learning, and neural networks that paved the way for large language models (LLMs; Christie, 2023).

Unlike previous AI systems or chatbots that rely on discriminatory modeling and predefined classifications (Adiguzel et al., 2023), GenAI tools use transformer-based machine learning algorithms to learn and create the context through predictive modeling. In other words, LLMs such as OpenAI's GPT-4 (generative pre-trained transformer) that is used to power ChatGPT are trained on copious amounts of textual data to 'learn' or better predict the next word in a sequence that is relevant to the users prompts that may or may not have explicit instruction. This adaptability, coupled with the integrative interface, provides greater flexibility than previous AI systems or chatbot iterations before it (Law, 2023). As a result, these recent advancements in LLMs and chatbot-creation platforms (e.g., Poe) mean that users can now build and access powerful, personalized chatbots, further enhancing their educational utility. Compared to chatbots created using Dialogflow, GenAI chatbots have shown an enhanced capability to understand utterances in context (Lee et al., 2023).

Since 2022, ChatGPT has further expanded the utility of chatbots in education, showing that they can serve as learning companions and provide students with an interactive, stress-free studying environment (El Shazly, 2020; Guo et al., 2023; Jeon et al., 2023). Recent research indicates how chatbots may help improve student motivation, engagement and learning outcomes (Jeon, 2021; Kim & Su, 2024; Kohnke, 2022). They lead to increased attention, reduced anxiety and a greater desire to communicate (Lee & Lim, 2023; Tai & Chen, 2023). They promote language skills, with studies reporting gains in speaking (Dizon, 2020; Yang et al., 2022) and listening scores (Tai & Chen, 2022). For example, ChatGPT has been effectively deployed in a range of disciplines to design educational content, create assessments and improve the curriculum (Cotton et al., 2023). Finally, chatbots such as ChatGPT reduce teachers' workload by automating routine tasks, allowing them to focus on critical human aspects of teaching.

Ethical considerations and concerns

While GenAI chatbots are promising, there are also challenges associated with GenAI chatbots, including a lack of contextual information – which can lead to inaccuracies or inappropriate suggestions – and outdated knowledge due to static training data (Huang et al., 2023; Kandpal et al., 2023). These constraints underscore the need for additional safeguards to ensure that chatbots can be deployed effectively in real-world educational settings (Gao et al., 2023). Other issues include artificiality, ambiguity and the lack of direct corrective feedback (Koç & Savaş, 2024). In some cases, the novel and unnatural speaking conditions can demotivate learners compared to human partners (Ericsson et al., 2023; Fryer et al., 2017). Studies have also shown that students only have a moderate interest in the prolonged use of AI chatbots and increased anxiety levels due to the fear of failure and lack of empathy (e.g., Çakmak, 2022; El Shazly, 2021). These challenges are also coupled with ethical issues that teachers and students must navigate when using GenAI tools.

The ethical issues associated with GenAI tools and their application in education have led the discussion within the recent literature (Adiguzel et al., 2023; Farazouli et al., 2024; Law, 2023). These issues relate to the reliability and timeliness of the training data, the lack of direct access to online databases, and insufficient transparency about data collection and handling practices (Ray, 2023). For instance, OpenAI provided the following answer concerning using users' content to train ChatGPT:

> We may use content submitted to ChatGPT, DALL·E, and our other services for individuals to improve model performance. For

example, depending on a user's settings, we may use the user's prompts, the model's responses, and other content such as images and files to improve model performance. (OpenAI, 2024a)

They further go on to state that users' must actively opt out by clicking on "do not train on my content" within the data controls (OpenAI, 2024a, b). As user prompts, conversations, files, and images can be used to train the tool, there are concerns about data privacy as users may reveal personal information while interacting with chatbots. This further raised concerns as a recent software "bug" or an unexpected outcome or error in the software resorted to other users unintentionally being able to see this collected information (OpenAI, 2023, March 24).

Due to the wide swath of information chatbots are trained on, the sources may be biased toward specific viewpoints or perspectives (e.g., in terms of history, politics, or religion), which may lead to discrimination or misinformation (Mhlanga, 2023). Algorithmic bias can occur when an LLM is trained on a dataset that is not representative of the population. For instance, if the training data primarily consists of teachers from Western countries, the LLM may fail to adequately represent or accurately interpret speakers of other languages, dialects, languages or ethnic backgrounds (Baker & Hawn, 2021). Another possibility is the phenomenon referred to as ChatGPT hallucinations, which are instances where GenAI tools generate information that seems scientifically plausible but is factually incorrect (Baker & Hawn, 2021; Selwyn, 2022; Surameery & Shakor, 2023). This is particularly concerning in educational contexts, where accuracy is critical, and both students and teachers need to develop the ability to critically evaluate and verify the information provided by a chatbot (Ray, 2023). This has resulted in colleagues call for students and teachers to develop AI literacy, or the ability to "critically evaluate AI technologies; communicate and collaborate effectively with AI; and use AI as a tool online" in all parts of their lives (Long & Magerko, 2020, p. 2).

Learners' beliefs toward GenAI

Regardless of the benefits or limitations associated with GenAI tools, the perceptions surrounding this tool have been multifaceted and informed the uptake and adoption within the classroom. While these perceptions have begun to be investigated concerning teachers' adoption and application within their classroom (e.g., Moorhouse & Kohnke, 2024; Wang & Chen, 2021), students' beliefs are still relatively underexplored (e.g., Kohnke, 2022, 2023b; Lee & Jeon, 2022; Stöhr et al., 2024). The studies that have explored learners' perceptions of non-GenAI tools have shown that students have conflicting views that impact their use of their online resources within their learning (e.g., Alm & Nkomo, 2020; Sydorenko et al., 2017). For instance, Sydorenko et al. (2017) conducted a survey-based study focusing on the beliefs of US university students towards computer-assisted language learning. The study found that students' perceptions of the benefits and importance of these tools, as well as how they were used in the classroom and the students' own experiences with them, were key factors influencing their motivation to use the tools for their own learning. These findings were similarly identified within Chan and Hu's survey-based study that explored 399 undergraduate and postgraduate students' perceptions of GenAI within Hong Kong. They found students' beliefs significantly influenced their willingness to use the tool as they had both positive and negative. Chan and Hu concluded their study by explaining, "Understanding students on their willingness and concerns regarding the use of GenAI tools can help educators to integrate these technologies into the learning process better, ensuring they complement and enhance traditional teaching methods" and learning outcomes (p. 14).

While there are many ways in which students perceptions have been termed and operationalized, this study defines the term as the regimes of values that are informed by their past experiences to shape their stance toward activities (e.g., learning in the classroom), languages (e.g., English), and tools (e.g., such as GenAI tools) with beliefs being socially constructed within their immediate context that they feel to be true (Barcelos, 2015; Montgomery et al., 2024). As many of the studies have taken a positivist or postpositivist approach to investigate students' perceptions outside of the classroom, there is a need to understand how students' perceptions of GenAI within the classroom (Chan & Hu, 2023; Kwok et al., 2024), specifically that focuses on developing learners' acquisition of an additional language. Therefore, this qualitative investigation study seeks to further explore and understand students' perceptions regarding GenAI while identifying the ethical challenges that arise within an English for Academic Purposes course in Hong Kong. Specifically, it addresses the following questions:

RQ1: How do students perceive that ChatGPT impacts their academic language development and engagement in an EAP course?
RQ2: What ethical challenges with using ChatGPT do students identify and how do they suggest addressing them?

Methodology

This study employed a case study design, ideal for exploring complex phenomena within their real-life context (Yin, 2018). This approach enabled an in-depth investigation of university students' perceptions of using GenAI tools, specifically ChatGPT, in an educational setting. The case study design facilitated a comprehensive understanding of the nuances and complexity involved in integrating GenAI into language learning.

Research context and participants

This study included nine first-year undergraduate students in Hong Kong taking a compulsory EAP course where the medium of instruction was in English. This course is designed to support students' academic language development by teaching them how to read and produce common genres of academic discourse. Students are exposed to both written (i.e., analytical report and exposition) and spoken media (i.e., oral presentation). They are required to think critically and make sound ethical judgments related to copyright and authorship by observing standards of academic integrity. Students used ChatGPT to assist with activities and assignments during the course, integrating GenAI into their learning process. This use of AI aimed to enhance their engagement and provide immediate feedback, helping them refine their writing and presentation skills.

All participants were 19–20 years old, originally from Hong Kong and had completed secondary school the previous year. The second author, who was teaching the EAP course, invited all 21 students in the course to participate. Nine students volunteered. Each participant received a letter outlining the purpose and procedure of the study, as well as a consent form to sign. Pseudonyms were used throughout the study to protect the participants' anonymity.

Data collection and analysis

The objectives of this study were to arrive at a rich understanding of the participants' lived experiences and perceptions related to the implementation of ChatGPT and explore strategies to address ethical issues, privacy and bias. Therefore, we adopted a qualitative approach, employing individual, semi-structured interviews (Creswell, 2008). An interview guide was developed to elicit responses. It comprised the following questions:

1. Can you describe your overall experience with using ChatGPT in the EAP course?
2. How has ChatGPT helped you improve your academic language skills?

3. How has ChatGPT influenced your engagement with course materials and activities?
4. Can you provide an example of a particular instance where ChatGPT significantly impacted your learning process?
5. What ethical issues have you encountered or considered while using ChatGPT in your coursework?
6. How do you feel about the privacy and security aspects of ChatGPT?
7. Do you think ChatGPT provides biased content or feedback? Can you give any examples?
8. What suggestions do you have for addressing the ethical challenges associated with using ChatGPT in educational settings?

The interviews were conducted in English and the mean length was 41 minutes. Each interview was audio-recorded and transcribed to facilitate the coding process. Participants were provided copies of the transcripts for an initial member check (Merriam & Tisdell, 2016). The data collected were subjected to iterative thematic analysis using the following steps, as proposed by Braun and Clarke (2006):

1. Reading the transcripts thoroughly to become familiar with the data.
2. Independently generating initial codes, sharing them using Google Docs and comparing them to the raw data to ensure salience and consistency.
3. Reviewing and organising the emerging themes.
4. Reaching a consensus on the themes and subthemes identified.
5. Selecting representative extracts to illustrate the themes and ensure the data reflected the participants' perspectives accurately.

To maintain transparency and trustworthiness, a follow-up member check was carried out (Merriam & Tisdell, 2016). Participants were given copies of the themes, subthemes and illustrative quotes identified. No participants asked for changes or offered additional suggestions.

Findings

This section presents the qualitative findings and is organized into four overarching themes, integrating students' comments to provide a rich understanding of their perspectives. Each theme incorporates answers to both RQ1 and RQ2.

Theme 1: Positive experience and engagement

All the students reported positive experiences in learning with ChatGPT. S1 shared that it was like 'having a teacher at my fingertips when I need to get help'. This sentiment was echoed by S3: 'because I can get comments right away from ChatGPT, I'm more sure of my writing'. Students found that ChatGPT made the learning process more interactive and engaging. S8 noted, 'I used to find reading [academic] articles boring and difficult, but now I can ask ChatGPT questions about them, it's not so bad'. Similarly, S9 shared that 'ChatGPT makes learning English more fun. It's like having someone to talk to who is willing to help, can explain things, and gives me so many different examples. ' S10 mentioned, 'ChatGPT makes learning feel more fun, almost like an adventure.' Students expressed feelings of empowerment and increased motivation, with S1 stating, 'It gives me the confidence to explore topics I usually avoid.'

S7 stressed, 'The rapid feedback from ChatGPT keeps me motivated and hungry to learn.' This demonstrates how immediate interaction can sustain interest and drive academic tasks. Five students volunteered that ChatGPT encouraged them to participate more actively in the class. S6 said, 'Because I train with ChatGPT before class, I'm better ready for discussions.' S4 added, 'It makes me feel more confident to share my ideas with my teacher and friends'.

Theme 2: Academic language development

In the interviews, the students also expressed that they had noted significant improvement in their academic language skills, particularly in writing and vocabulary. S7 gave the following example: 'ChatGPT helped me organise my writing better. It suggested signal words that helped me put my thoughts in a more organised way'. Another student, S5, added, 'I like it when it corrects my grammar and gives me examples of how to use certain phrases correctly'. S8 reflected, 'I feel proud when I see my writing improve, and ChatGPT really plays a big role in that.' S6 observed, "I feel like I can express myself better, and this makes me feel more confident.'

Students provided specific examples of how ChatGPT had enhanced their learning. For example, S1 recounted, 'It helped me develop some starting ideas to organise my outline. It made the assignment a lot less stressful'. S5 mentioned she used 'ChatGPT to write my presentation script' and 'show me what words I should stress to sound clearer.'

Theme 3: Ethical concerns

While the students were positive about their experience of using ChatGPT in their academic language development, several identified ethical issues. A primary concern was academic integrity. S8 talked about how she was 'afraid that some students will use ChatGPT to do their assignments.' S6 acknowledged that 'It is very tempting to rely on ChatGPT...yes, it is cheating, but it can also be a helpful tool to generate ideas or improve our writing'. Despite these concerns, S3 felt, 'I believe in using it responsibly, but it's hard when others might not.' Students discussed how some students may use it excessively due to their heavy workload and academic expectations.

They were also concerned about privacy and data security. Several students argued that they were unsure how the data was being used. S3 wondered, 'Who has access to the conversations with ChatGPT?' and S9 shared, 'I'm worried about the privacy of my information. I don't know if sharing personal information with ChatGPT is safe. Others felt that 'sometimes ChatGPT ideas seem very western or biased' (S7). S4 added, 'Some of the responses are outdated or don't fit with Hong Kong,' and S5 noted that 'ChatGPT sometimes suggests phrases that are not culturally appropriate.' Students highlighted the importance of adapting its suggestions to fit the local context and cross-checking its generated 'facts.'

Theme 4: Suggestions for improvement

Students offered several suggestions for addressing the challenges they faced using ChatGPT. To combat academic integrity issues, S7 proposed, 'It should be easy for us to know how to use ChatGPT in our courses, and our professors should teach us how to use it right'. All the participants also noted the lack of transparency and wanted clear information on how their data would be used and protected. S1 felt that 'There should be a way to delete our conversations after a certain time'.

Additionally, students expressed a desire for more control over the customization of ChatGPT's responses: 'It would be great if we could change the settings to fit the way we learn best or to focus on certain areas we need to work on' (S8). S5 added, 'Having more control makes me feel like ChatGPT understands me better.' This customization could further enhance the relevance and effectiveness of ChatGPT as a learning tool.

In summary, students perceive ChatGPT as a valuable tool that significantly contributes to their academic language development and engagement in EAP courses. However, they also recognize the importance of addressing ethical challenges such as academic integrity, privacy, and bias. By implementing clear guidelines, ensuring data security, minimizing bias through continuous updates and localization, and enhancing customization and interactivity, educational institutions can maximize the benefits of ChatGPT while mitigating ethical concerns.

Discussion and practical implications

As scholars begin to investigate strategies and approaches to integrating GenAI tools such as ChatGPT across education, we highlighted there is a need to couple these emerging developments by understanding students' perceptions and initial relationship with this tool to identify ways to make these findings not only sustainable but human-centered (Miao & Holmes, 2023). For this reason, we focused our investigation on understanding L2 learners' perceptions of this tool along with the ethical challenges they experienced regarding the tool as they attended an academic writing course where the medium of instruction was English.

As we found, students had a positive view of ChatGPT, and they used it as a scaffolding resource that they perceived supported the learning process in both content and language learning. As expected, given that our participants were taking an EAP course, most of these positive qualities revolved around acquiring and developing their academic language skills as they pertained to both vocabulary and the development of their writing. The students' lived experience revolved around using ChatGPT to supplement rather than replace their effort to complete the writing assignments. While this echoes similar findings that found students situated ChatGPT (or another GenAI tool) as an automated tutor or teacher that students can call when they need it (Ericsson et al. 2023; Jeon, 2021; Tai & Chen, 2022, 2023), our findings extend this understanding by strongly illustrating the emotional assurance that the tool provided students as they engaged in what they perceived to be as a high-stress activity (c.f., Çakmak, 2022; Ericsson et al., 2023). Specifically, the ability to have a teacher "at [their] fingertips when [they] need to get help" provided students what could be interpreted as emotional stability as they expressed feeling 'more confident', 'less stressed', and feeling reassured, presenting a qualitative dimension that is at times overlooked despite it having ramifications on students' performance (El Shazly, 2020; Kim & Su, 2024), especially within EMI classroom settings (see Hillman et al., 2023).

While students welcome the use of ChatGPT as a resource to enhance their learning rather than to replace it, they shared similar stresses and concerns as their teachers surrounding ethics, with both worrying about how to use this tool ethically (Barret & Pack, 2023; Chan & Hu, 2023; Farazouli et al., 2024; Kohnke et al., 2023a); however, the degree and focus of this worry for our participants differed (e.g., 'It is very tempting to rely on ChatGPT…yes, it is cheating, but it can also be a helpful tool…'). One unified concern our participants expressed was privacy, as many of the points they raised focused on how their data (i.e., their "conversations with ChatGPT") would be used (Cotton et al., 2023; Mahmud, 2024; Mhlanga, 2023). These findings echo Nemorin et al.'s (2023) points that any implementation of AI within education needs to be coordinated and focused on emphasizing students' agency who have control or, at the bare minimum, a full understanding concerning how these services could use their personal data. In doing so, educators can begin to equip students to combat being seen or used as "data nodes for extraction and exploitation of valuable data" (p. 48). While an already essential skill, the knowledge and understanding concerning AI safety to protect one's personal data and defend oneself from algorithmic bias and hallucinations (Baker & Hawn, 2021; Selwyn, 2022; Surameery & Shakor, 2023) will increase in necessity as AI is reoriented from a standalone product to that of a feature within everyday devices.

Due to these concerns, we strongly suggest that any approach or strategy incorporating GenAI should be accompanied by AI literacy to facilitate learners' understanding and intentional use of AI tools. AI literacy, as Long and Magerko (2020) define it, is "a set of competencies that enables individuals to critically evaluate AI technologies; communicate and collaborate effectively with AI; and use AI as a tool online, at home, and in the workplace" (p. 2). As GenAI continues to improve and becomes more effective in carrying out a range of tasks to a higher quality, there is a need to incorporate critical AI literacy before using it within the classroom, just as digital literacy (see Blake, 2013). Within multilingual and multicultural classrooms that implement de jure medium of instruction policies prioritizing a language, this literacy must incorporate intercultural communication that respects the cultural identities, linguistic repertoires, and practices learners bring with them (Piller 2017; De Costa et al., In Press). In doing so, learners can begin to negotiate the inherited cultural and linguistic differences they will encounter when using AI and chatbots.

In addition to structuring students' understanding of AI following Long and Magerko's (2020) overarching themes that range from getting familiar with AI to how to meaningfully use and perceive it throughout a course or semester, we also suggest structuring GenAI and chatbot usage within the classroom in the following ways based on the literature (Guo et al., 2023; Kong et al., 2024; Law, 2024; Ray, 2023):

- **Plan:** GenAI and Chatbots, along with any other digital resource and tool, should be the main vehicle of learning within an activity or lesson. In other words, these tools should have a clear and

intentional purpose that facilitates the learning outcomes of a lesson and enhances and personalises the learning experience to individual needs.
- **Compartmentalize**: Lessons that include GenAI and/or Chatbots should focus on ensuring that the steps for using the technology are streamlined, the tasks are manageable within one or two class sessions, and the procedures are simple and easy to follow.
- **Preview**: Explicit instruction and initial guided support on how to use and/or study with GenAI and/or chatbots. Part of this support should focus on prompt engineering, which entails showing learners how to develop and modify prompts, as even changing keywords and phrasing can impact the content and information the tool generates (see Poole & Coss, 2023). This is also where you show how to negotiate and critically evaluate the generated content. As such, this is where discussion of intercultural communication and strategies can begin to be implemented (Piller, 2017).
- **Prompt**: Just as Kong et al.' (2024) suggests, students take the lead and self-direct the engagement with the tool. Specifically, '[students] must integrate the ideas or themes in the tools output with those from academic sources, and then incorporate them into their writing [or content they are developing] alongside their personal insights and viewpoints' (pp. 8-9). During this time, the teacher should emphasize academic integrity. After this self-directed use, students should work together to engage with the developed material critically and discuss instances where the generated content was questionable and/or biased material and work together to critically assess it.
- **Repeat**: Using GenAI and/or Chatbots should be a regular (but intentional) part of the classroom that students can anticipate within a reasonable amount of time. We suggest at least including it at least once in each unit where the technology plays the same role. With each use, we also encourage you to build your own and your student's understanding of the tool by exploring additional avenues and strategies to create and engage with the generated material.

While the above strategies and considerations are a means to begin incorporating AI and chatbots within the classroom, incorporating these tools, as well as any digital resource, should be done with the student's needs in mind through the iterative implementation of a learner's needs analysis. We suggest incorporating enhanced digital literacy needs analysis that considers students' familiarity in terms of both usage and understanding of digital functionality for both AI-enhanced and non-enhanced digital resources in relation to their overall learning needs to develop comprehensive learning goals that prioritize and centers the learners as they enter an emerging 'smart' school space.

Lastly, to add to the perpetual list of future research (Chiu et al., 2023; Nah et al., 2023; Ray, 2023; Zawacki-Richter et al., 2019; Zhang & Aslan, 2021), more research is needed concerning students' perspectives and the emotional capital students attach and experience when using AI and chatbots within and outside of the classroom, as research has been limited (e.g., Barret & Pack, 2023b; Chen et al., 2023; Lee & Jeon, 2022; Kohnke, 2023b). Further research is especially needed within multilingual and multicultural contexts to understand how these tools assist students in lessening some of the cognitive load they may feel as they enter classrooms where the medium of instruction is not in their primary language. Another direction is to further experiment concerning how critical approaches related to language (see De Costa et al., In Press) can be coupled with AI and chatbot strategies and approaches as research concerning this intersection is still in a nascent stage of understanding.

> **Post-reading questions:**
>
> 1) What parameters or strategies would you put into place to make AI acceptable and ethical in writing and non-writing activities? How would these parameters achieve both goals?
> 2) When using GenAI tools to support one's writing, when does one's writing stop becoming one's own and become ChatGPT?
> 3) How would you address some of the students' ethical concerns and usage patterns as a teacher? What other, if any, ethical concerns or practices should students, teachers, and parents be aware of when using ChatGPT?

Further reading

Blake, R. J. (2013). *Brave new digital classroom: Technology and foreign language learning* (2nd edn). Georgetown University Press.

Despite its age, Blake's book provides clear guidance for teachers today to navigate how technology fits within education rather than education fitting within technology. He provides practical strategies and general guidelines that can help teachers ease GenAI within their classrooms and still feel empowered.

Kohnke, L. (2023). *Using technology to design ESL/EFL microlearning activities*. Springer.

This is a more recent and explicit resource for teachers on how to implement and design activities with technology in mind. This resource is picked because it has a clear chapter on integrating ChatGPT and a few sample activities ready to be used.

Miao, F. & Holmes, W. (2023). *Guidance for generative AI in education and research*. United Nations Educational, Scientific and Cultural Organization. https://doi.org/10.54675/EWZM9535

This short and free resource is great for both teachers and researchers to help them further understand GenAI tools and the new literacy you need with them, such as prompt writing, and the social issues that surround the emerging tool. Miao and Holmers provide some suggestions on creatively using, empowering, and facilitating the use of GenAI within the classroom while still focusing on human-centered learning and teaching.

References

Adiguzel, T., Kaya, M. H., & Cansu, F. K. (2023). Revolutionizing education with AI: Exploring the transformative potential of ChatGPT. *Contemporary Educational Technology, 15*(3), ep429. https://doi.org/10.30935/cedtech/13152

Ali, O., Murray, P. A., Momin, M., Dwivedi, Y. K., and Malik, T. (2024). The effects of artificial intelligence applications in educational settings: Challenges and strategies. *Technological Forecasting and Social Change, 199*, 123076. https://doi.org/10.1016/j.techfore.2023.123076

Alm, A. & Nkomo, L. M. (2020). Chatbot experiences of informal language learners: A sentiment analysis. *International Journal of Computer-Assisted Language Learning and Teaching (IJCALLT), 10*(4), 51–65. http://doi.org/10.4018/IJCALLT.2020100104

Baker, R. S., & Hawn, A. (2021). Algorithmic bias in education. *International Journal of Artificial Intelligence in Education, 32*, 1052–1092. https://doi.org/10.1007/s40593-021-00285-9

Barcelos, A. M. F. (2015). Unveiling the relationship between language learning beliefs, emotions and identities. *Studies in second language learning and teaching, 5*(2), 301–325. https://doi.org/10.14746/ssllt.2015.5.2.6

Barret, A., & Pack, A. (2023). Not quite eye to A.I.: Student and teacher perspective on the use of generative artificial intelligence in the writing process. *International Journal of Educational Technology in Higher Education, 20*. https://doi.org/10.1186/s41239-023-00427-0

Bridgeman, B., Trapani, C., & Attali, Y. (2012). Comparison of human and machine scoring of essays: Differences by gender, ethnicity, and country. *Applied Measurement in Education, 25*(1), 27–40. https://doi.org/10.1080/08957347.2012.635502

Çakmak, F. (2022). Chatbot-human interaction and its effects on EFL students' L2 speaking performance and speaking anxiety. *Novitas-ROYAL (Research on Youth and Language), 16*(2), 113–131.

Chan, C. K. Y., & Hu, W. (2023). Students' voices on generative AI: Perceptions, benefits, and challenges in higher education. *International Journal of Educational Technology in Higher Education, 20*(43), 1–18. https://doi.org/10.1186/s41239-023-00411-8

Chen, H. H.-J., Yang, C. T.-Y. & Lai, K. K.-W. (2023) Investigating college EFL learners' perceptions toward the use of Google Assistant for foreign language learning. *Interactive Learning Environments, 31*(3), 1335–1350. https://doi.org/10.1080/10494820.2020.1833043

Chiu, T. K. F., Xia, Q., Zhou, X., Chai, C. S., & Cheng, M. (2023). Systematic literature review on opportunities, challenges, and future research recommendations of artificial intelligence in education. *Computers and Education: Artificial Intelligence, 4*, Article 100118. https://doi.org/10.1016/j.caeai.2022.100118

Christie, A. (2023). Transformers and large language models. In D. Jurafsky & J. H. Martin (Eds) *Speech and Language processing* (pp. 1–30). Retrieved from https://web.stanford.edu/~jurafsky/slp3/10.pdf

Cotton, R. E., Cotton, P. A., & Shipway, J. R. (2023). Chatting and cheating: Ensuring academic integrity in the ear of ChatGPT. *Innovations in Education and Teaching International, 61*(2), 228–239. https://doi.org/10.1080/14703297.2023.2190148

Creswell, J. W. (2008). *Educational research: Planning, conducting, and evaluating quantitative and qualitative research* (3rd ed.). Pearson Education.

De Costa, P. I., Green-Eneix, C. A., Bupphachuen, P., Gregory, M., & Melgar, G. (In Press). Critical approaches to World Englishes. In C. Fäcke, A. Gao, and P. Garrett-Rucks (Eds), *the Handbook of Plurilingual and Intercultural language learning*. Wiley.

Dempere, J., Modugu, K. P., Hesham, A., & Ramasamy, L. (2023). The impact of ChatGPT on higher education. Dempere J, Modugu K, Hesham A and Ramasamy LK (2023) The impact of ChatGPT on higher education. *Frontiers in Education, 8*, Article e1206936. https://doi.org/10.3389/feduc.2023.1206936

Dizon, G. (2020). Evaluating intelligent personal assistants for L2 listening and speaking development. *Language Learning and Technology, 24*(1), 16–26. https://doi.org/10125/44705

El Shazly, R. (2020). Effects of artificial intelligence on English speaking anxiety and speaking performance: A case study. *Expert Systems, 38*(3), 1–15. https://doi.org/10.1111/exsy.12667

Ericsson, E., Sofkova Hashemi, S., & Lundin, J. (2023). Fun and frustrating: Students' perspectives on practising speaking English with virtual humans. *Cogent Education, 10*(1). https://doi.org/10.1080/2331186X.2023.2170088

Farazouli. A., Cerratto-Pargman, T., Bolander-Laksov, K., & McGrath, C. (2024). Hello GPT! Goodbye home examination? An exploratory study of AI chatbots impact on university teachers' assessment practices. *Assessment & Evaluation in Higher Education, 49*(3), 363–375. https://doi.org/10.1080/02602938.2023.2241676

Fryer, L. K., Ainley, M., Thompson, A., Gibson, A. & Sherlock, Z. (2017). Stimulating and sustaining interest in a language course: An experimental comparison of chatbot and human task partners. *Computers in Human Behavior, 75*, 461–468. https://doi.org/10.1016/j.chb.2017.05.045

Gallacher, A., Thompson, A., Howarth, M. (2018). "My robot is an idiot!" – Students' perceptions of AI in the L2 classroom. In P. Taalas, J. Jalkanen, L. Bradley, & S. Thouësny (Eds), *Future-proof CALL: language learning as exploration and encounters – short papers from EUROCALL 2018* (pp. 70–76). Research-publishing.net. https://doi.org/10.14705/rpnet.2018.26.815

Guo, K., Zhong, Y., Li, D., & Chu, S. K. W. (2023). Effects of chatbot-assisted in-class debates on students' argumentation skills and task motivation. *Computers & Education, 203*, Article e104862. https://doi.org/10.1016/j.compedu.2023.104862

Hillman, S., Li, W., Green-Eneix, C. A., & De Costa, P. I. (2023). The emotional landscape of English medium instruction (EMI) in higher education. *Linguistics and Education, 75*, e101178. https://doi.org/10.1016/j.linged.2023.101178

Huang, W., Hew, K. F., & Fryer, L. K. (2021). Chatbots for language learning–Are they really useful? A systematic review of chatbot-supported language learning. *Journal of Computer Assisted Learning, 38*(1), 237–257. https://doi.org/10.1111/jcal.12610

Hwang, G. J., Xie, H., Wah, B. W., & Gašević, D. (2020). Vision, challenges, roles and research issues of artificial intelligence in education. *Computers and Education: Artificial Intelligence, 1*, 100001. https://doi.org/10.1016/j.caeai.2020.100001

Jeon, J. (2021). Chatbot-assisted dynamic assessment (CA-DA) for L2 vocabulary learning and diagnosis. *Computer Assisted Language Learning, 36*(7), 1338–1364. https://doi.org/10.1080/09588221.2021.1987272

Jeon, J., Lee, S., & Choe, H. (2023). Beyond ChatGPT: A conceptual framework and systematic review of speech-recognition chatbots for language learning. *Computers & Education*, e104898. https://doi.org/10.1016/j.compedu.2023.104898

Kandpal, N., Deng, H., Roberts, A., Wallace, E., & Raffel, C. (2023). Large language models struggle to learn long-tail knowledge. In *International conference on machine learning* (pp. 15696–15707). PMLR.

Kim, A., & Su, Y. (2024). How implementing an AI chatbot impacts Korean as a foreign language learners' willingness to communicate in Korean. *System, 122*, Article e103256. https://doi.org/10.1016/j.system.2024.103256

Kim, H., Yang, H., Shin, D., & Lee, J. H. (2022). Design principles and architecture of a second language learning chatbot. *Language Learning & Technology, 26*(1), 1–18. http://hdl.handle.net/10125/73463

Koç, F. S., & Savaş, P. (2024). The use of artificially intelligent chatbots in English language learning: A systematic meta-synthesis study of articles published between 2010–2024. *ReCALL*, 1–18. https://doi.org/10.1017/S0958344024000168

Kohnke, L. (2022). A qualitative exploration of student perspectives of chatbot use during emergency remote teaching. *International Journal of Mobile Learning and Organisation, 16*(4), 475-488. https://doi.org/10.1504/IJMLO.2022.125966

Kohnke, L. (2023a). A pedagogical chatbot: A supplemental language learning tool. *RELC Journal, 54*(3), 828–838. https://doi.org/10.1177/00336882211067054

Kohnke, L. (2023b). L2 Learners' perception of a chatbot as a potential independent language learning tool. *International Journal of Mobile Learning and Organisation, 17*(1/2), 214–226. https://doi.org/10.1504/IJMLO.2023.10053355

Kohnke, L. (in-press). Generative AI. In A. Al-Hoorie., & L. McCallum. (Eds.), *The Palgrave encyclopedia of computer-assisted language learning*.

Kohnke, L., & Zou, D. (in-press). The role of ChatGPT in enhancing English teaching: A paradigm shift in lesson planning and instructional practices. *Educational Technology & Society*.

Kohnke, L., Moorhouse, B. L., & Zou, D. (2023a). ChatGPT for language teaching and learning. *RELC Journal, 54*(2), 537–550. https://doi.org/10.1177/00336882231162868

Kohnke, L., Moorhouse, B. L., & Zou, D. (2023b). Exploring generative artificial intelligence preparedness among university language instructors: A case study. *Computers and Education: Artificial Intelligence, 5*, Article 100156. https://doi.org/10.1016/j.caeai.2023.100156

Kong, S.-C., Lee, J. C.-K., & Tsang, O. (2024). A pedagogical design for self-regulated learning in academic writing using text-based generative artificial intelligence tools: 6-P pedagogy of plan, prompt, preview, produce, peer-review, portfolio-tracking. *Research and Practice in Technology Enhanced Learning, 19*(030). https://doi.org/10.58459/rptel.2024.19030

Kwok, A. P. K., Wong, Y. H., Wong, K. C., & Chan, C. H. (2024). AI meeting assistants in English-medium university lectures in Hong Kong, China: A double-edge sword for student perception.

International Journal of Information and Education Technology, 14(9), 1271–1276. https://doi.org/ 10.18178/ijiet.2024.14.9.2156

Law, L. (2024). Application of generative artificial intelligence (GenAI) in language teaching and learning: A scoping literature review. *Computers and Education Open, 6*, Article 100174. https://doi.org/10.1016/j.caeo.2024.100174

Lee, J. H., Shin, D., & Hwang, Y. (2023). Exploring the potential of large language model-based task-oriented dialogue chatbots from learner perspectives. *SSRN*. https://dx.doi.org/10.2139/ssrn.4644306

Lee, S., & Jeon, J. (2022). Visualizing a disembodied agent: Young EFL learners' perceptions of voice-controlled conversational agents as language partners. *Computer Assisted Language Learning, 194,* https://doi.org/10.1016/j.compedu.2022.104703

Long, D., & Magerko, B. (2020, April). What is AI literacy? Competencies and design considerations. In *Proceedings of the 2020 CHI conference on human factors in computing systems* (pp. 1–16).

Mahmud, S. (2024). *Academic integrity in the age of artificial intelligence*. IGI Global Publishing.

Merriam, S. B., & Tisdell, E. J. (2016). *Qualitative research: A guide to design and implementation* (4th ed.). Jossey Bass.

Mhlanga, D. (2023). Open AI in education, the responsible and ethical use of ChatGPT towards lifelong learning. In: *FinTech and artificial intelligence for sustainable development* (pp. 387–409). Sustainable Development Goals Series. Palgrave Macmillan. https://doi.org/10.1007/978-3-031-37776-1_17

Montgomery, D. P., Green-Eneix, C. A., Cinaglia, C., & De Costa, P. I. (2024). Ideology. In
C. A. Chapelle (Ed.), *The encyclopedia of applied linguistics* (2nd ed.). Wiley. https://doi.org/10.1002/9781405198431.wbeal20299

Moorhouse, B. L., & Kohnke, L. (2024). The effects of generative AI on initial language
teacher education: The perceptions of teacher educators. *System, 122*, e103290. https://doi.org/10.1016/j.system.2024.103290

Nah, F., Cai, J., Zheng, R., & Pang, N. (2023). An activity system-based perspective of generative AI: Challenges and research directions. *AIS transactions on human-computer interaction, 15*(3), 247–267. https://doi.org/10.17705/1thci.00190

Nemorin, S., Vlachidis, A., Ayerakwa, H.M., & Andriotis, P. (2023). AI hyped? A horizon scan of discourse on artificial intelligence in education (AIED) and development. *Learning, Media and Technology, 48*(1), 38–51. https://doi.org/10.1080/17439884.2022.2095568

OpenAI. (2023, March 24). *March 20 ChatGPT outage: Here's what happened*. https://openai.com/index/march-20-chatgpt-outage/

OpenAI. (2024a). *Data usage for consumer services FAQ*. OpenAI. https://help.openai.com/en/articles/7039943-data-usage-for-consumer-services-faq

OpenAI. (2024b). *How your data is used to improve model performance*. OpenAI. https://help.openai.com/en/articles/5722486-how-your-data-is-used-to-improve-model-performance

Piller, I. (2017). *Intercultural communication: A critical introduction*. Edinburgh University Press.

Poole, F. J., & Coss, M. (2023, December 19). Can ChatGPT reliably and accurately apply a rubric to L2 writing assessments? The devil is in the prompt(s). https://doi.org/10.35542/osf.io/3r2zb

Ray, P. P. (2023). ChatGPT: A comprehensive review on background, applications, key challenges, bias, ethics, limitations and future scope. *Internet of Things and Cyber-Physical Systems, 3*, 121–154. https://doi.org/10.1016/j.iotcps.2023.04.003

Selwyn, N. (2022). The future of AI and education: Some cautionary notes. *European Journal of Education: Research, Development and Policy, 57*(4), 620–631. https://doi.org/10.1111/ejed.12532

Stöhr, C., Ou, A.W., & Malmström H. (2024). Perceptions and usage of AI chatbots among students in higher education across genders, academic levels and fields of study. *Computers and Education: Artificial Intelligence, 7*, Article 100259. https://doi.org/10.1016/j.caeai.2024.100259

Surameery, N. M. S., Shakor, M. Y. (2023). Use ChatGPT to solve programming bugs. *International Journal of Information Technology & Computer Engineering (IJITC), 3*(1), 17–22. https://doi.org/10.55529/ijitc.31.17.22

Sydorenko, T., Hsieh, C.-N., Ahn, S., & Arnold, N. (2017). Foreign language learners' beliefs about CALL: The case of a U.S. Midwestern University. *CALICO Journal, 34*(2), 196–218. https://doi.org/10.1558/cj.28226

Tai, T.-Y. & Chen, H. H.-J. (2022) The impact of intelligent personal assistants on adolescent EFL learners' listening comprehension. *Computer Assisted Language Learning*. https://doi.org/10.1080/09588221.2022.2040536

Tai, T.-Y. & Chen, H. H.-J. (2023) The impact of Google Assistant on adolescent EFL learners' willingness to communicate. *Interactive Learning Environments, 31*(3), 1485–1502. https://doi.org/10.1080/10494820.2020.1841801

Wang, T., & Cheng, E. C. K. (2021). An investigation of barriers to Hong Kong K-12 schools incorporating artificial intelligence in education. *Computers and Education: Artificial Intelligence, 2*, e100031. https://doi.org/10.1016/j.caeai.2021.100031

Yang, H., Kim, H., Lee, J. H. & Shin, D. (2022) Implementation of an AI chatbot as an English conversation partner in EFL speaking classes. *ReCALL, 34*(3), 327–343. https://doi.org/10.1017/S0958344022000039

Yin, R. K. (2018). *Case study research and applications: Design and methods* (6th ed.). Sage.

Zawacki-Richter, O., Marín, V. I., Bond, M., & Gouverneur, F. (2019). Systematic review of research on artificial intelligence applications in higher education–Where are the educators? *International Journal of Educational Technology in Higher Education, 16*(1), 1–27. https://doi.org/10.1186/s41239-019-0171-0

Zhang, K., & Aslan, A. B. (2021). AI technologies for education: Recent research & future directions. *Computers and Education: Artificial Intelligence, 2*, Article e100025. https://doi.org/10.1016/j.caeai.2021.100025

15
AI-integrated language learning applications

Eneyire Godwin Omuya
Xin Zhao
Minna Rollins

Pre-reading questions:

1) How do AI-powered writing tools influence the writing process for students in academic settings?
2) What are some potential benefits and drawbacks of using AI tools in academic writing?
3) In what ways could AI tools shape students' writing practices, and how might this impact their long-term writing skill development?

Introduction

People express ideas, concepts, emotions, and experiences through writing (Alsariera & Alsaraireh, 2024; Zhou & Hiver, 2022). However, mastering academic writing poses significant challenges, especially for students learning English as a foreign language (EFL) (Campbell, 2019; Hanauer et al., 2019). These students often struggle with grammar, vocabulary, writing mechanics, and adhering to genre conventions (Finn, 2018; Phuong, 2021; Singh, 2017).

In recent years, artificial intelligence (AI) has emerged as a potential solution to support and enhance academic writing skills. AI-powered writing tools, such as Wordtune, offer innovative features like rephrasing, sentence restructuring, and vocabulary enhancement (Zhao, 2022). These tools have shown promise in helping EFL writers maintain consistent flow and clarity in their writing. However, concerns have been raised about potential drawbacks, including over-reliance on these tools and their impact on independent writing skills (Malinka et al., 2023; Iskender, 2023).

While previous studies have explored the impact of digital writing tools on student writing, research specifically examining how comprehensive AI-powered writing assistants like Wordtune aid international students in their academic endeavours remains limited. This study aims to fill this gap by investigating how students, both native English speakers and those using English as a second language, utilize Wordtune and perceive its contribution to their academic writing skills. By focusing on a specific AI-powered writing assistant and comparing its use across different student populations, our research builds upon existing studies and provides novel insights into the practical applications and implications of these tools in higher education settings. This study addresses the following research questions:

1. How do students (both native English speakers and those whose second language is English) use Wordtune?
2. How do students view Wordtune as contributing to their academic writing skills?
3. What were the relationships among international and native students and key variables such as English proficiency, Wordtune usage metrics, and perceived writing improvements?

AI-powered writing assistants and academic writing for international EFL students

International students pursuing higher education abroad often encounter significant challenges in academic writing (Singh, 2019; Flowerdew, 2019). These challenges include grappling with the expectations and norms of academic writing in English, along with issues related to grammar, vocabulary, and writing mechanics (Ankawi, 2020; Braine, 2002; Phuong, 2021; Singh, 2017). However, strong academic writing skills are essential for their success, as effective written communication is crucial for demonstrating mastery of course content and achieving academic goals (Geiser & Studley, 2001; Hartley, 2008).

Recent studies have examined the broader landscape of automated writing evaluation (AWE) systems and their impact on writing instruction. Ding and Zhou (2024) and Shi and Aryadoust (2024) have provided comprehensive analyses of AWE implementations in educational settings, highlighting the evolution from traditional grammar checkers to more sophisticated AI-powered writing assistance tools. Within this expanding ecosystem of writing technologies, specific AI-powered writing assistants such as Wordtune have emerged as valuable tools for enhancing writing skills. Mahmud (2023) conducted a mixed-methods study examining Wordtune's effectiveness, demonstrating improved writing performance among experimental groups compared to control groups through pre-tests, post-tests, and qualitative analysis of writing samples. Zhao et al. (2024), focusing on the experiences of Chinese international students, identified key benefits of Wordtune, such as enhanced grammatical accuracy, vocabulary improvement, and the generation of more coherent academic texts. These tools were particularly effective in addressing the challenges of crafting nuanced and contextually appropriate sentences in English, thereby fostering greater confidence and engagement among users.

Despite the potential benefits, challenges and limitations associated with the use of AI writing assistants cannot be overlooked. Cummings et al. (2024) employed a qualitative approach to explore the challenges and limitations of generative AI tools, highlighting concerns about their unreliability and time-consuming nature, leading to some students declining to use them. Additionally, concerns about overreliance on digital tools and the potential for them to undermine critical thinking skills in writing have been raised (Zhao et al., 2024). It is important to adopt a cautious and balanced approach in integrating AI writing assistants into academic writing instruction, particularly for international EFL students. Educators in many fields have started to explore various pedagogical strategies and technological innovations, including the empirical testing of new tools. However, additional support and training are often required to maximise the effective utilisation of these tools while minimising potential issues with academic integrity and bias (Bibi & Atta, 2024; Crompton & Burke, 2023).

Researchers suggest that future studies should focus on addressing the long-term impact of AI writing assistants on writing skills development, exploring effective pedagogical strategies for their integration into teaching practices, and examining the perspectives of both instructors and students on their effectiveness and limitations (Fitria, 2021; Mahmud, 2023; Zhao et al. 2024). Moreover, attention should be given to the development of digital literacy skills among international EFL students to promote responsible and effective use of AI writing assistants, not just in academic contexts, but also in real-world applications and everyday situations (Zhao et al., 2023).

Wordtune as a digital writing assistant

Wordtune (https://www.wordtune.com) is an AI-powered digital writing tool that assists users in rephrasing and enhancing their written content (Zhao, 2022; Mahmud, 2023). It employs natural language processing (NLP) and machine learning techniques to analyse extensive datasets of corpus of text, enabling it to generate naturalistic writing

(Zhao, 2022). Unlike conventional grammar checkers, Wordtune's primary function is to suggest alternative ways of expressing ideas by restructuring sentences or replacing words with synonyms, rather than solely focusing on grammar corrections (Zhao et al., 2024). The accessibility of Wordtune is facilitated through multiple platforms. Users can access it either through a web browser extension compatible with various online applications (e.g., Microsoft Word, Gmail, social media platforms), or a dedicated web-based editor (Zhao, 2022). This flexibility allows users to integrate Wordtune seamlessly into their existing writing workflows. When users highlight text within these applications, Wordtune provides a range of rewrite options, including basic rewrites, casual or formal tone variations, shortened or expanded versions of the text, and intelligent synonym suggestions (Zhao, 2022; Fitria, 2024), as illustrated in Figure 1. These features collectively aim to enhance the quality and clarity of written communication.

A notable feature of Wordtune is its ability to translate and rephrase text from various languages into English, catering specifically to the needs of EFL learners (Zhao, 2022). This functionality is particularly valuable for international students who often face challenges in navigating the intricacies of academic English (Alsied & Ibrahim, 2017; Hanauer et al., 2019). By offering multilingual support, Wordtune addresses a crucial gap in the toolkit of non-native English speakers striving to improve their academic writing skills. Wordtune offers both free and premium subscription options. The free version includes basic rewrite features with a daily sentence limit. Premium subscribers enjoy unrestricted access to advanced capabilities, including: (i) unlimited sentence rewriting; (ii) casual and formal tone options; (iii) text shortening or expansion; (iv) paragraph rewriting; and (iv) premium support.

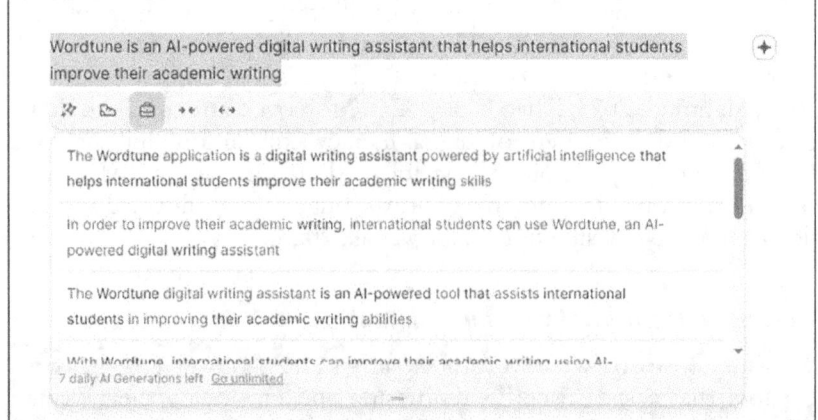

Figure 15.1 *Illustration of the free version of Wordtune rewrite suggestion in use (formal tone).*

Additionally, Wordtune provides customised enterprise programs for larger organisations, with pricing available upon request. However, like other AI-powered digital tools, Wordtune has certain limitations. These include occasional error messages, inaccuracies in rewriting sentences, and concerns about overreliance on these tools and their potential impact on academic integrity and unfair means (Zhao et al., 2024).

The integration of AI-powered writing assistants presents both opportunities and challenges for academic writing instruction, particularly for international EFL students. By understanding the perceived benefits, limitations, and pedagogical considerations associated with these tools, educators can effectively harness their potential to enhance writing instruction and support students' development in English academic writing.

Methodology

Research design

The current study employed a mixed-methods approach, combining quantitative and qualitative data collection to explore how Wordtune users integrate the tool into their writing practices. An online survey was utilized, structured into three key sections: (1) Demographic Information, which gathered details about respondents' language background and proficiency; (2) Writing Practices and Tool Utilization, which used 5-point Likert scale questions to assess how Wordtune was employed in their writing processes; and (3) Perceptions and Experiences, which combined a 5-point Likert scale questions with open-ended responses to capture users' views on Wordtune. The survey was piloted with a small group of academics and postgraduate students to ensure the clarity and validity of the questions. Participant recruitment was facilitated by the Wordtune management team among all Wordtune subscribers.

Participants

The survey was emailed to 9,000 Wordtune subscribers in September 2022. By the conclusion of the survey period, 467 questionnaires were returned, resulting in a 5% response rate. However, only 209 questionnaire responses were deemed usable for analysis after removing incomplete or irrelevant responses. Employing a survey approach facilitated data collection across diverse countries and disciplines, resulting in a comprehensive dataset that effectively addressed the research inquiries.

Our participants study at the different levels in the university: undergraduates (41.6%), postgraduates (33%), and PhD candidates (25.4%)

Table 15.1 *Demographic characteristics of students (N = 209)*

		n (% of the sample)
Gender	Female	121 (57.9)
	Male	82 (39.2)
	Other	2 (1.0)
	Prefer not to say	4 (1.9)
Age of students	Under 18	10 (4.8)
	18–24	65 (31.1)
	25–34	77 (36.8)
	35–44	47 (22.5)
	45–54	5 (2.4)
	55 and over	5 (2.4)
Level of education	Undergraduate student	87 (41.6)
	Postgraduate student (e.g., Masters)	69 (33.0)
	Research student (e.g., PhD)	53 (25.4)
English proficiency	No proficiency	1 (0.5)
	Elementary proficiency	3 (1.4)
	Limited working proficiency	21 (10.0)
	Professional working proficiency	57 (27.3)
	Full professional proficiency	44 (21.1)
	Native / bilingual proficiency	22 (10.5)
English as first language	Yes	81 (38.8)
	No	128 (61.2)

(Table 1). The age of respondents varied from 16 to 62 years, with an average age of 29.4 years (SD = 9.056). The sample predominantly consists of younger adults, with 84.3% of participants being under 35 years old. This fits with the usual age group of students involved in higher education or starting their academic careers. The sample consisted predominantly of females (57.9%) and males (39.2%), with a small proportion of participants identifying as other (1.0%) or preferring not to disclose their gender (1.9%).

In our sample, nearly two-thirds of participants, 61.2%, reported a first language other than English, while a substantial minority, 38.8%, identified as native English speakers. This distribution suggests that Wordtune has broad appeal across diverse linguistic backgrounds. Interestingly, despite the high proportion of non-native English speakers, the overall English proficiency levels reported by participants were remarkably high. Among non-native English speakers, a combined 48.4% reported either professional working proficiency (27.3%) or full professional proficiency (21.1%). Based on their self-assessed proficiency, these individuals believe they can competently participate in workplace discussions, contribute to meetings, and manage difficult work-related activities in English. More so, an additional 10.5% of non-native speakers considered themselves to have native or bilingual proficiency, indicating a level of comfort with English comparable to native speakers.

When we factor in the participants who identified English as their native language, we see a sample population with a strong command of English across the board. This high level of English language competence across both native and non-native speakers is particularly noteworthy given the academic context of our study. The prevalence of advanced English skills among our participants raises intriguing questions about the relationship between language proficiency and engagement with academic resources or tools.

The frequency of Wordtune usage was measured on a 5-point scale, from "I hardly ever use it" to "All the time", with an average usage frequency of 3.96 (SD = 0.82), suggesting regular use among respondents. The duration of Wordtune usage was measured on a 4-point scale: "less than 3 months", "3-6 months", "6-12 months", and "more than a year", with the majority having used the tool for less than 3 months (M = 1.65, SD = 0.80). Regarding writing skill improvement, participants rated their perceived improvement on a 3-point scale: "No I have not learnt anything yet", "Yes, but I now depend on Wordtune to write", and "Yes, I have learnt to write better" (M = 1.68, SD = 0.58). Finally, 33% (N = 69) of participants were using the premium version of Wordtune, while 67% (N = 140) relied on the free version.

Ethical considerations

Ethical approval for the study was granted by the University of Sheffield (application no: 061282). The study adhered to ethical research principles by obtaining informed consent from participants before their involvement. Additionally, participant anonymity was guaranteed, and the right to withdraw from the study at any point without penalty was explicitly communicated.

Data analysis

We analysed data using SPSS Statistics 29. The initial phase involved checking the dataset for errors and out-of-range values, which were removed to ensure the accuracy and validity of the findings. Observations with missing data or responses deemed inconsistent with other parts of the questionnaire were excluded. Participants aged below 16 were excluded as they did not meet the minimum age threshold for Higher Education. In total, 258 observations were excluded from the original 467 returned questionnaires, resulting in a final dataset of 209 usable responses. Questionnaire items were grouped into constructs to reflect perceptions of Wordtune's use, benefits, and issues (See Appendix). Reliability analysis using Cronbach's alpha showed strong internal consistency ($\alpha > 0.8$). Descriptive statistics, including means, standard deviations, frequencies, and percentages, were generated. Comparative analyses using Mann–Whitney U-tests, Spearman's rank correlation coefficients, and chi-square tests of Independence were conducted to explore differences and relationships among various groups and variables. Qualitative content analysis complemented the quantitative data, providing deeper insights through selected representative quotes. The coding was done primarily by the first author, who has sound knowledge of content analysis, and was subsequently discussed thoroughly with the co-authors to achieve agreement. To provide context and highlight potential differences in usage patterns and perceived benefits, a subset of questions allowed for comparison between international students and native English speakers. This comparative approach offered valuable insights into how language background influenced the use and perceived effectiveness of AI-powered writing tools like Wordtune in academic settings.

Results

RQ1: Usage and integration of wordtune

Usage Metrics

Students used Wordtune for various purposes, particularly for academic and work-related tasks, including reports, assignments, blogs, social media, and composing emails or other forms of written communication. The usage patterns were measured on an ordinal scale with five distinct categories: "I hardly ever use it"; "When I remember"; "Occasionally"; "Intensively when working on a particular type of work"; and "All the time". A significant portion of students, especially international students, report frequent use of Wordtune. Specifically, 71.0% (N = 76) of non-native English speakers use Wordtune "intensively when working on a particular type of work" compared to 29.0% (N = 31) of native English speakers. Additionally, 76.2% (N = 32) of international students use Wordtune "occasionally", compared to 23.8% (N = 10) of native students, and 67.3% (N = 35) of international

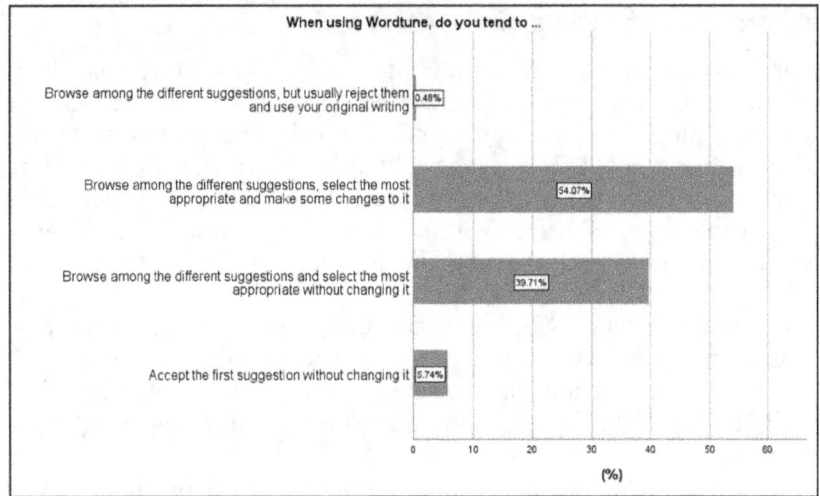

Figure 15.2 *Wordtune usage tendencies.*

students use it "all the time", versus 32.7% (N = 17) of native students. These findings underscore the central role of Wordtune in their writing processes, with only a few students indicating minimal use. These percentages were calculated within each usage category to examine the proportion of international versus native English speakers, rather than calculating distributions across all categories within each speaker group. This analytical approach was chosen to highlight the comparative usage patterns between international and native students within each specific usage category.[1]

Figure 2 illustrates students' usage tendencies of Wordtune's editing options. Most students either browse through the various suggestions, select the most appropriate one, and make some modifications (N = 113; 54.07%), or choose not to make any changes at all (N = 83; 39.71%). A smaller number accept the first suggestion without alterations, while a few typically reject the suggestions and stick with their original writing.

---

[1] While the percentages sum to 100% within each individual category (e.g., within "intensive use"), they are not intended to sum to 100% across all usage categories. Moreover, 67% of respondents used the free version of Wordtune, which, as highlighted in the literature review, is capped at a daily sentence limit, offering fewer features, such as limited rewrite options and fewer rewrites per session. In contrast, premium users frequently employed the tool's function to rewrite sentences in a more formal tone (39.2%), mirroring academic writing.

Integration with other digital writing tools

Our participants used Wordtune with other tools. More than half of the respondents who answered the question (86 of 162; 53.1%) reported using Wordtune in combination with other writing software. The coverage provided by using multiple tools, which helps users feel more confident in the accuracy and readability of their writing. Some participants reported using Wordtune in conjunction with Grammarly, highlighting the complementary functionalities of the two tools:

> "Grammarly and Wordtune are GREAT together, because Wordtune edits the perfect sentence, and Grammarly can help with small corrections like commas, spaces, and capitalizations." (Participant 209, Female, Undergraduate student, Native English Speaker)
> "I write sentences and get them improved by Wordtune, and then I check it in Grammarly for additional mistakes or fluency." (Participant 9, Female, Masters student, Full professional proficiency)
> "Yes, I use Wordtune with Google Docs, Google Translate, and Grammarly." (Participant 6, Female, Vietnamese, PhD student, Professional working proficiency)

For some EFL students, the process often begins with translation from their native language, followed by refinement using Wordtune:

> "I sometimes write in my native language using Google Translate. After that, I edit the text using Wordtune." (Participant 54, Female, not specified, PhD student, Full professional proficiency)
> "Separately. I would start writing on Scrivener. When I have a rough draft, I start editing and when it is difficult to draft, I usually write sections in Spanish and translate in Deepl. Then Use Wordtune to get a better way of writing it." (Participant 63, Female, Spanish, PhD student, Native / Bilingual proficiency)

One participant also described a sequential process of using multiple tools to enhance their writing:

> "Yes, first I use Wordtune to craft my piece of article. Then, I pass it through Grammarly in order to check any mistakes." (Participant 56, Male, PhD student, Full professional proficiency)
> "I first translate the sentences with Google Translate, then I copy them into Wordtune for rephrasing, and finally use Grammarly to check for grammatical mistakes." (Participant 130, Female, Masters student, Professional proficiency)

RQ2: Perceived influence on academic writing skills

When asked if they have improved their own skills with Wordtune, 73.7% (N = 151) of respondents reported that they have learned to write better through their use of Wordtune. Among the three response options provided ("no learning", "dependency", and "learning"), 20.5% (N = 42) of users selected the option "Yes, but I now depend on Wordtune to write", indicating a self-reported dependency alongside perceived improvement. This dependency raises questions about the long-term effects of AI writing tools on users' autonomous writing abilities. Only a small fraction of respondents (N = 12, 5.9%) reported no learning benefit from using Wordtune. Figure 3 illustrates the perceived benefits of Wordtune among all respondents, both international and native students. The tool's ability to offer diverse rephrasing options and prompt new ideas was highly appreciated, aiding in overcoming writer's block and enhancing creativity, while its accuracy in improving grammar and sentence structure further boosted users' confidence in their writing.

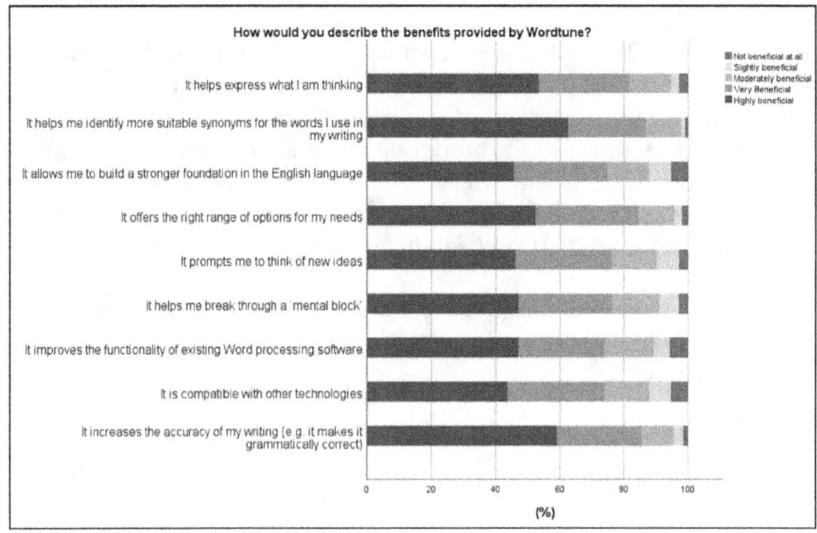

Figure 15.3 *Benefits of using Wordtune.*

Issues related to wordtune use

Participants reported various issues with using Wordtune (Figure 4). The tool's handling of complex sentences emerged as a notable

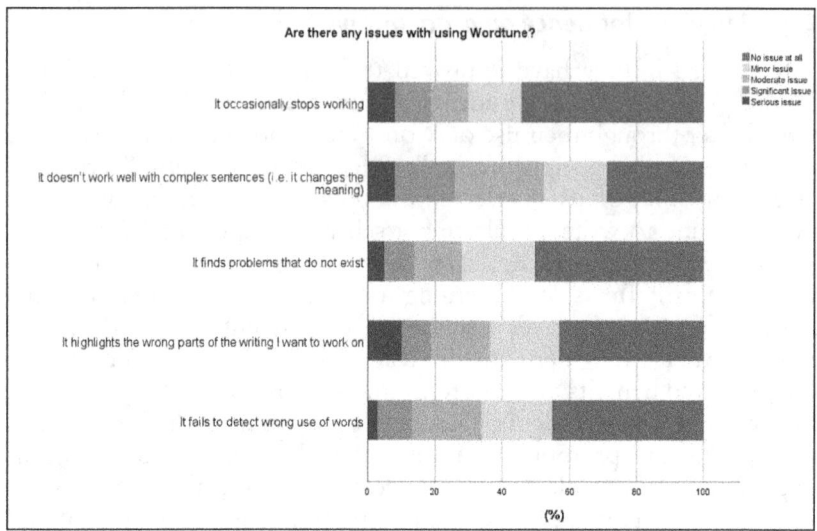

Figure 15.4 *Issues with using Wordtune.*

concern, with 28% of users reporting significant issues. Similarly, 25% of respondents noted problems with occasional operational failures. Interestingly, the issue of Wordtune finding problems that do not exist was reported as a moderate to serious concern by roughly 24% of users. While many users (40–50%) reported no major issues, these concerns suggest inconsistencies in Wordtune's performance, particularly with sophisticated language structures typical in academic writing.

In addition, several insightful comments emerged regarding these issues. Users reported several issues related to Wordtune's interface and user experience:

> "After highlighting sentences, the rewritten phrases appear. But that window is very small, and I have to drag the bottom handle to make it bigger. But in doing so, sometimes a minor click on the sides makes that window disappear and I lose 1 credit out of 20 without getting it done." (Participant 66, Female, Igbo, Undergraduate student, Limited working proficiency)
>
> "When you click on a part to rewrite if you scroll down, it will click off and if you're using the free version it uses up one of your uses. Or even if you don't click on one it will still use one of them" (Participant 117, Female, Undergraduate student, Native English speaker)

Several participants expressed a desire for more advanced features:

"The function I want the most is to combine 2 or more sentences into 1 or the other way around. But you do not offer this." (Participant 81, Male, Hebrew, Research student (e.g., PhD), Limited working proficiency)

"Sometimes I want to rewrite only part of the sentence, but the suggestion changes it as a whole. Also, sometimes I'd like to combine 2 or 3 suggestions- and take some words from each suggestion. But it is not comfortable to do so." (Participant 112, Female, Hebrew, Undergraduate student, Limited working proficiency)

"It analyses only one sentence at the time. Sometimes, to better understand the meaning, the whole picture should be taken in exam" (Participant 56, Male, Research student (e.g., PhD), Full professional proficiency)

Concerns about Wordtune's accuracy and contextual understanding were also noted:

"Sometimes it suggests wrong abbreviation even after I write the whole words with the abbreviation. Or sometimes, it suggests better ways of saying things but delete ideas in the original text." (Participant 12, Female, Arabic, Postgraduate student, Full professional proficiency)

"Scrambles sentence already made" (Participant 166, Female, Undergraduate student, Native English Speaker)

Participants also noted issues with Wordtune's integration with other tools and compatibility across platforms:

"As a matter of fact, I use the Grammarly and Wordtune Chrome extensions. It would appear that Grammarly will check and correct my writing as I type. I have to manually highlight the paragraphs in order to use Wordtune." (Participant 81, Male, Hebrew, PhD student, Limited working proficiency)

While these issues highlight user concerns, they also suggest opportunities for improvement. Many users expressed a desire for Wordtune to analyse larger chunks of text:

"To give suggestions to the whole paragraph instead of sentences. Also, to show statistics dashboard such as time spent and how many suggestions as well as number of words" (Participant 18, Female, Undergraduate Student, Native English Speaker)

Some users requested features specifically tailored to academic or specialized writing:

> "I would love to have an "academic tone" feature, similar to formal and casual tone." (Participant 28, Female, PhD student, Native English Student)
> "It need more academic and maybe need topic to paraphrase such as: AI, structure health monitoring, medical, ..." (Participant 47, Male, Vietnamese, PhD student, Limited working proficiency)

Some users requested additional language support and translation capabilities:

> "A translation option to Portuguese." (Participant 99, Female, Postgraduate student, Native / Bilingual proficiency)
> "My suggestions is regarding spelling and rewriting from native-to-native language. not only from native to English." (Participant 101, Female, Hebrew/Russian, Postgraduate student, Limited working proficiency)

The subject on pricing seemed to be a recurring concern, as many students suggested more affordable options:

> "You should provide student version at lower free of cost." (Participant 31, Male, Hindi, PhD student, Limited working proficiency)
> "Maybe make it free with premium services to students that are in school, college high school etc." (Participant 141, Female, Not specified, Undergraduate student, Native English Speaker)
> "To make it popular you should give it free to students." (Participant 115, Male, Undergraduate student, Native English Speaker)

Wordtune is generally seen as a valuable tool, these issues highlight areas for improvement, particularly in handling complex sentences, enhancing user experience, and expanding functionality. Addressing these concerns could enhance Wordtune's effectiveness, especially in academic settings.

RQ3: Relationships between student groups and writing tool variables

We examined the interactions between distinct groups (EFL versus native students) and critical variables (English competence, Wordtune usage patterns, and perceived writing enhancements), along with the interconnections among these variables. The analysis employed various statistical approaches to thoroughly investigate these connections.

Although a chi-square test (using linear-by-linear association) revealed no significant association between the frequency of Wordtune usage and English proficiency ($\chi^2 = 0.002$, df = 1, p = 0.965), descriptive trends suggested that participants with higher proficiency tended to use the tool for longer periods. However, this finding should be interpreted with caution due to violations of chi-square test assumptions, with 18 cells (64.3%) having expected counts below 5. Additionally, more than half of the participants (51.3%) reported using Wordtune for less than three months, while only 4.7% had used it for over a year, reflecting the tool's relatively recent launch in 2020. These findings highlight the nascent stage of AI-powered writing assistant adoption in academic contexts at the time of the survey.

When comparing perceived benefits between international and native English-speaking students, Mann–Whitney U-tests found no significant differences for most benefits. However, international students reported significantly greater perceived advantages in building a stronger foundation in English than native speakers (U = 4,103.00, n1 = 128, n2 = 80, p = 0.010). This indicates that while both groups see value in Wordtune, international students find it especially helpful for language skill enhancement.

Further analysis using chi-square tests showed a significant association between language background and perceived benefits related to vocabulary, particularly identifying synonyms ($\chi^2 = 13.416$, df = 1, p < 0.001). International students with higher English proficiency valued Wordtune's synonym suggestions more than native speakers, highlighting the tool's relevance for non-native users seeking language development.

Finally, while another chi-square test found no significant relationship between the duration of Wordtune usage and perceived improvement in writing ($\chi^2 = 0.625$, df = 1, p = 0.429), this result should be interpreted with caution due to violations of test assumptions (53.3% of cells had expected counts below 5). Despite the lack of statistical significance, all participants who used Wordtune for more than three months reported becoming dependent on it for writing, suggesting that prolonged use may lead to reliance rather than independent skill development.

Discussion

In investigating the usage patterns and integration of Wordtune with other digital writing tools among students and academics, our study explored the impact of this AI-powered writing assistant on academic writing skills. Although AI-powered writing tools in university settings have been extensively studied (Shi & Aryadoust, 2024; Barrot, 2024), this research adds to the ongoing discourse by focusing on the specific impact of Wordtune on both native and international students' academic writing skills, making it a valuable contribution to the field.

Our study had five key findings. First, Wordtune appears to have broad appeal across diverse linguistic backgrounds, with nearly two-thirds of participants reporting a first language other than English. This aligns with previous research highlighting the challenges faced by EFL learners in academic writing (Ankawi, 2020; Phuong, 2021; Singh, 2017). Interestingly, despite this high proportion of non-native English speakers, the overall English proficiency levels were remarkably high, with a combined 48.4% reporting either professional working or full professional proficiency. This suggests that individuals with strong English abilities may be more inclined to seek out and utilize advanced academic support systems, echoing the observations of Geiser & Studley (2001) on the correlation between English proficiency and academic success.

Second, regarding usage patterns, many students, especially international students, reported frequent use of Wordtune in all writing tasks. 71.0% of non-native English speakers use Wordtune 'intensively when working on a particular type of work,' compared to 29.0% of native English students. These findings underscore the central role of Wordtune in their writing processes of non-native English speakers. This high usage rate among international students aligns with the findings of Zhao et al. (2024), who noted the propensity of Chinese international students to utilize digital tools for academic writing support.

Third, the integration of Wordtune with other digital writing tools emerged as a common practice among participants. Many reported using Wordtune with tools like Grammarly, Google Translate, and DeepL. This complementary use of multiple tools could be attributed to students' desire for comprehensive coverage in their writing process, addressing various aspects such as grammar, translation, and stylistic improvements. This finding aligns with the observations of Zhao et al. (2024) on the diverse digital tool usage patterns of international students.

Fourth, regarding the influence on academic writing skills, 73.66% of respondents reported learning to write better through their use of Wordtune, while 20.49% indicated dependency on the tool for their writing tasks. This high percentage suggests both Wordtune's perceived usefulness and potential concerns about over-reliance on AI tools in academic writing. The tool's ability to offer diverse options for rephrasing and prompt new ideas was particularly appreciated by international students with high English proficiency, aligning with observations by Bibi & Atta (2024) on the favourable perception of AI writing tools. Our study revealed that 93.8% of students browse through Wordtune's suggestions, selecting the most appropriate option with or without modifications. This behaviour mirrors paraphrasing techniques described by Fitria (2021), such as using synonyms and changing word order, suggesting active engagement in language learning. Our analysis showed no significant association between the duration of Wordtune usage and perceived improvement in writing skills. This discrepancy between users' self-reported improvement and the lack of statistical correlation with their duration of usage presents an intriguing paradox. It suggests that although students perceive benefits from using Wordtune, these benefits may not be directly proportional to the duration of use. This raises concerns about the balance between tool usage and skill development. As highlighted by Zhao et al. (2024), it's crucial to consider the potential for overreliance on digital tools. The percentage of students reporting dependency on Wordtune underscores the need for cautious integration of such tools in academic settings, balancing their perceived benefits with the development of independent writing skills.

Last, participants' perceptions of Wordtune's utility in enhancing academic writing were primarily associated with its capacity to provide alternative phrasings and synonyms, a feature particularly valued by non-native English speakers. However, it is important to note that this study relied on self-reported survey data, which reflects subjective experiences rather than empirical evidence of Wordtune's efficacy in improving academic writing skills. No direct assessments were conducted to measure improvements in academic writing, necessitating cautious interpretation of any conclusions regarding the tool's impact. While the data suggests that participants perceived value in Wordtune's functionality, further research is required to determine the tool's actual effectiveness in fostering long-term improvements in writing proficiency.

Practical implications

Based on our results, we propose the following pedagogical strategies to balance the benefits of AI writing assistants with the need to develop students' independent writing skills and critical thinking abilities:

- **Digital Literacy and Critical Evaluation:** Students should be trained to use AI writing assistants as learning tools, not just editing devices. They should critically evaluate AI-generated suggestions to avoid blindly accepting them. This will help them develop digital

literacy, and critical thinking skills (Tseng & Warschauer, 2023; Crompton et al., 2023).
- **Scaffolded Approach**: Instructors could implement a phased approach where students are initially allowed to use AI assistants freely, but gradually reduce their reliance as the course progresses. This could help develop their writing skills without becoming over-reliant on the AI tool (Cummings et al., 2024).
- **Comparative Writing Workshops:** Organize sessions where students compare their original drafts with AI-assisted versions, encouraging them to reflect on the changes and develop a deeper understanding of effective writing techniques (Shi & Aryadoust, 2024).

Conclusion and Limitations

Our study explored the usage patterns and impact of Wordtune, an AI-powered writing assistant, among university students. Our findings reveal that Wordtune has broad appeal across diverse linguistic backgrounds. The tool's ability to offer alternative phrasings and synonyms was highly appreciated, particularly by non-native English speakers with high proficiency levels.

Our study has some limitations that open avenues for future research. First, the self-reported nature of proficiency levels and perceived benefits introduces potential bias into the results. The study's assessment of improvement in writing skills was limited by the three-point scale used ("no learning", "dependency", and "learning"), where the middle option inherently presumed dependency rather than allowing participants to independently report their level of tool reliance. This methodological constraint may have affected our ability to accurately assess the true extent of user dependency. Additionally, recruiting participants from active Wordtune subscribers may have led to an overrepresentation of users who find the tool beneficial, potentially skewing the results towards more positive perceptions. Future studies could study the perceptions of AI powered writing tools among students in higher education.

Our study used cross sectional data, which limits our ability to draw conclusions about the long-term effects of Wordtune use on writing skills development. We asked participants to self-evaluate the impact of the use of Wordtune. Future studies could address the skills development using longitudinal research design, for instance, by comparing the writing assignments before and after using Wordtune for a certain period. Furthermore, future studies could examine how multiple AI writing assistants could effectively be integrated into academic writing instruction without compromising skill development. Although this study is a relatively small project, it would be useful to have more members to be involved with the coding process to establish intercoder reliability rate.

> **Post-reading questions:**
>
> 1) Considering the potential for AI tools like Wordtune to enhance writing processes, how might educators develop assessment strategies that evaluate creativity and originality, beyond just technical proficiency?
> 2) With the rise of AI-assisted writing, what ethical considerations should universities address regarding student dependency on AI tools, particularly in terms of academic integrity?
> 3) Reflecting on the study's findings, how can AI-powered tools be leveraged to support students in developing not only language skills but also critical thinking and self-editing abilities?

Further reading

Tseng, W., & Warschauer, M. (2023). AI-writing tools in education: if you can't beat them, join them. *Journal of China Computer-Assisted Language Learning*, *3*(2), 258–262. https://doi.org/10.1515/jccall-2023-0008

Cummings, R. E., Monroe, S. M., & Watkins, M. (2024). Generative AI in first-year writing: An early analysis of affordances, limitations, and a framework for the future. *Computers and Composition*, *71*, 102827.

Shi, H., & Aryadoust, V. (2024). A systematic review of AI-based automated writing evaluation tools. *Computers & Education*.

References

AbdAlgane, M., & Othman, K. A. J. (2023). Utilizing artificial intelligence technologies in Saudi EFL tertiary level classrooms. *Journal of Intercultural Communication*, 92–99. https://doi.org/10.36923/jicc.v23i1.124

Alsariera, A. H., & Alsaraireh, M. Y. (2024). Advancing EFL writing proficiency in Jordan: Addressing challenges and embedding progressive strategies. *International Journal of Arabic-English Studies*, *22*(2). https://doi.org/10.33806/ijaes.v24i2.664

Alsied, S. M., & Ibrahim, N. W. (2018). Exploring challenges encountered by EFL Libyan learners in research teaching and writing. *IAFOR Journal of Language Learning*, *3*(2). https://doi.org/10.22492/ijll.3.2.06

Andersson, R., Ringhagen, A., & Tapper, A. (2024). Exploring the integration of artificial intelligence tools in English as a foreign language (EFL) pedagogy. A literature review. *Gupea.ub.gu.se*. https://hdl.handle.net/2077/79561

Anjana Susarla, Gopal, R., Bennett Thatcher, J., & Sarker, S. (2023). The Janus effect of generative AI: Charting the path for responsible conduct of scholarly activities in information systems. *Information Systems Research, 34*(2). https://doi.org/10.1287/isre.2023.ed.v34.n2

Ankawi, A. (2020). The academic writing challenges faced by Saudi students studying at a university in New Zealand. *International Journal of English Language Education, 8*(2), 117. https://doi.org/10.5296/ijele.v8i2.17342

Balida, A. R., & Encarnacion, R. (2020). Challenges and relationships of e-learning tools to teaching and learning. In *European Conference on e-Learning* (pp. 48–XIX). Academic Conferences International Limited.

Balida, A. R., & Encarnacion, R. (2020). Challenges and relationships of e-learning tools to teaching and learning. In *European Conference on e-Learning* (pp. 48–XIX). Academic Conferences International Limited.

Barrot, J. S. Leveraging Google Gemini as a research writing tool in higher education. *Tech Know Learn* (2024). https://doi.org/10.1007/s10758-024-09774-x

Baskara, R. (2023). Exploring the implications of ChatGPT for language learning in higher education. *Indonesian Journal of English Language Teaching and Applied Linguistics, 7*(2), 343–358.

Bibi, Z., & Atta, A. (2024). The Role of ChatGPT as AI English writing assistant: A study of student's perceptions, experiences, and satisfaction. *Annals of Human and Social Sciences, 5*(1). https://doi.org/10.35484/ahss.2024(5-I)39

Bland, J. M., & Altman, D. G. (1997). Statistics notes: Cronbach's alpha. *BMJ, 314*(7080), 572.

Braine, G. (2002). Academic literacy and the nonnative speaker graduate student. *Journal of English for Academic Purposes, 1*(1), 59–68. https://doi.org/10.1016/s1475-1585(02)00006-1

Caldarini, G., Jaf, S., & McGarry, K. (2022). A literature survey of recent advances in chatbots. *Information, 13*(1), 41. mdpi. https://doi.org/10.3390/info13010041

Campbell, M. (2019). Teaching academic writing in higher education. *Education Quarterly Reviews, 2*(3).

Chiu, M.-C., Hwang, G.-J., Hsia, L.-H., & Shyu, F.-M. (2022). Artificial intelligence-supported art education: a deep learning-based system for promoting university students' artwork appreciation and painting outcomes. *Interactive Learning Environments*, 1–19. https://doi.org/10.1080/10494820.2022.2100426

Coenen, A., Davis, L., Ippolito, D., Reif, E., & Yuan, A. (2021, July 15). *Wordcraft: a Human-AI Collaborative Editor for Story Writing*. ArXiv.org https://doi.org/10.48550/arXiv.2107.07430

Crompton, H., & Burke, D. (2023). Artificial intelligence in higher education: The state of the field. *International Journal of Educational Technology in Higher Education*, *20*(1). https://doi.org/10.1186/s41239-023-00392-8

Cummings, R. E., Monroe, S. M., & Watkins, M. (2024). Generative AI in first-year writing: An early analysis of affordances, limitations, and a framework for the future. *Computers and Composition*, *71*, 102827.

Ding, L., & Zou, D. (2024). Automated writing evaluation systems: A systematic review of Grammarly, Pigai, and Criterion with a perspective on future directions in the age of generative artificial intelligence. *Education and Information Technologies*, *29*, 14151–14203. https://doi.org/10.1007/s10639-023-12402-3

Divan, A., Bowman, M., & Seabourne, A. (2013). Reducing unintentional plagiarism amongst international students in the biological sciences: An embedded academic writing development programme. *Journal of Further and Higher Education*, *39*(3), 358–378. https://doi.org/10.1080/0309877x.2013.858674

Finn, H. B. (2018). Articulating struggle: ESL students' perceived obstacles to success in a community college writing class. *Journal of Second Language Writing*, *42*, 101–106. https://doi.org/10.1016/j.jslw.2018.09.001

Fitria, T. N. (2018). Error analysis found in students' writing composition of simple future tense. *ELS Journal on Interdisciplinary Studies in Humanities*, *1*(3), 240–251. https://doi.org/10.34050/els-jish.v1i3.5028

Fitria, T. N. (2019b). Students' error analysis in writing English composition of 'My Self-Description'. *Proceeding SENDI_U*, (pp. 453–460).

Fitria, T. N. (2021). QuillBot as an online tool: Students' alternative in paraphrasing and rewriting of English writing. *Elsya: Journal of Language, Education, and Humanities*, *9*(1), 183. https://doi.org/10.22373/ej.v9i1.10233

Fitria, T. N. (2022). Avoiding plagiarism of students scientific writing by using the QuillBot Paraphraser. *Elsya: Journal of English Language Studies*, *4*(3), 252–262.

Fitria, T. N. (2024). Using Wordtune as an AI-powered writing tool how is the performance in rewrite and rephrase English writing? *Journal Pendidikan Bahasa English Proficiency*, *6*(1), 117–149.

Flowerdew, J. (2019). The linguistic disadvantage of scholars who write in English as an additional language: Myth or reality. *Language Teaching*, *52*(02), 249–260. https://doi.org/10.1017/s0261444819000041

Geiser, S., & Studley, R. (2001). UC and the SAT: Predictive validity and differential impact of the SAT I and SAT II at the University of California. Retrieved March 1, 2002, from the University of California, Office of the President website: www.ucop.edu/sas/research/ researchandplanning/pdf/sat_study.pdf

Haddaji, H., (2024). Pedagogical potentials of technological facilities in developing the writing skills of L2 learners: AI-era writing. *International Journal of Innovative Research in Multidisciplinary Education*, *3*(02). https://doi.org/10.58806/ijirme.2024.v3i2n08

Hanauer, D. I., Sheridan, C. L., & Englander, K. (2019). Linguistic injustice in the writing of research articles in English as a second language: Data from Taiwanese and Mexican researchers. *Written Communication*, *36*(1), 136–154. https://doi.org/10.1177/0741088318804821

Hartley, J. (2008). *Academic writing and publishing*. Routledge. https://doi.org/10.4324/9780203927984

Iskender, A. (2023). Holy or unholy? Interview with Open AI's ChatGPT. *European Journal of Tourism Research*, *34*(3414), 1–11. https://doi.org/10.54055/ejtr.v34i.3169

Ito, T., Yamashita, N., Kuribayashi, T., Hidaka, M., Suzuki, J., Gao, G., Jamieson, J., & Inui, K. (2023). Use of an AI-powered rewriting support software in context with other tools: A study of non-native English speakers. *Association for Computing Machinery*, 1–13. https://doi.org/10.1145/3586183.3606810

Jasper, R., Renandya, W., & Jacobs, G. (2023). A review of AI-powered writing tools and their implications for academic integrity in the language classroom. *Journal of English and Applied Linguistics Journal of English and Applied Linguistics*, *2*(1). https://doi.org/10.59588/2961-3094.1035

Leyland, C. (2020). Academic writing tutorials for international students: Deferring to an expert and follow-up advice. *Language and Education*, *34*(3), 212–230. https://doi.org/10.1080/09500782.2019.1682008

Mahammoda, S. A. (2016). Factors affecting the quality of undergraduate research work in Bahir Dar University, Ethiopia. *International Journal of Innovative Research and Development*, 23–27.

Mahmud, F. A. (2023). Investigating EFL students' writing skills through artificial intelligence: Wordtune application as a tool. *Journal of Language Teaching and Research*, *14*(5), 1395–1404. https://doi.org/10.17507/jltr.1405.28

Malinka, K., Peresíni, M., Firc, A., Ondrej Hujnák, & Janus, F. (2023). On the educational impact of ChatGPT: Is artificial intelligence ready to obtain a university degree? *On the Educational Impact of ChatGPT: Is Artificial Intelligence Ready to Obtain a University Degree?* https://doi.org/10.1145/3587102.3588827

Marzuki, Utami Widiati, Diyenti Rusdin, Darwin, & Inda Indrawati. (2023). The impact of AI writing tools on the content and organization of students' writing: EFL teachers' perspective. *Cogent Education*, *10*(2). https://doi.org/10.1080/2331186x.2023.2236469

McDonough, K., De Vleeschauwer, J., & Crawford, W. J. (2018). Exploring the benefits of collaborative prewriting in a Thai EFL context. *Language Teaching Research*, *23*(6), 685–701. https://doi.org/10.1177/1362168818773525

Mohamed, A. M. (2023). Exploring the potential of an AI-based Chatbot (ChatGPT) in enhancing English as a Foreign Language (EFL) teaching: perceptions of EFL Faculty Members. *Education and Information Technologies*, *29*, 3195–3217. https://doi.org/10.1007/s10639-023-11917-z

Nah, F. F.-H., Zheng, R., Cai, J., Siau, K., & Chen, L. (2023). Generative AI and ChatGPT: Applications, challenges, and AI-human collaboration. *Journal of Information Technology Case and Application Research*, *25*(3), 1–28. https://doi.org/10.1080/15228053.2023.2233814

Nazari, N., Shabbir, M. S., & Setiawan, R. (2021). Application of Artificial Intelligence powered digital writing assistant in higher education: Randomized controlled trial. *Heliyon*, *7*(5), e07014. https://doi.org/10.1016/j.heliyon.2021.e07014

Osawa, K. (2023). Integrating automated written corrective feedback into e-portfolios for second language writing: Notion and notion AI. *RELC Journal*, *55*(3). https://doi.org/10.1177/00336882231198913

Ouyang, L., Wu, J., Jiang, X., Almeida, D., Wainwright, C., Mishkin, P., & Lowe, R. (2022). Training language models to follow instructions with human feedback. *Advances in Neural Information Processing Systems*, *35*, 27730–27744. https://rb.gy/na5bs

Perkins, M. (2023). Academic integrity considerations of AI Large Language Models in the post-pandemic era: ChatGPT and beyond. *Journal of University Teaching and Learning Practice*, *20*(2). https://doi.org/10.53761/1.20.02.07

Phuong, W. T. N. (2021). Difficulties in studying writing of English-majored sophomores at a university in Vietnam. *European Journal of Education Studies*, *8*(10). http://dx.doi.org/10.46827/ejes.v8i10.3962

Rad, H. S., Alipour, R., & Jafarpour, A. (2023). Using artificial intelligence to foster students' writing feedback literacy, engagement, and outcome: a case of Wordtune application. *Interactive Learning Environments*, *10*(2), 1–21. https://doi.org/10.1080/10494820.2023.2208170

Selim, M. (2024). The transformative impact of AI-powered tools on academic writing: perspectives of EFL university students. *International Journal of English Linguistics*, *14*(1), 14–14. https://doi.org/10.5539/ijel.v14n1p14

Shi, H., & Aryadoust, V. (2024). A systematic review of AI-based automated written feedback research. *ReCALL, 36*(2), 187–209. https://doi.org/10.1017/s0958344023000265

Singh, M. K. M. (2017). International EFL/ESL master students' adaptation strategies for academic writing practices at tertiary level. *Journal of International Students, 7*(3), 620–643. https://doi.org/10.32674/jis.v7i3.291

Singh, M. K. M. (2019). Academic reading and writing challenges among international EFL master's students in a Malaysian university. *Journal of International Students, 9*(4), 972–992. https://doi.org/10.32674/jis.v9i3.934

Strobl, C., Ailhaud, E., Benetos, K., Devitt, A., Kruse, O., Proske, A., & Rapp, C. (2019). Digital support for academic writing: A review of technologies and pedagogies. *Computers & Education, 131*, 33–48. https://doi.org/10.1016/j.compedu.2018.12.005

Surden, H. (2019). Artificial intelligence and law: An overview. *Georgia State University Law Review, 35*, 19–22.

Tavakol, M. & Dennick, R. (2011). Making sense of Cronbach's alpha. *International Journal of Medical Education, 2*, 53–55. https://doi.org/10.5116/ijme.4dfb.8dfd

Tseng, W., & Warschauer, M. (2023). AI-writing tools in education: If you can't beat them, join them. *Journal of China Computer-Assisted Language Learning, 3*(2), 258–262. https://doi.org/10.1515/jccall-2023-0008

Xin, Z., Sbaffi, L., & Cox, A. (2023). *The digitisation of writing in higher education: Exploring the use of Wordtune as an AI writing assistant*. https://doi.org/10.31219/osf.io/uzwy7

Xu, L., Lu, Y., & Li, L. (2021). Embedding blockchain technology into IoT for security: A survey. *IEEE Internet of Things Journal, 8*(13), 1–1. https://doi.org/10.1109/jiot.2021.3060508

Zhao, X. (2022). Leveraging artificial intelligence (AI) technology for English writing: Introducing Wordtune as a digital writing assistant for EFL writers. *RELC Journal, 54*(3), 003368822210940. https://doi.org/10.1177/00336882221094089

Zhao, X., Sbaffi, L., & Cox, A. (2023). The digitisation of writing in higher education: Exploring the use of Wordtune as an AI writing assistant.

Zhao, X., Xu, J., & Cox, A. (2024). Incorporating artificial intelligence into student academic writing in higher education: The use of Wordtune by Chinese international students. In *scholarspace.manoa.hawaii.edu*. Hawaii International Conference on System Sciences 2024. https://hdl.handle.net/10125/106712

Zhou, S. A., & Hiver, P. (2022). The effect of self-regulated writing strategies on students' L2 writing engagement and disengagement behaviors. *System, 106*, 102768. https://doi.org/10.1016/j.system.2022.102768

Appendix

Table 1 *Questionnaire items*

	Items
1	Response ID
2	Date submitted
3	Last page
4	Start language
5	Seed
6	Date started
7	Date last action
8	Referrer URL
9	Taking part in the project:
10	Your gender:
11	Your age:
12	Your role:
13	Your role: [Other]
14	What is your major/degree subject or area of interest?
15	Is English your first language?
16	If English is not your first language, what is your first language?
17	If English is not your first language, how would you define your proficiency?
18	What is your use of the following tools when you write? (1 = Not used at all; ... 5 = High level of use) [Voice recognition software (e.g.: Dragon dictate, speech note, Google voice)]
19	What is your use of the following tools when you write? (1 = Not used at all; ... 5 = High level of use) [Handwriting recognition software]
20	What is your use of the following tools when you write? (1 = Not used at all; ... 5 = High level of use) [Websites such as dictionaries or thesauruses]
21	What is your use of the following tools when you write? (1 = Not used at all; ... 5 = High level of use) [Digital writing assistants / software]
22	What is your use of the following tools when you write? (1 = Not used at all; ... 5 = High level of use) [Translation tools]
23	What is your use of the following tools when you write? (1 = Not used at all; ... 5 = High level of use) [Text summarisation tools]

Continued

Continuation

	Items
24	What is your use of the following tools when you write? (1 = Not used at all; ... 5 = High level of use) [Pen and paper]
25	What is your use of the following tools when you write? (1 = Not used at all; ... 5 = High level of use) [Whiteboard / blackboard / flip charts]
26	What is your use of the following tools when you write? (1 = Not used at all; ... 5 = High level of use) [University writing services, writing tutorials, workshops on writing practices]
27	What is your use of the following tools when you write? (1= Not used at all; ... 5 = High level of use) [Human proofreaders]
28	What is your use of the following tools when you write? (1= Not used at all; ... 5 = High level of use) [Visualisation tools (e.g.: mind mapping, Padlet, Google whiteboard, Jamboard)]
29	What is your use of the following tools when you write? (1 = Not used at all; ... 5 = High level of use) [Books (including dictionaries, writing guides, etc.)]
30	Other tools used (please specify):
31	What platform are you usually writing in? (e.g. Google doc, Word, Overleaf, etc.)
32	What other writing software do you use apart from Wordtune and for what purpose (e.g. Grammarly, Google translate, etc.)?
33	If you use other software, do you use them & Wordtune together? If so, how?
34	In general, how often do you use Wordtune?
35	How long have you used Wordtune for?
36	What version of Wordtune are you using?
37	Did you switch from another tool when joining Wordtune? If so, please specify which one.
38	If you are using the Premium subscription version, why did you decide to purchase the subscription?
39	If you are using the Premium subscription version, what built-in features do you tend to use? [Casual tone]
40	If you are using the Premium subscription version, what built-in features do you tend to use? [Formal tone]
41	If you are using the Premium subscription version, what built-in features do you tend to use? [Shorten]
42	If you are using the Premium subscription version, what built-in features do you tend to use? [Expand]

Continued

Continuation

	Items
43	If you are using the Premium subscription version, what built-in features do you tend to use? [N/A (I do not use the Premium subscription version)]
44	How would you describe how you use Wordtune? (1 = Not used for this; ... 5 = High level of use) [I use it in every aspect of my writing (i.e. grammar, syntax and content)]
45	How would you describe how you use Wordtune? (1 = Not used for this; ... 5 = High level of use) [It helps me write more clearly]
46	How would you describe how you use Wordtune? (1 = Not used for this; ... 5 = High level of use) [It helps me fix grammar mistakes]
47	How would you describe how you use Wordtune? (1 = Not used for this; ... 5 = High level of use) [It helps me translate words from my native language into English]
48	How would you describe how you use Wordtune? (1 = Not used for this; ... 5 = High level of use) [It helps me fine tune the wording for a particular audience]
49	How would you describe how you use Wordtune? (1 = Not used for this; ... 5 = High level of use) [It helps me avoid plagiarism]
50	How would you describe how you use Wordtune? (1 = Not used for this; ... 5 = High level of use) [It helps me express myself in a polite way]
51	Other uses of Wordtune (please specify):
52	When using Wordtune, do you tend to…
53	For what purposes do you use Wordtune? [Rank 1]
54	For what purposes do you use Wordtune? [Rank 2]
55	For what purposes do you use Wordtune? [Rank 3]
56	For what purposes do you use Wordtune? [Rank 4]
57	For what purposes do you use Wordtune? [Rank 5]
58	For what purposes do you use Wordtune? [Rank 6]
59	For what purposes do you use Wordtune? [Rank 7]
60	How would you describe the benefits provided by Wordtune? (1 = Not beneficial at all; ... 5 = Highly beneficial) [It helps express what I am thinking]
61	How would you describe the benefits provided by Wordtune? (1 = Not beneficial at all; ... 5 = Highly beneficial) [It helps me break through a 'mental block']
62	How would you describe the benefits provided by Wordtune? (1 = Not beneficial at all; ... 5 = Highly beneficial) [It prompts me to think of new ideas]

Continued

Continuation

	Items
63	How would you describe the benefits provided by Wordtune? (1 = Not beneficial at all; ... 5 = Highly beneficial) [It helps me identify more suitable synonyms for the words I use in my writing]
64	How would you describe the benefits provided by Wordtune? (1 = Not beneficial at all; ... 5 = Highly beneficial) [It allows me to build a stronger foundation in the English language]
65	How would you describe the benefits provided by Wordtune? (1 = Not beneficial at all; ... 5 = Highly beneficial) [It offers the right range of options for my needs]
66	How would you describe the benefits provided by Wordtune? (1 = Not beneficial at all; ... 5 = Highly beneficial) [It increases the accuracy of my writing (e.g. it makes it grammatically correct)]
67	How would you describe the benefits provided by Wordtune? (1 = Not beneficial at all; ... 5 = Highly beneficial) [It improves the functionality of existing Word processing software]
68	How would you describe the benefits provided by Wordtune? (1 = Not beneficial at all; ... 5 = Highly beneficial) [It is compatible with other technologies]
69	Other benefits of Wordtune (please specify):
70	Have you improved your own skills with Wordtune?
71	Have you improved your own skills with Wordtune? [Other]
72	If you are an educator/teacher, would you recommend the use of Wordtune by students?
73	If you are an educator and answered the question above, can you please elaborate on your answer?
74	If you no longer had access to Wordtune, what would the overall effect on your writing be? (1= No impact at all; ... 5 = Serious impact) [Reduced confidence in writing]
75	If you no longer had access to Wordtune, what would the overall effect on your writing be? (1= No impact at all; ... 5 = Serious impact) [Reduced ability to spell]
76	If you no longer had access to Wordtune, what would the overall effect on your writing be? (1= No impact at all; ... 5 = Serious impact) [Less clear writing]
77	If you no longer had access to Wordtune, what would the overall effect on your writing be? (1= No impact at all; ... 5 = Serious impact) [Less motivation to write]

Continued

Continuation

	Items
78	Other effects on your writing (please specify):
79	Are there any issues with using Wordtune? (1 = Not an issue at all; ... 5 = Serious issue) [It occasionally stops working]
80	Are there any issues with using Wordtune? (1 = Not an issue at all; ... 5 = Serious issue) [It highlights the wrong parts of the writing I want to work on]
81	Are there any issues with using Wordtune? (1 = Not an issue at all; ... 5 = Serious issue) [It doesn't work well with complex sentences (i.e. it changes the meaning)]
82	Are there any issues with using Wordtune? (1 = Not an issue at all; ... 5 = Serious issue) [It fails to detect wrong use of words]
83	Are there any issues with using Wordtune? (1 = Not an issue at all; ... 5 = Serious issue) [It finds problems that do not exist]
84	Other issues with Wordtune (please specify):
85	Would you recommend Wordtune to a friend? Why or why not?
86	Do you have any suggestions for the improvement of the tool? Is there anything you are missing and would like to see?
87	Is there anything else you would like to add?

16
Feedback and Automated Writing Evaluation (AWE)

Inyoung Na
Mahdi Duris
Volker Hegelheimer

> **Pre-reading questions:**
>
> 1) How can *ChatGPT* benefit second language (L2) learners in receiving writing feedback?
> 2) What factors might influence learners' attitudes towards using *ChatGPT* as a tool for improving English writing skills?

Introduction

Automated Writing Evaluation (AWE) systems, such as Grammarly and ETS's Criterion, have gained considerable interest for integration into language classrooms to provide second language (L2) learners with corrective and diagnostic feedback. The practical benefits of these systems were recognized for alleviating the workload of instructors, enabling them to focus their feedback efforts on aspects of writing that require human evaluation, such as discourse features of writing, rather than on sentence-level issues like grammar, word choice, and mechanics (Ranalli et al., 2017). Students receiving immediate and frequent feedback through AWE tools showed enhanced L2 development, increasing autonomy and motivation to write (Warschauer & Grimes, 2008).

With the recent release of highly sophisticated large language models (LLMs), such as OpenAI's GPT series and Google's PaLM2, AWE seems to be entering a new era. These models are trained on vast amounts of text data from the internet to understand and predict language patterns, generating coherent human-like text in response to user prompts. Simple chat interfaces like ChatGPT by OpenAI and, more recently, Google's Gemini and Microsoft's Copilot have allowed an increasing number of users to interface with LLMs to perform tasks as if they are interacting with a human. When this capability is used in L2 writing contexts, particularly for automated writing evaluation and feedback, LLMs may provide students with support like what they receive from teachers. This allows them to request feedback about various aspects of their writing, including global aspects such as organization and flow, in addition to the sentence-level error corrections offered by traditional AWE tools. Thus, we aimed to explore what interactions between L2 learners and LLMs look like and the extent to which LLMs offer the support that students need, potentially leading to revisions across different aspects of writing. Given that ChatGPT has been available the longest (since November 2022) and is the most widely used, we chose ChatGPT based on GPT-3.5 as the AI chat platform for learners to interact within our study.

To evaluate ChatGPT's effectiveness as an AWE tool, it is crucial to examine the interaction between the learner and ChatGPT due to its reactive nature. Specifically, the effectiveness of ChatGPT's feedback is largely determined by the user prompt, as it responds based on what is requested. Therefore, we investigated learner-ChatGPT interactions using Chapelle's (2001) CALL evaluation framework, adopting an interactionist approach to focus on ChatGPT's language learning potential. Additionally, it is essential to explore learners' detailed perspectives and attitudes towards ChatGPT, as these can provide insight into why students engage with ChatGPT in particular ways, such as accepting or ignoring its feedback.

However, it is important to emphasize that our intention is not solely to advocate for the benefits of using LLMs. A growing body of literature addresses concerns associated with LLMs in English writing, such as academic malpractice, inaccuracies, reduced learning, and misinformation (e.g., Fuchs, 2023; Song & Song, 2023). The findings of this study also highlight these issues, particularly in relation to plagiarism concerns. In what follows, the literature review will discuss AWE studies, LLMs in L2 Writing, and Chapelle's CALL Evaluation Framework.

Literature review

Automated writing evaluation

Automated Writing Evaluation (AWE) tools are digital writing environments that provide automated feedback (Cotos, 2023). AWE has been found to be more adept at providing feedback on sentence-level correctness than on higher-level concerns (Ranalli et al., 2017; Weigle,

2013), leading us to question whether ChatGPT is effective at one and/ or the other. Moreover, learners' engagement levels and the subsequent effectiveness of AWE can be influenced by individual differences, highlighting the importance of researching students' variability, such as their learning orientations, proficiency, and perceptions of AWE's efficacy (Chen et al., 2022; Ranalli, 2021; Zhang & Hyland, 2018; Zhang, 2020), and through a qualitative and close lens (Godwin-Jones, 2022). For instance, even though students may revise their drafts using the AWE feedback, a closer look might tell us that they do not necessarily engage more deeply with and learn from the feedback than just adopting a quick proofreading orientation to the drafts (Stevenson & Phakiti, 2019), not going beyond sentence-level changes.

Learners perceiving ChatGPT as an effective writing tool are more likely to continue to use the AI tool and benefit from it further as a complement to the teacher's feedback and/or outside the language classroom.

LLMs and L2 writing

Recently, more studies have started to explore LLMs in the context of L2 writing, highlighting the benefits of ChatGPT's feedback enhancing students' skills in coherence, organization, vocabulary, grammar, and organization as well as students' positive perceptions of its use (e.g., Ali et al., 2023; Boudouaia et al., 2024; Mahaptara, 2024; Song & Song, 2023). For instance, Mahapatra (2024) evaluated ChatGPT's effectiveness in improving the writing skills of undergraduate ESL students in India, finding that those who received ChatGPT's feedback significantly outperformed a control group on writing tasks and expressed positive perceptions of its assistance with content, organization, and grammar. Similarly, Boudouaia et al. (2024) reported that EFL students in Algeria who used ChatGPT-4 for revising their texts over a 10-week intervention showed notable improvements in both local (e.g., grammar) and global (e.g., coherence) aspects of writing, compared to a control group that received traditional teacher feedback. Questionnaire results further revealed growing acceptance of ChatGPT's feedback among students, particularly regarding its perceived usefulness and ease of use. While it serves as an effective tool for writing practice and feedback that supplements teacher's feedback (Guo & Wang, 2023), some studies have also raised concerns about potential issues such as plagiarism, inaccuracies, over-reliance, and unoriginality in students' work (Fuchs, 2023; Kohnke & Moorhouse, 2023; Mahapatra, 2024; Xiao & Zhi, 2023).

However, the methodologies employed in these studies have been limited to experimental designs, intervention studies, and survey-based approaches. Many, including Mahapatra (2024), Boudouaia et al. (2024), and Song and Song (2023), used pre-test and post-test designs to evaluate changes in writing proficiency, comparing experimental groups receiving ChatGPT feedback with control groups receiving traditional teacher feedback. Yet, this focus on test scores and group comparisons alone does not provide detailed insights into how students engaged with and used ChatGPT's feedback. As with previous AWE studies, a qualitative lens may suggest only a quick proofreading orientation using ChatGPT's feedback to the draft (Ranalli, 2021; Stevenson & Phakiti, 2019) rather than deep engagement with the writing process. More detailed explorations of the nature of learner-ChatGPT interaction are needed.

Chapelle's CALL evaluation framework

To evaluate ChatGPT's potential as an AWE system for promoting language learning, we applied Chapelle's (2001) Computer-Assisted Language Learning (CALL) evaluation framework. This framework provides six criteria for evaluation: language learning potential, meaning focus, learner fit, impact, authenticity, and practicality. Our study focuses on the evidence of language learning potential (LLP) through a detailed investigation of learners' patterns of using ChatGPT and their perceptions of its effectiveness. Here, LLP is broadly defined as the potential of feedback to facilitate a beneficial focus on form and discourse features (e.g., organization and development). Using the interactionist approach (Gass & Mackey, 2006; Long, 2007) to assess LLP, we examined learners' interactions with ChatGPT, focusing on how they attended to and noticed the feedback, as well as how they engaged with the modified input (i.e., learners' original output analyzed and returned with feedback by the system) to negotiate meaning and modify their output (see Figure 1 for this interaction process). It is important to note that since ChatGPT is reactive rather than proactive, the nature and quality of its feedback greatly depends on the types of feedback sought through user prompts. Therefore, our particular interest was to see how learners and ChatGPT co-construct the feedback and add another mechanism to maximize learning opportunities.

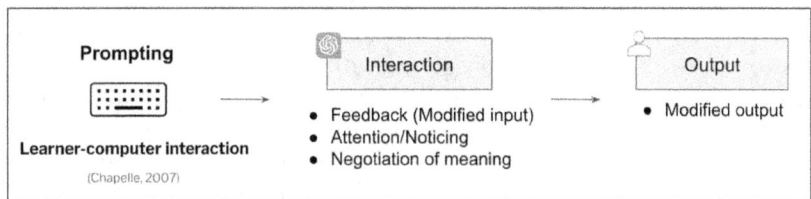

Figure 16.1. *Diagram of interaction between learner and ChatGPT.*

To the best of our knowledge, no prior study has rigorously examined how learners interact with ChatGPT for English writing revisions based on a theoretical framework such as Chapelle's CALL framework or the interactionist approach. Such detailed explorations will provide a better understanding of what aspects of the nature of learner-ChatGPT interaction shape learners' modified output–something that cannot be revealed through mere quantitative comparisons between experimental and control groups. Researching this topic is timely, considering the growing interdisciplinary interest in LLMs and attention to providing a detailed perspective from learners who currently or potentially use ChatGPT as an AWE tool. Insights from our study are also expected to help language teachers guide students to use ChatGPT more effectively with appropriate prompts and recognize its benefits for ongoing language development. Therefore, our exploratory study investigates the usage patterns and perceived effectiveness of ChatGPT, examining eight international students from two university-level ESL writing courses at different levels. Using student-ChatGPT conversation logs, semi-structured interviews, surveys, and screen recordings, we explored how these students interacted with and evolved their views on ChatGPT's support for their L2 writing across three revision sessions. The following research questions guided our study:

1. What interaction patterns are observed between the L2 learners and ChatGPT? What prompts do they use, what feedback do they receive, and how do they respond to this feedback?
2. What are the L2 learners' perceived effectiveness and attitudes towards ChatGPT in writing revisions and improvement?

Based on our findings from research questions 1 and 2, we evaluated the LLP of ChatGPT for improving English writing.

Methodology

Participants

The participants were eight international students (male = 6, female = 2) at a large university in the Midwestern U.S. They were recruited from a two-course ESL writing program, with five participants from the lower-level course and three participants from the higher-level course in that program. Participants completed background questionnaires through Qualtrics (https://qualtrics.com). All had experience using either the basic or plus version of ChatGPT except for participant B05. The characteristics of participants are summarized in Table 1.

Table 16.1 *Characteristics of participants*

ID	L1	Sex	Age	Student Level	TOEFL/IELTS/ etc. (converted to TOEFL score in parentheses)	Major	Type of ChatGPT user
B01	Arabic	Male	25	G	TOEFL 84	Community and regional planning	Weekly
B02	Telugu, Hindi	Female	25	G	IELTS 6.5 (79–93)	Information systems and business analytics	Weekly
B03	Telugu	Male	24	G	TOEFL 99	MBA	Daily
B04	Tamil	Male	23	G	IELTS 7 (94–101)	Industrial Design	Daily
B05	Portuguese	Male	29	G	Duolingo 105 (70–75)	Mechanical Engineering	Inactive
C06	Korean	Female	21	U	Duolingo 130 (98–103)	Statistics	Daily
C07	Bangla	Male	21	U	Cambridge-B (80–96)	Mechanical Engineering	Weekly
C08	Nepali	Male	18	U	SAT 590	Computer Engineering	Weekly

Note. B and C indicate whether the participant was from the lower writing course (B) or higher writing course (C); U=Undergraduate and G=Graduate.

Data collection

Four data collection sessions were conducted over three weeks: the first included a tutorial and was held in the first week, the second and third sessions in the second week, and the final session in the third week. Participants completed a revision task using ChatGPT during the first three sessions, followed by a brief Qualtrics survey about their experience. In the final session, participants engaged in semi-structured interviews along with stimulated recalls, individually with the researcher. Each session lasted between 45 and 60 minutes.

Tutorial and biography task

In the first session, participants watched a 5-minute tutorial on using ChatGPT to revise their essays. The tutorial provided an example of basic prompting, such as, "Could you give me general feedback on this essay?" and more specific prompting to direct the feedback toward their needs and problems, including, "How can I make my thesis statement stronger?" "Can you provide feedback on the organization of my essay?" and "Are there any grammatical errors?" The same example prompts were also provided as written instructions. The purpose of the study was to observe how learners would interact with ChatGPT without being encouraged to use specific prompts. Therefore, no additional instructions were given beyond these examples, aside from emphasizing that ChatGPT's feedback is co-constructed through interaction with the user. This approach was taken to avoid influencing how participants used the tool and to prevent any potential skewing of the results. After watching the tutorial, participants were asked to write a short biography of 150–200 words in 20 minutes and then revise it using feedback obtained from ChatGPT in another 20 minutes. They submitted their work when ready and completed a short survey about their experience. This session lasted 50 minutes.

Revision task

In the subsequent two sessions, the participants completed a revision task using texts they had recently written or were in the process of writing for the course they were currently enrolled in. The decision to have participants bring their own authentic texts rather than assigning a task in a controlled setting was intended to encourage them to invest more fully in the revision process. Because they finished revising the texts earlier than expected, all participants revised one text per session, resulting in two texts each across the two sessions. Each participant worked individually on a provided computer in a private lab. The researcher was available for technical assistance but did not observe the tasks directly. The participants submitted their texts to ChatGPT-3.5, prompted it at their discretion to receive feedback, and revised their texts accordingly in a Google Docs document. They worked through the feedback until they were satisfied with their writing or reached the 40-minute time constraint. The participants submitted their completed drafts, and conversations between them and ChatGPT were automatically archived. After submission, they completed the same survey regarding their experience.

Survey questions

The survey included 10 Likert-scale questions regarding participants' general views on ChatGPT and its feedback, their perceived effectiveness, and attitudes and reactions towards using ChatGPT for English writing revision. Survey questions were adapted from Cotos (2010) and

Escalante et al. (2023). Each question was rated on a five-point scale, with one being the lowest (not at all or very poor) and five being the highest (very good or very much). Four questions focused on perceived effectiveness as an indirect measure of ChatGPT's potential for language learning, leading to four variables: the extent of changes learners made based on ChatGPT's feedback (change), the extent to which ChatGPT helped learners notice sentence-level errors (local) or global concerns such as content and organization (global), and the development of English writing skills overall (development). Another four questions focused on participants' attitudes towards using ChatGPT, including their satisfaction with ChatGPT's feedback (satisfaction), preference for using ChatGPT over teacher feedback (preference), trust in ChatGPT's feedback (trust), and willingness to use ChatGPT for future writing tasks (future).

Screen recording

The default screen recording function of the desktop was used to capture the data on participants' interaction with ChatGPT, producing video files that document all visible actions on their computer screens.

Semi-structured interviews/stimulated recalls

In the final session, semi-structured interviews were conducted with each participant individually. The participants were asked about how they interacted with ChatGPT and their perceived effectiveness and attitudes towards using ChatGPT for language learning purposes. To further contextualize their responses, participants were also asked about the text they had provided, their previous experiences with ChatGPT, and their experience with English writing and receiving written feedback.

After the interview, stimulated recalls were conducted. Individualized questions were prepared based on researchers' notes about interesting points in the participants' patterns of using ChatGPT, as observed in the screen recordings. Participants were shown these parts of the recordings and prompted to verbalize their thoughts as needed. The questions focused on why the participants addressed the feedback in a particular way, for example, "Why did you ignore this feedback?" and "Why did you type out ChatGPT's output rather than copying and pasting it into your draft?" Other questions aimed to determine whether the participants noticed the errors or changes made by ChatGPT and whether they learned from the feedback. Semi-structured interviews and stimulated recalls were all audio-recorded.

Data coding

To address RQ1, the student-ChatGPT conversation logs were annotated using MAXQDA 2024 (VERBI Software, 2024) to capture two variables:

- **Prompt Type**: What prompt learners used or the specific interaction they sought with ChatGPT (e.g., asking for feedback, revision).
- **Feedback Type**: What types of feedback or output ChatGPT produced in response to the prompts (e.g., summative comment, revision).

Response type, or how the learner reacted to ChatGPT's feedback, was identified through an analysis of screen recordings. We compiled all segments of prompts, outputs, and responses, created initial codes, and then recoded based on a refined list of codes.

To address RQ2, audio recordings of the stimulated recalls/semi-interviews were transcribed and imported into MAXQDA. The transcripts were analyzed following Corbin and Strauss (2007), which involved open coding (identifying relevant units and initial codes for analysis) and axial coding (making connections between codes to create categories). The categories identified during the axial coding stage were refined into a final set of eight codes: effectiveness/ineffectiveness of feedback, liking/disliking about the feedback, learning/no learning, learning to use ChatGPT, perception of ChatGPT, emotional reactions, trust/partial trust, preference and continued use. These codes were then used to recode the dataset.

Data analysis

To address RQ1, percentages were calculated for the occurrence of each type of prompt and feedback coded in the student-ChatGPT conversation logs, allowing for a quantitative analysis of patterns and trends in interactions with ChatGPT. Response types were identified through the screen recordings. To address RQ2, descriptive statistics for Likert-scale responses in the survey were calculated and compared. Qualitative analyses involved writing analytic memos for each of the eight participants based on the coded transcriptions, biodata from the interviews, and survey data analyzed for each participant.

Results

Interaction with ChatGPT: prompt, feedback, and response

RQ1 addressed the interaction patterns between the learner and ChatGPT, specifically focusing on learners' prompt types, ChatGPT's

Table 16.2 *Prompt types and descriptions*

Prompt Type	Description	Count (%)
Asking for Feedback	The participant asks for feedback on their text. (e.g., *provide specific feedback on the fourth paragraph; can you provide me some examples?*)	143 (45.25)
Revision Request	The participant asks ChatGPT to rewrite the text. (e.g., *make it better and polished in 200–250 words; rewrite the second paragraph with all your suggestions*)	75 (23.73)
*Follow-up	The participant follows up on ChatGPT's response with a further request or meaning negotiation. (e.g., *I don't feel that giving examples is a good point; with more simple language*)	73 (23.10)
Information Search	The participant searches for general information not related to the target language. (e.g., *how much CO2 is produced to make one car*)	12 (3.80)
Evaluation Request	The participant asks ChatGPT to grade their paper. (e.g., *Would you rate this out of 100?*)	7 (2.22)
Text Generation	The participant asks ChatGPT to generate new text without basing it on their own text. (e.g., *write your response on the findings*)	6 (1.90)
		Total: 316 (100%)

Note: Follow-up was double-coded with any other type.

feedback types, and learners' response types. We identified six prompt types (Table 2). Among the 316 prompts identified, 'asking for feedback' was used the most (45.25%), followed by 'revision request' (23.73%), and 'follow-up' with another prompt (23.10%). Among 'follow-up', there were 9 instances (12.33%) of meaning negotiation.

Regarding 'Feedback' (Table 3), among ChatGPT outputs, we identified nine methods for how ChatGPT addressed participants' prompts for a total of 282 coded segments. In most cases, prompt type and feedback type corresponded to each other. However, even in cases where the participant only asked for feedback, ChatGPT sometimes provided fully revised text. As shown in Table 3 below, 'Revision' was the most frequently used method (40.43%), followed by 'Suggestion' (26.60%) and 'Summative comment' (15.10%).

Lastly, through the analysis of screen recordings, we identified three 'Response' types (Table 4), or in what ways participants made use of ChatGPT's feedback, along with other interesting behaviors (Table 5) we observed. For 'No modified output', participants either ignored the

Table 16.3 *Feedback types and descriptions*

Feedback Type	Description	Count (%)
Revision	ChatGPT produces the revised text.	114 (40.43)
Suggestion	ChatGPT gives suggestions for improvement, usually providing a bulleted list of points. (e.g., *Vocabulary Enhancement: Introduce more diverse and sophisticated vocabulary where appropriate to add depth and nuance to the text.*)	75 (26.60)
Summative comment	ChatGPT provides a summary of evaluative comments on the writing. (e.g., *The biography is clear and well-structured.*)	44 (15.60)
Direct correction	ChatGPT indicates that there was an error in the writing with the correct form. (e.g., *Changed "comes" to "stems" for better tense agreement.*)	13 (4.61)
Information	ChatGPT provides general knowledge not related to the target language. (e.g., *Red symbolizes passion, energy, and good fortune in Korea.*)	12 (4.26)
Metalinguistic information	ChatGPT gives information on language and writing. (e.g., *Subject-Verb Agreement: Ensure that the subject and verb agree in number and tense; Question Hook: Pose a thought-provoking question that encourages readers to consider the impact of technology on children's development.*)	12 (4.26)
Summary	ChatGPT provides a summary of the content of the participant's writing. This usually is a breakdown of the text. (e.g., *Here's the breakdown of the essay: …*)	6 (2.13)
Generation	ChatGPT generates the text upon request, not based on the original text. (e.g., *Certainly, I'll provide responses to two of the findings from the study: …*)	5 (1.77)
Locating	ChatGPT visually highlights the location of what it's indicating with bolded text. (e.g., *Here's the highlighted thesis statement: …*)	1 (0.35)
		Total: 282 (100%)

feedback entirely or followed up by clarifying their previous prompt (also double-coded as 'follow-up' as a prompt type). In cases of 'Modified output,' changes were primarily made to content and vocabulary but less to mechanics, grammar, and structure. 'Full modified output' occurred in 21.5% of the total responses. In other instances, participants chose to type out ChatGPT's revised version rather than copy and paste it. During stimulated recalls, they explained that they wanted to proofread what ChatGPT wrote and selectively replaced some words or portions they didn't want (i.e., selective adjustment). Paraphrasing, or making more extensive modifications (both lexically and syntactically) than in selective adjustment, was observed particularly for B05, who expressed strong motivation to learn English. B05 also mentioned concerns about plagiarism, which further motivated his preference for paraphrasing over directly copying and pasting:

> Researcher: Why did you not copy and paste?
> B05: Because I wanted to improve this, like paraphrasing skills. Because it's very important in the research, right? And if you want to copy and paste, I will not improve those skills. (Participant B05)

Table 16.4 *Response types and descriptions*

Response Type	Description	Count (%)
No modified output	The learner does not make any modifications to the text or follow up with another request (double-coded with the prompt type, "Follow-up")	144 (29.27)
Modified output	The learner partially implemented ChatGPT's feedback at five levels:	
	Grammar (e.g., verb tense/form, SV agreement, plurals)	22 (9.09)
	Mechanics (e.g., citation format, punctuation)	33 (13.64)
	Lexical (e.g., replacement of words or phrases)	50 (20.66)
	Structure (e.g., sentence and paragraph structures)	18 (7.44)
	Content (e.g., additions, deletions, modified ideas)	119 (49.17)
	Modified output total	242 (49.19)
Full modified output	The learner fully implemented ChatGPT's feedback (i.e., copy and paste)	106 (21.54)
		Total: 492 (100%)

Table 16.5 *Other response behaviors*

Response Behaviors	Description	Count
Typing	The participant copies and pastes but through typing it in.	16
Viewing	The participant copies and pastes ChatGPT's output above or below their own text during revisions to easily view and implement the feedback into their writing.	12
Reverting	The participant initially does not but later implements the feedback.	11
Comparing	The participant compares ChatGPT's output with their text.	2
		Total: 41

Perceived effectiveness and attitudes

RQ2 addressed the perceived effectiveness of and attitudes towards ChatGPT for language learning. Qualitative insights from semi-structured interviews and stimulated recalls are presented alongside relevant survey response data, with the mean score out of 5 for each variable across three sessions provided in parentheses (e.g., 'local' = x.xx). Note that due to the small sample size, no statistical significance was assumed in the survey results; instead, the survey data serves to complement the qualitative findings by highlighting trends.

Perceived effectiveness

Analysis of semi-structured interviews and stimulated recalls revealed that most participants found ChatGPT's feedback effective at the global level ('global' = 4.17) but less so at the local level ('local' = 3.92) of their writing. Six participants appreciated ChatGPT's effectiveness at the global level. They frequently mentioned its effectiveness in improving structure, overall coherence, and flow of ideas, and particularly addressing the content matter in their writing, such as suggesting elaborations with examples. More importantly, five participants highlighted the benefit of using ChatGPT when integrated into their writing processes for tasks like generating ideas and creating outlines. C07 expressed his struggles with English writing, especially when he had to start with a blank piece of paper. He said ChatGPT helped him overcome that by giving him "a booster" at the beginning stage of writing. B03 and B01 further highlighted ChatGPT's importance in process writing sharing: "I feel ChatGPT is good in the process. [...] It helps you think about things while writing. (Participant B03)." and "For final editing, I would not use ChatGPT because I feel ChatGPT is a process tool, not an outcome tool. That's why I use it while writing, because it helps me with the process. (Participant B01)."

However, as mentioned by B01 above, participants were not as satisfied with ChatGPT's feedback at the final editing stage and regarding sentence-level errors. Five participants pointed out that ChatGPT was less effective in addressing sentence-level errors, often comparing its performance to other tools such as Grammarly. B01, stating, "grammars were not helpful at all," pointed out that ChatGPT's inability to locate errors might be an issue:

> But I felt like the way that ChatGPT writes and how they edit it, it was like a lot of work to know where the errors were. Whereas with Grammarly, you need to follow each suggestion to see where to compare. (Participant B01)

Four participants expressed mixed feelings about ChatGPT's word choice suggestions, noting issues with repetition, complexity, and inaccuracy. While B01 and C06 found some synonyms and word choices overly complex and repetitive, B03 highlighted inaccuracies in context-specific suggestions, emphasizing a need for more practical and precise word options. Consequently, participants relied on their own judgment in this area, not accepting ChatGPT's suggestions entirely. Instead, they selected appropriate words from the synonym suggestions or replaced overly complex words from ChatGPT's output to make their writing less "artificial." This highlights the limitation of ChatGPT as a chatbot, with participants describing it as "robotic" (B02), a "machine" (C08), and an AI "thing" (B04). As C06 remarked:

> I wish it could diversify words. Because, as a student, the essays should look like I wrote them. But when I use ChatGPT, it kind of shows that ChatGPT wrote it. [...] Since it uses certain words repetitively, if the teacher or another person has used ChatGPT before, they can quickly discern that it is a ChatGPT-written essay. (Participant C06)

Most notably, all participants also reported issues with the feedback, such as it being too general and often overly positive, making it less relatable or applicable to their writing. B02 expressed her frustration about general feedback, finding it too lengthy, not understandable, and not pointing out specific problems in her writing. As the feedback got too lengthy and complicated, participants were often observed to skip it entirely: "I was too lazy to read it. I felt like I couldn't really understand it. I mean, I could, but I felt like I didn't need to. So, I just didn't (Participant C06)."

When the participants only wanted to hear about the weaknesses in their writing to make improvements, ChatGPT often gave them excessive positive feedback, requiring participants to prompt it again for more specific and actionable suggestions. As noted by our participants, this might be because: "[...] ChatGPT wants to keep you positive in general as a human (Participant B01), and thus, "[...] It doesn't tell you. It's not honest. (Participant C07)."

One prominent theme that emerged from the analysis was learning and adaptation in using ChatGPT over time, which may help overcome the limitations in ChatGPT's feedback and thus explain the overall increase in survey scores across different sessions (with the overall 'perceived effectiveness' score improving from 4 to 4.31). Six participants mentioned their realization that the quality of ChatGPT's feedback depended on their prompts and how they improved their prompts to be more specific and straightforward, resulting in more precise and helpful feedback. For instance, B01 noted that he learned to provide smaller text portions instead of the entire text for better results and developed the skill of translating thoughts into clear, actionable prompts. As B04 commented about prompting techniques, "It comes with practice (Participant B04)."

However, some participants reported that ChatGPT's perceived effectiveness did not necessarily lead to actual learning of the language or enhancement in writing skills. Specifically, four participants mentioned "partial" or "no learning" from ChatGPT; while they acknowledged that ChatGPT "helped" with their writing, they could not say they learned from it:

> I would say that ChatGPT gives me an understanding of how to make my paragraphs more descriptive or write more details, but I don't really feel like it helps me to enhance my English. (Participant C07)

Survey responses support this, showing a greater extent of changes based on ChatGPT's feedback ('change' = 4.38), while participants were less able to 'notice' sentence-level errors and global issues that could lead to learning gains ('local' = 3.91; 'global' = 4.17).

Nonetheless, four participants acknowledged that they learned implicitly by comparing their writing with ChatGPT's refined version, as indicated by the following excerpts:

So now I've known how to write this particular sentence in this way, so now I can use it in my future writing. So whenever I have an instance of writing a similar sentence or similar content, I can use the sentences or words from these versions, and then I can use them for my future writing. (Participant B03)

> Sometimes it might be a small grammatical thing, like I used to write two different words with a hyphen in between. […] I learned that, okay, this is how it is written. And whenever I'm writing now, I'm unconsciously just typing it in the same way ChatGPT does. (Participant B04)

Attitudes towards ChatGPT

All participants had at least some trust in ChatGPT and its capabilities ('trust' = 3.46). Those with strong trust, like B04 and C06, highlighted its accuracy, effectiveness with specific prompts, and overall reliability for certain tasks like English writing (as opposed to, for instance, math problems). For instance, B04, identified as an experienced and skilled user in our observation of screen recordings, expressed the highest level of trust among all participants. When asked whether there were any instances of feedback that were not helpful, he said: "It was all the prompts I used that I knew would work perfectly there, so I tried to use them instead of other prompts (Participant B04)," suggesting that perceived effectiveness and attitudes can improve with increased proficiency in prompting skills. B04 seemed to have strong confidence in his prompting skills and awareness of common system errors and bugs in ChatGPT so that even in cases where he encountered such problems, he could make things work out or avoid writing the prompts that might cause those issues in the first place.

However, two participants expressed reduced trust in ChatGPT due to inconsistent, irrelevant, and inaccurate responses, as shared in these two excerpts:

> And if I ask a question and then I know that question is not correct, if I again ask ChatGPT, 'Are you sure?' then I see that it changes the answer and says, 'I'm sorry for that sentence.' So, I don't completely trust ChatGPT. (Participant C07)
>
> When I put things in ChatGPT, it tries to take it away from what I'm trying to write and posts a bunch of stuff from the internet, which I don't think fits in there. […] I can't really trust everything because I have to look it up and manage it that way. (Participant C08)

As indicated by C08 in the previous excerpt, participants said they tended to double-check with other sources or tools as a cautious approach. Even B04, who expressed very strong trust in ChatGPT, mentioned that he used Grammarly for final proofreading even after ChatGPT.

When asked about their preference between teacher feedback and ChatGPT's feedback, five participants preferred teacher feedback ('preference' for ChatGPT = 3.25), finding it more specific and contextually informed. C08, referring to ChatGPT as a "machine" said "Humans, they know better. I still say they know better than machines, they will be able to make you understand the things they are saying. (Participant C08)." However, even those who favored teacher feedback acknowledged ChatGPT's advantage of increased consistency and accessibility, allowing them to ask for feedback as many times as they wanted. B01 noted:

> But also, it depends on the teacher. Some teachers will not be. So, the good thing about ChatGPT is that it's consistent. Even if it's not the best quality, it's always there. And that's something that gives it a big advantage. (Participant B01)

Despite its limitations, all participants expressed a desire to continue using ChatGPT ('future' = 3.83), whether strongly or, to some extent, viewing it as a valuable supplementary tool in their writing process.

Discussion

This study examined how L2 English learners interacted with ChatGPT in terms of prompt, feedback, and response types across three revision sessions, as well as their perceived effectiveness of ChatGPT as an AWE tool. In answering RQ1, we found that 'Revision request' was the second most used prompt type, often leading to full modified output as observed in the screen recordings. However, contrary to the positive implication of the term, 'full' was not ideal, as it indicated that participants had directly copied and pasted ChatGPT's revised text without making any modifications on their end. Interestingly, in many cases, even when students asked for feedback, ChatGPT provided fully revised versions of their drafts. As a result, many participants skipped reading the feedback and simply adopted the revised version. However, a full or near copy of ChatGPT's output can hardly be considered modified output (Keck, 2014), thereby limiting learning opportunities. This also raises plagiarism concerns caused by ChatGPT, as noted by the students in our study and in previous research (Xiao & Zhi, 2023). Nevertheless, about half of the responses (49.19%) resulted in modified output, where students implemented the feedback on their own, particularly with content-level changes (49.17% across all five levels; grammar, mechanics, lexical, structure, and content). This suggests the potential for learners' engagement with ChatGPT to contribute to writing skills development. As some participants noted in interviews, this might not result in explicit language learning; however, implicit learning may still occur through repeated exposure to correct language forms in ChatGPT's feedback.

In answering RQ2, we found participants often found ChatGPT's feedback too general and overly positive, making it less actionable for students. Additionally, the feedback was often lengthy and complicated, which may have increased the cognitive load on the learners and complicated comprehension (Ranalli et al., 2017; Weigle, 2013). This may have further reduced ChatGPT's LLP, leading participants to take shortcuts rather than engage with the feedback. However, as participants mentioned in interviews, the effectiveness of feedback would depend on how much the learner cares about the text and their motivation to learn the language. More motivated learners are more likely to attend to ChatGPT's feedback (Xiao & Zhi, 2023).

Regarding local versus global aspects of writing, ChatGPT was perceived as less effective in addressing local errors due to its limited perfection, which does not align with previous research (Ali et al., 2023; Mahapatra, 2024; Song & Song, 2023). This perception is supported by findings from RQ1, which showed relatively low percentages of modified output at the grammar (9.09%) and mechanics (13.64%) levels. Unlike tools such as Grammarly, which provides visual aids like flagging and highlighting, ChatGPT lacks features that make it easier for learners to identify where errors occurred, or changes were made. Integrating these types of visual aids with ChatGPT's feedback could help learners produce more appropriately modified outputs, leading to more effective learning outcomes.

In terms of global aspects, learners found ChatGPT effective in refining their drafts by improving the flow of ideas and enhancing overall delivery; this aligns with previous literature (Boudouaia et al., 2024; Mahapatra, 2024; Song & Song, 2023). Unlike previous AWE tools, which excelled at addressing sentence-level correctness, ChatGPT's more advanced technology allows it to provide customized feedback on global writing concerns, adapting to each student's unique text. Therefore, integrating ChatGPT into classroom teaching could further reduce teachers' workloads while enhancing students' L2 writing development by providing continuous access to an AI writing assistant.

Moreover, despite not being directly related to LLP, our findings suggest the potential for using ChatGPT to promote a process-oriented writing approach in classroom settings. As highlighted by our participants, students can use ChatGPT at any stage of their writing process as a personal writing assistant. They found it particularly useful when beginning their writing, as it helps in generating ideas on the topic and organizing thoughts by outlining their drafts.

Given these benefits, despite ChatGPT's limitations, we suggest that teachers collaborate with ChatGPT in providing feedback on student writing. Teachers should aim to help students set up ChatGPT to become an effective tool that complements their feedback and maximizes actual learning. We acknowledge that the use of AI in student work poses challenges to academic integrity, as evidenced in our study where students often copied and pasted directly from ChatGPT into their writing. Therefore, it is the responsibility of instructors to decide whether to allow the use of ChatGPT in their courses. However, as it is nearly impossible to ban students from using ChatGPT without a reliable means of detecting LLM-generated content, the key question concerns how teachers can guide students to use such tools in a legitimate way. Based on our findings, we encourage teachers to consider the following points to guide students:

- Encourage students to practice their prompting skills to make their prompts more specific and straightforward. Emphasize that it is really a communication between them and ChatGPT, and the results depend on their prompt. For example, instead of prompting, "Give me feedback on this writing," more specific prompts indicating which aspects they want feedback on work better, such as "Give me feedback on the flow of this writing." Students can also provide context or the purpose of their writing to get more individualized feedback. If their prompt does not work out, students should be encouraged to negotiate the meaning with ChatGPT through iterative interactions until they are satisfied with the results.
- Teachers should emphasize using ChatGPT as a learning tool to assist students throughout the entire writing process. Students can generate ideas and outlines to ease the burden of writing from scratch. During the writing stage, students should be guided to ask for feedback on various aspects of their writing, from mechanics and grammar errors to more global aspects, including connectivity between sentences and overall coherence. Let students be cautious when using ChatGPT for final proofreading, however, as sometimes, ChatGPT was found to have errors. They should double-check with other tools that are more specialized for those purposes.
- To increase the noticing of errors for actual learning gains, students can ask ChatGPT to locate the errors or changes made using a simple prompt like "highlight the errors/changes."
- Teachers should discuss with students when and when not to use ChatGPT for their writing. Students should be cautioned against

Insights into AI and Language Teaching and Learning 309

copying and pasting behavior. Rather than generating the full draft or seeking a fully revised text from ChatGPT, students should view ChatGPT as a personal writing teacher that is easily accessible as needed for their writing process. Teachers should make it explicit that misuse of ChatGPT, such as copying and pasting, constitutes cheating and plagiarism, as it involves presenting ChatGPT's output as their own work, and there would be a lack of learning from it.

- Teachers can provide students with default prompts to be used with the customization feature in ChatGPT, which would yield more structured feedback. This feature can be found under Profile > Customize ChatGPT. Refer to Figure 2 below for an example:

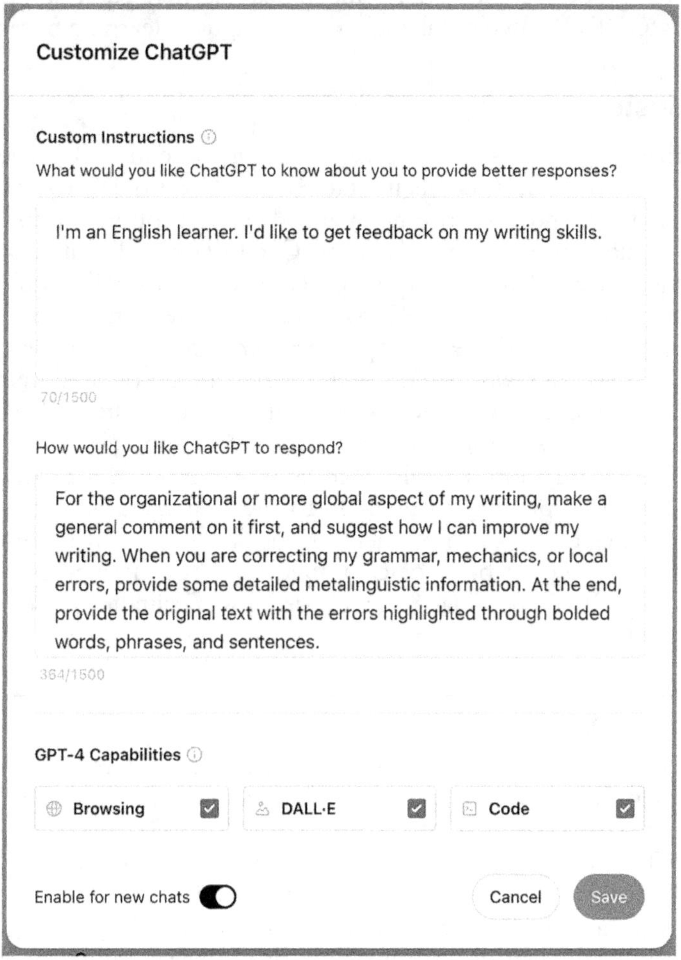

Customize ChatGPT

Custom Instructions
What would you like ChatGPT to know about you to provide better responses?

> I'm an English learner. I'd like to get feedback on my writing skills.

70/1500

How would you like ChatGPT to respond?

> For the organizational or more global aspect of my writing, make a general comment on it first, and suggest how I can improve my writing. When you are correcting my grammar, mechanics, or local errors, provide some detailed metalinguistic information. At the end, provide the original text with the errors highlighted through bolded words, phrases, and sentences.

364/1500

GPT-4 Capabilities

- Browsing ✓
- DALL·E ✓
- Code ✓

Enable for new chats ●   Cancel   Save

Figure 16.2 *Customization feature in ChatGPT.*

Noting that this study has some limitations is important for future research. First, our sample size is very small, with only eight participants, which limits the generalizability of our findings. More participants are needed to improve this aspect. Second, in our effort to explore overall trends, we did not fully focus on individual participants when reporting our findings. Future research should include a more detailed qualitative exploration of each individual learner as a case study. Last, our study was conducted over a short period, which may not have been sufficient to observe changes in learners' interaction patterns and perceptions of ChatGPT. Future research should include longitudinal studies to address this gap. Despite these limitations, our exploratory study aims to provide a foundation for researching the most recent AI technology as an AWE tool. Additionally, it aims to help teachers guide students to use ChatGPT effectively, enhancing their language learning potential.

Conclusion

This chapter explores the language learning potential of ChatGPT, focusing on how L2 students interacted with ChatGPT (prompt type, feedback type, and response type) and their perceptions of its effectiveness and attitudes towards using ChatGPT for English writing. Findings indicate that the learning potential of ChatGPT is limited, as students often asked ChatGPT to produce revised drafts, frequently copying, pasting, and merely replacing some words from the generated text. Feedback was often found overwhelming or predominantly positive, making it less applicable for revising their writing. While less effective in addressing local errors, L2 students appreciated the value of ChatGPT for more global concerns of writing and a process-oriented writing approach, particularly for generating ideas and outlining at the beginning stage of their writing. We hope that the findings of our study suggest pedagogical implications for instructors intending to use ChatGPT in language classrooms, facilitating its effective implementation.

Post-reading questions:
1) Based on the findings, how do learners' interactions with ChatGPT vary in terms of prompt types and feedback received?
2) What were some common issues learners experienced with ChatGPT's feedback, and how did they address them?
3) What are the key recommendations for teachers to help students use ChatGPT more effectively in their writing processes?

Further reading

Barrot, J. S. (2023). Using ChatGPT for second language writing: Pitfalls and potentials. *Assessing Writing*, *57*, 100745. https://doi.org/10.1016/j.asw.2023.100745

Yan, D. (2023). Impact of ChatGPT on learners in a L2 writing practicum: An exploratory investigation. *Education and Information Technologies*, *28*(11), 13943–13967. https://doi.org/10.1007/s10639-023-11742-4

References

Ali, J. K., Shamsan, M. A., Hezam, T. A., & Mohammed, A. A. (2023). Impact of ChatGPT on learning motivation. *Journal of English Studies in Arabia Felix*, *2*(1), 41–49. https://doi.org/10.56540/jesaf.v2i1.51

Boudouaia, A., Mouas, S., & Kouider, B. (2024). A study on ChatGPT-4 as an innovative approach to enhancing English as a foreign language writing learning. *Journal of Educational Computing Research*, *62*(6), 1509–1537. https://doi.org/10.1177/07356331241247465

Chapelle, C. A. (2001). *Computer applications in second language acquisition: Foundations for teaching, testing, and research*. Cambridge University Press.

Chapelle, C. A. (2007). Technology and second language acquisition. *Annual Review of Applied Linguistics*, *27*, 98–114. https://doi.org/10.1017/S0267190508070050

Chen, Z., Chen, W., Jia, J., & Le, H. (2022). Exploring AWE-supported writing process: An activity theory perspective. *Language Learning & Technology*, *26*(2), 129–148. https://doi.org/10125/73482

Corbin, J., & Strauss, A. (2007). *Basics of qualitative research: Techniques and procedures for developing grounded theory* (3rd edition). Sage.

Cotos, E. (2023). Automated feedback on writing. In *Digital writing technologies in higher education: Theory, research, and practice* (pp. 347–364). Springer International Publishing.

Escalante, J., Pack, A., & Barrett, A. (2023). AI-generated feedback on writing: Insights into efficacy and ENL student preference. *International Journal of Educational Technology in Higher Education*, *20*(1), 57. https://doi.org/10.1186/s41239-023-00425-2

Fuchs, K. (2023). Exploring the opportunities and challenges of NLP models in higher education: Is ChatGPT a blessing or a curse? *Frontiers in Education*, *8*, 1166682. https://doi.org/10.3389/feduc.2023.1166682

Gass, S., & Mackey, A. (2006). Input, interaction and output: An overview. In K. Bardovi-Harlig and Z. Dörnyei (Eds.), *Themes in SLA research* (pp. 3–17). John Benjamins.

Godwin-Jones, R. (2022). Partnering with AI: Intelligent writing assistance and instructed language learning. *Language Learning & Technology, 2*(26), 5–24. https://doi.org/10125/73474

Guo, K., & Wang, D. (2023). To resist it or to embrace it? Examining ChatGPT's potential to support teacher feedback in EFL writing. *Education and Information Technologies*, 1–29. https://doi.org/10.1007/s10639-023-12146-0

Keck, C. (2014). Copying, paraphrasing, and academic writing development: A re-examination of L1 and L2 summarization practices. *Journal of Second Language Writing, 25*, 4–22. https://doi.org/10.1016/j.jslw.2014.05.005

Kohnke, L., Moorhouse, B. L., & Zou, D. (2023). ChatGPT for language teaching and learning. *RELC Journal, 54*(2), 537–550. https://doi.org/10.1177/00336882231162868

Long, M. H. (2007). *Problems in SLA*. Lawrence Erlbaum.

Mahapatra, S. (2024). Impact of ChatGPT on ESL students' academic writing skills: A mixed methods intervention study. *Smart Learning Environments, 11*(1), Article 9. https://doi.org/10.1186/s40561-024-00295-9

Ranalli, J., Link, S., & Chukharev-Hudilainen, E. (2017). Automated writing evaluation for formative assessment of second language writing: Investigating the accuracy and usefulness of feedback as part of argument-based validation. *Educational Psychology, 37*(1), 8–25. https://doi.org/10.1080/01443410.2015.1136407

Ranalli, J. (2021). L2 student engagement with automated feedback on writing: Potential for learning and issues of trust. *Journal of Second Language Writing, 52*, 100816. https://doi.org/10.1016/j.jslw.2021.100816

Song, C., & Song, Y. (2023). Enhancing academic writing skills and motivation: Assessing the efficacy of ChatGPT in AI-assisted language learning for EFL students. *Frontiers in Psychology, 14*, 1260843. https://doi.org/10.3389/fpsyg.2023.1260843

Stevenson, M., & Phakiti, A. (2019). Automated feedback and second language writing. In K. Hyland, & F. Hyland (Eds.), *Feedback in second language writing: Contexts and issues* (pp. 125–142). Cambridge University Press.

VERBI Software. (2024). MAXQDA 2024 [computer software]. VERBI Software. Available from maxqda.com

Wang, Z. (2022). Computer-assisted EFL writing and evaluations based on artificial intelligence: A case from a college reading and writing course. *Library Hi Tech, 40*(1), 80–97. https://doi.org/10.1108/LHT-05-2020-0113

Warschauer, M., & Grimes, D. (2008). Automated writing assessment in the classroom. *Pedagogies: An International Journal, 3*(1), 22–36.

Weigle, S. C. (2013). English as a second language writing and automated essay evaluation. In M. D. Shermis & J. Burstein (Eds.), *Handbook of automated essay evaluations: Current applications and new directions* (pp. 36–54). Routledge.

Xiao, Y., & Zhi, Y. (2023). An exploratory study of EFL learners' use of ChatGPT for language learning tasks: Experience and perceptions. *Languages, 8*(3), 212.

Zhang, Z., & Hyland, K. (2018). Student engagement with teacher and automated feedback on L2 writing. *Assessing Writing, 36*, 90–102. https://doi.org/10.1016/j.asw.2018.02.004

Zhang, Z. (2020). Engaging with automated writing evaluation (AWE) feedback on L2 writing: Student perceptions and revisions. *Assessing Writing, 43*, 100439 https://doi.org/10.1016/j.asw.2019.100439

Index

21st-century skill, 102

academic dishonesty, 102, 105
academic integrity, 2, 4–5, 34–35, 83, 102, 104–106, 108, 185, 241, 246, 249, 252, 263, 265, 279, 308
academic writing, 6, 83–85, 88, 194, 205, 250, 261–265, 269, 271–272, 276–278
accuracy, vi, 2, 15, 53, 68–69, 81, 89, 101–102, 104–105, 107–108, 122, 156, 175–176, 180, 211, 221–224, 231, 233, 244, 263, 268, 270–271, 273, 288, 305
action research, 125–126
adaptive learning, 2, 135, 240
affordance, vii–viii, 1–2, 4, 18, 45, 54, 56, 58, 68–69, 73, 78, 80, 91, 106, 116–117, 141, 143, 157, 159, 178, 197
agency, 54, 60–61, 63, 67, 69–73, 83, 137, 147, 158, 165, 251
AI literacy, 3–6, 60–62, 72–73, 107–108, 143, 147, 154, 156–157, 159–160, 162, 165, 186, 198, 211, 244, 251
anxiety, 34–35, 44, 71, 119, 139–141, 143–146, 222, 224, 226, 228, 230–232, 243
artificial intelligence in education (AIED), 240
asynchronous, viii
synchronous, viii
attitude, 99, 109, 118–119, 102, 122, 124, 139–140, 145, 190, 195, 197, 206–207, 213, 222, 224, 231, 290–291, 294, 296–297, 302, 305, 310

automated essay scoring (AES), 3, 77–79, 104
automatic speech recognition (ASR), 1, 3–4, 77–78, 98–101, 106, 192
automated writing evaluation (AWE), 1, 77, 79, 95, 99, 103, 105, 121, 262, 290–294, 306–307, 310
autonomy, vi, viii, 2–3, 32, 43, 57–58, 69–70, 73, 91, 103, 107, 119–120, 124, 136–137, 145–146, 212, 290

chatbot, 15–18, 25, 71, 73, 91, 101, 103, 117, 122, 153, 155-156, 179, 187, 191, 194, 204–205, 210, 214, 240–244, 251–253, 303
ChatGPT, 1, 7, 12, 15, 35, 37, 40–41, 43, 54, 59–61, 80–82, 84, 87, 89–91, 97, 103–105, 115, 118, 122, 125, 135, 137, 148, 153, 155–157, 161, 173, 176, 185–187, 186–189, 191–194, 199, 204–205, 240–251, 253, 246–247, 290–310
ChatGPT literacy, 82, 89, 91
Claude, 15, 37, 40, 205, 241
Copilot, 15-16, 21, 103, 191, 205, 291
cognitive skill, 2
collaborative learning, 24–25, 161
co-literacy, viii, 3, 53, 54, 63, 67–73
Communities of Practice (CoP) framework, 4, 154–155, 160
Computer-Assisted Language Learning (CALL), v, 1, 3, 12, 171, 245, 293
 Tutorial CALL, 12, 23–25
 Intelligent CALL (ICALL), 3, 12–14, 16–19, 21–26, 116

Index

confidence, 4–6, 56, 67, 107, 119, 144, 146, 222, 224, 226, 228, 230–234, 248, 263, 271, 288, 305
contingent feedback, 13, 19, 25
corpora, 14–15, 84, 187
corrective feedback, vii, 19, 21–22, 37, 79, 156, 223, 225, 243
creativity, vi, viii, 2, 36, 43, 57–59, 62–72, 86, 147, 176, 179, 211, 215, 271, 279
critical thinking, 2, 5, 36, 59, 62–63, 66, 68, 83, 87–89, 106, 147, 171–174, 177–181, 204, 211–213, 215, 263, 277–278, 279

data privacy, 116, 123, 211–212, 244
DeepL, 101, 191, 270, 276
deep learning, 15, 27, 78–79, 88
Dialogflow, 242
digital divide, 42, 116, 123
digital literacies, 3, 54, 56–57, 59–60, 62, 68–69, 72
Duolingo, 36, 77, 79, 295

Education 4.0, 214
effectiveness, ix, 4, 6, 108, 116–117, 119, 122, 124, 126, 214–215, 224–225, 231, 233–234, 249, 263, 268, 274, 277, 290–294, 296–298, 302, 304–307, 310
emotion, 5, 141, 206–207
engagement, ix, 2–3, 5, 7, 36, 54, 56–59, 64–69, 71–72, 83, 85, 88–89, 104, 106, 116, 118, 121, 124–125, 146–147, 157, 164–165, 175, 190, 192, 208, 241, 243, 245–249, 252, 263, 267, 277, 292–293, 307
English for Academic Purposes (EAP), 5–6, 137, 185–186, 188–194, 196–200, 241, 245–246, 249–250
enjoyment, ix, 4, 139, 141, 143, 145
ethical issues, 4, 45, 98, 100, 102, 105–107, 157, 213, 222, 241–243, 246–247, 249

equity, 3, 61–62, 90–91, 104, 123
error analysis, 19
error correction, viii, 13, 19, 21, 25, 223–224
Expectancy-Value Theory (EVT), 120, 138, 140

game-based language learning, 26
Gemini, 15, 103, 191, 205, 241, 291
Google Translate, 33, 54, 101, 119, 191, 270, 276
grammar checking, 190, 224
Grammarly, 121, 205, 270, 273, 276, 286, 290, 303, 306–307

hallucination, 40–41, 179
higher education (HE), 5, 98, 140, 185–186, 207, 241, 262, 266, 268, 278

independent learning, vii, 24–25, 165
intelligent personal assistant (IPA), 99, 117
intelligent tutoring system (ITS), 22–23, 79, 142, 137
interactive speech technologies, 1
intercultural awareness, 106
intercultural communication, 37, 61, 251–252

Large Language Model (LMM), vi, 1, 3, 15, 19, 21–23, 25–26, 35, 37, 38, 40–41, 43–44, 60, 65, 77–78, 80, 90, 97, 101–106, 135, 187, 191, 235, 237, 242, 290–292, 294, 301
languages other than English (LOTE), 14, 90, 125
learning styles, 13
lifelong learning, 213, 215 listening comprehension, 79

machine translation (MT), 4, 6, 11, 16, 32, 98, 101, 104, 155, 161, 187–188, 190–193, 221, 223
metaverse, vi

mindset, viii, 44, 46, 73, 213, 225
motivation, v, ix, 4, 35–36, 44, 65, 99, 117–120, 136–138, 140–143, 145, 147, 222, 225–226, 228, 230–232, 241, 243, 245, 248, 288, 290, 301, 307
  demotivation, 34, 36
multimodal learning, vii, 146

natural language processing (NLP), 12, 14, 15–17, 19, 23, 77–79, 81, 115, 122, 125, 153–154, 174, 210, 242, 263
natural language understanding (NLU), 17, 21, 25, 153–154
neural machine translation (NMT), 101

OpenAI, 15, 42, 115, 179, 243–244, 291
over-reliance, 2, 4, 34, 36, 72, 119, 147, 156–157, 151–152, 195–196, 262–263, 265–277, 292

perception, viii, ix, 4–7, 102, 107, 117–118, 125, 134–135, 139–140, 143–144, 214–215, 217, 221–222, 224, 227-228, 231–234, 241, 244–246, 250, 265, 268, 277–278, 290, 292–293, 298, 307, 310
personalized learning, 33, 115, 120, 122, 145, 241
professional development, ix, 3, 5, 44–45, 47, 56, 82, 91, 157–158, 171, 198, 200, 203–215
pronunciation, 99, 101, 117, 119, 122, 124, 156

reading comprehension, 80, 89, 119, 143, 223
reinforcement learning with human feedback (RLHF), 103

self-determination theory (SDT), 120, 136–137
self-directed learning, 32
self-efficacy, ix, 4, 137–138, 142–144, 162

Situated Expectancy–Value Theory (SEVT), 138
social influence, 121, 140–142, 144–145
sociality, 58–59, 69, 71–72
speaking, 2, 16, 78, 81–82, 99–100, 117, 125, 170, 175, 189, 243, 275
student modeling, 13, 22, 26

Task-Based Language Teaching (TBLT), 39
teacher communities, ix, 4–5, 153–155, 158–163, 165
Technology Acceptance Model (TAM), vii, 121, 139–140
theory for reasoned action (TRA), 138-141
theory of planned behavior (TPB), 139, 141, 206–207
Technological, Pedagogical, and Content Knowledge (TPACK), viii, 5, 170–175, 177–181,
Turing Test, 12

UTAUT (Unified Theory of Acceptance and Use of Technology), vii, 121, 140–141

vocabulary, 6, 14, 37, 89–90, 99, 102, 119, 143, 156, 215, 222, 224, 228–229, 242, 248, 250, 261–263, 275, 292, 3009–301

well-being, 45
Wordtune, 6, 261–279, 286–288
writing skills, 7, 221, 223, 226, 261–264, 271, 276–278, 290, 292, 297, 304, 307

YouTube, 46, 58, 70

Zone of Proximal Development (ZPD), 126

www.ingramcontent.com/pod-product-compliance
Lightning Source LLC
Chambersburg PA
CBHW051559230426
43668CB00013B/1905